John Eadie, John M. Mason

Sermons, Lectures, and Orations

John Eadie, John M. Mason

Sermons, Lectures, and Orations

ISBN/EAN: 9783337242657

Printed in Europe, USA, Canada, Australia, Japan

Cover: Foto ©ninafisch / pixelio.de

More available books at **www.hansebooks.com**

SERMONS, LECTURES, &c.

SERMONS,

LECTURES, AND ORATIONS.

BY

JOHN M. MASON, D.D.,

LATE OF THE ASSOCIATE REFORMED CHURCH, NEW YORK.

WITH

MEMOIR AND INTRODUCTORY ESSAY,

BY JOHN EADIE, D.D., LL.D.

PROFESSOR OF BIBLICAL LITERATURE TO THE UNITED PRESBYTERIAN CHURCH.

EDINBURGH:
OGLE & MURRAY, AND W. OLIPHANT & CO.
GLASGOW: M. OGLE & SON. LONDON: HAMILTON, ADAMS, & CO.

MDCCCLX.

A. AND W. R. WILSON, PRINTERS, HIGH STREET, EDINBURGH.

CONTENTS.

	PAGE
MEMOIR OF THE AUTHOR,	v
SERMON I.—The Gospel for the Poor,	1
II.—Divine Judgments,	20
III.—Mercy Remembered in Wrath,	48
IV.—Hope for the Heathen,	63
V.—Pardon of Sin,	86
VI.—Living Faith,	105
VII.—Messiah's Throne,	125
VIII.—Christian Mourning,	143
IX.—Full Assurance of Faith and Hope,	168
X.—Evangelical Ministry Exemplified,	186
XI.—Salvation by Grace,	204
LECTURE—Psalm XXIII.,	218
Psalm VIII.,	244
Matthew XXVII. 1-5,	259
SERMON XII.—Ministerial Fidelity,	269
XIII.—The Christian Warfare,	282
XIV.—Do. do.	297
XV.—Nature and Necessity of Regeneration,	308
XVI.—Works of the Flesh and Spirit Distinguished,	322
XVII.—True Honour,	336
XVIII.—Apostolic Commission,	349
XIX.—Nonconformity to the World,	359
XX.—The Fountain of Life,	372
XXI.—The Gospel Offer,	388
XXII.—The Gospel no Cause of Shame,	401
XXIII.—On Steadfastness in Religious Sentiment,	415
ORATION on the Death of Washington,	429
ORATION on the Death of Hamilton,	440

MEMOIR OF THE AUTHOR.

My late revered colleague Dr John Brown, had undertaken to write a few introductory pages to this volume, and from his admiration of the eloquence and genius of Dr Mason he would have paid a grateful and ardent tribute to his memory. But his last illness prevented him from even beginning the task, and on his death-bed he earnestly commended it, nay, virtually handed it over to me.

The fame of Dr Mason has not been eclipsed by any of his successors in America, and it is almost superfluous to say a word about one whose praise is still in all the churches. He needs no " epistle of commendation,"—no herald to bespeak attention for him. Yet a few sentences on his life, character, and position, may not be deemed out of place as a preface to the following discourses.

Dr Mason's father, the Rev. John Mason, was a native of Mid-Calder. On leaving the University of Edinburgh, he studied theology at Abernethy, under Moncrieff of Culfargie, and himself taught for a period a class of philosophy in the same seminary, in connection with what was then called the Anti-Burgher or General Associate Synod. On the 5th of August 1760, he was ordained at Perth as minister of the Associate Congregation, New

York; and in the following spring he sailed with two other missionaries for the sphere of his labours. His infant church rose rapidly in numbers and influence. The place of worship was at first a small frame building in Cedar Street, and this, in 1768, was succeeded by a stone erection on the same site. It may be added that in 1837 the congregation moved "up town" to Grand Street, and in 1853 moved farther "up town" still, to Fourteenth Street, where they continue to worship under the care of their fourth pastor, the able and excellent Dr M'Elroy. The various sects of Scottish Seceders, though they had changed their country, yet retained their minor denominational peculiarities in the New World; but Mason and others effected, after the Revolution, a union among a portion of them, and Burghers, Anti-Burghers, and Covenanters were merged into a new body—the Associate Reformed Church. This new organization gave great offence to the Anti-burgher Church at home, and Adam Gib proposed in synod that Mr Mason "should be laid aside from a seat among them." A letter of solemn rebuke was sent across the Atlantic, and, in 1784, Mason replied in a noble and masterly vindication, addressed to his Professor of Theology, the Rev. Wm. Moncrieff, and the Rev. John Heugh, father of the late Dr Heugh of Glasgow. This rupture seems to have led him to attach himself to the other or Burgher branch of the Secession.

The elder Mason was a man of sound and vigorous intellect. His learning was far above mediocrity, and his style of thought and utterance was in advance of his day. His prelections as tutor in philosophy at Abernethy were always spoken of in high terms by his students, such as the late Dr Young of Hawick, and they were all delivered in Latin with remarkable fluency and correctness. Indeed, as Dr Miller of Princeton has said of him,—"few ministers have ever lived in New York in so high esteem, or died so generally and deeply lamented."

John Mitchell Mason, the subject of this brief sketch, was born at New York, March 19, 1770. The influence and training of his mother, Catherine Van Wyck, of one of the old Dutch families of New York, was one prime source of what was good and great about him. Early impressions, in happy union with the heart's desire of his parents, led him to study for the ministry. Perhaps his most effective mental discipline was enjoyed under his father's roof. In 1791, after passing through college in America, he came over to Edinburgh, to pursue a more formal course of literary and theological preparation, carrying with him a long letter of instructions from his father, whom he was never to see again—a letter which is full of minute and sage counsels as to reading and study, composition and delivery, conduct and prospects, and having this postscript: "Read these advices once a-month; carefully preserve them as a memorial of me." In the Divinity Hall of Edinburgh University Mason had as his intimate companions such men as the late Ewing and Dick of Glasgow, and Innes of Edinburgh. He was noted in his class for his boldness of speech, and for his keen and unsparing criticisms on such of the discourses as indicated vicious taste, or which, with literary pretensions, did not contain a distinct exhibition of evangelical truth. His father having died during the son's absence, the vacant congregation waited the youth's return from Scotland which he left in August 1792. On being licensed by the presbytery of Pennsylvania, he was soon after ordained as his father's successor. The well-known Mrs Isabella Graham says of him at this time,—" He is reckoned a lad of great talents, and an orator, and many of even the idle and careless go to hear him." The sub-

a

ject of missions soon began to engross him, and to draw out his eloquence; and the third discourse which he published was the famous one, "Hope for the Heathen," preached before the New York Missionary Society in 1797. Such was his growing fame, that his church found it necessary to "swarm," as he phrases it, and both congregations remained for some time under his sole pastoral care.

Preachers were still scarce in the States, and there were hardly any means for training them; while appeals to the old country did not always induce students and ministers to emigrate. It was, therefore, resolved by the synod of the Associate Reformed Church to send "Brother Mason" as a deputy to Scotland, in order not only to secure a supply of pastors for pressing vacancies, but also to solicit donations for the erection and support of a native theological seminary. Dr Mason arrived in Scotland in October 1801, met with a very cordial welcome, appealed to the Burgher Synod, visited the Hall under Dr Lawson at Selkirk, was delighted "with the correct principle, literary acquirement, and pulpit talent exhibited among the students," and used all his eloquence to induce some young men to leave "their country, and their kindred, and their father's house." He made tours into various parts of the country, and preached with extraordinary popularity, particularly at Stirling, where he "was more than usually affected by the spot, the building, and the people, through their connection with Ebenezer Erskine." In consequence of a recent Act of the General Assembly, through fright "at the Tabernacle men," he was excluded from all the pulpits of the Establishment. In a letter to Mrs Mason, he gives a graphic account of the epithets in which some good men in the Church of Scotland condemned the Act which "tied up their hands"—an Act yet unrepealed— or rather repealed for a brief season and speedily reintroduced. ' "That wicked Act!" exclaimed Dr Balfour; "That stupid Act!" cried Dr Kemp; "That nonsensical Act!" added Mr Jones. "What a pity! how foolish! how unkind!" said Mr Bonar, clasping his hands together, and lifting up his angel face toward heaven: "I am a man under authority," uttered Dr Love, with the profoundest gravity.' He also went up to London, and preached, by request, the annual sermon for the London Missionary Society, in Tottenham Court chapel, to an audience of five thousand. This discourse, named "Messiah's Throne," made a prodigious impression, and he became an idol in the metropolis, followed by crowds wherever he happened to preach. The late Dr Hamilton of Leeds used to tell many anecdotes of his powerful oratory on those occasions. "The grandeur of his conceptions," says one of his auditors, "was equalled by the dignity of his utterance." When in London, he writes his sister that he had seen George the Third; but, like a true republican, he adds, "the king is a fine-looking man; but I sighed and felt proud when I recalled the majesty of Washington." During his brief residence in this country, his great fame induced some persons to publish a small volume containing a few of his sermons and some minor pieces already printed in America. This procedure annoyed him as a great injustice, especially as the volume was accompanied with a brief and faulty biography. He thus wrote to his friend Mr Hardcastle: "Your London type-setters are sorry blades; they make no more difficulty of sporting with one's feelings than of trussing up a chicken. It was surely enough to cabbage the goods without caricaturing the owner."* Dr Mason returned to America in

---

* The volume referred to is "First Ripe Fruits; being a collection of Tracts, to which are added two Sermons." By the Rev. John M. Mason. With a short Memoir of the Author. London, R. Ogle, Great Turnstile, Holborn; Ogle & Aikman, Edinburgh; and M. Ogle, Glasgow, 1803."

the autumn of 1802, taking with him six preachers, and having collected nearly a thousand pounds for the projected Divinity Hall. He cherished a vivid recollection of the Scottish and English friends he had met with, and often corresponded with them—with Balfour, Dick, Hall, Peddie, Waugh, Hardcastle, Davidson, and Hunter.

He was at once chosen professor in the new seminary, which he had helped so powerfully to establish. His labours had now become very onerous, for they included his pastorate, his professorate, the advocacy of public objects, the editorship of a religious magazine, the secretaryship of the New York Missionary Society, and the larger proportion of the business of the growing ecclesiastical body to which he belonged—the care, in short, " of all the Churches."

Though of a catholic spirit, he was no latitudinarian, but held fast by the doctrine and discipline of his own denomination. We enter not into his famous controversy on Episcopacy with Bishop Hobart—an antagonist every way worthy of him. Suffice it to say that he was not the aggressor—that provocation called him into the field—that he fought with gallant heart and brawny arm—that his weapons were as sharp as they were massive—and that the might of his argument was equalled by the point of his invective; for his whole nature was roused by the arrogance of a system which virtually deposed him and all other ministers on whom no bishop's hands had been laid, and unchurched all the congregations that did not submit themselves to prelatic superintendence.

From a variety of causes, both personal and public, he was led, in 1810, to resign his pastoral charge; but another church was speedily erected for him. His appearances at the presbytery, when he tendered his resignation were characteristic of his high bearing and undaunted nature; for he feared nothing but God and sin. Several bursts of eloquence sped in torrents from his lips, when his statements were commented on, or his sincerity seemed to be suspected. As he raised himself to his full stature and lifted his arm, there was a hush deep as death, and then rolled out those periods of rebuke and self-vindication the thunder-tone of which bore down all opposition, and commanded universal assent. Thus he speaks, in one of his addresses, of himself,—

"Moderator, I have served this people for more than seventeen years. Malevolent eyes have continually watched me, and I challenge the world to produce a single plan or measure of mine to justify in the slightest degree the gentlest of all those foul insinuations. Opulence and grandeur I have sacrificed to the church of God, to this people, and they know it. Talent in our country need not enter the pulpit without being in some degree allied to the spirit of martyrdom. The road to wealth and honours takes another direction; other things being equal, the ministry, of all human professions, is the most helpless and unfriended. Since the time of my settlement here, lawyers, merchants, physicians, have made their fortunes; not an industrious and prudent mechanic but has laid up something for his family. But should God call me away to-morrow, after expending the flower of my life, my family could not show a single cent for the gain of more than seventeen years' toil. And were it not for some private property, quite insufficient for their maintenance and education, my wife and her children would be set adrift upon the world, without bread to eat, or raiment to put on. And yet, after my giving one of the strongest possible proofs of disinterestedness, men who have been accumulating the good things of this world, and enjoying their religion too, come forward to show their Christian zeal, by charging me with motives not only selfish, but meanly and basely selfish. One would hope that the charity which thinketh no evil, might put a good construction where it is easy; and not rack its invention in search of an evil one, when it has first to get rid of both presumption and proof to the contrary."—[*Works, vol. IV. p.* 284.]

In 1811, he was appointed Provost of Columbia College, in addition to all his other duties; and he set himself at once to liberalize the course of study, and make the literary training more effective. He held this office for above five years—attending three recitations of the senior class every week in the college, preaching three times a-week in his new church in Murray Street, and lecturing five times a-week as professor of theology. But these duties were too heavy and multifarious, and in five years he resigned the Provostship of the college, from failing health and other causes. Those other causes were the perpetual scenes of disunion at the Board—the one half being Episcopalians and the other half belonging to other denominations. The cautious, busy, and persevering Hobart was more than a match for the open, fervid, and impatient Mason. To recover his health a voyage to Europe was thought of; and as he had for eleven years discharged gratuitously the duties of theological professor, the synod voted him a gift of five hundred dollars. Accordingly, Dr Mason, his son Ebenezer, and Matthias Bruen, came over to England in August 1816, visited various parts of Scotland, and crossed to France, Belgium, Switzerland, and Italy. He was greatly benefited by the journey, and returned full of hope to New York in the end of 1817. He had met, as on his previous visit, with very great kindness, and had been received into wider society He took to Cæsar Malan at Geneva, and he heard Chalmers with rapture. Chalmers was equally captivated with him, and spoke in high terms of his "colloquial talents," his "masculine vigour," and an "eloquence which he had rarely known surpassed." But the strong man was obliged to bow, nay, the very impetus which had given such power to his eloquence, and such passion to his unwritten discourses, showed his constitutional liability to cerebral disease. It was not so much incessant wear as periodical excitement and effort strained to its maximum that wore him out,—

> All the soul in rapt suspension,
> All the quivering, palpitating

> Cords of life in utmost tension,
> With the fervour of invention,
> With the rapture of creating.

In the month of February 1820, his mind suddenly failed in the pulpit, and his train of thought had vanished beyond recall,—when, bursting into tears, he told the audience of his mental prostration, and abruptly dismissed them. He recovered, but very slowly, and though the measure was like "tearing the flesh from his bones," he purposed to demit his charge. But before the period to which he pointed had come, he received an invitation to the presidency of Dickenson College, Carlisle, in the State of Pennsylvania. He at once acceded to the request, saying, "It will employ me usefully in a work to which I find myself adequate, but which will not oppress me." The College, which had been suspended for some time, immediately revived, an able staff of professors was chosen, and students flocked to it from all parts of the country. But, in a few months, he met with an accident which long confined him to his bed, and crippled him for life. A paralytic affection, also, that "lurked about his frame," awakened in his constitution the symptoms of a previous malady. Domestic trials fell upon him at the same time,— a married daughter died, and "the heart of a father over his daughter responded to every moan of a husband's heart over his beloved wife." Not many weeks after, a promising son, James Hall, was also taken away by fever, and this stroke shattered him. As the fellow-students of the youth were about to take the first step in bearing his remains to the tomb, the father, in the anguish of his heart, suddenly exclaimed, "Tread lightly, young men, tread lightly; you carry a temple of the Holy Ghost."—"My heart bleeds," he wrote to a friend, "O pity me, I am very weak: the blossom, the blossom of my hopes gone, cut down in its richest bloom, yet I hope, and I hope not without reason, to be transplanted to a kindlier soil, to shed fresher fragrance in the paradise of God." Crushed so sorely by affliction, his constitution fast losing its nervous power, and a dimness gathering round his genius, he was heard to say, "My morn was joyous, my noon was brilliant, but clouds and shadows rest upon the evening of my days." And they were never fully lifted, though they might be raised for a moment to show the splendours which they only veiled. He resigned his situation in 1824, and returned to New York. But his great powers were permanently impaired, and the last years of his life were spent in comparative retirement. Now and then the old spirit would flash up at the sight of a friend, and a happy sentence or image would find a tremulous and imperfect utterance. But his Bible was his treasure, and amidst all his lassitude he never failed to enjoy it. What he had known and preached as truths, he now felt and enjoyed as comforts. He was able till within a very short time of his death to conduct worship in his family, and usually with correctness and ease. The time of his release came at length and he died on the 26th of December 1829, in the sixtieth year of his age.

The influence of Dr Mason during his life was very great. His name was a tower of strength. Universally acknowledged as the first preacher in the States, he gathered audiences of the high and educated classes—lawyers, senators, merchants, and scholars—men who, as they receive impressions themselves, naturally and unconsciously impart them to those around them. His noble nature, unsullied character, impulsive spirit, and tongue of fire,—his generous patriotism and chivalrous love of spiritual freedom, gave him a place far beyond the reach of vulgar ambition. He lived and laboured for the Church, either in its pulpits or colleges, with entire and self-denying devotedness, with an energy which seldom paused, and with a zeal which consumed him, wore out his nervous strength by repeated strokes of paralysis, and eventually shortened his days. He could not refuse his aid to any good work, and his services were in continual requisition. So highly, indeed, were his pleadings valued, and so constantly were they in demand for all forms of benevolent and missionary enterprise, that, as we have seen, he fell a sacrifice to his obliging temper and earnest love of usefulness, while the plaudits of thousands were weaving the garland for the victim which the patrons of charities and leaders of churches were conducting to the altar.

Dr Mason took an intense interest in theological tuition, —bent his whole mind to the discovery of the best plans, and urged the Church to adopt and support them. His sagacious addresses, in connection with Columbia and Dickenson Colleges, exhibit correct and comprehensive views of education, as being that harmonious culture by which the entire nature is developed, so as to be qualified in the highest degree for the service of the "great taskmaster." He exposed the error into which so many institutions in his own country have since been betrayed—that of hurrying a youth through his preparatory studies, and sending him "deformed, unfinished," into the public arena. Such premature dismissal from school, college, or hall, inevitably begets sciolism, one-sidedness, and smartness without solidity—acts as if precocity were a universal gift, and saves pence in the meantime at the expense of pounds at a subsequent period. In applying the sickle to the green ears and cutting them down, it may boast of superior husbandry in forcing an early harvest, but the garner will not be filled, nor the hopes of the sower realized, "with the finest of the wheat." Or, to give the figure an American aptness, a structure of logs is soon erected, and timber is far more easily shaped than marble; but the edifice of stone, which rises slowly and with toil, preserves its stateliness long after the other has been beaten down by the storm, covered with fungi, or pierced with worms.

Dr Mason was not one of those men whose forms of thought are stereotyped, who tremble at the idea of innovation, and shrink from the prospect of opposition—who take things as they are, and will not try to make them what they should be—who may have impulses and convictions, but stifle them, and ultimately coffin them in their torpid bosoms; who prefer ease to progress, and, on the pretext of alarm at disturbing others, are only courting an ignominious quiet for themselves. He burst through the shackles of his denomination, practised free communion, and published an excellent treatise on the subject. Indeed, his name is identified with that volume, and the practice which it advocates. It is not remarkable for flights of oratory, but it is cautious in its statements, though weighty in its arguments, appealing to the facts and doctrines of Scripture, and to the opinions and usages of the early Church, and refuting such objections as sectarian bias and custom were in the habit of offering with no little petulance and ingenuity. He pleaded for frequent as well as free communion, and bears hard on those good people who would not go to the Lord's table without observing a regular number of preparatory services, and could not think of lessening the full "tale of bricks" in any circumstances.

It is, however, as a Christian orator that Dr Mason is chiefly known. Not a few of his sermons are masterpieces. Their power lies in their directness—in their glowing imagery and style. They are not elaborate disquisitions, better fitted for study in the closet than recitation in the pulpit. Nor are they pieces of meretricious declamation—empty, tricksy, and gaudy—trading in oddities, and affecting dramatic variety and construction—crossing and recrossing the boundary between licit humour and buffoonery. Neither are they orations with a clause of Scripture prefixed for a motto, but neither expounding its meaning nor enforcing and illustrating its lessons. They are sermons, not academic treatises, subtle and erudite in structure, and presupposing a high cultivation on the part of the audience. It is not pathos which distinguishes them, though they excite emotion, nor yet is it fancy, though figures sparkle in every page. They are not noted as chains of argument, though every paragraph either furnishes premises, points home a conclusion, or shows a wise and warranted deduction. They are popular addresses, and all about them partake of this character. There is no technicality in the reasoning, nor abstruseness in the argument; no glitter in the ornament, nor mawkishness in the sentiment. Their power, indeed, is clothed with splendour, as the most brilliant of metals is the heaviest of metals. Dr Mason's eloquence was characterized by power, not dull vigour, but the energy which glows while it strikes, and coruscates while its forces are developed. It was not like a well whose stillness must be disturbed by a bucket, but a fountain fresh and overflowing, whose living waters gleam and sparkle as they pour themselves through the rocky channel. What Dr Mason preached was the gospel in its majesty,—truth explained, argued, defended, adorned and urged out of a heart on fire, and from lips touched with a live coal from off the altar. He does not beat about, but his words are bold and mighty. He spoke divine truth in a divine style,—simple, without sinking into common-place, vehement, but not evaporating into boisterous extravagance—original, but scorning eccentricity, for the man stamped the image of himself on his oratory. That oratory rose far above rhetoric.

The uniform rumour is, that his unprinted sermons were his greatest ones. His son tells us that for the last twenty-five years of his life he did not write one discourse for the pulpit.* Those sermons delivered without the intervention of manuscript are said to be but feebly represented by his published works. Then he was untrammelled by any effort to recollect and recite what he had composed. His mind threw off its fervid thoughts in simple grandeur, and in somewhat irregular profusion, borrowing imagery and illustration from Scripture and also from common life, not affecting classical allusions nor disdaining colloquial familiarity,—now searching the objections of the sceptic with a withering glance, and now denouncing the folly of the worldling with the wisdom of a sage and the elevation of a prophet,—calm and conversational these two minutes, and then soaring into gorgeous description, or whetted into vehement accusation, or melting in intense and final appeal.

Dr Mason had, moreover, the advantage of a princely figure,—being six feet in stature, with a high forehead, and a noble carriage. As we have heard from one who, for a brief period, enjoyed his ministrations, his deep blue eye was keen and expressive, and often more eloquent than his tongue. As it glanced and kindled, darkened and glowed again under every variety of emotion, it told more of the inner world than the more passive periods rolling from his tongue. "What lofty enthusiasm!"—"What courage and confidence!"—"What entire self-abandonment to his theme!"—"What bold conceptions and felicitous words!"—"What a tender and generous bearing!"—"What a solemn and stirring style!"—"What a subduing and captivating address!"—"What a combination of sympathy and power!"—"What an atmosphere of love and majesty he sheds around the gospel!"—were the frequent excla-

* Memoirs of J. M. Mason, D.D., by Jacob Van Vechten, New York, 1856.

mations of his hearers. His incidental remarks were like flashes of fire, if he referred to anything indecorous in appearance or manner in the house of God. More than the offender winced, smitten as if by a careless back-handed stroke. The biographer, one might almost say the idolater, of Bishop Hobart, is forced to admit no little of what we have said of Dr Mason's ready eloquence and intellectual supremacy. Alluding to the quarrels at the Board of Columbia College, he bears this testimony,—" Dr Mason was a man well calculated to wield influence in either a popular or an intellectual assembly. Powerful with his pen, he was still more powerful in speech, for a commanding figure and stentorian voice such as he possessed, are never without their influence in debate; while, at the same time, his truly great powers both of argument and sarcasm, seemed to justify him in that disdainful tone and manner with which he was wont to put to silence opponents of whom he stood not in awe." Again, " His powers, however great, were roused into action more by impulse than calm resolve;" and again, " Towering in his strength, he joined Warburtonian coarseness of manner to unquestioned learning and overbearing talent."* If we deduct the element of exaggeration infused into these sentences by an opponent, we have a strong and unpartial testimony to Dr Mason's power and influence.

In short, the eloquence of Dr Mason closely resembles that of the great Lord Chatham. It had the same grandeur and opulence of unpremeditated sentiment and graceful elocution—the same richness and variety of intonation, though the trumpet note predominated—the same lofty and generous style of thought—the same self-possession and

* Life of Bishop Hobart, by John M'Vicar, D.D., Columbia College, New York.

absence of all embarrassment—the same easy play of whispered illustration succeeded by paroxysms of excitement that subdued and entranced the hearer—the same slight tone of exaggeration blending with assertion and apostrophe, and perhaps the same consciousness of producing and intending to produce overwhelming effect. Dr Mason's style is in harmony. It is not smooth and monotonous, but living and fresh—words fitting in to the various thoughts with marvellous precision and power—calm when the orator is didactic—eager when he is impetuous—now like the crags and precipices through which the river foams and leaps—and now like the green banks fringed with willows and olives by which it glides in its level course.

His oratory has thus a character of its own. It does not resemble Hall's, which was characterized more by beauty than by force—more by refinement than by depth and vehemence; his rigid taste keeping him at once from tawdry embellishment and rugged coarseness. But while he combines ease with elegance and fluency with precision, there is a monotonous tone in his sentences, little variety in his cadences, and a want of relief generally in his composition. There lacks the flavour of almonds to his sweetnes: so that he sometimes resembles the placid sameness of Isocrates—sometimes the gentle and graceful rapidity of Cicero—rarely, if ever, like Mason, the abrupt, argumentative, intense, and irresistible periods and interrogations of Demosthenes.

No mean judge has said, indeed, that Hall's style combines the beauties of Burke, Johnson, and Addison without their defects. To this dictum we should demur. The imperial fancy of Burke laid all nature under contribution. He did not need to grapple with images and agonize till he had enthralled them, for they crouched in groups around him with oriental obeisance. These images are inwoven with his abstract reasonings, and impart vigour and stateliness to a style, which is not clipped and trimmed, but spread out like the irregular boughs and foliage of a lofty tree. He rioted in this opulence; but the mind of Hall had not such a range, and was more fastidious in its limited choice. Johnson was sonorous and solemn; his words adjusted into measured clauses, not unlike the modulation and parallelism of Hebrew poetry. His huge soul still kept its heights, and linked together its sounding epithets, whatever might chance to be the theme. His zephyrs play with sedateness, his squirrels have the unwieldy gambols of an elephant, his children have an old head on young shoulders. Hall is vastly more natural and never turgid. Still the influence of Johnson may be seen not only in Hall, but in the laboured and rythmical construction in which Mason sometimes indulges. Addison was all ease and sprightliness, with graceful negligence; and Hall and Mason resemble him when they are off their guard and give free and unrestrained expression to their thoughts. Hall and Mason were both unlike Chalmers in form of thought, style, and delivery. The Scottish preacher seized upon a primary thought, and held it and turned it in all its aspects, and still struggled with it and dwelt upon it as he pressed it with impetuous argument and luxuriant illustration on his audience—heaving forth vehement words from his impassioned soul—his rhetoric, like a "rushing mighty wind," carrying the fire of inspiration on its wings. Hall was ever calm and collected—Mason was not always under the afflatus, but often had a breathing time. The three great orators have erected for themselves imperishable monuments. If we should say that Hall's is of Parian marble, polished with exquisite skill and chaste-ness, then Mason's, though not of so fine and rich a material, has a nobler sweep and freer outline,—while that of Chalmers is of his own granite, wrought and hewn after no order, but a massive structure set upon a bold and rugged hill, where the eagle has its eyrie, and the thunder-cloud its throne.

Of living orators we speak not. Nor does our space allow us to refer to Massillon, Bourdaloue, or Saurin, nor to Reinhardt, Dräseke, Herder, or Schleiermacher.

The reader of these reprinted discourses of Dr Mason will assuredly find delight and spiritual profit in them.

JOHN EADIE.

GLASGOW,
13 LANSDOWNE CRESCENT,
APRIL 1860.

SERMON I.

THE GOSPEL FOR THE POOR.

LUKE VII. 22.

" To the poor the gospel is preached."

The Old Testament closes with a remarkable prediction concerning Messiah and his forerunner: " Behold, I will send you Elijah the prophet before the coming of the great and dreadful day of the Lord: and he shall turn the heart of the fathers to the children, and the heart of the children to their fathers, lest I come and smite the earth with a curse." Accordingly, at the appointed time, came John the Baptist, " in the spirit and power of Elias," saying, "Repent ye, for the kingdom of heaven is at hand." In his great work of *preparing the way of the Lord*, he challenged sin without respect of persons. The attempt was hazardous; but, feeling the majesty of his character, he was not to be moved by considerations which divert or intimidate the ordinary man: name, sect, station, were alike to him. Not even the imperial purple, when it harboured a crime, afforded protection from his rebuke. His fidelity in this point cost him his life: for having reproved " Herod, for Herodias, his brother Philip's wife, and for all the evils which Herod had done," he was thrown into prison, and at length sacrificed to the most implacable of all resentments,—the resentment of an abandoned woman.

It was in the interval between his arrest and execution that he sent to Jesus the message on which my text is grounded. As his office gave him no security against the workings of unbelief in the hour of temptation, it is not strange, if, in a dungeon and in chains, his mind was invaded by an occasional doubt. The question by two of his disciples, " Art thou he that should come, or do we look for another?" has all the air of an inquiry for personal satisfaction; and so his Lord's reply seems to treat it. "Go your way, and tell John what things ye have seen and heard; how that the blind see, the lame walk, the lepers are cleansed, the deaf hear, the dead are raised, to the poor the gospel is preached." The answer is clear and convincing. It enumerates the very signs by which the church was to know her God, *for whom she had waited;* and they were enough to remove the suspicions, and confirm the soul, of his servant John.

Admitting that Jesus Christ actually wrought the works here ascribed to him, every sober man will conclude with Nicodemus, "We know that thou art a teacher from God; for no man can do these miracles that thou doest, except God be with him." It is not, however, my intention to dwell on the miraculous evidence of Christianity. The article which I select as exhibiting it in a plain but interesting view, is, THE PREACHING OF GOSPEL TO THE POOR.

In scriptural language, "the poor," who are most exposed to suffering and least able to encounter it, represent all who are destitute of good necessary to their perfection and happiness; especially those who feel their want and are disconsolate; especially those who are anxiously *waiting for the consolation of Israel.* Thus in Ps. xl. 17: "I am poor and needy, yet the Lord thinketh upon me." Thus, in Is. xli. 17: "When the poor and needy seek water, and there is none, and their tongue faileth for thirst, I the Lord will hear them, I the God of Israel will not forsake them." Thus also, ch. lxi. i.: "The Lord hath anointed me to preach good tidings to the MEEK;" the same word with that rendered "poor;" and so it is translated by Luke, ch. iv. 18, "to preach the gospel to the POOR;" which is connected, both in the prophet and evangelist, with *healing the* BROKEN-HEARTED. Our Lord, therefore, refers John, as he did the Jews in the synagogue at Nazareth, to this very prediction as fulfilled in himself. So that his own definition of his own religion is, *a system of consolation for the wretched.* This is so far from excluding the *literal poor*, that the success of the gospel with them is the pledge of its success with all others: for they not only form the majority of the human race, but they also bear the chief burden of its calamities. Moreover, as the sources of pleasure and pain are substantially the same in all men; and as affliction, by suspending the influence of their artificial distinctions, reduces them to the level of their common nature;

whatever, by appealing to the principles of that nature, promotes the happiness of the multitude, must equally promote the happiness of the residue; and whatever consoles the one, must, in like circumstances, console the other also. As we cannot, therefore, maintain the suitableness of the gospel to the literal poor, who are the mass of mankind, without maintaining its prerogative of comforting the afflicted; nor, on the contrary, its prerogative of comforting, separately from its suitableness to the mass of mankind, I shall consider these two ideas as involving each other.

I. With this explanation, the first thing which demands your notice, is the FACT ITSELF—GOSPEL PREACHED TO THE POOR.

From the remotest antiquity there have been, in all civilized nations, men who devoted themselves to the increase of knowledge and happiness. Their speculations were subtle, their arguings acute, and many of their maxims respectable. But to whom were their instructions addressed? To casual visitors, to selected friends, to admiring pupils, to privileged orders! In some countries, and on certain occasions, when vanity was to be gratified by the acquisition of fame, their appearances were more public. For example, one read a poem, another a history, and a third a play, before the crowd assembled at the Olympic games. To be crowned there, was, in the proudest period of Greece, the summit of glory and ambition. But what did this, what did the mysteries of pagan worship, or what the lectures of pagan philosophy, avail the *people?* Sunk in ignorance, in poverty, in crime, they lay neglected. Age succeeded age, and school to school; a thousand sects and systems rose, flourished, and fell; but the degradation of the multitude remained. Not a beam of light found its way into their darkness, nor a drop of consolation into their cup. Indeed a plan of raising them to the dignity of rational enjoyment, and fortifying them against the disasters of life, was not to be expected: for as nothing can exceed the contempt in which they were held by the professors of wisdom; so any human device, however captivating in theory, would have been worthless in fact. The most sagacious heathen could imagine no better means of improving them than the precepts of his philosophy. Now, supposing it to be ever so salutary, its benefits must have been confined to a very few; the notion that the bulk of mankind may become philosophers, being altogether extravagant. They ever have been, and, in the nature of things, ever must be, unlearned. Besides, the grovelling superstition and brutal manners of the heathen, presented insuperable obstacles. Had the plan of their cultivation been even suggested, especially if it comprehended the more abject of the species, it would have been universally derided, and would have merited derision, no less than the dreams of modern folly about the perfectibility of man.

Under this incapacity of *instructing* the poor, how would the pagan sage have acquitted himself as their *comforter?* His dogmas, during prosperity and health, might humour his fancy, might flatter his pride, or dupe his understanding; but against the hour of grief or dissolution he had no solace for himself, and could have none for others. I am not to be persuaded, in contradiction to every principle of my animal and rational being, that pain, and misfortune, and death, are no evils; and are beneath a wise man's regard. And could I work myself up into so absurd a conviction, how would it promote my comfort? Comfort is essentially consistent with nature and truth. By perverting my judgment, by hardening my heart, by chilling my nobler warmth, and stifling my best affections, I may grow stupid; but shall be far enough from consolation. Convert me into a beast, and I shall be without remorse; into a block, and I shall feel no pain. But this was not my request. I asked you for consolation, and you destroy my ability to receive it. I asked you to bear me over death, in the fellowship of immortals, and you begin by transforming me into a monster! Here are no glad tidings: nothing to cheer the gloom of outward or inward poverty. And the pagan teacher could give me no better. From him, therefore, the miserable, even of his own country, and class, and kindred, had nothing to hope. But to *lift the needy from the dunghill,* and wipe away the tears from the mourner; to lighten the burdens of the heart; to heal its maladies, repair its losses, and enlarge its enjoyments; and that under every form of penury and sorrow, in all nations, and ages, and circumstances; as it is a scheme too vast for the human faculties, so, had it been committed to merely human execution, it could not have proceeded a single step, and would have been remembered only as a frantic reverie.

Yet all this hath Christianity undertaken. Her voice is, without distinction, to people of every colour, and clime, and condition: to the continent and the isles; to the man of the city, the man of the field, and the man of the woods; to the Moor, the Hindoo, and the Hottentot; to the sick and desperate; to the beggar, the convict, and the slave. She impairs no faculty, interdicts no affection, infringes no relation; but, taking men as they are, with all their depravity and woes, she proffers them peace and blessedness. Her boasting is not vain. The course of experiment has lasted through more than fifty generations of men. It is passing every hour before our eyes: and, for reasons to be afterwards assigned, has never failed, in a single instance, when it has been fairly tried.

The design is stupendous; and the least success induces us to inquire, by whom it was projected and carried into effect. And what is our astonishment, when we learn, that it was by men of obscure birth, mean education, and feeble resource; by men from a nation hated for their religion, and proverbial for their moroseness; by carpenters, and tax-gatherers, and fishermen of Judea! What shall we say of this phenomenon? A recurrence to the Jewish scriptures, which had long predicted it, either surrenders the argument, or increases the difficulty. If you admit that they reveal futurity, you recognise the finger of God, and the controversy is at an end. If you call them mere conjectures, you are still to account for their correspondence with the event, and to explain how a great system of benevolence, unheard, unthought of by learned antiquity, came to be cherished, to be transmitted for centuries from father to son, and at length attempted among the *Jews!* And you are also contradicted by the fact, that however clearly such a system is marked out in their scriptures, they were so far from adopting it, that they entirely mistook it; rejected it, nationally, with disdain; persecuted unto death those who embarked in it; and have not embraced it to this day! Yet in the midst of this bigoted and obstinate people, sprang up the deliverance of the human race. *Salvation is of the Jews.* Within half a century after the resurrection of Christ, his disciples had penetrated to the extremes of the Roman empire, and had carried the *dayspring from on high* to innumerable tribes who were *sitting in the region and shadow of death.* And so exclusively *Christian* is this plan, so remote from the sphere of common effort, that after it has been proposed and executed, men revert perpetually to their wonted littleness and carelessness. The whole face of Christendom is overspread with proofs, that, in proportion as they depart from the simplicity of the gospel, they forget the multitude as before, and the doctrines of consolation expire. In so far, too, as they adapt, to their own notions of propriety, the general idea, which they have borrowed from the gospel, of meliorating the condition of their species, they have produced, and are every day producing, effects the very reverse of their professions. Discontent, and confusion, and crimes, they propagate in abundance. They have smitten the earth with curses, and deluged it with blood; but the instance is yet to be discovered, in which they have *bound up the broken-hearted.* The *fact,* therefore, that Christianity is, in the broadest sense of the terms, *glad tidings to the poor,* is perfectly original. It stands without rival or comparison. It has no foundation in the principles of human enterprise; and could never have existed without the inspiration of that *Father of lights from whom cometh down every good and every perfect gift.*

II. As the Christian FACT is original, so the REASONS OF ITS EFFICACY ARE PECULIAR. Christianity can afford consolation, because *it is fitted to our nature and character.* I specify particulars:

First. The gospel proceeds upon the principle of *immortality.*

That our bodies shall die is indisputable. But that reluctance of nature, that panting after life, that horror of annihilation, of which no man can completely divest himself, connect the death of the body with deep solicitude. While neither these, nor any other merely rational considerations, ascertain the certainty of future being; much less of future bliss. The feeble light which glimmered around this point among the heathen, flowed not from investigation, but tradition. It was to be seen chiefly among the vulgar, who inherited the tales of their fathers; and among the poets, who preferred popular fable to philosophic speculation. Reason would have pursued her discovery; but the pagans knew not how to apply the notion of immortality, even when they had it. It governed not their precepts; it established not their hope. When they attempted to discuss the grounds of it, *they became vain in their imaginations, and their foolish heart was darkened.* The best arguments of Socrates are unworthy of a child who has *learned the holy scriptures.* And it is remarkable enough, that the doctrine of immortality is as perfectly detached, and as barren of moral effect, in the hands of modern infidels, as it was in the hands of the ancient pagans. They have been so unable to assign it a convenient place in their system; they have found it to be so much at variance with their habits, and so troublesome in their warfare with the scriptures, that the more resolute of the sect have discarded it altogether. With the soberer part of them it is no better than an opinion; but it never was, and never will be, a source of true consolation, in any system or any bosom, but the system of Christianity and the bosom of the Christian. *Life and immortality*, about which some have guessed; for which all have sighed; but of which none could trace the relations, or prove the existence; are not merely hinted, they *are brought to light by the gospel*. This is the parting point with every other religion; and yet the very point upon which our happiness hangs. That we shall survive the body, and pass from its dissolution to the bar of God, and from the bar of God to endless retribution, are truths of infinite moment, and of pure revelation. They demonstrate the incapacity of temporal things to content the soul. They explain why grandeur, and pleasure, and fame, leave the heart sad. He who pretends to be my comforter without consulting my immortality, overlooks my essential want. The gospel supplies it. Immortality is the basis of her fabric. She resolves the importance of man into its true reason—the *value of his soul*. She sees under every human form, however rugged or abused, a spirit unalterable by external change, unassailable by death, and endued with stupendous faculties of knowledge and action, of enjoyment and suffering; a spirit, at the same time, depraved and guilty; and therefore liable to irreparable ruin. These are Christian views. They elevate us to a height, at which the puny theories of the world stand and gaze. They stamp new interest on all my relations, and all my acts. They hold up before me objects vast as my wishes, terrible as my fears, and permanent as my being. They bind me to eternity.

Secondly. Having thus unfolded the general doctrine of immortality, the gospel advances further, informing us, that although a future life is sure, *future blessedness is by no means a matter of course*. This receives instant confirmation from a review of our character as *sinners*.

None but an atheist, or, which is the same thing, a madman, will deny the existence of moral obligation, and the sanction of moral law. In other words, that it is our duty to obey God, and that he has annexed penalties to disobedience. As little can it be denied, that we have actually disobeyed him. Guilt has taken up its abode in the conscience, and indicates, by signs not to be misunderstood, both its presence and power. To call this superstition, betrays only that vanity, which thinks to confute a doctrine by giving it an ill name. Depravity and its consequences meet us, at every moment, in a thousand shapes; nor is there an individual breathing, who has escaped its taint. Therefore our relations to our Creator as innocent creatures have ceased; and are succeeded by the relation of rebels against his government. In no other light can he contemplate us, because his *judgment is according to truth.* A conviction of this begets alarm and wretchedness. And whatever some may pretend, a guilty conscience is the secret worm, which preys upon the vitals of human peace: the invisible spell, which turns the draught of pleasure into wormwood and gall. To laugh at it as an imaginary evil, is the mark of a fool: for what can be more rational than to tremble at the displeasure of an Almighty God. If, then, I ask how I am to be delivered? or whether deliverance is possible? human reason is dumb: or if she open her lips, it is only to tease me with conjectures, which evince that she knows nothing of the matter. Here the Christian verity interferes; showing me, on the one hand, that my alarm is well founded; that my demerit and danger are far beyond even my own suspicions; that God, with whom I have to do, *will by no means clear the guilty;* but on the other hand, revealing the provision of his infinite wisdom and grace, for releasing me from guilt. "God so loved the world, that he gave his only begotten Son, that whosoever believeth in him should not perish, but have everlasting life." The more I ponder this method of salvation, the more I am convinced that it displays the divine perfection, and exalts the divine government; so that "it became him, for whom are all things, and by whom are all things, in bringing many sons unto glory, to make the Captain of their salvation perfect through sufferings." Now I know where to obtain the first requisite to happiness, pardon of sin. In Christ Jesus the Lord, is that justifying righteousness, the want of which, though I was ignorant of the cause, kept me miserable till this hour. I cling to it, and am safe. His precious blood *purges my conscience. It extends peace to me as a river, and the glory of redemption like a flowing stream.* My worst fears are dispelled: *the wrath to come* is not for me: I can look with composure at futurity, and feel joy springing up with the thought that I am immortal.

Thirdly. In addition to deliverance from wrath, Christianity provides relief against the *plague of the heart.*

It will not be contested, that disorder reigns among the passions of men. The very attempts to rectify it are a sufficient concession; and their ill success shows their authors to have been *physicians of no value.* That particular ebullitions of passion have been repressed and particular habits of vice overcome, without Christian aid, is admitted. But if any one shall conclude, that these are examples of victory over the *principle* of depravity, he will greatly err. For, not to insist that the experience of the world is against him, we have complete evidence that all reformations, not evangelical, are merely an exchange of lusts; or rather, the elevation of one evil appetite by the depression of another; the *strength* of depravity continuing the same; its *form* only varied. Nor can it be otherwise. Untaught of God, the most comprehensive genius is unable either to trace the original of corruption, or to check its force. It has its fountain where he least and last believes it to be—but where the omniscient eye has searched it out—in the human heart: the heart, filled with *enmity against God*—the heart, *deceitful above all things, and desperately wicked.* "But the discovery being made, his measures, you hope, will take surer effect." Quite the contrary. It now defies his power as it formerly did his wisdom. How have disciples of the moral school studied and toiled! how have they resolved, and vowed, and fasted, watched and prayed, travelling through the whole circuit of devout austerities! and set down at last, *wearied in the greatness of their way!* But no marvel! the *Ethiopian cannot change his skin, nor the leopard his spots.* Neither can impurity purify itself. Here again, light from the footsteps of the Christian truth breaks in upon the darkness; and gospel again flows from her tongue; the gospel of a *new heart*—the gospel of regenerating and sanctifying grace; as the promise, the gift, the work of God. " I will sprinkle clean water upon you, and you shall be clean : from all your filthiness, and from all your idols will I cleanse you; a new heart also will I give you, and a new spirit will I put within you; and I will take away the stony heart out of your flesh; and I will give you a heart of flesh; and I will put my spirit within you, and cause you to walk in my statutes, and ye shall keep my judgments and do them." Here all our difficulties are resolved at once. The spirit of life in Christ Jesus quickens *the dead in trespasses and sins*. *The Lord, our strength, works in us all the good pleasure of his goodness, and the work of faith with power.* That which was impossible with men, is not so with him; for *with him all things are possible; even the subduing our iniquities;* creating us anew, after his own image, *in knowledge, righteousness, and true holiness;* turning our polluted souls into his own *habitation through the Spirit;* and making us *meet for the inheritance of the saints in light.* Verily *this is gospel;* worthy to go in company with remission of sin. And shall I conquer at last? Shall I, indeed, be delivered from the bondage and the torment of corruption? A new sensation passes through my breast. *I lift up mine eyes to the hills from whence cometh my help;* and with the hope of *perfecting holiness in the fear of God,* hail my immortality.

Fourthly. Having thus removed our guilt, and cleansed our affections, the gospel proceeds to put us in possession of *adequate enjoyment.* An irresistible law of our being impels us to seek happiness. Nor will a million of frustrated hopes deter from new experiments; because despair is infinitely more excruciating than the fear of fresh disappointment. But an impulse, always vehement and never successful, multiplies the materials and inlets of pain. This assertion carries with it its own proof; and the principle it assumes is verified by the history of our species. In every place, and at all times, ingenuity has been racked to meet the ravenous desires. Occupation, wealth, dignity, science, amusement, all have been tried; are all tried at this hour; and all in vain. The heart still repines: the unappeased cry is, Give, give. There is a fatal error somewhere; and the gospel detects it. Fallen away from God, we have substituted the creature in his place. This is the grand mistake: the fraud which sin has committed upon our nature. The gospel reveals God as the satisfying good, and brings it within our reach. It proclaims him reconciled in Christ Jesus, as our father, our friend, our portion. It introduces us into his presence with liberty to ask in the Intercessor's name, and asking, to *receive, that our joy may be full.* It keeps us under his eye; surrounds us with his arm; feeds us upon *living bread* which he *gives from heaven:* seals us up to an eternal inheritance; and even engages to reclaim our dead bodies from the grave, and fashion them in beauty, which shall vie with heaven! It is enough! My prayers and desires can go no further: I have got to the *fountain of living waters—Return to thy rest, O my soul, for the Lord hath dealt bountifully with thee!*

This gospel of immortality, in righteousness, purity, and bliss, would be inestimable, were it even obscure, and not to be comprehended without painful scrutiny. But I observe again,

Fifthly. That, unlike the systems of men, and contrary to their anticipations, the gospel is as *simple,* as it is glorious. Its primary doctrines, though capable of exercising the most disciplined talent, are adapted to the common understanding. Were they dark and abstruse, they might gratify a speculative mind, but would be lost upon the multitude, and be unprofitable to all, as doctrines of consolation. The mass of mankind never can be profound reasoners. To omit other difficulties, they have not leisure. Instruction, to do them good, must be interesting, solemn, repeated, and plain. This is the benign office of the gospel. Her principal topics are few; they are constantly recurring in various connections; they come home to every man's condition; they have an interpreter in his bosom; they are enforced by motives which honesty can hardly mistake, and conscience will rarely dispute. Unlettered men, who love their Bible, seldom quarrel about the prominent articles of faith and duty; and as seldom do they appear among the proselytes of that meagre refinement which arrogates the title of *Philosophical Christianity.*

From its simplicity, moreover, the gospel derives advantages in consolation. Grief, whether in the learned or illiterate, is always simple. A man, bowed down under calamity, has no relish for investigation. His powers relax; he leans upon his comforter; his support must be without toil, or his spirit faints. Conformably to these reflections, we see, on the one hand, that the unlearned compose the bulk of Christians; the life of whose souls is in the substantial doctrines of the cross—and on the other, that in the time of affliction even the careless lend their ear to the voice of revelation. Precious, at all times, to believers, it is doubly precious in the hour of trial. These things prove, not only that the gospel, when understood, gives a peculiar relief in trouble, but that it is readily apprehended, being most acceptable, when we are the least inclined to critical research.

Sixthly. The gospel, so admirable for its simplicity, has also the recommendation of *truth.* The wretch who dreams of transport, feels a new sting in his wretchedness, when he opens his eyes and the delusion is fled. No real misery can be removed, nor any real benefit conferred by doctrines which want the seal of certainty. And were the gospel of Jesus a human invention! or were it checked by any rational suspicion, that it may turn out to be a fable, it might retain its brilliancy, its sublimity, and even a portion of its interest; but the charm of its consolation would be gone. Nay, it would add gall to bitterness, by fostering a hope, which the next hour might laugh to scorn. But we may dismiss our anxiety: for there is no hazard of such an issue. Not only " grace," but " truth," came by Jesus Christ. *The gracious words which proceeded out of his mouth,* were words of the *Amen, the faithful and true witness* ; and those which he has written in his blessed book, are *pure words, as silver tried in the furnace, purified seven times.* His promises can no man deny to be *exceeding great;* yet they derive their value to us from assurances, which by satisfying the hardest conditions of evidence, render doubt not only inexcusable, but even criminal. *By two immutable things in which it was* IMPOSSIBLE FOR GOD TO LIE, *we have a strong consolation who have fled for refuge to lay hold upon the hope set before us.* Now, therefore, the promises of the gospel, which are " exceeding great," are also " precious." We need not scruple to trust ourselves for this life and the life to come, upon that word which shall stand when *heaven and earth pass away.* Oh, it is this which makes Christianity glad tidings to the depressed and perishing! No fear of disappointment! No hope that shall *make ashamed!* Under the feet of evangelical faith is a covenant-promise, and that promise is everlasting Rock. *I know,* said one, whose testimony is corroborated by millions in both worlds, *I know whom I have believed, and I am persuaded that he is able to keep that which I have committed unto him against that day.*

Lastly. The gospel, as a system of consolation, is perfected by the *authority* and *energy* which accompany it. The devices of man originate in his fancy, and expire with his breath. Destitute of power, they play around depravity, like shadows round the mountain-top, and vanish without leaving an impression.

Their effect would be inconsiderable, could he manifest them to be true; because he cannot compel the admission of truth itself into the human mind. Indifference, unreasonableness, prejudice, petulance, oppose to it an almost incredible resistance. We see this in the affairs of every day, and especially in the stronger conflicts of opinion and passion. Now, beside the opposition which moral truth has always to encounter, there is a particular reason why the truth of the gospel, though most salutary, though attested by everything within us and around us: by life and death; by earth and heaven and hell; will not succeed unless backed by divine energy. It is this. Sin has perverted the understanding of man, and poisoned his heart. It persuaded him first to throw away his blessedness, and then to hate it. The reign of this hatred, which the Scriptures call *enmity against God*, is most absolute in every unrenewed man. It teaches him never to yield a point unfriendly to one corruption, without stipulating for an equivalent in favour of another. Now, as the gospel flatters *none* of his corruptions in *any* shape, it meets with deadly hostility from *all his corruptions* in *every* shape. It is to no purpose that you press upon him the "great salvation;" that you demonstrate his errors and their corrective; his diseases and their cure. Demonstrate you may, but you convert him not. He will occasionally startle and listen; but it is only to relapse into his wonted supineness: and you shall as soon call up the dead from their dust, as awaken him to a sense of his danger, and prevail with him to embrace the salvation of God. "Where, then," you will demand, "is the pre-eminence of your gospel?" I answer, with the apostle Paul, that *it is the power of God to salvation.* When a sinner is to be converted, that is, when a slave is to be liberated from his chains, and a rebel from execution, that same voice which has spoken in the scriptures, speaks by them to his heart, and commands an audience. He finds the word of God to be *quick and powerful, and sharper than any two-edged sword.* It sets him before the bar of justice; strips him of his self-importance; *sweeps away his refuge of lies!* and shows him that death which is *the wages of sin.* It then conducts him, all trembling, to the divine forgiveness; reveals Christ Jesus in his soul, as his righteousness, his peace, his hope of glory. Amazing transition! But is not the cause equal to the effect? *Hath not the potter power over the clay?* Shall God draw, and the lame not run? Shall God speak, and the deaf not hear? Shall God breathe, and the slain not live? Shall God *lift up the light of his countenance* upon sinners reconciled in his dear Son, and they not be happy? Glory to his name. These are no fictions. *We speak that we do know, and testify that we have seen. The record, written not with ink, but with the Spirit of the living God; not in tables of stone, but in fleshly tables of the heart,* is possessed by thousands who have *turned from the power of Satan unto God,* and will certify that the revolution was accomplished by his word. And if it perform such prodigies on corruption and death, what shall it not perform in directing, establishing, and consoling them, who have already obtained a *good hope through grace?* He who thunders in the curse, speaks peace in the promise; and none can conceive its influence but they who have witnessed it. For proofs you must not go to the statesman, the traveller, or the historian. You must not go to the gay profession, or the splendid ceremonial. You must go to the chamber of unostentatious piety. You must go to the family anecdote, to the Christian tradition, to the observation of faithful ministers. Of the last there are many who, with literal truth, might address you as follows: "I *have seen* this gospel hush into a calm the tempest raised in the bosom by conscious guilt. I *have seen* it melt down the most obdurate into tenderness and contrition. I *have seen* it cheer up the broken-hearted, and bring the tear of gladness into eyes swollen with grief. I *have seen* it produce and maintain serenity under evils, which drive the worldling mad. I *have seen* it reconcile the sufferer to his cross, and send the song of praise from lips quivering with agony. I *have seen* it enable the most affectionate relatives to part in death; not without emotion, but without repining; and with a cordial surrender of all that they held most dear, to the disposal of their heavenly Father. I *have seen* the fading eye brighten at the promise of Jesus: 'Where I am, there shall my servant be also.' I *have seen* the faithful spirit released from its clay, now mildly, now triumphantly, to enter into the joy of its Lord."

Who, among the children of men, that *doubts* this representation, would not *wish* it to be correct? Who, that thinks it only *probable,* will not welcome the doctrine on which it is founded, as *worthy of all acceptation?* And who, that *knows* it to be true, will not set his seal to that doctrine as being, most emphatically, *gospel preached to the poor?*

In applying to practical purposes the account which has now been given of the Christian religion, I remark,

1. That it fixes a criterion of Christian ministrations.

If he, who *spake as never man spake*, has declared his own doctrine to abound with consolation to the miserable, then, certainly, the instructions of others are evangelical, only in proportion as they subserve the same gracious end. A contradiction, not unfrequent among some advocates of revelation, is to urge against the infidel its power of comfort, and yet to avoid, in their own discourses, almost every principle from which that power is drawn. Disregarding the mass of mankind, to whom the gospel is peculiarly fitted, and omitting those truths which might revive the grieved spirit, or touch the slumbering conscience, they discuss their moral topics in a manner unintelligible to the illiterate, uninteresting to the mourner, and without alarm to the profane. This is not " preaching Christ." Elegant dissertations upon virtue and vice, upon the evidences of revelation, or any other general subject, may entertain the prosperous and the gay; but they will not *mortify our members which are upon the earth;* they will not unsting calamity, nor feed the heart with an imperishable hope. When I go to the house of God, I do not want amusement. I want *the doctrine which is according to godliness.* I want to hear of the remedy against the harassings of my guilt, and the disorder of my affections. I want to be led from weariness and disappointment, to that *goodness which filleth the hungry soul.* I want to have light upon the mystery of providence; to be taught how the *judgments of the Lord are right;* how I shall be prepared for duty and for trial—how I may *pass the time of my sojourning here in fear,* and close it in peace. Tell me of that Lord Jesus, *who his own self bare our sins in his own body on the tree.* Tell me of his *intercession for the transgressors* as their *advocate with the Father.* Tell me of his Holy Spirit, whom *they that believe on him receive,* to be their preserver, sanctifier, comforter. Tell me of his chastenings; their necessity, and their use. Tell me of his presence, and sympathy, and love. Tell me of the virtues, as growing out of his cross, and nurtured by his grace. Tell me of the glory reflected on his name by the obedience of faith. Tell me of vanquished death, of the purified grave, of a blessed resurrection, of the life everlasting—and my bosom warms. This is gospel; these are glad tidings to me as a sufferer, because glad to me as a sinner. They rectify my mistakes; allay my resentments; rebuke my discontent; support me under the weight of moral and natural evil. These attract the poor; steal upon the thoughtless; awe the irreverent; and throw over the service of the sanctuary a majesty, which some fashionable modes of address never fail to dissipate. Where they are habitually neglected, or lightly referred to, there may be much grandeur, but there is no gospel; and those preachers have infinite reason to tremble, who, though admired by the great, and caressed by the vain, are deserted by the poor, the sorrowful, and such as *walk humbly with their God.*

2. We should learn from the gospel, lessons of active benevolence.

The Lord Jesus, who *went about doing good, has left us an example that we should follow his steps.* Christians, on whom he has bestowed affluence, rank, or talent, should be the last to disdain their fellow-men, or to look with indifference on indigence and grief. Pride, unseemly in all, is detestable in them, who confess that *by grace they are saved.* Their Lord and Redeemer, who humbled himself by assuming their nature, came to *deliver the needy, when he crieth, the poor also, and him that hath no helper.* And surely an object, which was not unworthy of the Son of God, cannot be unworthy of any who are called by his name. Their wealth and opportunities, their talents and time, are not their own, nor to be used according to their own pleasure; but to be consecrated by their vocation *as fellow-workers with God.* How many hands that hang down would be lifted up; how many feeble knees confirmed; how many tears wiped away; how many victims of despondency and infamy rescued by a close imitation of Jesus Christ. Go, with your opulence to the house of famine, and the retreats of disease. Go, *deal thy bread to the hungry: when thou seest the naked, cover him; and hide not thyself from thine own flesh.* Go, and furnish means to rear the offspring of the poor; that they may at least have access to the word of your God. Go, and quicken the flight of the Angel, who has the *everlasting gospel to preach* unto the nations. If you possess not wealth, employ your station in promoting good will toward men. *Judge the fatherless; plead for the widow.* Stimulate the exertions of others, who may supply what is *lacking on your part.* Let the *beauties of holiness* pour their lustre upon your distinctions, and recommend to the unhappy that peace which yourselves have found in the salvation of God. If you have neither riches nor rank, devote your *talents*. Ravishing are the accents, which dwell on the *tongue of the learned*, when it *speaks a word in season to him that is weary*. Press your genius and your eloquence into the service of the *Lord your righteousness*, to magnify his word, and display the riches of his grace. Who knoweth whether he may honour you to be the minister of joy to the disconsolate, of liberty to the captive, of life to the dead? If he has denied you wealth, and rank, and talent, consecrate your *heart*. Let it dissolve in sympathy. There is nothing to hinder your *rejoicing with them that do rejoice, and your weeping with them that weep;* nor to forbid the interchange of kind and soothing offices. *A brother is born for adversity;* and not only should Christian be to Christian *a friend that sticketh closer than a brother*, but he should exemplify the loveliness of his religion to *them that are without*. An action, a word, marked by the sweetness of the gospel, has often been owned of God for producing the happiest effects. Let no man, therefore, try to excuse his inaction; for no man is too inconsiderable to augment the triumphs of the gospel, by assisting in the consolation which it yields to the miserable.

3. Let all classes of the unhappy repair to the Christian truth, and "draw water with joy out of its wells of salvation!" Assume your own characters, O ye children of men! Present your grievances, and accept the consolation which the gospel tenders. Come, now, ye tribes of pleasure, who have exhausted your strength in pursuing phantoms that retire at your approach! The voice of the Son of God in the gospel is, "Wherefore spend ye your money for that which is not bread, and your labour for that which satisfieth not; hearken diligently unto me, and eat ye that which is good, and let your soul delight itself in fatness." Come, ye tribes of ambition, who burn for the applause of your fellow-worms! The voice of the Son of God to you is, "The friendship of this world is enmity with God; but if any serve me him will my Father honour." Come, ye avaricious, who pant after the dust of the earth on the head of the poor! The voice of the Son of God is, Wisdom is "more precious than rubies; and all the things thou canst desire are not to be compared unto her" —but "what shall it profit a man if he shall gain the whole world,

and lose his own soul?" Come, ye profane! The voice of the Son of God is, "Hearken unto me ye stout-hearted, that are far from righteousness; behold I bring near my righteousness. Come, ye formal and self-sufficient, who say *that ye are rich, and increased with goods, and have need of nothing; and know not that you are wretched, and miserable, and poor, and blind, and naked!* The voice of the Son of God is, "I counsel you to buy of me gold tried in the fire that ye may be rich; and white raiment that ye may be clothed; and that the shame of your nakedness do not appear; and anoint your eyes with eye-salve, that ye may see. Come, ye, who, being convinced of sin, fear lest the *fierce anger of the Lord fall upon you!* The voice of the Son of God is, "Him that cometh unto me I will in no wise cast out. I, even I, am he that blotteth out thy transgressions for mine own sake, and will not remember thy sins." Come, ye disconsolate, whose souls are sad, because the Comforter is away! The voice of the Son of God is, The Lord "hath sent me to appoint unto them that mourn in Zion, beauty for ashes, the oil of joy for mourning, and the garment of praise for the spirit of heaviness." Come, ye tempted who are borne down with the violence of the *law in your members*, and of assaults from the evil one! The voice of the Son of God is, "I will be merciful to your unrighteousness, and the God of peace shall bruise Satan under your feet shortly." Come, ye children of domestic woe, upon whom the Lord has made a breach, by taking away your counsellors and support! The voice of the Son of God is, "Leave thy fatherless children with me; I will preserve them alive; and let thy widows trust in me." Come, ye, from whom mysterious providence has swept away the acquisitions of long and reputable industry! The voice of the Son of God is, "My son, if thou wilt receive my words thou shalt have a treasure in the heavens that faileth not; and mayest take joyfully the spoiling of thy goods, knowing that thou hast in heaven a better and enduring substance." Come, ye poor, who without property to lose, are grappling with distress, and exposed to want! The Son of God, though the heir of all things, *had not where to lay his head;* and his voice to his poor is, "Be content with such things as ye have, for I will never leave thee nor forsake thee; thy bread shall be given thee, and thy water shall be sure." Come, ye reproached, who find *cruel mockings* a most bitter persecution! The voice of the Son of God is, "If ye be repreached for the name of Christ happy are ye, for the Spirit of God and of glory resteth upon you." Come, in fine, ye dejected, whom the fear of death holds in bondage! The voice of the Son of God is, " I will ransom them from the power of the grave, I will redeem them from death. O death, I will be thy plagues! O grave, I will be thy destruction! repentance shall be hid from mine eyes;"—Blessed Jesus! thy loving-kindness shall *be my joy in the house of my pilgrimage;* and I will praise thee *while I have any being,* for that gospel which thou hast preached to the poor!

SERMON II.*

DIVINE JUDGMENTS.

HAB. ii. 3.

"O Lord, in wrath remember mercy."

AT the time when our prophet directed to the throne of grace that sublime and affecting petition of which our text is a part, the circumstances of his country were calamitous, and her prospects alarming. The Most High God, provoked at her unfaithfulness, had withdrawn the smiles of his countenance, and the protection of his arm. To make her know, by sad experience, that it is indeed an evil thing and bitter to depart from God, he commissioned his servant Habakkuk to foretel the speedy invasion of the Chaldeans, and to declare that he would yield her a helpless prey to this fierce and unpitying foe. The posterity of Abraham, like all other sinners, were the authors of all the woes which they felt or expected. Regardless of the first principle of sound policy, that "righteousness exalteth a nation, but sin is a reproach to any people," the generality of the Jews had abandoned the God of their fathers, and *turned aside like a deceitful bow.* Not only were they blind to the typical nature of their economy, and the spiritual sense of their peculiar observances; but they threw off the restraint of moral principle, and indulged, with unblushing impudence, their criminal passions. To such an awful height had impiety and profligacy risen, that they were chargeable with "transgressing and lying against the Lord, and departing from their God; speaking oppression and revolt, conceiving and uttering from the heart words of falsehood. Yea, judgment was turned away backward, and justice stood afar off; for truth was fallen in

---

* Preached 20th September, 1793, a day set apart in the city of New York for Public Fasting, Humiliation, and Prayer, on account of the Yellow Fever in the city of Philadelphia.

the street, and equity could not enter; yea, truth failed, and he that departed from evil made himself a prey. In vain did God warn by his providence; in vain remonstrate by his prophets: these sons of rebellion and obstinacy persisted in their crimes, till *the sin of Judah*, no longer tolerable, was *written with a pen of iron, and with the point of a diamond.* Abused patience aggravated, and hastened, the doom of this guilty people. Since they hardened their hearts against mild expostulation and gentle correction, the Lord God thundered his threatenings, and in terrible indignation said, " Shall I not visit for these things? And shall not my soul be avenged on such a nation as this?" Pious Habakkuk, who clearly saw the impending ruin, wept, in secret, over the infatuation of his countrymen; acknowledged the justice of Jehovah's controversy; and wrestled in fervent prayer for devoted Israel: "O Lord, I have heard thy speech," the sentence which thou hast denounced against my people, "and was afraid: O Lord," we indeed deserve all the evils to which it condemns us: yet cast us not, I pray thee, out of thy sight, but " revive thy work in the midst of the years," these years of trouble which are coming upon us; " in the midst even of these years, make known" thyself and thy tender compassions: " in wrath," merited wrath, " remember," and testify, unmerited " mercy."

The words *wrath, mercy, remember*, which occur in the text, must be understood and explained in a sense which will not militate against the purity and simplicity of the divine nature. It would be both ignorant and impious to ascribe to Jehovah those emotions which agitate the bosom of a mortal. In the uncreated mind, there is, properly speaking, neither passion nor affection, but all is pure *act.* The *wrath* of God, then, as it respects himself, in his *holy determination to punish sin;* and, as it respects his creatures, is the *execution* of that determination. *Mercy*, in Him, is that perfection which is ever ready to relieve the miserable; and when it regards misery connected with *guilt*, it is termed *grace.*

As everything is invariably present to the infinite mind, God cannot be strictly said to *forget:* and therefore to *remember mercy* is the same as to *show mercy.* And the prayer of the prophet is briefly this, that the Lord would graciously remove from the Israelites the punishment of their sin, or would soften, with kindness, the rigour of his chastisements.

Let us not imagine, my brethren, that *we* have no concern in a petition which refers immediately to an occasion that existed many centuries past. To all who "discern the signs of the times," the judgments of God, which are abroad in the land, furnish an ample proof that this is a day of rebuke, and of the Lord's anger. And, therefore, every one who is under the power of godliness, will immediately see that the inquiries, and the exercises suggested by the prayer of the prophet, are peculiarly adapted to the serious purpose for which we have this morning assembled. "O Lord, in wrath remember mercy."

In applying these words to the service of the day, we are naturally led to contemplate our *situation* and our *duty*. By adverting to the former, we will find that *wrath* is upon us from the Lord; and therefore our duty is to plead with him for *mercy*.

First, with respect to our *situation:* the Lord is dealing with us in wrath.

Here lend me your attention whilst I briefly prove the fact; and vindicate the divine procedure, by showing the righteous reasons on which it is founded.

I. The Lord is dealing with us in wrath.

Let the careless, if they please, contemn the assertion as of no importance; or the profane deride it as the child of superstition; it is a solemn truth that Jehovah *has* a controversy with America. Very suitable to her condition is the spirit of the prophetic exclamation "Hear ye, O mountains; and ye strong foundations of the earth! for the Lord hath a controversy with his people, and he will plead with Israel." For the confirmation of what has now been advanced, it is not necessary to recur to scenes which time has almost buried in oblivion, and which are nowhere preserved but in the records of the historian. Those symptoms of the divine displeasure on which I insist, are such as have recently occurred, and must be fresh in the memories of all who have arrived at the age of manhood.

It is not long since war desolated our country. We saw her invaded by a numerous and disciplined army, trained to be the tool of oppression, and hired to commit deeds of blood, in order to insure success to schemes of iniquity—We saw our suffering citizens driven from their homes by these sons of plunder, and obliged to seek, among strangers, an asylum from the wintry blast, and relief from the miseries of poverty and exile—We saw the temples of the living God wrested from the peaceful worshipper; ravaged and wrapt in flames, by wretches whose senselessness could be equalled only by their impiety—We saw a part at least of the States overrun by banditti, whose conduct was marked with perfidy and violence—We saw the sword of slaughter drawn, and the fields of America drenched with the blood of her children. For more than seven years did woe stream her bitterness into our daily cup.* At length the Lord was pleased to remove

* The Author has learnt that some persons, whose partiality to Great Britain will not permit them to enter into the views and feelings which *ought* to predominate in the breast of every American citizen, have taken umbrage at the foregoing sentences, which allude to the devastation committed by the British army. To make truth and duty the basis of his public discourses, is a maxim to which he would preserve the most rigid adherence; and if any are offended at him for freely declaring the one or fulfilling the other, it cannot be helped. It never has been, and he hopes never shall be, his practice to model his discourses upon a previous calculation whom they may please, or whom displease. He has, however, reviewed with cool deliberation the obnoxious passages, and cannot find, after the strictest examination, one assertion false, or uncharitable, or unseasonable; and therefore is not at liberty to make the least alteration. But while the consciousness that he has said no more than can be well defended, or was exacted by fidelity to his trust, forbids him to apologize; yet respect for some whose judgment he reveres, and whose friendship he values, induces him to explain. Such he assures, that nothing was further from his mind than an intention to wound the feelings of any person whatever—that he throws no *national* reflections: sensible that such reflections are at all times unjust and illiberal; and that among the disinterested, the judicious, and unprejudiced, those who were *well-informed*, were, even in Britain, the friends of America—that what he says, even of the army, is meant of the army in *general*. There were, he is happy to acknowledge, some noble exceptions; and that he does not enter into the merits of a political controversy, but simply states matters of notorious fact. He must detain the reader a little longer, while he vindicates the expressions themselves, as well as the spirit which they breathe; and if he advance any things which look like political discussion, it is not his fault; he is compelled to do it.

The army destined to subdue America, he styled, and rightly styled, *a tool of oppression*. Such, standing armies have always been, and, in the nature of things, always must be. It is nothing but the tameness of slavery, or the sottishness of prejudice, which can inspire a thinking being with a different sentiment. Their whole history, from their first institution till this hour, is little else than the history of destructive machines in the hands of intrigue and cruelty. And whether the standing army of Britain is *now* guided by better principles, or employed to better purposes, let the occurrences of every day attest. That army, with respect to America, was "hired to commit deeds of blood in order to insure success to schemes of iniquity." Did they not fight for their from us the rod of his anger; to respite us from affliction, and to give peace in our borders. The happy effects of a change so de-

pay, and because they were *ordered* to fight? Were they not sent for the express purpose of cannonading and bayoneting, and burning the Americans into *unconditional submission to arbitrary measures?* And was not that scheme itself, independently on any other sufficiently iniquitous? Was it not iniquitous to trample under foot every principle of natural right, in refusing the Americans a voice when their *own* property was to be given away? And to tear from their hands the rewards of honest industry, with the imperiousness of masters, and the rapacity of robbers? If this is not iniquity, it will be hard to find a crime.

Were not multitudes of our citizens, whose only fault was the love of their country, the love of justice, "driven from their homes?" Were they not stripped of their all, and reduced from ease and affluence to extreme penury? And were not those by whom they were thrown destitute upon the world, and who seized their possessions, "sons of plunder?" In the name of common sense, what were they?

Were not "the temples of the living God ravaged and wrapped in flames?" Every one knows that the British troops betrayed, on almost all occasions, the most implacable virulence against places dedicated to divine worship, and against those servants of the Most High God, who there showed their flocks the way of salvation. "In the course of the war they utterly destroyed more than FIFTY places of public worship in these States. Most of them they burned; others they levelled with the ground, and in some places left not a vestige of their former situation; while they have wantonly defaced, or rather destroyed others, by converting them into barracks, jails, hospitals, riding schools, &c. Boston, Newport, Philadelphia, and Charleston, all furnished melancholy instances of this prostitution and abuse of the House of God. And of the nineteen places of public worship in this city, when the war began, there were but nine fit for use when the British troops left it. And were not the men who could be guilty of such conduct "wretches?" Who can tell whether more "senseless" or "impious."

Of what kind were the transactions of this same army when they traversed the Jerseys? "Many thousands of the inhabitants received printed *protections, signed by order of the commander-in-chief.* But neither the proclamations of the commissioners, nor protections, saved the people from plunder, any more than from insult. Their property was taken or destroyed without distinction of persons;" and this with their protections in their hands. The goodly example was set by *officers* and *general officers.* "The soldiery, both British and foreigners, were shamefully permitted, with unrelenting hand, to pillage *friend* and *foe*, in the Jerseys. Neither age nor sex was spared. Infants, old men and women, were left in their shirts, without a blanket to cover them, under the inclemency of winter. Every kind of furniture was destroyed and burnt: windows and doors were broken to pieces: in short the houses were left uninhabitable, and the people without provision; for every horse, cow, ox, and fowl, was carried off." Was not the shameless violation of faith publicly plighted, "perfidy?" Were not villanies like these, "violence?" And the men who could perpetrate them, in the fullest sense of the word, "banditti?" It is plain, then, that the author, while he has spoken truth, has not spoken *half* the truth. Many other feats sirable, were immediately and sensibly felt. As soon as the pressure of external calamity was taken off, languishing commerce

of a similar kind he might have mentioned; he might have adverted to the butchery of prisoners in cool blood; he might have touched on the history of sugar-houses and prison-ships, &c. But he delights not to dwell on these scenes of horror; and therefore, as he could not, consistently with his duty, omit noticing the miseries of the war, he expressed himself in *general* terms. It is to no purpose to say, as it may be said, that this is a subject on which the best of men have differed, and will ever differ. Granted; but let it be remembered, that those good men who were on different sides of the *question*, were also on different sides of the *Atlantic*. Among the pious and devout in *this* country, there was, generally speaking, but one sentiment. The opinions of the best of men, who were 3000 miles from the scene of action, and whose confidence in their government was abused by a perpetual slander on the principles and conduct of the Americans, can be of no weight at all. Besides, the point before us is not a matter of opinion, but of *fact;* and the opinion of no man could either replace the property, or restore the lives, of our citizens.

With respect to the *spirit* which the expressions under consideration breathe, it is proper to remark, that they were designed not to provoke bitterness, or to enkindle resentment, but to awaken recollection. They can be fully supported by scripture *principle*, and scripture *precept*, and scripture *example*. The scripture *principle* on which they are advocated, is the wise improvement of God's judgment and mercies. But how can they be improved, if we bury them in oblivion? How can we duly appreciate a mercy, if we do not preserve a lively sense of the evil from which that mercy delivered us? It is impossible. The miseries, therefore, which we suffered during the war *must* be remembered, and mentioned, and *discoursed of;* and the American who forgets or overlooks them is a traitor to the God who saved his country. For this reason the lawless behaviour of the British army was *purposely* described in forcible language. Since the more horrible were their outrages, the heavier was the judgment upon this land; the more signal her deliverance, and of course the more criminal her subsequent ingratitude.

Scripture *precepts*, by which the author is warranted to speak as he has spoken, may be found in Deut. vi. 12, 20, 23; Ex. x. 2; Deut. xxxi. 26, &c., and scripture *example* throughout the Bible. And why any *Britons*, above all others, should be offended, is truly mysterious. No people on earth record more carefully, or repeat more frequently and feelingly, their *own* sufferings than they. Do, reader, take the trouble to look into some of the revolution and fast-day sermons, which have been preached in Britain; and you will see the tyranny, the cruelty, and the multiplied horrors of Popery, painted in colours black enough. Hervey himself, in whom were united all those gracious tempers, and all those gentle virtues which adorn and dignify the human character; even the mild, the meek James Hervey, speaks very strongly on this subject. Glance over the speeches of some *Honourables* and *Right Honourables* in the British Parliament, and some of the fast-day sermons occasioned by "*the rebellion in America*," and you may find not a few hard speeches uttered without any just provocation at all. All this is good; this is patriotic, this is glorious. But if an *American* ventures recovered her vigour; agriculture was prosecuted with safety and success; science resumed her wonted seats; and all the arts of peace were cultivated, and flourished. He who should compare our unpromising condition with our miraculous preservation, would be ready to conclude, that Americans, above all others, would most affectionately remember a favour so great and unexpected. Yet, to our shame be it spoken, when our enemies were gone, we neglected the God of our deliverance. But he soon made it evident, by another alarming providence, that he had not forgotten our past transgressions, and that he did not overlook our present unthankfulness. The enviable blessings which his bounty bestowed we had reason to fear would again be torn from us. The storm once more thickened, and lowered, and threatened. Four years, from the restoration of peace, had not elapsed, when the reflecting patriot foresaw the rapid approach of danger more formidable than that which we had escaped. The bond of general union proved too feeble for the important purposes for which it was formed. Clashing interests and turbulent spirits foreboded the introduction of

to mention what his country endured from the oppressions of a venal court, and the depredations of an unprincipled soldiery; this is mean, this is bigoted, this is intolerable! Kind reader, if your property be pillaged, and your life destroyed, what is the difference whether the mischief be done by a popish inquisitor, or a British soldier.

The author feels persuaded, that what has now been said will satisfy the *candid;* for no candid person will attempt to deny facts which are familiar to every child; or undertake the defence of what is wholly indefensible. It is really strange that any, be their attachments to Britain ever so great, should so far make themselves a *party* in the vile proceedings of her agents, as to be offended when these proceedings are mentioned. If, however, they *must* be angry, let resentment fall where resentment is due. Let them be vexed that the armies of a nation which boasts her humanity and generosity, should stain, by a more than savage barbarity, the pretensions in which she glories; but let them not unjustly quarrel with Americans, for exposing in the blaze of day the wickedness which seeks shelter in the dark thickets of oblivion. The author only remarks further, that there was a period when America thought her sufferings of sufficient moment to consecrate a day for the express purpose of publicly thanking the God of heaven for her salvation; and when *some* persons were happy in the safety they enjoyed. But, *tempora mutantur.* It is *now* become a crime for an American so much as to hint at the misfortunes of his country under British usurpation, and at the goodness of God in delivering her—a crime in the eyes of men who, during the time of her calamity, were her implacable foes; who were afterwards protected by her clemency; and who have since grown luxurious and wanton upon the fat of the land.

anarchy, with all the curses that follow in his train. But the Lord, long suffering, did not pour out upon us the fury of his anger. He shook the rod over us that we might observe it, and laid it aside without chastising. Loth to make us the monuments of his wrath, and willing to reclaim us from our guilty indifference, he tried the arguments of mercy. He dissipated the blackening clouds, and gave us a constitution which secures, to all ranks of citizens, every species of right; which combines wisdom with energy; and connects the dignity of the government with the safety and happiness of the individual. The prospect of evil had awakened the sensibility of the public mind, and the prompt salvation obliged even politicians to acknowledge "the finger of God." But when the panic subsided, the devotion subsided with it; and America quickly relapsed into her former lethargy.

To chastise the hypocrisy, and cure the indifference which all orders of men had betrayed, Jehovah commissioned his army, against which valour and skill are no defence, to avenge his quarrel. A host of destructive insects, sporting with the puny efforts of human exertion, traversed the country, and mowed down, in their march, the staff of life. "The land was as the garden of Eden before them, and behind them a desolate wilderness." Had they continued their devastations, we could have expected little "but cleanness of teeth in all our dwellings."* Startled at the alarming progress of this minute yet invincible foe, our citizens, who were not wholly dead to religious principle, were constrained to remark the judgment of the Most High, and to implore the aid of him whom they had offended. But the pang of penitence was no longer felt when the affliction ceased, and the return of prosperity was accompanied with a return of transgression.

To remind us of our sin and of our duty, the monitions of Providence were *again* employed. In just indignation, God sent upon our frontiers the Indian tribes. War lighted, once more, his hostile torch, and death unfurled his banners. Our western brethren were exposed to the indescribable horrors of a savage warfare,—a warfare of which the unvarying maxim is an indiscriminate murder of every age and sex. Elated with the persuasion that their power was irresistible by the hordes of the wilderness, the State resolved to crush at a blow the troublesome combination which was formed against them. But they trusted in an arm of

* See the History of the *Hessian Fly*, vol. iv. p. 302.

flesh; the God of battles fought for their enemies, and what was the issue? Let the banks of St. Mary, and the adjacent grounds which now whiten with the bones of our youth, tell the tale of woe!* From that disastrous period to this, the vengeful barbarian has more or less committed depredations on our borders; pillaging the property and destroying the lives of our citizens. What shall we say to the *present* aspect of Providence? You all know the deplorable condition of our neighbouring city. A few weeks ago she was a city of prosperity and joy—Commerce crowded her harbour and thronged her streets—Mechanic industry boasted her useful though humbler toil—Literature saw, with delight, her growing honours—Amusement led up her sportive train—Jollity assembled the sons of mirth: All was life—all was ardour. But, how sad the change! The hurry of business has ceased—the hands of industry are idle—Gaiety is fled. All faces gather blackness; and the theatre of pleasure is converted into one great house of mourning. "The mirth of tabrets ceaseth: the noise of them that rejoice endeth: the joy of the harp ceaseth: They shall not drink wine with a song: strong drink shall be bitter to them that drink it: every house is shut up, that no man may come in. In the city is left desolation; and the gate is smitten with destruction." Death has erected, in the midst of her, his gloomy throne. With fury uncontrolled, he rages through all descriptions of men. In all directions fly the shafts of this unerring archer. Every day he multiplies his triumphs. The young, the old, the honourable, and the vile, fall the undistinguished prey of this remorseless tyrant. Vain, as yet, have been all human expedients to arrest his progress and baffle his power. He mocks opposition—He strews the earth with slain—He numbers among his victims even the "masters of the healing art."

---

* The affecting catastrophe here alluded to, happened on the 4th of November 1791. On that inauspicious day the American army which General St. Clair led against the western Indians was entirely defeated. The battle was fought at the river St. Mary, about 15 miles from the Miami village. The army consisted of about 1400 effective men. No less than 38 officers and above 1100 men were killed: and it was with difficulty that the miserable remnant made good their retreat. See General St. Clair's official letter, vol. 10, appendix. Quarter-Master Hodgson's return of the officers killed and wounded, p. 28. The "Report of a Committee of Congress respecting the failure of the expedition under General St Clair," ib. vol. 9, appendix 2d, p. 79—83; and also appendix 3d, p. 2.

Let none consider this dire calamity as an event in which only the immediate sufferers are concerned. To punish *their* iniquities it has, doubtless, been sent. But are they *single* in transgression? Have *we* escaped because we are better than they? No, in no wise. A sovereign God has made them an example of his righteous vengeance. The evil under which they languish is one of those awful dispensations by which Jehovah speaks in thunder to a guilty people. The destroying angel, who is now executing upon our fellow-citizens and fellow-sinners the awards of Heaven, looks terribly on *us*, looks terribly on *all.* Whether he will bend his course hither, God only knows.

Now, my brethren, lay all these things together, and ask your own consciences, whether the Lord has not been, and is not at this moment dealing with us in wrath? Assuredly, "for all this his anger is not turned away, but his hand is stretched out still."

Philosophers may speculate and argue as they please. They may pretend to assign merely natural causes for all these events. But let it be remembered, that GOD ACTUATES NATURE. Nature without God is a word either destitute of meaning, or replete with blasphemy. Jehovah accomplishes, by *natural means*, the wise and holy ends of his moral government. By natural means he preserves the righteous: by natural means he punishes the guilty. "Shall there be evil in a city, and the Lord hath not done it?" But why accumulate arguments to prove that the affliction which we deplore is not a chance, but a divine appointment? Your very appearance in the sanctuary this morning is a public testimony of your deep conviction that "this also cometh forth from "Jehovah, who is terrible in his doing toward the children of men."

Since, then, the distresses under which we have formerly smarted, and that which now afflicts some of our citizens, and threatens more, is "the doing of the Lord," permit me,

2. To vindicate the ways of God to man, by showing what righteous reasons he has for dealing with us in wrath.

We need not go far to look for causes: They are within us and around us. We will find abundant reasons to justify the divine procedure, if we advert to our *ingratitude,* our *insincerity,* our *pride,* our *obstinacy,* and the *prevalence of various kinds of moral evil.*

It is but too evident to any one who cursorily inspects the conduct of God to us, and our conduct to him, that we have been *very ungrateful.*

There is no nation under heaven for which God had done so much in so short a time as he hath done for America. In the season of our danger, when our *hope was* almost *as the giving up of the ghost*, and we felt ourselves unable to work out our own deliverance, we supplicated his aid. Memorable, to distant ages should be the 20th of July, 1775 :* when the injured millions of America, prostrate before the throne of the Eternal, poured out their complaint, and sent their cry to him *that judgeth rightly*. Jehovah heard our cry. *He bowed his heavens and came down.* Our armies, destitute of discipline, of arms, of ammunition, of food, of clothing, fainting with hunger and freezing with cold, he crowned with victory the most signal and decisive. He restored peace to our borders: He blessed our commerce: He opened the windows of heaven, and poured plenty into our dwellings: He kept us from the confusion, and tumult, and miseries, of civil feuds: He has preserved us, hitherto, from being involved in the broils and bloodshed of Europe. He has sweetened all these mercies by fixing us in the secure enjoyment of every privilege our hearts can wish: He has given us the everlasting gospel, we trust, in its purity; and has been inviting, by the allurements of his love, to the enjoyment of his rest. But where has been our gratitude? What have we rendered to the Lord for this profusion of benefits? Let us appeal to the most interesting, important, and solemn business in which we have been engaged since our national existence. One would imagine that no occasion of making a pointed and public acknowledgement of the divine benignity, could have presented itself so obviously, as the framing an instrument of government, which, in the nature of things, must be closely allied to our happiness or our ruin. And yet that very constitution, which the singular goodness of God enabled us to establish, does not so much as recognise his *being!*† Yes, my brethren, it is a

---

* Observed throughout the continent as a day of fasting, humiliation, and prayer; and one of the most solemn days she ever saw.

† While many, on various pretences, have criminated the federal constitution, one objection has urged itself forcibly on the *pious* mind. That no notice whatever should be taken of that God who planteth a nation and plucketh it up at his pleasure, is an omission which no pretext whatever can palliate. Had such a momentous business been transacted by *Mahometans*, they would have begun, "In the name of God." Even the savages whom we despise, setting a better example, would have paid some homage to the *Great Spirit*. But, from the constitution of the United States, it is impossible to ascertain *what* God we wor-

lamentable truth: a truth, at the mention of which shame should crimson our faces; that, like Jeshurun of old, we have *waxed fat and kicked.* "Of the rock that begat us we have been unmindful, we have forgotten his works, and the wonders that he hath showed us."

There is a connection between crimes as well as between graces. Never will we find, either in individuals or communities, a solitary sin. In the conduct of America, particularly, there has been a most unworthy combination. Little is necessary to prove, that if we have been ungrateful, we have also been *insincere.*

Who does not remember the professedly penitential tears which streamed from every eye, and the groans which burst from every heart, when the hand of the Lord lay heavy upon us. Our rulers and public men led the way to acts of solemn devotion, and invited their fellow-citizens to join together in *humbling themselves under the mighty hand of God?* Who proscribed, as far as their authority could reach, those guilty amusements and practices which provoke the Most High to pour out his fury upon a people? *Who* reprobated, and exhorted others to discountenance that seminary of vice, that corrupter of moral principle, that parent of profligacy, the *theatre? Who* condemned *games of chance, horse-racing,*[*] and

ship; or whether we own a God *at all.* It is a very insufficient apology to plead, that the devotion which political institutions offer to the Supreme Being, is, in most cases, a matter of mere form; for the hypocrisy of one man, or set of men, is surely no excuse for the infidelity of another. Should the citizens of America be as irreligious as her constitution, we will have reason to tremble, lest the Governor of the universe, who will not be treated with indignity by a people, any more than by individuals, overturn, from its foundation, the fabric we have been rearing, and crush us to atoms in the wreck.

[*] To some it may appear strange that games of chance, such as *cards, dice,* &c., were ranked among the sins of the land. The usual pretext that they are harmless pastimes, is very flimsy, and altogether inadmissible. Independently of the odious consequences, with which they are generally connected, they are much more criminal than many are inclined to allow. It may safely be affirmed that they are palpable violations of the third precept of the decalogue. What is a *name?* It is a distinguishing mark. What is the name of God? It is anything by which he *makes himself known.* Now he makes himself known as the God of *Providence;* and therefore to sport with his providence, is equivalent to sporting with his divinity. But with this all games of chance are chargeable. If the providence of God extends to the *fall of a sparrow,* why not to the shuffle of a card, or the cast of the dice? But the former cannot happen without a divine appointment (Mat. xii. 10); therefore the latter cannot. We are positively assured that "the whole disposing of the lot is from the Lord." (Prov. xvi. 33.) And all games of chance are lots. On some occasions it may not only be lawful,

other kinds of immoral behaviour? Did not the representatives of the community? *Who*, since the restoration of peace, have been the first to throw off every appearance of respect for the authority of the great God, and to treat his ordinances and his word with contempt? Have they not too often been those to whom the most important interests of the country were committed?

but a duty, to refer certain cases, by religious lot, to the decision of God's tribunal. This is a mode of acknowledging his supremacy, which he has honoured with his approbation under the dispensation both of the Old Testament and the New, and which, under the former, he expressly commanded. The religious *lot*, then, it is plain, is an act of worship precisely of the same kind with the religious *oath*. Both are solemn and *direct* appeals to Omniscience and Omnipotence. And games of chance bear, in every particular, the same relation to the former which profane swearing bears to the latter; whence the conclusion, however uncomfortable, is inevitable, that if profane swearing is criminal, so are games of chance; nay, that these games are every jot as wicked as common customary imprecation. It is foolish to say, "We *mean* no evil." Every cursing reprobate pleads the same excuse. "This mode of arguing," it may be said, "draws very deep, and involves in the guilt of sporting with Divine Providence, not only games of chance, but all amusements of skill; and, eventually, all, even the most innocent actions of our lives, since the issue of them all must be determined by the superintendence of Divine Providence; and therefore, that either this dreadful consequence must be admitted, or the principle on which games of chance are condemned given up; and these games, of course, justified." But the objection proves by far too much. No man will deny murder to be a horrible crime. Now, as it can be, and often has been, demonstrated, that all *spontaneous* motion, to which belongs all *muscular* and *vital* motion, is the effect of the immediate agency of the Deity,* we must either, according to the doctrine of the objection, allow murder to be an innocent action, or throw the blame of it upon God himself. The truth is that the objection confounds two things essentially different. In games of chance, the principle which *makes* them such, and *without* which they would cease to be such, is the *appeal to God:* The decision is *designedly* put out of the reach of human foresight; and should a man use any precaution to determine the chance in his own favour, he would be accused of *unfair* play. This forms the *character* of the games in question, and distinguishes them from trials of skill, and all the common actions of life, the issue of which depends upon the providence of God. In the *former*, an appeal to God constitutes the *nature* of the game. In the *latter*, there are only some *circumstances* which his providence disposes: circumstances which necessarily attend our actions as the actions of *dependent* beings.

As to *horse-racing*, it is a sin almost too flagrant to require any proof. God gave us his creatures to use for our good, not to torment for our diversion. And if the scripture says true, that "the righteous man regardeth the life of his beast," he who can habitually indulge himself, or countenance others, in a wanton, cruel abuse of one of the most generous animals that alleviate his toil and promote his comfort, has a wretched claim to the character of a Christian.

* Baxter's Matho. vol. i. p. 331—339.

Have not men in office, and numbers of our principal citizens, been foremost to observe, in the face of day, that very conduct which formerly they decried as unlawful in its nature and destructive in its influence? Is this carriage which becomes those who vowed to live for God, if he would save them from their distress? We may see upon ourselves the black mark of Israel's duplicity and treason. "When he slew them, then they sought him; and they returned and inquired early after God: and they remembered that God was their rock, and the Most High God their Redeemer: Nevertheless, they did flatter him with their mouth, and lied unto him with their tongues; for their heart was not right with him, neither were they steadfast in his covenant."—"Be not deceived, God is not mocked: These things we wickedly have done, and he kept silence; we thought that he is altogether such a one as ourselves, but *now, by his providence,* he is reproving us, and setting our iniquities in order before our eyes."

One who reflects upon the majesty of God, and the evil of sin, will see, in such vile ingratitude and hypocrisy, abundant reason to justify him for pleading with us in wrath; and instead of wondering that we are chastised, will wonder that the divine patience permits us to exist, when he surveys our *unbecoming pride.*

Have we not, my brethren, in numberless instances, acted as if we were the sources of our own happiness, and the sovereigns of our own conduct? As if we were neither subject to the jurisdiction, nor amenable to the tribunal of "the God in whom we live, and move, and have our being?" Has not America, in the fulness of her prosperity, virtually said, "Who is the Lord that I should obey him?" Has she not said, "My power, and the might of my hand, have gotten me this wealth?" Has she not said, with imperious Babylon, "I shall be a lady for ever; I am, and there is none else?" Is it anything strange then, that "mischief which she is unable to put off, has fallen upon her?" My brethren, God is jealous of his glory. He will not suffer the creature to affect independence on the Creator. He will make us know that "Jehovah reigns, and, therefore, the people must tremble."

These abominations, too notorious to be denied, and too shocking to be palliated, are rendered still more heinous by the *obstinacy* which has uniformly characterized them.

What means have been neglected to show us our sin, to warn us of our danger, and bring us back to our duty? Has not God spoken to us both in judgment and in mercy? Has he not alternately inflicted his chastisements, and lavished his bounties? Has he not "many a time turned his anger away, and refrained from stirring up all his wrath?" And have we not persisted in walking contrary to him. Have we not made our "neck an iron sinew and our brow brass?" Sins abound, but where are the penitent? Who "sigh and cry for the abominations done in the land?" Who appropriates to himself *his* share of the general guilt? Where is the humbled heart, where the contrite spirit, occasioned by such an appropriation? Shall the abuse of God's amazing patience and lenity, and our unfruitfulness under all the pains he has taken with us, go unpunished? No certainly! We may forget, but the Lord remembers: And if he sweep us not away with *the besom of destruction*, it is because he is the *Lord long-suffering*. But woe to him who argues from the divine forbearance, that he shall pass with impunity. The longer Justice spares, the higher does she lift her arm, and the heavier will be her stroke at the last. "He that, being often reproved, hardeneth his neck, shall suddenly be destroyed, and that without remedy."

Such has been our behaviour, and such behaviour has drawn upon us the vengeance of Heaven. Here, then, our inquiries into the cause of the Lord's displeasure might end; but we may properly go a step farther, and observe that he is justly angry with us on account of the *prevalence of various kinds of moral evil*.

What respect is paid to those fundamental principles of moral rectitude upon which is founded, not only the prosperity, but the existence, of a commonwealth? Is not truth between man and man the basis of mutual confidence, and the life of society shamefully violated? Are not unmeaning professions, and gross adulation, too general in the circles of fashion? Is not the breach of absolute promise, particularly among debtors and tradesmen, become so common, that it is scarcely considered as a fault? Is not the bond of all civil union, the solemn appeal to Omniscience by oath, fallen almost into contempt, from the irreverent manner in which it is both administered and taken? Is not the name of the great and terrible God wantonly and outrageously blasphemed? Are not even children, who, it is probable, were never taught to put up one prayer to the Author of their being, expert in the infernal science of profane imprecation? Do not our "streets resound with this language of hell?" Is it not heard even from the lips of many who presume to call themselves by the name of Christ? Yes, my brethren, "Because of swearing the land mourneth."

What regard is shown to the important duties which are reciprocally incumbent upon the different members of families? Where are the watchful, circumspect, conscientious, praying parents? Where the humble, dutiful, pious children? What is become of family devotion? What, of family discipline? What, of the engagements into which parents at the baptism of their infants entered to observe both? Is not neglect, in these particulars, a fatal source of youthful dissipation?* And what shall we say of that profligacy of principle and manners which is everywhere observable. Who "rises up before the hoary head, and honours the face of the old man?" On the contrary, are not the aged often treated with disrespect; the maxims of wisdom ridiculed, and the counsels of experience despised? Are there not multitudes who scarcely behave with common civility to the magistrate whom God has commanded us to revere? Are not intemperance, impurity, and debauchery hardy enough to face even the light? Do we not hear repeatedly of the lawless rabble, and the midnight revel? Are not these deeds of darkness and obscenity deemed, by too many, the marks of a generous spirit? And those who will not "run to the same excess of riot," vilified as contracted bigots or superstitious fools?

In what manner is the SABBATH observed? "Remember," is

---

* Families supply both church and state: and if genuine religion and strict morality be wanting there, society is poisoned at the fountain-head. Through disrespect to *family religion*, the young grow up profoundly ignorant of their Creator, and unimpressed with reverence for his law; and surely we cannot expect that they who fear not God will regard man. *Family discipline* also is of the utmost moment. Parental vigilance and care, form useful members of the community. We have no right to flatter ourselves that disorderly, disobedient, uncontrolled children will become good citizens. To a criminal, a very criminal inattention in these two particulars, may be ascribed, in a great measure, that trifling character, and that vicious conduct, which mark the fopling and the rake, and of which the pious and observing so generally and so justly complain. Vain are the wisest laws without *virtuous habits;* and these habits must be formed in *early* life. Where the reverse obtains, the energy of law must necessarily be enfeebled, and the arm of justice unnerved. But although the fear of public ignominy *should*, in most cases (for sometimes it certainly does *not*), restrain from the commission of enormous outrages, it will be but a slender proof of social probity, that the terrors of penal statutes are barely sufficient to keep men from the gallows.

the divine injunction, remember "the Sabbath day to keep it holy." Is it indeed kept holy? Do men indeed "call the Sabbath a delight, the holy of the Lord, honourable?" Do they "honour him, not doing their own ways, nor finding their own pleasure, nor speaking their own words?" Do not many waste the day in idleness? Are not some so indolent or carnal, or both, that they will not wait upon God, that day, in the ordinances of his grace? Or that they too frequently allow their seats to be vacant at least one half of the day? Or esteem any pretext weighty enough to excuse their absence from the sanctuary? Let none hope to palliate their conduct by pretending that they improve themselves at home. It is altogether incredible, that he who will not sanctify the Sabbath in God's house, will sanctify it in his own. This profanation of the Sabbath is truly deplorable; but in not a few instances the profanation is still more gross. Do not some make it a day of business? Others a day of feasting? And others a day of visiting and amusement? Have not salutary laws been enacted to protect the Sabbath from this open and shameless indignity?* Do our citizens regard these laws? Do our magistrates find fault with the breach of them? Whatever be the opinions of men, the Lord God will not suffer this iniquity to pass unpunished; for he has sworn "if ye will not hearken unto me to hallow the Sabbath-day, then will I kindle a fire in your gates, and it shall devour your palaces."†

---

* See, in the laws of the State of New York, an act passed Feb. 23, 1788.

† Jerem. xvii. 27. The enforcement of the observation of the Sabbath, by civil authority, cannot be viewed as an unwarranted interference of the magistrate in matters of religion, or an infringement of the rights of conscience. For respect to this divine institution is a point in which all denominations of Christians are agreed. Apart from Christian principle, the due observation of the Sabbath has the happiest influence upon civil society *as such;* and therefore it merits the most vigilant and unintermitted attention of the civil magistrate. "It has been observed by the wisest men, that were the celebration of this weekly festival totally neglected, religion would not long survive its disuse." *(Venn's Tracts*, p. 170.) And no society can exist without religion; because the members of it can have no hold upon each other. On proper inquiry it would perhaps appear; it has, in fact, appeared, that a great majority of those unhappy men who are abandoned to infamy, or who terminate their days in a sacrifice to public justice, commenced the career of their crimes with the violation of the Sabbath. "Consider those who help to fill the jails, and furnish the gallows, and it will be found (upon their own confession) they are such as have neglected the observation of the Lord's day, by following their own pleasures." (*Sabbatum redivivum, p.* 660.)

What reception is given to the everlasting Gospel? "Who hath believed our report, and to whom is the arm of the Lord revealed?" Who "fly as a cloud, and as doves to their windows?" Who glories in the cross of Christ? Who takes refuge from the curse of the law in his covenant righteousness? Who bends the knee to a *sanctifying* Saviour? Whose holy ambition spurns the dregs of earth, and soars to the kingdom above? Where are those "crowns of glory, the hoary heads found in the way to righteousness?" Where the hopeful youth who dedicate themselves to the

To these remarks may be added a short extract from a published pamphlet. It is too much in point to be omitted, and too excellent to need an apology. "One Christian Institution alone," says the ingenious author, "the sanctification of the Christian Sabbath, diffuses a more benign influence on society, and has a greater efficacy on the morals of mankind to purify and refine them, than all the institutions of civil policy, or terrors of civil government, put together. The pauses it creates in human transactions; the interruptions it makes in our worldly cogitations and earthly cares; its fixing or keeping alive in the mind, the impressions of a God infinitely great and dreadful, whose we are, and to whom we must be accountable for all our ways; and who will most dreadfully punish the wicked, and plentifully reward the good; its tendency to keep constantly in our view the immortality of the soul, and a future state of retribution; its being connected with such religious services as reading the holy scriptures, in which the most august, grand, and awfully sublime ideas of the Almighty are exhibited—its relation to the infinite love of Christ to mankind—and the peremptory and awful injunctions of this Divine Saviour, that men love one another—together with our joining in solemn heartfelt supplications, confessions, and thanksgivings at the Throne of Grace; these things, I believe, have had, and still have, an efficacy on the minds of the great body of the people in Christian nations, I was almost going to say infinitely great—and I firmly believe, that no man who ever became very vile and profligate, could possibly be so, till he renounced all solemn and serious attention to the Lord's day. A question has some time employed my thoughts, what in human nature it is that will account, in a rational manner, for the generally extreme wickedness of soldiers and sailors? The true solution of this problem, I believe, is this. They do not carefully observe the Lord's day: they have no opportunity, or very little, of attending the worship of God: consequently the impressions of a God; of the worth of their souls; the evil of sin; and the infinite importance of a future state, are either very faint in their minds, or perhaps in some scarcely existent. In this respect, the institutions of Christianity have a most benign influence on society; and wise rulers, who wish rather to prevent crimes than to punish them, *will take care, both by precept and example to promote the sanctification of the Christian Sabbath,*—this is the best security of our life, property, and liberty, This is like the wings of the Almighty spread over us. No man who conscientiously, and with knowledge, sanctifies the Sabbath, will find a liberty in his mind to injure us through the week.—This is God's shadow extended over us; it is Heaven's protection." (*A concise and faithful Narrative,* &c., p. 68—70.)

Lord God of their fathers : and who are not ashamed of Jesus and his works before a crooked and perverse generation?

On the contrary, what is the frequent treatment of the Bible? This blessed Bible which unfolds the counsels of Heaven, and proclaims the glad tidings of salvation? Is it not despised as the parent of enthusiasm, and calumniated as the offspring of fraud? Are not the exercises of that serious godliness which it inspires, which purifies the human mind, and ennobles the human character, reviled as the whine of fanaticism, or the cant of imposture? Is not infidelity the *fashion?* Is not the profession of a Christian thought to degrade the dignity of a *gentleman?* Is not the bold blasphemer of the holy oracles admired by many as a man of genius? Is not the rude and impious jeer, at all which the wise and good hold sacred, applauded for *wit?* Is not the paltry witticism, if it be but levelled against religion, complimented with the name of invincible argument? Does not every unfledged sciolist, every ignorant retailer of the sophisms of a Hume, or the quibbles of a Voltaire, set up for a philosopher, and think himself entitled to laugh at the faith of the saint? Is not the progress of principles so pernicious an awful symptom of deep degeneracy? And is not the fact as notorious as it is distressing? "If it be not so now, who will make me a liar, and make my speech nothing worth?"

When we turn our eyes from these miserable mortals who carry the mark of hell on their foreheads, and survey the generality of professed believers, is there not reason to fear that a large proportion of them have only "a name to live, while they are dead?" How many call themselves *Christians,* while their whole deportment proves that they are, in truth, the enemies of Christ? No subject so tedious and irksome as redeeming love. Speak to them of the ideal scenes of a romance, and they are all attention and activity. But speak of the sweet realities of the gospel; of the height, the depth, the length, the breadth, of the love of Christ, and immediately they are languid and listless. Set before them the fooleries of the stage, and their bosoms will be agitated with alternate and violent emotions. Now they will be softened into pity, or roused into rage: Anon, they will melt in grief, or be transported with joy. But conduct them to Calvary: Show them that real tragedy which clothed all heaven in sackcloth—show them a bleeding Saviour—show him stretched on the accursed tree; bowing in agony his guiltless head ; and pouring out his soul unto death, a victim to divine wrath, a sacrifice for sin; and they will be cold and unfeeling as a stone. Not a pang of remorse will shoot through the flinty heart, nor a tear of contrition steal down the iron cheek.

Do even the disciples of Jesus, who love him in sincerity, walk as he also walked? Do they live, as habitually as they ought, by faith, and not by sight? Do they improve, as they are bound, the precious promises? Do they apply to the fulness which is laid up for them in their new covenant head? Are congregations entirely free from these iniquities for which the Lord is visiting our land? Are there no ministerial transgressions? Yes, my brethren, the humiliating truth must be told, "The Lord is righteous, I and my people have sinned."

It is, therefore, undeniable that the Lord is speaking to us in wrath, and that his controversy is holy and just. Let us, then, attend,

Secondly, To the duty which our circumstances and our text point out; and that is, to plead with him for mercy,—"O Lord, in wrath remember mercy!"

Here it is requisite to elucidate some of those principles which the petition implies; and the temper with which we should employ it.

1. With respect to the principles of the petition.

It plainly implies that there *is* mercy, pardoning mercy, which may, consistently with both the divine attributes and the divine government, be freely communicated to the sinner.

Dreary, my brethren, would be our prospect, and miserable our consolation, were it absolutely necessary for the God whom we have offended to reward us exactly according to our deserts: Then, indeed, might we close our eyes on peace, and lie down in sorrow. "If thou, Lord, shouldst mark iniquity; O Lord, who could stand?" Certainly *we* could not stand; *we*, whose conduct has been little else than a series of transgressions; and whose crimes have been attended with every hateful circumstance which can aggravate guilt, or increase punishment. Unable to answer our Judge "one of a thousand" of the accusations he may bring against us, if we attempt to "justify ourselves, our own mouths will condemn us." But, glory, eternal glory, be to God in the highest! *There is* FORGIVENESS *with him that he may be feared.* There is a Saviour *for whose righteousness' sake* the Father *is well pleased.* Through this Saviour we may safely approach that inflexible justice, and unspotted purity, which are otherwise *a consuming fire.* Our condition, therefore, though sad, is not hopeless. We are guilty, indeed, but not wholly cast off: We are afflicted, 'tis true, but not abandoned to despair. How great, how unequalled soever our provocations have been, we are encouraged to "hope in the Lord, for with the Lord there is mercy, and with him there is plenteous redemption."

But, it may be asked, "Is there any reason for us to hope when we are visibly the objects of the divine displeasure? May we repair to mercy's throne, when slighted mercy has kindled the vengeful flame?" We may, for our text farther implies, *That the present wrath of God is no obstruction to the exercise of his mercy.*

This, the very prayer of Habakkuk, which was penned under the influence of the Holy One, manifestly supposes. This is supposed by all the prayers which, the scripture informs us, were directed to heaven for deliverance from affliction. This is supposed by the design of all God's wrathful dispensations, which are intended not only to *correct man, with rebukes, for his iniquity,* but to humble the arrogance of his spirit—to teach him his entire and universal dependence upon the one supreme—to create in his mind religious sensibility, and bring the thankless prodigal back to the God from whom he has *deeply revolted.* "I will go," says Jehovah by his prophet, "and return to my place, till they acknowledge their offence, and seek my face: In their affliction they will seek me early." This same principle is supposed by his own positive injunction, recorded in the prophecy of Joel: "Therefore also now, saith the Lord, turn ye even to me with all your heart; and with fasting, and with weeping, and with mourning; and rend your heart and not your garments and turn unto the Lord your God; for he is gracious and merciful, slow to anger, and of great mercy, and repenteth him of the evil. Who knoweth if he will turn and repent, and leave a blessing behind him."—" Peradventure I shall live" is higher encouragement than the best of us merits: Upon this *peradventure* must a sinful man make an experiment of the divine mercy for the salvation of his soul, and a sinful land for her deliverance from trouble; it is enough for us to know that God can be just in pardoning the ungodly; it is enough for us to know that Jesus Christ, the propitiation for sin, hath broken down the barriers which hindered our access to God, and the access of his mercy to us, and hath opened, by the blood of Calvary, *a new and living way to the Father.* From the invitation to this way of life, none, no not the most worthless and vile, are excluded. Even those who are slaves of corruption, and prisoners of the curse, are exhorted to lay hold of the great salvation. No sins can surpass the merit of our Lord Jesus. The grace of God, that reigns by his cross, is never so gracious, never shines with such glorious splendour, as when she holds back the arm of justice, rushes through the fire of wrath, snatches the criminal as a brand out of the burning, and heaps countless blessings on his head.

This doctrine, so rich with instruction and comfort, we should never forget. It is at all times important; at all times needful. Particularly in seasons of wrath, it is the precious doctrine which brightens the gloom of guilt, and revives expiring hope. The prophet, by his own example, has taught us the truth, and how to employ it; for the text implies,

Lastly, That *when the Lord is dealing with us in wrath, mercy is our* ONLY *plea.*

As sinners we have no claim of right to any of God's benefits. Fallen, by apostasy, from our state of probation, we cannot acquire, by our own obedience, a title to the blessings which were promised in the covenant of works. It is, therefore, of infinite moment to our most valuable interests, not only to confess with our mouths, but to feel in our hearts, that we lie at mercy. Above all, upon a day of fasting and humiliation, it accords not with our circumstances and profession to foster the opinion that God will forgive our iniquities, and receive us into favour, on account of our sincere though imperfect services. Who is he that presumes upon the sincerity and goodness of a heart which the spirit of inspiration has pronounced "deceitful above ALL things, and desperately wicked?" Who is he that would offer to his Creator a righteousness which has been rejected already *as filthy rags?* Know, vain man, that every expectation which does not rest upon mercy, mere mercy, undeserved mercy, is more perishing than the fleeting cloud. Thou must bow to sovereignty. "The loftiness of man shall be brought down, and the haughtiness of man shall be made low, and the Lord alone shall be exalted." Every durable comfort; every solid joy; every hope that will abide the rude shock of death, or the burning trial of the judgment-day, is built upon this divine assurance, not that with us there is *merit,* but that *with the Lord there is mercy.*

With these principles, that are evidently implied in the text, is intimately connected,

2. The *temper* with which it becomes us to present the prayer of the prophet.

If we admit, (and who dares deny?) that the Lord is speaking to us in wrath, and that our only refuge is his mercy, we cannot resist the conviction, that an essential part of the temper which should influence us in suing for mercy, consists in *an ingenuous confession of guilt.*

To frame excuses for our rebellion against the majesty in the heavens; or to soften down, by partial tenderness, our heinous violations of the divine law, discovers an ignorant mind, and an unhumbled heart: It is in effect to say, *the ways of the Lord are not equal.* We may, indeed, imagine ourselves hardly treated: but if we compare the best of our fancied claims to the indulgence of God with the tremendous charges he may justly bring against us, the lips of murmur will be silenced; the rising discontent suppressed; and, overwhelmed with deep confusion, we will be constrained to acknowledge the rectitude of Jehovah's appointments. The "Judge of all the earth," who invariably does right, must "be justified when he speaketh, and be clear when he judgeth." Before his equal bar "every mouth shall be stopped, and all the world become guilty."—"Woe, then, to him that striveth with his Maker." The wisest, the safest, the most honourable conduct, in this hour of peril, is *to humble ourselves under the mighty hand of God,* and to plead guilty to the heavy accusations which are written, in large and luminous characters, on his providential dealings. He virtually addresses us in this piercing language, "Have I not nourished and brought you up as children, and have ye not rebelled against me?" If we act honestly, we must reply, Truth, Lord! Did I not "make known unto you my holy Sabbath, and command you precepts, statutes, and laws, and give you my good spirit to instruct you; and have you not been disobedient, and cast my law behind your backs, and wrought great provocations?" Truth, Lord! "Did I not deliver you, for your sins, into the hand of your enemies, who vexed you: and in the time of your trouble, when you cried unto me, did I not hear you from heaven, and, according to my manifold mercies, give you saviours, who saved you out of the hand of your enemies; and after you had rest, did you not do evil again before me?" Truth, Lord! "Thou art just in all that is brought upon us; for thou hast done right and we have done wickedly: Neither have our" rulers, our magistrates, our priests, nor our citizens, "kept thy law, nor hearkened unto thy commandments; for they have not served thee in the large and fat land which thou gavest them; neither turned they from their wicked works."

But let us not suppose, my brethren, that we fulfil our duty by a *general* confession of guilt. We plead not for mercy with a proper temper, unless we individually bring home the charge of guilt to our own consciences. Our national sins are enormous; their cry ascends to the very heavens: and we all have had our share in them. Let us every one turn his eyes in upon his own heart, and, willing to know the worst of his character, ask, with solemn impartiality, "What have I done?" There is no citizen present, who will not find, upon fair inquiry, that he has abundant reason to say, not only as a *man*, but as an *American*, "God be merciful to me a sinner." The public iniquity is, in fact, an accumulation of private transgressions. They are the drops of individual contrition, which constitute the flood of national repentance; and if we expect ever to see a general reformation, we must pray every one for *himself*, "O Lord, in wrath remember mercy."

These reflections lead us directly to observe, that a part, the chief part, of the temper which should predominate in our applications to the mercy-seat, is a fervent desire, that the Lord would remove from us, first of all, the guilt for which he is now punishing us.

If our humiliation, this day, proceeds from a dread of evil, rather than from a cordial hatred of the sin which is the parent of all evil, we mock God; we wound our own souls; we prepare for ourselves a more terrible condemnation. The God of holiness will never deem himself honoured by the feigned devotion of those who *roll sin as a sweet morsel under their tongues*—who grieve, not because *he* is offended and insulted, but because *they* are chastised—who are deterred from the indulgence of their lusts only by the fear of vengeance; and who will probably return, when their alarm subsides, to those unhallowed practices which they now affect to renounce. Unpardoned sin is a perennial source of sorrow: and it is but a small consolation to be freed from an existing plague while an angry cloud, charged with ten thousand woes, hovers over us, and threatens every moment to burst in curses on our heads.

Acquaint thyself NOW *with him and be at peace;* haste, for pardon, to the blood of sprinkling, and leave it to the wisdom and sovereignty of God to remove, in his own good time, the rod of affliction.

Finally: In pleading for mercy, we should be anxious that the Lord would *sanctify* his providence: that is, would bless it as an effectual means of rendering our hearts more tender, and our lives more holy.

Chastisements unimproved swell, in proportion to their severity, the guilt of an individual or a people, and are a prelude to calamities doubly dreadful. If men will not *learn righteousness* when God's *judgments are abroad in the earth*—if they *will not behold the majesty of the Lord*, and when his hand is lifted up, obstinately refuse to see it—he may say in righteous indignation, *Let them alone*: LET THEM FILL UP THE MEASURE OF THEIR INIQUITIES: And what the consequence may be, none can tell but he who knows perfectly the evil of sin, and the limits of his own forbearance. Should we revert to our former sloth and impiety, after this solemn warning from the God of heaven, our condition will be worse, much worse, than before. He may, indeed, permit us to enjoy tranquillity for a while; but, in the meantime, he is storing a magazine of fury. If his unexampled goodness do not *lead us to repentance*, we will "treasure up to ourselves wrath against the day of wrath, and revelation of the righteous judgment of God." For aught we can tell, the period may be near, when seven thunders shall utter our doom; and seven vials pour out upon us their united plagues. In the day of our distress God may stand afar off: "When we spread forth our hands, he may hide his eyes from us, yea, when we make many prayers, he may not hear." He may strike into our souls the chill of death, by addressing us in this style of affronted patience,—"Because I called and ye refused, I stretched out my hand and no man regarded; but ye have set at nought all my counsel, and would none of my reproof; I also will laugh at your calamity; I will mock when your fear cometh: when your fear cometh as desolation, and your destruction cometh as a whirlwind; when distress and anguish come upon you."

The facts and the doctrines on which we have been meditating suggest, very plainly, the *improvement* we ought to make of them.

If wrath is upon us from the Lord every man of reflection will feel that it becomes us to be very *serious*.

My brethren, God does not trifle with us, and he will not permit us to trifle with him. His government is not a phantom, nor his judgments a farce. Both are awful realities: Sooner or later shall every accountable creature know, that the former cannot be rejected, nor the latter despised, with impunity. The divine law is a serious thing: sin, which is a transgression of the law, is also a serious thing; and *that* death, which is the wages of sin, is as serious a thing as either: And now, that we have violated the law; have made ourselves sinners; are obnoxious to the penalty of the law, and have before our eyes a signal proof of the Lord's anger against the very sins with which we are chargeable; surely, surely we ought to be serious. To be careless and indifferent when the cry of anguish pierces our ears is cruelty: To frolic on the brink of ruin is madness. The Spirit of God has marked it as one of the last stages of human obduracy, when men have "the harp, and the viol, the tabret, and the pipe, and wine in their feasts; but regard not the doing of the Lord, neither consider the operation of his hands." God forbid that we should imitate the folly described by the prophet; "And in that day," a day of wrath, "did the Lord God of hosts call to weeping, and to mourning, and to baldness, and to girding with sackcloth: and, behold joy and gladness, slaying oxen, and killing sheep, eating flesh and drinking wine;" a conduct which proclaimed more loudly than any words the maxim of the libertine: "Let us eat and drink, for to-morrow we die." May the woe denounced against such offenders penetrate our inmost souls: "Surely this iniquity shall not be purged from you, TILL YE DIE, saith the Lord God of hosts."

But let none mistake the intention of these remarks, or pervert their use. If we are called from unseasonable inattention and levity, we are not called to the sullenness, the gloom, the inaction, of despondence. We must be serious, but not idle. And one of the most profitable purposes for which we can improve the subject which we have been considering, is *a strict examination of our own characters.*

My brethren, the dispensations of Divine Providence proclaim, as with the voice of an archangel's trump, "Prepare to meet thy God, O Israel." Are we prepared to meet him in confidence, and with comfort? Pause, ye votaries of pleasure—interrupt, ye gay, the round of vanity—suspend, ye men of business, the anxieties of gain, and retreat for a while into your own bosoms: summon your consciences before that tribunal, the decisions of which are all according to truth; and ask, ask solemnly, for ye know not how soon it may be asked at the bar of God, What arrangements have ye made for an eternal world? Amidst all your acquirements, have ye obtained the *one thing needful?* Amidst all your pursuits, have ye sought *first the kingdom of God, and his righteousness?* Are ye *in Christ Jesus?* Are ye justified by his blood, and sanctified by his Spirit? Have ye devolved the whole weight of your acceptance with the Father, of your perseverance in holiness, and your arrival at glory, on him " who is able to save to the uttermost all who come unto God by him."

To these interrogations very different answers must be given by two classes of hearers. To each of them our subject furnishes a suitable exhortation. To those, who *have a good hope through grace,* it addresses the command of the Apostle Peter, " Give all diligence to make your calling and your election sure." In seasons of wrath it is peculiarly needful for believers to have their faith strengthened; their title to their inheritance fully ascertained, and their way to the possession of it freed from all obstruction. Trim, then, your lamps, ye wise virgins. Gird on your armour, ye soldiers of the living God: " Be sober, be vigilant."—" Watch and pray, that ye enter not into temptation."—" Let your loins be girded about, and your lights burning; and ye yourselves like unto men that wait for their Lord; Blessed are those servants, whom the Lord, when he cometh, shall find watching." And when ye supplicate for yourselves, intercede for your fellow-citizens, with whom you profess to sympathize. " The effectual fervent prayer of a righteous man availeth much." Say, " Spare thy people, O Lord, and give not thine heritage to reproach." Say, " O remember not against us former iniquities: Let thy tender mercies speedily prevent us, for we are brought very low."—" Help us, O God of our salvation, for the glory of thy name: and deliver us and purge away our sins, for thy name's sake."—" Let the sighing of the prisoner come up before thee; according to the greatness of thy power, preserve thou those that seem appointed to die." Intercede for your country: Say, "Turn us again, O Lord God of hosts; cause thy face to shine, and we shall be saved." Say, " Forgive our sin, and heal our land. Let thy work appear unto thy servants, and thy glory unto their children: and let the beauty of the Lord our God be upon us, and establish thou the work of our hands; yea, the work of our hands establish thou it." Intercede for the church of Christ: say, "Do good, in thy good pleasure, unto Zion: build thou the walls of Jerusalem. O Lord, revive thy work in the midst of the years; in the midst of the years make known: in wrath remember mercy."

To those who are "aliens from the commonwealth of Israel, and strangers to the covenant of promise," the dispensations of Providence speak in a most alarming style, and the doctrine of the text offers salutary counsel. *Wherewithal, my brethren, will ye come before the Lord, and bow yourselves before the Most High God?* Unprovided with that *robe of righteousness, and those garments of salvation,* without which none can enter *the palace of the king,* what will ye do in the day of visitation? Are ye able to contend with your Maker? Are ye able to *abide the fierceness of his anger?* O put not from you the evil day. Multitudes of your neighbouring city, who were as careless and secure as yourselves, have been hurried away with scarce a warning to the bar of God. What assurance have ye that this shall not very shortly be your own case? Death is now doing his work among our fellow-citizens; and before we are aware he may *come up into our windows.* Perhaps—God grant that the fear be not realized!—perhaps the destroyer has already received his commission to clear these seats of their useless possessors; to cut down the cumberers of the Lord's vineyard; and to cast them into the fire. My brethren, as your souls live, there is but a step between you and death: critical is your condition; and precious your time. Haste, then, *flee for your lives; flee from the wrath to come!* "But whither shall we flee?" Whither? To the mercy-seat! "To the blood of sprinkling, which speaketh better things than the blood of Abel. To Jesus, the mediator of the new covenant. Him hath God exalted to be a Prince and a Saviour, to give repentance unto Israel and remission of sins." This, this is the only channel through which the mercy of God can flow to the sinner: "For there is no other name given under heaven among men, whereby we can be saved." The only alternative is, to receive the Saviour, or perish. Receive him without delay. "Now is the accepted time; now is the day of salvation. To-day if ye will hear his voice, harden not your hearts." He has said, that "them who come to him he will in no wise cast out." Having such high encouragement, fasten your hope on his atoning blood; throw yourselves unreservedly upon his precious merits; and plead, "O Lord, in wrath remember mercy." Amen.

SERMON III.*

MERCY REMEMBERED IN WRATH.

PSALM CIII. 10.

"He hath not dealt with us after our sins, nor rewarded us according to our iniquities."

My Brethren,—The providence of God, which threatened the speedy punishment of our sins, lately called us to humble ourselves under his mighty hand. We came to his sanctuary in the character of penitents; we professed to afflict our souls for the evil we had done in his sight; we addressed his throne in the language of contrition; we implored respite; we implored pardon. Abstinence from bodily food, in the self-denial of fasting, we employed as the symbol of inward bitterness, and as an aid in the mortification of sin.

For purposes of a different nature do we this day tread the courts of the Most High. "*The oil of joy* succeeds to *mourning;* and *the garment of praise* to *the spirit of heaviness.* We come to *offer unto God thanksgiving:* We come to celebrate his recent benefits: We come to kindle on the altar of common gratitude the mingled incense of our praise.

But where, may some ask, where is the propriety of bringing, at this time, *the sacrifices of joyfulness?* Is Jehovah's controversy with our guilty land completely removed? " Is his anger turned away, and his hand stretched out no longer?" Have our citizens, "breaking off their sins by repentance, returned to him from whom they have deeply revolted? From his judgments, which are abroad in the earth, do they appear to have learned righteousness? And has the Spirit of grace shed down the large effusion of his quick-

---

* The substance of this Sermon was preached on 19th February 1795, observed throughout the United States as a day of Thanksgiving and Prayer.

ening and purifying influence? Would to God, my brethren, that facts could warrant a prompt and exulting affirmative. But truth obliges us to confess, with blushes, that we have little reason to boast of rectified principle and new obedience. We are still a "sinful nation, a people laden with iniquity, a seed of evil-doers; children that are corrupters; we have forsaken the Lord; we have provoked the Holy One of Israel to anger; we have gone away backward. It is of the Lord's mercies that we are not consumed." But this cannot supersede the necessity, nor lessen the propriety of thanksgiving. It is rather one of the most cogent reasons for singing aloud of His mercy. Besides, we are to consider, that within a short time the procedure of holy Providence, contrary to our most distressing fears, hath, in matters intimately affecting our happiness, assumed a more favourable aspect. Therefore, although we are not authorized to conclude that the Lord is pacified towards us for all that we have done, yet we may and ought to utter abundantly the memory of his goodness; we may and ought to thank Him, and thank Him publicly, that "He hath not dealt with us after our sins, nor rewarded us according to our iniquities."

The text, which significantly describes our condition, asserts that God hath not treated us according to our desert; and strongly implies that this dispensation is replete with singular kindness; subjects which lead to discussion profitable in itself, and obviously corresponding with the design of this day.

1. Let us endeavour to be deeply impressed with the *fact*, that the Lord hath not dealt with us after our sins, nor rewarded us according to our iniquities.

How numerous our sins are, how black their atrocity, how peculiar and malignant their aggravations, it is neither my intention nor my business to state. This would lead us again over the ground of which, not long ago, we had occasion to take a sorrowful review. That we have merited those varied plagues by which the Eternal scourges a rebellious and stiff-necked people, we may not deny, for we have already confessed. The symptoms of their approach startled the most thoughtless; our hearts throbbed with painful apprehension; and we hastened to the mercy-seat to deprecate those evils of which even the remote appearance filled us with terror. That He *hath* had compassion; that in wrath He *hath* remembered mercy, we are all witnesses; for we are all living monuments of His forbearance. The gathering darkness hath not

D

been permitted to concentrate and pour down its tempest. It hath ceased, in part, to overcloud our sky; and, in some degree at least, hath yielded to brighter prospects.

Without dwelling minutely on that kind interposition which hath checked the ravages of disease, hath calmed the tumult of the presaging breast, and recalled to languishing multitudes the glow and the vigours of health—without expatiating on the successes which have attended an enterprise against the western foe: successes that make some amends for the dishonour and loss of former defeats; and encourage us to hope for a solid and permanent peace, which may prevent the effusion of blood hereafter; without insisting on any of those things which, however estimable, occupy a middle or inferior place in the scale of national benefit, allow me to direct your attention to two distinguishing blessings: preservation from foreign war, and deliverance from domestic discord.

It is a mysterious arrangement of the government of God, by which He makes one sin the corrective and the punishment of another. If nation rise against nation, and kingdom against kingdom; if dissensions grow into animosities; and animosities, inflamed by mutual irritation, break out into open and destructive hostility; let it not be supposed that such deplorable events proceed merely from the jarring interests and jarring passions of men. Ambition of power, the fascinations of grandeur, or the lust of fame often set the world on fire, and swell the huge catalogue of human miseries. "Wars and fightings come from our lusts." But in these disasters a higher agency is concerned. God, who "sitteth upon the floods,"—God, "whose kingdom ruleth over all,"—God, who causeth even "the wrath of man to praise him," marks out the path of the warrior, selects the objects of his prowess, and fixes the bounds of his triumph. *His* design may be evil; *his* aggressions unprovoked, and, from *him*, unmerited by those against whom they are directed, every step of *his* procedure may be scored with crimes; and yet God, unimpeachably righteous, brings light out of this darkness; by such evil instruments accomplishes wise, and good, and holy ends; and when He has accomplished them, He visits the iniquities of the instruments themselves, and breaks them to pieces with his rod of iron. The truth is painted in strong colours, by the prophet Isaiah: "O Assyrian, the rod of mine anger, and the staff in their hand is mine indignation. I will send him against an hypocritical nation, and against the people of my wrath will I give him a charge, to take the spoil, and to take the prey, and to tread them down like the mire of the streets. Howbeit, he meaneth not so, neither doth his heart think so; but it is in his heart to destroy and cut off nations not a few. Wherefore it shall come to pass, that, when the Lord hath performed his whole work upon Mount Zion and on Jerusalem, I will punish the fruit of the stout heart of the king of Assyria, and the glory of his high looks. For he saith, By the strength of my hand I have done it, and by my wisdom, for I am prudent: and I have removed the bounds of the people, and have robbed their treasures, and I have put down the inhabitants like a valiant man. And my hand hath found, as a nest, the riches of the people: and as one gathereth eggs that are left, have I gathered all the earth, and there was none that moved the wing, or opened the mouth, or peeped. Shall the axe boast itself against him that heweth therewith? or shall the saw magnify itself against him that shaketh it? as if the rod should shake itself against them that lift it up, or as if the staff should lift up itself as if it were no wood. Therefore shall the Lord, the Lord of hosts, send among his fat ones leanness; and under his glory he shall kindle a burning like the burning of a fire; and it shall burn and devour his thorns and his briers in one day."—Isaiah x. 5-8; 12-17.

This is one of those "terrible things in righteousness," by which, when he "cometh forth out of his place, God punishes the inhabitants of the earth." Thus sinners become to each other angels of cursing; and thus He delegates one guilty nation, as ministers of His quarrel to another; and sends them to execute His threatenings upon their brother in transgression. The sword never comes to devour, but when He appoints it; for every fatal thrust, it hath His high commission; and with the blood which rushes through the portals of death, does He write the crimson history of His wrath.

Brethren, need I remind you, that this dreadful plague was at our doors? Have ye forgotten the chilling anticipations which lately obtruded themselves, unsought, on your minds? Already did the frenzied imagination re-display those scenes of horror of which the remembrance will live with our memories! Already did we hear the burst of hostile thunder; already did we see our temples desolated; our dwellings sinking in the flames, and our families fugitives from the burning ruin!

But the storm has blown over, and done no harm. The sound of alarm, retreating from our shore, grew fainter and fainter, till it expired on the listening ear. No angry banner waves in our eye; no cruel foe ravages our possessions. All is serene; all secure. This day is witness that peace dwells in our land, and enjoys the quiet exercise of her confirmed reign. Give glory to Him who hath commanded the deliverance! "O bless our God, ye people, and make the voice of His praise to be heard; who holdeth our soul in life, and suffereth not our feet to be moved."

Tremendous as foreign war is, it is yet preferable to domestic discord. Internal union is the bond of social strength. When mutual confidence hath fled; and coldness, and jealousies, and opposition come in its place; when professed anxiety for the public welfare degenerates into the strife of partial policies; and unanimity of measures gives way to the violence of faction, the firmest sinews of the national energy are cut, and the richest veins of national prosperity sluiced.

It was a serious thing, my brethren, for our country, to see, in a neighbouring state, four large counties, including great numbers of inhabitants, throw off submission to the law, and rise in the contumacy of revolt. The season at which this ominous event happened was peculiarly unfavourable. Pressed on one side with savage depredations; vexed, on another, with daring and shameless encroachment; fretted and soured with maritime insult and plunder; torn, at the same time, with intestine feud; and ill provided with the means of defence, we invited the assaults of any adversary who was in a condition to improve our disunion and perplexity. Nor was it easy to calculate what would be the extent of the calamity, or what its issue. Men of similar habits, and in similar circumstances, readily unite in similar undertakings. Cherished by the wicked assiduity of those sons of Belial, who had been industrious in creating it, the dissension, spreading like a flame through the dried leaves of autumn, might have divided the children of America, not into the parties of opinion, but into the armies of civil war. Despots would have exulted in this consequence, as it would have ruined the fairest experiment which the sun ever beheld, of a government reared on the equal rights of men. But to their confusion, and our triumph, the tumult has subsided. The temperate, yet firm; the vigorous, yet unbloody manner in which this rebellion was subdued, is fraught with delight to ourselves, and furnishes a useful lesson to mankind. It is the victory of principle over passion, of order over confusion, of laws over licentiousness.

Such a joyful issue of such an afflictive commotion, has filled united America with admiration and applause. To those patriots who, to enforce the sovereignty of the law, exchanged the comforts of domestic life for the rigours of military service, the tribute due to their spirited exertion is cheerfully paid. Above all, our eyes involuntarily fasten on THAT MAN, whose timely application of the severe but salutary discipline intrusted to his prudence, was the happy means of restoring peace—on THAT MAN, whom God had honoured to be the instrument of countless blessings to this land; whose name will live, and whose memory will be revered, when the blighting eye of malignity is sealed up in darkness, and the tongue of calumny fettered with the irons of death.

The facts now mentioned are luminous events, which, at present, absorb in their lustre all other political incidents relating to us. They cannot but fix in astonishment the gaze of the most careless; and impress the hearts of the most hardened. How powerful obligations to gratitude to our God are created by such benefits, will appear from contemplating the *singular mercy of that providential dispensation from which they flowed.* The illustration of this mercy is the

II. Second branch of our subject.

Sources of illustration are numerous and fruitful—you will all acknowledge.

1. *The divine clemency which has distinguished us from other nations.*

Several countries on the eastern shores of the Atlantic, have scarcely time to breathe, much less to recruit, from the wounds and sufferings of one war, before they are precipitated into another. It is a foul stain on the civilisation of Europe, as well as an awful judgment for her sins, that she is almost continually weltering in blood. Her infatuated sons fly to arms, and slaughter each other, as the caprice or the politics of their tyrants ordain. Besides two rash and formidable preparations* which began in

---

* The Russian and Spanish armaments in Britain: the former of which was requipped to aid the Turks against Russia, and the latter, to fight the Spaniards of the privilege of killing "whales in the South Seas, and wild cats at Nootka Sound."

bravado, and ended in expense; the present* are two of six †
wars which, more generally or partially, have flooded their curses
on Europe in less than ten years. Wars, all of them wicked,
most of them mad, and none of them necessary. At this moment,
some of the fairest fields that ever rejoiced the eye, or repaid the
labour of man, instead of being cultivated by the husbandman and
the vine-dresser, are trodden down by the martial steed, and
strewed with the bodies of the slain. "Come, behold the works
of the Lord, what desolations He hath made in the earth. He
cuts off the spirit of princes: He is terrible to the kings of the
earth."

How preferable, my brethren, is our condition! How gentle
the dispensations of God towards us! It is now above one
hundred and sixty years since the chief settlement of this country;
and, excepting Indian hostilities on the frontier, we have not been
engaged in war more than three or four times at furthest; and
have never been compelled to it, but either by foreign connection,
or the rigour of foreign exaction. Why do we prosper whilst other
lands are covered with desolation? Why does not the sword thin
our families, and hew down our gallant youth, their parents' pride,
and their country's hope? Why are we permitted to till our
grounds without molestation, and to eat the fruit of our industry?
Why, through the medium of commerce, to keep up an amicable
and lucrative intercourse with distant places? Why to foster the
arts of peace, which refine the manners, and improve the mind?
Why to assemble, without interruption or fear, in the house of
God; to sing his praises, to supplicate his favour, to learn the
words of everlasting life? Is it because we are better than
others? No, in no wise. We merit a harsher lot; but the Lord
hath not dealt with us after our sins, nor rewarded us according to
our iniquities. It is undeserved mercy; therefore, Hallelujah!

2. The *eminent danger* in which we lately were, highly exalts
the mercy of our deliverance.

---

* The war of France against the combined powers; and of Poland against
Russia and Prussia.

† In addition to the wars mentioned in the preceding note, there have been—
1. The war of Sweden with Russia. 2. That of Russia and the Emperor with
the Turks. 3. That of the Emperor with the Netherlands. 4. That of Poland
and Russia, in 1792—all within the short space of eight years; viz. from 1786
to 1794! besides the troubles in Holland, and some disorders of less importance.

However imagination might depict the horrors of war, before they had a real existence, yet the strong apprehension of their approach was not chimerical: affairs, both abroad and at home, were fast verging to a dreadful crisis. Various indignities and spoliations, by land and sea, unprovoked, in the midst of painful exertions to maintain our tranquillity, bespoke, too evidently, designs unfriendly to our happiness. It is an agreeable dream of benevolence to suppose, that if the plans of confederated oppression had succeeded, we should have been unmolested. When we consider the grudge entertained by most of the establishments of the Old World against these States, for breaking the political spell, by which, for ages, man had been enchanted; and showing him what he *is*, and what he *ought to be*, in society; it is a more probable conjecture, that the conquerors, flushed with victory, would have turned their arms hither, and endeavoured, by one mighty effort, to crush the nursery of freedom, and extirpate from the globe its generous plants.

Connectively with symptoms of disaffection abroad, we must view the unruly and turbulent dispositions of many at home. In every community there are multitudes who have a much greater share of good intention than discernment. Their honest credulity, unguided by judgment and untempered with caution, draws them into the plots of others whose less upright principles take an eager advantage of their simplicity. An appeal to popular prejudice, calculated to inflame popular passion, is an engine which craft always employs, and generally finds effectual, for enlisting both under the banners of intrigue. There will ever be some, in all parts of the world, to whom, from natural unhappiness of mind, or from less venial causes, order will be imprisonment, and peace a torture—some, who sicken to see the gallant vessel riding securely at anchor, or flitting before the favouring gale, and who pray for an adverse blast to dash her on the reef, that while the crew perish in the waters, they may pillage the wreck. The mischievous projects of such as these, aided by the imprudent zeal of others, are sufficient, in ordinary cases, to force almost any nation into war. And when we add to their machinations the external exasperating treatment which gave union to their counsels, and colour to their pretexts, it seems little short of a miracle that we have escaped. We stand astonished at the precipice over which we were nearly hurried—a precipice that would have plunged us into evils for which their immediate authors could never have atoned: no, not though they wept in sackcloth the remainder of their lives: no, not though their heads were waters, and their eyes fountains of tears; tears streaming in perpetual succession, and every drop embittered with the gall of heart-wringing penitence. It was God's unspeakable mercy that interfered to save us: and the greater our danger, the more beneficent was the interference, and the more precious the salvation. Surely He hath not dealt with us after our sins,—therefore, again Hallelujah!

3. The *complicated evils which attend war*, whether foreign or domestic, show, in an amiable and affecting life, the mercy which has prevented them. These evils, both political and moral, it would require a volume fully to enumerate and to display. Nor, were it possible, would it be improper here to unfold them. I might call your attention to its pernicious influence on the population of your country, not only by increasing the difficulty of comfortable subsistence, but by the shocking waste it occasions of human life; I might remind you, (for you would not demand proof,) that it breaks up the happiest arrangements of society; that it arrests the progress of the arts; that it retards and ruins the improvements of science; that it weakens, and often destroys, the efforts of commercial, manufacturing, and agricultural genius; that it creates perplexing revolutions in the state of property; that it impedes, if it does not frustrate, the regular administration of civil and criminal justice; that it frequently subjects many of the citizens to the stern jurisdiction and the summary proceedings of martial law; that, while it puts a stop to national improvement, it dries up the ordinary streams of national resource: that it oppresses the community with odious but necessary exactions, in order to maintain their military establishments, and give energy to their hostile operations; and that it generally entails upon them a burden which the wisdom and exertion of ages may be unable to throw off.

The moral evils which spring from war are neither fewer nor less baneful than the political. As it nurtures all the fierce and violent passions, it wrests from society the benefit of many advances of civilisation, and drives it, in a retrograde motion, back towards barbarism. By interrupting the quiet pursuit of enlarged and generous education, it keeps the young in ignorance, and withholds from them the means of respectability and usefulness.

In hindering general and uniform attendance on the social worship of God, it suspends the benign influence of the Christian Sabbath, relaxes the bonds of religious duty; deadens the acute sensibilities of conscience; and tends to subvert the steady dominion of moral principle. Standing armies, moreover, and navies, are seminaries of vice. There are some examples, glorious examples, of men who hold fast their integrity even here. But in general the predominance of iniquity is so great, that the virtue of most is quickly contaminated, and blended with the common mass of corruption. 'Here the profligate and profane tutor each other in the arts of impiety and debauch. Infrequency of pure example lessens its efficacy; while freedom from pious restraint gives the rein to the more worthless propensions of the heart. Wickedness generates infidelity, and infidelity emboldens wickedness. Hence, as from a root, unbelief in speculation, and immorality in practice, are propagated in every direction, and scatter their poison to a prodigious extent. Besides all this, with men who are accustomed to works of death, the life of man loses its value. And this is one of the chief causes of that inexcusable, that atrocious, that detestable crime, the murder of single combat: a crime which bids equal defiance to laws human and divine, and which spills the blood of a friend, to maintain a point of frivolous honour, or to gratify the impulse of diabolical revenge. To add no more, an army is almost as dangerous when disbanded, as it is expensive and troublesome when organized. Men who live in idleness when they are not called to the activity of military duty, who are provided for without any thought of their own, who have acquired habits of plunder as well as of sloth, can with difficulty apply to laborious occupations. These render us unsafe in the midst of prosperity: these furnish the street with thieves, the highway with robbers, and the dungeon with criminals. It is the ignominy of not a few who escape the perils of the field, to fall under the stroke of the executioner; and the laurels which the soldier won are entwined by the ruffian round his gibbet.*

Such are some of the evils common to all wars; but war among brethren has peculiar miseries. Experience, that faithful monitor, had shown that the wounds inflicted by civil war are far deeper, and of more difficult cure, than any that can be received from the

---

* From this general censure, the body of the late revolutionary army of America are entitled to an honourable exception.

hand of foreign violence. The murderous tempers which, in other wars are indulged, in this are wrought up to the height of fury. Resentments are more keen, revenge more implacable, and hatred more lasting. The aggressor is more injurious, and the injured more unforgiving. Amidst mutual reproaches and accusations of violating the most sacred ties, they appear to each other wretches unworthy of esteem, and incapable of faith. Reconciliation is hard to be effected; and, when effected, is scarcely ever sincere. The body politic may, indeed, reassume its healthful complexion; but the poison, rankling within, is ready to burst out with renewed violence: for we find, in fact, that when men have once broken the cords of amity, they are easily impelled to repeat the sacrilege. It is, moreover, a melancholy reflection, that it makes little difference to the community at large how the quarrels of its contending parties are decided. Whoever is victorious, or whoever is vanquished, all suffer. While they struggle against each other, they rend the vital system by which all are nourished; and the triumph of any over the rest is but the success of a mad conspiracy against themselves. Nor does the mischief end here. In silent ambush the common foe marks the origin of disunion, its progress, and its consequences. He patiently waits for the moment of opportunity: and when the combatants, exhausted and fainting, are incapable of resistance, he springs from his concealment, and seizes them for his prey. We cannot be sufficiently thankful that the mercy of God, in keeping the great body of our citizens united, has kept us from self-procured ruin.

4. The divine goodness, which to-day we celebrate, is rendered still more affecting, *by contrasting it with our own stubborn and rebellious conduct.*

In the course of His providence, God has given us "line upon line, and precept upon precept;" but "line upon line, and precept upon precept," were in vain. Alternate judgment and love, neither awed into submission, nor allured to penitence. Hardened in transgression, we persisted to provoke Him, to defy His threatenings, and trample on His bounties. Nor have we any reason to believe that His former dispensations, whether of terror or of joy, have been really sanctified. Guilty, but not abashed; afflicted, but not reformed; neither humbled by chastisement nor softened by kindness, we were entitled to no favour at the hand of God. Pregnant with great futurities, the phenomena of His providence bid us to prepare for their development; and each succeeding day, bringing with it new discouragements, led us to contemplate an issue as mournful as it was near. But while at a distance the thunders rolled; while our heavens blackened, and the woe-fraught clouds stretched over our heads; while our citizens, some in trembling, and others in sullen suspense, were expecting their fate, God—for surely it was the work of no created wisdom or power—God sent help from His holy hill. The arm of vengeance, raised to hurl its wrathful bolt, He suddenly arrested. Through the opening gloom, the light of His deliverance beamed; and so brilliant was the interposition, that nothing but atheistic impiety could forbear exclaiming, "This salvation is from the Lord!" Towards other nations He hath exercised less patience. Their sin, in itself, was no greater than our own; their means of knowledge were inferior; nor were they so often admonished with solemn and pointed rebuke; yet they have perished by the frown of the Eternal, and their memorial is blotted from under heaven. But *we* are spared, are protected, are prospered! Americans, the lenity is divine! Because the Lord delighteth to do us good, is He thus indulgent. He prevents us with His mercies. He surrounds us with His compassions: He loads us with His benefits. "Nay," said His reprieving sentence, "slay them not. Let grace be magnified in their preservation. Though they have richly merited the punishment which hangs over them, and merited a thousandfold more, though they have hitherto set at nought my instruction, let the dispensation of love heap coals of fire upon their heads." My brethren, that heart which is not, in any degree, melted by such goodness, must lie under the curse of triple hardness; and if it have no influence in leading to repentance, every possible excuse will be taken from **us**; and when God arises to judgment, we will stand without an extenuating plea before the bar of righteousness.

Finally, by the continuance of peace, *numbers have access to the privileges of the gospel, who, otherwise, would not only have been deprived of them, but would have fallen a sacrifice to the sword of war:* and this is a display of the mercy of God, which, on the present occasion, we may not overlook.

A sinner receives a boon for which he cannot be sufficiently thankful, when he is permitted to have *a nail in God's holy place*, and to attend on the ministrations of life: when his days are lengthened out in the enjoyment of those precious means by which pardon is communicated to the guilty, and purity infused into the vile: by which the slaves of Satan are made Christ's free men; and felons of the pit, constituted citizens of heaven, and heirs of God. Had the removal of providential restraint left us as ready to wage war as the intemperance of some and the wickedness of others were to urge it, many who now worship in the house of prayer would have been numbered with the dead. Many, to whom the redemption of the blessed Jesus and all the glories of His covenant were freely offered, would have been this day writhing in the place of torment. Unprepared to die, multitudes would have gone to death, and in one hour been swept, by hundreds, into the world of spirits; all their hopes of mercy blasted, and their immortal souls undone for ever.

And now, my brethren, since "the Lord hath done great things for us, whereof we are glad," how shall we express our gratitude? What shall we "render to Him for all His benefits?" Taking that "cup of salvation," which His own hand hath tendered to us, let us "call upon His name." This, beyond controversy, is an immediate and essential part of our duty, *to pay him explicit and public homage: to recognise, by devout and marked acknowledgment, our dependence in His favour, and the blessings we have reaped from His protection.*

There is a religion of society, as such, a tribute of reverence, which it owes to the living God. Formed under His auspices, and nurtured by His care, preserved by His power, and replenished with His bounty, He requires from it, on these accounts, social worship and the social vow. The honour of His sovereign rule He cannot relinquish, and the confession of it we may not withhold. It is true that our excellent chief magistrate, in those critical circumstances into which he was thrown, by the danger of foreign war, and the madness of insurrection among ourselves, displayed, in a conspicuous manner, those governmental virtues which are at once the duty and the glory of his official pre-eminence. The other magistrates, who acted in concert with him, imbibed the spirit of their station, and showed themselves " a terror to evil-doers." The citizens by whose military co-operation their patriotic efforts were carried into complete effect, brought into splendid action the principles of men who enjoy true liberty, and know how to value and defend it. They have all deserved well of their country; but their exertions, sublime and heroic as they were, would have been utterly fruitless without the countenance of Him who is the "governor among the nations." Let us not, therefore, rest in second causes, nor limit our praise to human instruments. Let us not disregard them, but look beyond them. Let us make our boast in God, who, in the day of trouble, covered us with the shield of His omnipotence. "If it had not been the LORD who was on our side," now may the Americans say, "if it had not been the LORD who was on our side, when men rose up against us: then they had swallowed us up quick, when their wrath was kindled against us: then the waters had overwhelmed us, the stream had gone over our soul: then the proud waters had gone over our soul. Blessed be the LORD, who hath not given us as a prey to their teeth. Our soul is escaped as a bird out of the snare of the fowlers; the snare is broken, and we are escaped. Our help is in the name of the LORD who made heaven and earth." Therefore, "Give unto the LORD, O ye kindreds of the people, give unto the LORD glory and strength. Give unto the Lord the glory due unto His name; bring an offering, and come into His courts. O worship the LORD in the beauty of holiness; fear before him, all the earth!"

Another becoming expression of our gratitude to God, for the goodness which we are met to commemorate, is to *keep at a cautious distance from the "arrogance of prosperity."*

If we are elevated to a dignified rank among the nations of the earth; if our *goodly heritage* contains a larger proportion of freedom and happiness than has fallen to the lot of others; if our privileges—civil, religious, and political, secured "under the shadow of the Almighty—have hitherto repelled the weapons of every assailant, and have received recent and strong confirmation, let us beware of *dealing foolishly,* and vaunting away our mercies. To communities, not less than to individuals, insolence is the forerunner of shame. "Pride," saith the wise man, "goeth before destruction, and a haughty spirit before a fall."

Interest combines with duty to enforce compliance with the injunction of inspired prudence,—"Lift not up your horn on high: speak not with a stiff neck, for promotion cometh neither from the east, nor from the west, nor from the south: but God is the judge —He putteth down one, and setteth up another." The rebellious, who exalt themselves, He will teach to bend before His authority, by the sad experience of His displeasure. Without His direction, the sagacity of the profoundest politician is but another name for stupid infatuation. He "turneth wise men backward, and maketh their knowledge foolish." Without HIM, the most intrepid "bow down under the prisoners, and fall under the slain." Abandoned by HIM, the most stable fabrics of earthly contrivance totter on their bases, moulder into dust, and become the sport of every wanton breeze. Let us not flatter ourselves, that however others suffer, we may safely walk after the imagination of our own hearts. We have no charter of immunity in sin. Without discrimination, "our haughty shall be humbled," and the froward cut off; "for the mouth of the Lord hath spoken it!"

Once more: If we would demonstrate our gratitude to God for averting those evils which we could not have shunned, let us "study to be holy in all manner of conversation."

Sincere profession is best evinced by the simplicity of pure obedience. Genuine gratitude will ever be accompanied by an unaffected desire of pleasing, and a fear equally unaffected of offending our benefactor. Be not deceived. If men love God, they will keep His commandments; if they are thankful for His benefits, they will respect His law. Sins of enormous turpitude are still chargeable upon us, and sooner or later the day of visitation will come. More than once or twice we have confessed our guilt, and vowed amendment. On this very subject does the Most High expostulate with us. He calls us by His providence to realize our confessions, to pay what we have vowed. Let us implore the grace and attempt the duty of penitence, while space is given us to repent. The Holy One of Israel will not be mocked with empty promises. When the hour of judgment arrives, His ear will be deaf to entreaty, and the pleadings of mercy will end. Those floods of ruin, which are now held back by His forbearance, will pour in their waters with augmented fury. Heaven will call upon earth, and earth reply to heaven, in conspiring the destruction of the irreclaimable transgressors. Improve the means of obtaining present peace and of insuring final salvation while ye have opportunity. Before the season of acceptance expire, flee to that Lord Jesus who is the "hiding-place from the storm, and the covert from the tempest:" and prove that ye receive the Saviour by walking in him. "HE HATH SHOWED THEE, O MAN, WHAT IS GOOD; AND WHAT DOTH THE LORD REQUIRE OF THEE, BUT TO DO JUSTLY, TO LOVE MERCY, AND TO WALK HUMBLY WITH THY GOD?" Amen.

SERMON IV.*

HOPE FOR THE HEATHEN.
ISAIAH XXV. 6, 7.

"The Lord of Hosts will destroy in this mountain the face of the covering cast over all people, and the vail that is spread over all nations."

The exercise of divine mercy toward man is coeval with his need of it. The shock of the fall was hardly felt; remorse had only begun to prey upon the conscience, and guilt to rally his terrors, when a hope, as consoling as it was unexpected, dawned from heaven upon our revolted race. "I will put," said God to the tempter, "I will put enmity between thee and the woman, and between thy seed and her seed: it shall bruise thy head, and thou shalt bruise his heel." In this original promise were included all subsequent revelations concerning the redemption of sinners. The doctrine of Messiah's person, of his sacrifice, of his triumph; together with that vast system of prediction which extends from the beginning to the end of time, and all the corresponding dispensations of the new covenant, are nothing but its regular development. But this being slow as well as regular, and all flesh corrupting his way, the Lord selected the family of Abraham to be, for ages, both the witnesses of His grace and the depositaries of His truth. To them were committed His living oracles; to them the ordinances of His worship; to them the symbols and doctrines of the great atonement. Among them He deigned to dwell, and to raise up an illustrious line of prophets, who should direct their faith and hope to Jesus the Saviour. "To Him," saith Peter, "give *all* the prophets witness, that, through *His* name, whosoever believeth in Him shall receive remission of sins."

* Preached in the First Presbyterian Church, before the New York Missionary Society, at their Annual Meeting, November 7, 1797.

But though the children of Israel enjoyed these privileges, while other nations were " suffered to walk in their own ways," they were taught that the covenant of peculiarity should one day be abrogated, and be succeeded by a more general and more glorious economy. " In thee, and in all thy seed, shall *all* the nations of the earth be blessed," was the catholic promise to Abraham their father. As the time of its accomplishment approached, the circle of prophetic vision grew brighter and larger. Later prophets were enabled to explain the enigmas of their predecessors, and to speak with precision and clearness, both of the coming of the Messiah and of the glory that should follow. Isaiah, in particular, appears to have been favoured with the most liberal disclosure of the divine purposes. Borne on high by the revealing Spirit, he sees far beyond the common horizon. The extremes of the earth and the ages of futurity are commanded into his view. He sees the " Sun of Righteousness" ascending the heavens, and breaking in upon the thick darkness which enwraps the globe. He sees the fiends of night stretch their foul wings, and fly from the spreading day. He sees the tabernacle of God descending to dwell among men; his eye rolls ardent over the wondrous scene; his bosom heaves with mighty emotions; and when utterance is granted, he bursts forth in the language of the text, " In this mountain will the Lord of Hosts destroy the face of the covering cast over all people, and the vail that is spread over all nations."

The Lord hath not been slack concerning His promise, nor have the words of His servant fallen to the ground. The elementary dispensation of Moses is no more; its shadows have received their substance, and its types their truth, in the person and offices of the WORD *made flesh.* Millions of Gentiles, and among them believers of this assembly, who were once " afar off, are now brought nigh by the blood of Christ," and are " no more strangers, and foreigners, but fellow-citizens of the saints, and of the household of God."

But though all this hath happened, according to the scriptures, much is yet required to their complete fulfilment. Many families of the earth are still unblest: These, too, are reserved for the trophies of Emanuel's grace, and are to be subjected to His authority, by the same means which He hath ever employed in convertting sinners—the gospel of His cross: three topics of discourse, not less appropriate to the design of our meeting, than plainly suggested by the text: for "in this mountain shall the Lord of Hosts destroy the face of the covering cast over all people, and the vail that is spread over all nations."

I. Many families of the earth are yet unblest. They are described as destitute of spiritual and saving knowledge; an idea obviously conveyed by the figures of a vail and a covering—darkness, thick darkness, enshrouds their minds, and conceals from them those facts and principles which it most interests them to know and to improve.

Of the nations thus under a vail we reckon four classes.

1. The families which adhere to the "man of sin:" Enticed by his lying wonders, and given up to strong delusions, they have deviated into the paths of apostacy; they are under the vail of antichristian error.

2. The families of rejected Israel: Having disowned their Messiah when he came, and being disqualified, by judicial blindness, for discerning the real sense of their Scriptures, which testify of him; the vail upon their hearts is the vail of obstinate belief.

3. The families which embrace the doctrines of Mohammed: turned aside after fables, and amusing themselves with the belief of lying vanities, they are under the vail of gross imposture.

4. The families which are usually called Pagan: With no other instruction than the glimmerings of natural reason, and the refracted rays of distant tradition; they are covered with the vail of deplorable ignorance.

All these are characterised in the text. But our attention is invited more immediately to those who are without any scriptural revelation. Though true of all, it is of them pre-eminently true, that they are under the double vail of a benighted understanding and an erring conscience.

God is the source of intellectual light, for he alone is perfect reason. Wisdom in natural things is his gift; much more that wisdom which is spiritual and divine. Loss of ability to discover the chief good, was at once the just reward and the native consequence of revolt. For as all spiritual light in the creature beams from the effulgence of the Godhead, whenever sin had intercepted the communion of man with his Maker, the day which shone around him vanished; the gloom of the pit thickened on his soul; and from that accursed hour to this, unless illumined from above, he hath wandered out of the way, and his feet have "stumbled upon the dark mountains." Does the assertion need proof? Proofs innumerable are furnished by the unhappy heathen. Of the very God who "breathed into their nostrils the breath of life," on whose bounty they are continual pensioners, and at whose tribunal they must shortly stand, they are fatally ignorant. The "heavens may declare his glory, and the firmament show forth his handiwork;" but the Pagans, unaccustomed to decipher their language and to study their lessons, do not thence derive, in fact, just and clear perceptions even of his eternal power and Godhead; far less of his moral character; less still can they learn that he is the only satisfying portion of rational beings; and least of all, that he is accessible to the rebellious. Those general notices of his being which have prevailed in all countries and at all times, have never sufficed to direct men aright in their inquiries after him; nor do they now prevent the most foolish, the most extravagant, the most abominable conceptions of his nature and of his operations.

Mistake in the first principles of religion and of morals must generate uncertainty in all the subordinate principles of both. The rule of obedience is, therefore, at best, a subject of conjecture. What is the genius, measure, and manner of acceptable worship? What are the relative duties of society? Wherein they come short? and what shall be the fruit of transgression? few of the heathen ask, and none can tell. Yet they are under a law of righteousness which saith, "the soul that sinneth shall die." The origin of their wants and woes they are unable to explore. To the demerit and wages of sin they are utter strangers: the consequences of death they are equally unprepared to meet or to estimate. All beyond the grave is impenetrable obscurity. Their notions of immortality are less a speculation than a dream. When called hence, they plunge into the world of spirits, unconscious of their destiny; and, till that consummation of sorrows, they grope, at a venture, after the path of life, but grope, alas! in vain; "having the understanding darkened; being alienated from the life of God, through the ignorance that is in them, because of the blindness of their heart."

Of this intellectual darkness the inseparable companion is an erring conscience.

Although light in the understanding does not, of course, imply moral excellence, yet, without the former, there can be none of the latter. To this it is necessary not only that there be a law of morals, but that it be obeyed from a regard to the authority of the lawgiver. Both the lawgiver and the law must, therefore, be known, or conscience will inevitably go astray. The general sentiment of right and wrong, though sufficient, if violated, to leave men without excuse, will by no means conduct to the proper discharge of duty. The fact is notorious, and a glance at the heathen will descry a thousand monuments of it. To those who have the advantage of revelation, no truths appear more simple and luminous, than that there is but one God, and that he only is entitled to religious homage. Yet how dubious, on these points, were the most celebrated heathen philosophers! how embarrassed their research! how conjectural their opinion! And of that spiritual devotedness which is the life of real religion, they had as little knowledge as the sons of modern unbelief. If from them we turn to the mass of their cotemporaries, or to those who are now in a similar condition, we are startled and shocked to see them " worship and serve the creature more than the Creator, who is blessed for ever." One poor idolater bows to the " host of heaven;" another trembles before an evil spirit—Here, he finds his divinities in birds, and beasts, and reptiles; "there, he "changes the glory of the incorruptible God into an image made like unto corruptible man," and lies prostrate before a deity of stone or of wood, the work of his chisel or his axe. " He heweth him down cedars, and taketh the cypress and the oak; he burneth part thereof in the fire; with part thereof he eateth flesh; he roasteth roast, and is satisfied; yea, he warmeth himself, and saith, Aha, I am warm, I have seen the fire: And the residue thereof he maketh a god, even his graven image: he falleth down unto it, and worshippeth it, and prayeth unto it, and saith, Deliver me, for thou art my god. And none considereth in his heart, neither is their knowledge nor understanding to say, I have burnt part of it in the fire; yea, I have also baked bread upon the coals thereof: I have roasted flesh, and eaten it: and shall I make the residue thereof an abomination? shall I fall down to the stock of a tree?"

The rites of paganism are worthy of its creed. Instead of a worship—reasonable, reverend, and pure—it exhibits all the frightful varieties of whatever is absurd, or blasphemous, or obscene. Its effects on individual and social character, are precisely such as we might anticipate. Unrestrained by any just apprehensions of God, of his law, or his government, the most baleful passions domineer in the heart, and the most horrible excesses pollute the life. Moral distinctions confounded, the sense of relative obligation extinguished, crimes the most atrocious perpetrated with deliberation, and upon principle, are, among the heathen, the result of being without God.* If, in the midst of this degradation and these enormities, the thought should occur, "that they who do such things are worthy of death," a secret horror creeps through the blood; conscience, the scorpion of guilt, strikes his sting into the bosom; forebodings, equally dark and intolerable, the mysterious presentiment of judgment to come, harrow up the soul. Whither, in this extremity, shall they turn for succour? All around them is one dreary waste,—the reign of silence and of desolation. No friendly voice is borne to the listening ear; no tower of help rises up to the anxious eye. The Comforter, who should comfort their souls, is afar off. They have not heard, like you, of the name of Jesus. They have none to tell them of "redemption through his blood, even the forgiveness of sins, according to the riches of his grace." And the termination of their mortal course—O brethren, how tremendous? The heavens blacken, the tempest roars, the whirlwind rushes by, down pours the torrent, and without a refuge, and without a hope, they are swept away in the ruin of the nations that forget God.

Exposed to this melancholy fate, the heathen claim our sympathy; and we eagerly ask, is their doom to such woe irreversibly sealed? Are they shut out for ever from the divine compassions? No! To the praise of his grace, Jehovah hath thoughts of mercy, rich mercy towards them. He will destroy, saith the prophet, "the covering cast over all people, and the vail that is spread over all nations"—a design, the contemplation of which forms the second part of discourse.

Ii. From the days of eternity, the Father has given to Messiah

* Ward's History of the Law of Nations.

"the heathen for his inheritance, and the uttermost parts of the earth for his possession." The whole earth, therefore, being included in the covenant-grant, shall be filled with the knowledge, and subdued to the obedience of Jehovah. On the maxims of carnal wisdom, the fact is, indeed, impossible, and the expectation wild. To extirpate prejudices implanted in infancy, nurtured by habit, confirmed by example, and consecrated by tradition—to enlighten the stupid idolater, and soften the ferocious savage—to persuade men to despise as contemptible, and loathe as abominable, the objects of their respect and veneration—in a word, to change the opinions, the customs, the characters of nations, and unite them in a religion, simple, holy, heavenly—a religion opposed to every vicious principle, and every vicious act—a religion which proscribes all human merit, and prostrates all human pride—this is an undertaking which equally defies the policy and the power of man. And the belief that it shall, at any time, be attended with success, furnishes incessant matter of derision to the philosopher, and of sneer to the witling. Their mistake lies in supposing the God who made them to be as foolish and as feeble as themselves, or as little concerned in the salvation of sinners. But we, according to his promise, look for the interposition of his arm, by which, however mean the instruments, this prodigious revolution shall be effected with no less ease than certainty. For,

1. He directs the complicated movements of the universe. However confused and contradictory things may appear to our little minds, with him whose "understanding is infinite," there is neither surprise, perplexity, nor chance. "Known unto the Lord are all his works from the beginning of the world." Not only are the laws of matter his sovereign will, and their operation his continual agency, but the whole system of intellect is under his control. All the discordant passions, interests, designs, which dash, in eternal collision, the affairs of men; all the activities of superior intelligences, as well the enmity of fiends as the ministry of angels, are combined, in the harmony of Providence, to produce the result which he hath ordained; and hither every occurrence irresistibly tends. "He doth according to his will in the army of heaven, and among the inhabitants of the earth." He causeth "the wrath of man to praise him, and the remainder of wrath he will restrain." The unpromising situation, therefore, of the heathen

is no obstacle to Israel's God, and should be none to Israel's faith. Be the mountains of difficulty ever so impassable, at his presence they flee away. Let the "nations rage, and the kingdoms be moved," if he "utter his voice, the earth is melted."

2. The glory of Messiah is a chief end of the dispensations of Providence.

The vicissitudes of kings and kingdoms, and all the stupendous events which shine in ancient annals, were important chiefly as they served to prepare the way, and to spread the triumphs of him who was "a light to lighten the Gentiles." For this God gave the learning of the world to Greece, and its empire to Rome. Both contributed to facilitate and extend the victories of the gospel. The same design is prosecuted in the events which, at this moment, astonish the world. If "nation rise up against nation, and kingdom against kingdom"—if establishments, imposing from their antiquity, and formidable from their strength, be undermined by the progress of opinion, or shattered by violent explosion—if impiety and ambition, and all the infuriate passions, be permitted to take their course, and scenes of desolation and blood, such as history hath not learnt to record, nor imagination to paint, be opened to our view; it is, that God may destroy the dominion of hell by her own chosen legions, and make them subserve the introduction of that kingdom, which is "righteousness, and peace, and joy in the Holy Ghost." Thus saith his high decree, "I will overturn, overturn, overturn, until he shall come whose right it is, and I will give it him."

3. In the scriptures of the prophets, this spiritual revolution by which the "kingdoms of this world shall become the kingdoms of our Lord and of his Christ," is frequently predicted and strongly marked. "All the ends of the world shall remember, and turn unto the Lord; all the kindreds of the nations shall worship before thee. It shall come to pass, in the last days, that the mountain of the Lord's house shall be established in the top of the mountains, and shall be exalted above the hills, and all nations shall flow unto it: And many people shall go and say, come ye, and let us go up to the mountain of the Lord, to the house of the God of Jacob: and he will teach us of his ways, and we will walk in his paths:" So that "from the rising of the sun even unto the going down of the same, his name shall be great among the Gentiles;

and in every place incense shall be offered unto his name, and a pure offering." Is there then a nation that yet "sit in darkness and the shadow of death;" for them "light is sown," and to them shall "light spring up." Is there a nation "mad upon their idols?" Jehovah shall "famish all the gods of the earth," and teach their votaries that he is "the God of salvation," and that "there is none beside him." Is there a nation enslaved to superstition, or abused by imposture? He shall "frustrate the tokens of the liars, shall make the diviners mad," and convert the bondage of their followers into the liberty of his dear children. "Rejoice, therefore, ye Gentiles, with his people. Faithful is he that hath promised, who also will do it."

But here occurs an important query. By what means are these predictions to be fulfilled, and these prospects to be realized? The means are prepared; they are extremely simple; they are in your hands—even "the doctrines of the gospel of peace." And this is the

III. And last topic which I proposed to discuss—In this mountain, saith the prophet, "shall the Lord destroy the vail that is spread over all nations?"

Mount Zion, to which Isaiah refers, is a figure, most familiar to the Scripture, of the Church of Christ. The Apostle Paul, addressing believers under the New Testament, says, "Ye are come unto Mount Zion." And the plain sense of the text is, that the Lord will bless the heathen outcasts, by "causing them to pass under the bond of his covenant," and to inherit the privileges of his house: and this shall be effected, by diffusing among them the glad tidings of salvation through our Lord Jesus Christ. "Behold," saith the sure word of prophecy, "behold, thou shalt call a nation that thou knowest not, and nations that know not thee shall run unto thee, because of the Lord thy God, and for the Holy One of Israel, for he hath glorified thee."

Our faith on this point will, indeed, provoke the ridicule of a tribe equally vain and licentious, who claim to be the exclusive benefactors of mankind. Rejecting, with opprobrium and insult, the gospel of Christ, they hail, as they speak, a new order of things, and the world is to be regenerated by a reason without conscience, and a philosophy without religion. "No doubt ye are the people, and wisdom shall die with you." But after all the ostentation and clamour of infidels, what reformation has been wrought by their doctrines or by their spirit? During forty centuries, reason and philosophy had the world almost to themselves. Where did they overthrow the reign of idolatry? From what vice did they reclaim the nations? One sect of philosophers rose on the ruin of another, to be itself the aggrandizement of a third. But the world lay still in wickedness, its diseases rankled with increasing fury, and struck deeper and deeper their poisonous roots, under the successive treatment of these "physicians of no value." Eighteen centuries more have nearly elapsed since "God manifested in the flesh put away sin by the sacrifice of himself:" and what has been done in elevating the character, in purifying the morals, in ameliorating the condition of man, that has been done without the aids of his gospel? What countries have the priesthood of unbelief rescued from barbarism? Where have they resisted the influence, or wiped off the shame of profligacy? Where have they promoted either happiness or virtue in public or in private? Whom have they taught to "deny ungodliness and worldly lusts, and to live soberly, righteously, and godly? By their fruits ye shall know them."

How different is the genius, and how different has been the career, of the Gospel of Christ! When it was promulgated to the heathen, the philosopher pronounced it folly, and stalked disdainfully by the missionary of the cross: yet through the cross did the missionary preach forgiveness of sins, and life everlasting; and lo, the throne of darkness tottered to its fall; the Gentiles "turned from idols to serve the living God." Abandoning, at once, their prejudices, their delusions, and their lusts, they "fled for refuge to lay hold on the hope set before them." The face of the world was changed, and the worldling knew not how. No deep speculations, no subtle reasoning, no displays of science, converted the nations. The process was very short, and very simple. Their guilt and their depravity—their certain destruction without pardon and renovation—the grace of God in sending Christ Jesus to die for sinners—his ability to save unto the uttermost; and the freedom of his salvation to the most worthless and vile, are the truths which won the Gentiles to the obedience of Christ. It is this same gospel which, at this hour, turns men "from darkness to light," and which is destined to " carry the banners of the cross victorious round the globe." Those refined moral disquisitions which, under the garb of sermons, expel vital godliness from the Church, will never introduce it among the heathen. Whoever hopes to gain them to the faith must imitate the Apostle Paul. He must " preach Christ crucified, to the Jews a stumbling-block, and to the Greeks foolishness; but to them who are called, both Jews and Greeks, Christ, the power of God, and the wisdom of God." Adapted to every clime of the earth, to every stage of society, and to all descriptions of its members, unavailing their real misery, and bringing near the only remedy,—discovering, at once, their wants, and the means of supplying them; and, seconded by the energy of the quickening Spirit, this precious Gospel fastens on the conscience, melts the heart, thrills the very bones and marrow, and transforms the most obdurate rebel into a willing subject of Jesus Christ. When the Lord " gives testimony to the word of his grace," it shall have " free course, and be glorified." No darkness too dismal for it to dispel—no prejudices too obstinate to subdue. " Mighty, through God, to the pulling down of strongholds," this very Gospel shall force its way through every physical and every moral difficulty; and in his name and strength shall its messengers cast down imaginations, and every high thought that lifteth itself up against the obedience of Christ. " Every valley shall be exalted, and every mountain and hill shall be made low; and the crooked shall be made straight, and rough places plain. And the glory of the Lord shall be revealed, and all flesh shall see it together; for the mouth of the Lord hath spoken it."

Come then, my brethren, let us ascend the hill of God; and, aided by the torch of the skies, let us look through the surrounding gloom, to the glories that lie beyond. See! an " angel flies through the midst of heaven, having the everlasting gospel to preach to every nation, and kindred, and tongue, and people." The standard of Shiloh is reared: his banner waves on high: the great trumpet is blown: the nations hear, and gather unto him. From the east, from the west, from the north, from the south, they press into the kingdom. On the one hand is the plundering Arab: on the other, the pitiless savage. Here, are the frozen children of the Pole; there, the sable tribes of Afric; and yonder, the long disinherited Jew steals silently to his Messiah, weeping as he goes. Hark! the din of arms, and the tumult of battle cease; discord and war retreat back to hell; and again that hymn of angels is heard below, "Glory to God in the highest, on earth peace, good-will towards men." The redeemed of the Lord raise their responsive song, "Now is come salvation and strength, and the kingdom of our Lord, and the power of his Christ." Brethren, 'tis no illusion; 'tis "the sober certainty" of truth divine. The zeal of the Lord of hosts will perform this—Hallelujah!

And now, dear brethren, shall not the first sentiment of our hearts be a sentiment of gratitude for the grace of God manifested unto us?

Let it never be forgotten, that we, in our ancestors, were among the perishing outcasts. Yet to us hath the word of salvation been sent. Without the gospel of Jesus, we should this day have been burning incense unto idols: without the gospel of Jesus, we should have been strangers to that blessed hope which gives to life its best relish, and takes from death both his terrors and his sting. O Christian, Christian, remember, that if thou hast escaped the wrath to come, and art made "an heir of God, and a fellow-heir with Jesus Christ," it is to the praise of sovereign mercy. Thy father was an Amorite, and thy mother a Hittite; and thou mightest have been left, with the Amorites and Hittites, to die in thine iniquity. Yet thou livest; livest unto God; livest for glory; and shalt never come into condemnation, and never taste of the second death. Thrice blessed gospel, which "hath brought life and immortality to light!" Thrice glorious grace, which hath constrained any of us to receive "the truth in the love thereof:" And thrice condescending Saviour, who hath "washed us from our sins in his own blood, and hath made us kings and priests unto God and his Father."

2. Since the Lord hath destroyed the vail that was spread over us, by revealing to us the great salvation, let all who have hitherto been indifferent about it be deeply impressed with the duty of embracing it without delay; and with the sin and danger of neglecting it.

"It is a faithful saying, and worthy of all acceptation, that Christ Jesus came into the world to save the chief of sinners." On the authority of the most high God, that gospel which we preach tenders to you, my brethren, to every one of you, a free grant of this Saviour, and, in him, of eternal life; and suffer me to add with all solemnity, enjoins your acceptance of it at the peril of your souls. This is his commandment; this, therefore, is your duty, your immediate, your indispensable duty, to believe on the name of his Son, Jesus Christ, that you may be saved. A refusal is the most aggravated crime which you can possibly commit. For it not only approves, with deliberation, all your deeds of rebellion against the God of your mercies, but pours contempt on the riches of his grace, and throws scornfully away the only hope that ever has been, or ever shall be, proposed to guilty men. The experiment, therefore, is not less dangerous than sinful. For if ye reject Christ Jesus, the Lord, "there remaineth no more sacrifice for sin." And when Jehovah writeth up the people, he will count that ye "trampled under foot the Son of his love, and deemed the blood of the covenant wherewith he was sanctified an unholy thing; and did despite unto the spirit of grace." Think not that this is a matter of trifling moment. If the gospel, which you hear from day to day, be not the instrument of your conversion to God, it shall be the occasion of your more dreadful condemnation. If not "the savour of life unto life," most certainly the savour of death unto death. The heathen will rise up in the judgment against you, and will condemn you, for they never shared your means of salvation. The devils will rise up in the judgment against you, and will condemn you, for no Saviour was provided for them; and, therefore, whatever be their crimes, the rejection of a Mediator's blood will be none of them. Now, then, "as though God did beseech you by us, we pray you in Christ's stead, be ye reconciled unto God." O that ye may know, in this your day, the "things that belong to your peace, before they be hid from your eyes!"

3. In the assurance that Jehovah will destroy, by the prevalence of his gospel, the vail spread over the nations, believers may see how little they have to fear for the existence or for the triumph of their religion.

Infidelity, it is true, prospers, and hath assumed a most effrontful air, and a most imperious tone. Her threats are loud, and her expectations sanguine. But threats as loud have, more than once, been put to shame, and expectations as sanguine, more than once been blasted. Seventeen centuries ago did the adversaries of the

Church predict her speedy downfall; but, unlike the prophets of Jehovah, they proved to be the seers of a lie: she hath lived to see their rage perish, the monuments moulder, their names sink into oblivion: and such shall be the issue of her present conflict. She can meet with no assault more furious and formidable than those which she hath a thousand times met and a thousand times foiled. "God is in the midst of her; she shall not be moved; God shall help her, and that right early." Therefore, "no weapon that is formed against her shall prosper; and every tongue that riseth in judgment against her, she shall condemn." The temporary success of the infidel should, indeed, confirm our faith, because it verifies the Scriptures. Our Master, Christ, hath told us, that this shall be one of the signs of his approach: "when the Son of man cometh, shall he find faith on the earth?" Every infidel under heaven is, then, a witness for Christianity, and carries in his forehead the proclamation that it is divine—Let him enjoy his exultation. Under a control which he can neither elude nor resist, he is really, though ignorantly, working his own destruction, and the aggrandizement of Messiah. His progress shall be arrested, and his boast confounded, whenever he shall have performed the part allotted to him in the determinate counsel and foreknowledge of God. In our patience, therefore, let us possess our souls. What, though blasphemy display his columns in defiance to the armies of the living God? What, though disorder spread from pole to pole, and mingle the nations in universal uproar? What, though the foundations be destroyed, their fabrics overturned, and earth quiver under the falling wreck? That Jesus, whom we worship, sitteth king for ever: he

"Rides in the whirlwind, and directs the storm."

With all power in heaven and earth, he will bring order out of confusion, and light out of darkness. In the moment of decision he will arise and plead his own cause. When he appears, in glory, to build up Zion, his enemies shall lick the very dust. The infidel, to his astonishment, will find that, in planting the seeds of unbelief, he was planting laurels for the cross; and the believer, to his unspeakable joy, that all the trials of the Church, and all the tumults of the world, were but preparative to the reign of righteousness in the ages of peace.

4. The subject which has this evening occupied our attention, places in a strong light both the obligation which lies on Christians to evangelize the heathen, and their encouragement to attempt it.

If we count it life eternal to know the only true God, and Jesus Christ, whom he hath sent, our bowels must yearn over those who are acquainted with neither. But it would be more than unkind, and worse than reproachful, were our best sympathies to evaporate in empty words or empty wishes. We are called not merely to condolence, but to action. A number of the families yet under the vail are our neighbours. They border on our country; they are accessible to our enterprise. Prompt and spirited measures for introducing among them the gospel of Christ, are our bounden duty.

Our duty—because we have the means of grace, and they have not. The unsearchable riches of Christ have been poured in upon us, while they are languishing in spiritual poverty. They must address themselves for help to some more favoured than themselves: and to whom with a more imperious claim than to us? The very difference of our situation creates us their debtors: the vicinity of our residence doubles the debt. The word and ordinances were bestowed upon us, not only that ourselves might be saved, but that we might minister to the salvation of others. Our possession, therefore, of the glorious gospel, implies, in the very nature of the privilege, an obligation to extend it as far as possible. Freely ye have received, freely ye must give. This is the way in which the gospel ever hath been and ever must be diffused. Though the employment would dignify angels, God has committed it to men. They who possess the treasure must impart it to others, and these again to more; till passing, in earthen vessels, from people to people, and from clime to clime, it enrich the world. An attempt to monopolize, or, which amounts to the same thing, a refusal to circulate it, is treason against the law of the kingdom. And let it not, my brethren, be our dishonour and our crime, to betray both ingratitude to our Redeemer, and cruelty to our fellowmen, by declining to communicate to them the mercies which, through the instrumentality of others, he hath lavished upon us.

With the superiority of our privileges, the genius of our profession conspires to challenge our interference in behalf of the heathen. As Christians, we profess that the glory of the Lord Jesus is the object most dear to our hearts, and most worthy of our pursuits. We profess to believe that the redemption of the soul is precious, and that, without the virtue of his blood, it ceaseth for ever. Is this a sincere profession? Can it at all consist with unwillingness to use every means in our power for diffusing, far and near, the sweet savour of his name? Must not a guilty blush crimson our faces, if we presume to pray "Thy kingdom come," when we are conscious that we have done nothing, are doing nothing, endeavour to do nothing, for the promotion of his kingdom? Do we, in very deed, believe that there is no salvation in any other—no other name given under heaven whereby sinners can be saved, but the name of Jesus Christ, and yet look coolly on, while multitudes of the heathen are perishing within our reach, nor ever stretch out a hand for their relief? Yes, my brethren, a generous and persevering attempt to proclaim among them the glad tidings of a Saviour, is a tribute to the decency of our Christian profession; and it is a tribute which their most afflicting necessities forbid to be deferred any longer.

If you heard of a number of human beings shut out from every sustenance, and falling, in rapid succession, the victims of famine, and knew, at the same time, that vigorous exertion might rescue the survivors, what anxiety would thrill every heart, what eagerness animate every countenance! How would the hand pour forth its spontaneous benefactions! How speedily would messengers be despatched with the staff of life! Alas! my brethren, we speak to you of a more terrible famine—a famine, not of bread, nor of thirst for water, but of hearing of the word of the Lord. We plead with you not for expiring bodies; it is the spirit, the spirit that dies! To the heart of the Christian be our appeal. Suppose thy Bible taken from thee; thy Sabbaths blotted from thy days; the mercies of the sanctuary fled; thy Father's fellowship denied; thy hopes, full of immortality, vanished; the shadows of eternal night stretching over thy soul: and if the thought be more intolerable than ten thousand deaths, think of yonder pagans, without God, and without hope. Ah! while the sentence is on my lips, they are passing, by hundreds, into that world unseen, with no renewing spirit, and no atoning blood! "O that mine head were waters, and mine eyes a fountain of tears," that I might weep unceasingly over the mighty ruin!

If any additional argument can be needed to render the proof of our duty, on this point, completely triumphant, that argument is supplied by the command of our Lord Jesus Christ. When he left this world, and went unto the Father, his parting injunction to his followers was,—"Go ye and teach all nations." And that the precept is binding upon the whole Church to the end of time, the promise of his presence and support most clearly evinces,—"Lo, I am with you always, even unto the end of the world." The command, being express and full, leaves no room for evasion. It either obligates all, or obligates none. If we may be exempted without sin, the exemption must extend to every Christian society under heaven; and then the Master's commandment would be a nullity, and his promise have neither grace nor meaning. In this matter, therefore, my brethren, we are by no means guiltless. With a single exception,* all denominations of Christians among us have violated their faith to their Lord, and are now chargeable with habitual disrespect to his authority. Instead of hastening, with generous emulation, to the aid of the heathen, we have gone, one to his farm, and another to his merchandise: we have clamoured for the shibboleths of party, and have been unanimous (ah, shameful unanimity!) in declining, on carnal and frivolous excuses, that work of faith, that labour of love. Now, therefore, thus saith the Lord, consider your ways. If we persist in neglecting these heathen, while we have the means of sending the gospel to them, they shall die in their iniquity; but their blood may be required at our hands.

Let no one object difficulties.† In a question of plain duty, a

* The honour of this exception belongs to the Moravian brethren.

† An objection to missions among the Indians, or other savages, which many view as unanswerable, is, "that some considerable progress in civilisation is previously necessary to prepare a people for the reception of Christianity. You must first make them men, say the patrons of this opinion, before you make them Christians You must teach them to live in fixed habitations, to associate in villages, to cultivate the soil, and then you may hope that they will hear and understand when you unfold the sublime principles of the gospel."*

Plausible and popular as this objection is, it is equally unsupported by reason, by scripture, or by fact.

If the gospel cannot succeed among the Indians, for example, the obstacle must be either in their understandings or in their manner of life.

* Dr Hardy's (of Edinburgh) Sermon before the Society, in Scotland, for Propagating Religious Knowledge, p. 14.

believer is not to be deterred by difficulties. Thus saith the Lord, is his warrant: and as long as there is nothing too hard for

The former opinion "supposes a wider difference between the understanding of the man of the woods and the man of the city, than what does, in fact, take place. The human mind is not, in any country, below the reach of discipline and religious instruction. The American Indian, the Pacific Islander, and the African negro, are shrewd men, whose intellectual capacity will not suffer in comparison with the uneducated classes of people on the continent of Europe."* Why should it, since it is culture, and that alone, which destroys the level of abilities naturally equal? Surely the Indian, whose necessities compel him not only to hunt and fish for his subsistence, but to be, in a great measure, his own artificer, as well as the guardian of his public and private right, must be superior, in point of general understanding, to those vast bodies of Europeans whose intelligence the division of labour has confined to a detached article of manufacture, or to the merely servile operations of agriculture. Indeed, all the national transactions with the Indians show them to possess great acuteness, and no small share of what learning cannot bestow—common sense. How seldom will you find, I do not say among the vulgar, but among the polished orders of society, better specimens of well-formed idea, and of genuine eloquence, than are frequent in the Indian talks?

If, on the other hand, their manner of life be considered as presenting the decisive obstacle, this opinion supposes it much more difficult to alter outward habits than inward principles. Christians will not dispute that the gospel can and does transform both the heart and the character; yet it is thought unable to overcome a propension to wandering from place to place. The plain meaning of the objection, therefore, is this, that some means *more powerful than the gospel*, must be applied to civilize the Indians, and prepare them for its reception. For if it be admitted, that the gospel can civilize as well as save, the objection falls at once to the ground. But if its power to civilize be denied, while its power to save is admitted, it becomes the objectors to show the reason of this distinction, and also what those more effectual means of civilisation are. Be they what they may, since the gospel is excluded, they must be merely human; and then the principle of the objection turns out to be this, that the wisdom of man is better adapted to civilize the Indians, than the wisdom of God.

Further: the objection supposes that savages are to be civilized without *any* religious aid. For whatever arguments prove the utility, in this matter, of religion at all, conclude, with tenfold energy, in favour of the religion of Christ. But to neglect the religious principle, would be to neglect the most potent auxiliary which can be employed in managing human nature; and to act in the spirit of that wise philosophy which would erect civil society upon the basis of atheism.

It would swell this note into a dissertation, to state the various considerations which militate against the idea of civilizing the Indians before we attempt to Christianize them. But granting this, for a moment, to be necessary, who shall

---

* Dr Hardy's Sermon, p. 15.

Omnipotence, there is nothing to justify disobedience or demur. Unbelief looks at opposition, and faints. Faith looks at the pro-

effect it? Philosophers? Merchants? Politicians? If we wait for them, the sun will expend his own light, and the business be unfinished. The Indians have had intercourse with the whites, in the concerns of trade and policy, nearly two hundred years, and most of them are as wild as ever. To put off evangelical missions to them, till, in the ordinary course of things, they become civilized, is, therefore, equivalent to putting them off forever.

2. If the opinion that the gospel can succeed only among civilized people, receives little countenance from reason, it receives less from scripture.

No such restriction of its influence is contemplated in prophecy. Its universal reception is the subject of numberless predictions; but they contain not a hint that the want of civilisation shall be such a bar to its progress as is commonly imagined. On the contrary, it is expressly declared, that the most roving and untutored tribes shall rejoice in Messiah's salvation, even while they retain their unpolished characters and manners. "Sing unto the Lord a new song: Let the wilderness and the cities thereof lift up their voice, the villages* that Kedar doth inhabit: Let the inhabitants of the rock sing; let them shout from the top of the mountains." Beyond all controversy, the general sense of the prophet, in the words of that elegant scholar, Bishop Lowth, is, that "the most uncultivated countries, and the most rude and uncivilized people, shall confess and celebrate, with thanksgiving, the blessing of the knowledge of God graciously imparted to them."† And he particularizes, as an example, those wild Arabs, who, in every point of comparison, were as inaccessible to the gospel as the American Indians.

No such restriction was thought of by the Apostle Paul. He was a debtor not more to the Greeks than to the barbarians. He maintains, that in the body of Christ "there is neither Greek nor Jew, barbarian, Scythian, bond nor free." A position which evidently assumes, that barbarians or Scythians might be Christians no less than Jews or Greeks, bondmen or free.

No such restriction is to be found in the commission which the Lord Jesus hath left his church. Thus it runs, "Go and teach all nations—Go ye into all the world, and preach the gospel to every creature," manifestly, every human creature, for such only are objects of the gospel salvation. Not a syllable about civilization. And unless it can be proved, that Indians, and other savages, are neither nations nor human creatures, or, if they are, that they are in no part of the world, the prejudice we are combating must be abandoned as in direct opposition to the will and the commandment of Christ.

Such a restriction, moreover, effaces the chief character and glory of the gospel, viz., "that it is the power of God to salvation." Were it what many take it to be, a system of mere moral suasion, of cool, philosophic argument, the case would be different, and the prejudice just. Indians and Hottentots are, indeed, rather rough materials for a religion cantly styled "rational." But whoever knows anything of real Christianity, knows that the conversion of a sinner is the exclusive work of Jehovah the Spirit. It is this principle, and this

* Or tents. † Translation of Isaiah. Notes, p. 19b, 4to.

mise of God, and conquers. In the strength of the promise, worm Jacob thrashes the mountains, and beats them small as chaff. It is the way of the Holy One of Israel to order his servants on difficult duty, without showing them immediately how they are to succeed. Reserving to himself the manner and the praise of their victory, he lays upon them a necessity of trusting his faithfulness; and they never did and never shall trust it in vain.

But why do I speak of difficulties? The most formidable ones which must be encountered in a mission to the heathen, have been overcome, and are daily overcome, by the firmness and intrepidity of carnal men. They can visit the savage tribes, can cross their rivers, climb their mountains, traverse their forests; can learn their language, conform to their manners, acquire their confidence;

alone, which makes the preaching of the word to men "dead in trespasses and sins," a reasonable service Now, to say that the gospel cannot succeed among a people not previously civilized, is to say, either that it is not the power of God, or that there are some things too hard for Omnipotence.

3. This opinion, dissonant from reason and scripture, is also contrary to fact.

Was the world universally civilized when Christianity was promulgated? or did it prosper only in civilized countries? What were the ancient Getulæ, in Africa? the Sarmatians and Scythians, in Europe? If we can credit history, they were as remote from civilization as the American Indians. Yet among these, and other nations equally uncultivated and savage, had the gospel, in the time of Tertullian, established its reign * And in Britain it penetrated into those places which Roman arts and arms had never been able to reach.†

This general assertion might be amplified in an interesting detail, and might receive additional force from the sanctions of modern history But either would protract, to an immoderate length, a note already too long. We may, however, ask, why the gospel should be unequal to the effects which it formerly produced, and of which its friends made their just and unanswerable boast? Let us fairly risk the experiment, whether the cross of Christ has lost its influence on barbarian minds. Instead of waiting till civilization fit our Indian neighbours for the gospel, let us try whether the gospel will not be the most successful means of civilizing them. The grace of the Lord Jesus will do what philosophy and the arts will never do—tame the wild heart: and there is no doubt of a corresponding alteration in the conduct. One Christian institution alone, the holy Sabbath, will go farther to civilize them, in a year, than all human expedients in a century. Driven continually before an extending frontier; their manners debauched by the commerce of unprincipled whites; their numbers diminishing by war and by vice; the only alternative which seems to be offered them is, conversion or extermination.

* Tertull. adversus Judæos, cap. vii.

† Inaccessa Rominis loca. Id. ib. A number of testimonies to the same facts are collected in that learned work of Grotius, De veritate Religionis Christianæ.

can patiently submit to hunger and cold, fatigue and peril:—For what? To decorate earthly science, or to collect the dust of lucre or the vapours of fame. They pretend to no divine command; they think of no divine support. Yet we, who talk familiarly of both, turn pale at the mention of those obstacles which they continually surmount. Whence this resoluteness on the one side, and this timidity on the other! The uncourtly truth is, that the men of the world are in earnest, and we are not. And what must they, what can they, conclude from our supineness? Either that our religion is false, or that we do not believe it. How long ere this reproach be wiped away? Duty urges, misery implores, thousands of precious souls are the depending stake, and not a moment is to be lost. In the work before us, in the immortal work of evangelizing the heathen, let us rouse each latent energy, and brave opposition like good soldiers of Jesus Christ. And certainly the encouragement is as great as the call is pressing. As far as man, with the lights of prophecy, can judge, the time is not far distant, when God shall arise, and have mercy upon Zion. What mean these dire convulsions? this crash of kingdoms? these torrents of blood? He who can here discover only the shock of human interests, or the madness of human passions, hath not penetrated beyond secondary and instrumental agencies. From the eminence of scriptural prediction, a humble believer overlooks the mole-hill of worldly politics, and descries the moving power, and the necessary effect, of the machinery of Providence. To him it is evident that Jehovah shakes the nations, and is shaking them, that "the desire of all nations may come." And hence his faith derives an establishment, and his hope an elevation, which earth is as unable to destroy as to create. Impending calamity, then, should stimulate, and not dishearten, the disciples of Jesus. The walls of Jerusalem are commonly built in troublous times. Nor hath the career of the gospel been ever more ample and brilliant, than in the days which were memorable for "distress of nations, with perplexity; the sea and the waves roaring; men's hearts failing them for fear, and looking after those things which were coming upon the earth." In these circumstances of disaster and dismay, the people of God are charged to look up, and lift up their heads, because their redemption draweth nigh, and the Son of man is coming with great power and glory. If these are, in any degree, the signs of the times, then now is the time for the armies of Israel to gird every man his sword on his thigh, and follow David, his king, to conquest and glory.

If from the sphere of politics we turn to that of religion, we shall behold events which ought to convert every doubt into proof, and every wish into a vow. While the spirit of discord rages in the world, the spirit of union and of love descends upon the Church. Beyond the waters of the Atlantic, our brethren in the faith and patience of Jesus rejoice in his most benignant influences. Astonishing spectacle! The spell of party is broken, the antipathies of the cradle expire, the strife of ages ceases, and a sweeter harmony of heart and of measures, among Christians of different name, is produced in an hour, than has been granted to the intreaties, the labours, the prayers, of the best of men, for centuries together!

Do you demand the cause of this gracious unanimity? It is the doing of the Lord. Its object? It is the extension of the Mediator's kingdom. Its fruits? They are, already, embassies of peace to the heathen. Great is the company who have gone forth, with primitive zeal, to publish the word of life. The probability is that Christ crucified, that Christ whom our souls love, is, at this moment, preached to the barbarians of the southern seas; and that an evangelical mission is on its way to the interior of Africa? Ye servants of the Most High God, who shows unto the Gentiles the way of salvation, all hail! May the Breaker go up before you; even Jehovah on the head of you; may he cheer you with his presence, fill you with his spirit, clothe you with his blessing! And what more auspicious omen can we, my brethren, desire? When the work is actually begun, when it has received the most unequivocal tokens of divine approbation, shall we still linger, and tempt the Lord by asking any further signs? To him who is not blind, the finger of his providence points; to him who is not deaf, the voice of his providence calls. Incitement of a more imperious kind would encroach on the province of miracle.

If to these encouragements we add the promise of our Master in heaven, reluctance will be cut off from her last retreat. He hath said, "that he will be with his people in their attempts to teach the nations." If, on a design so truly Christian, we go in his name, and in his strength, we have a right to expect his aid; nor is it possible that he should abandon us, or put us to shame. He hath bound himself, by the oath of his covenant, to beat down opposition before those who, obedient to his authority, constrained by his love, and confiding in his truth, enter upon arduous duty; and the glory of his crown is staked on the issue. With the Lord of hosts on our side, whom or what shall we fear? To him all difficulties are alike. At his command the treasures of the earthling shall flow in the service of the cross; and hundreds shall arise to solicit, as an enviable distinction, the office of a gospel-herald to the savages. Clad in the armour of the sanctuary, and conducted by the "Captain of salvation," they shall go forth "conquering and to conquer." Ere his promise fail, the mountains shall sink, the valleys rise, the rivers be driven back to their sources, and ocean again divide his waters. Who, then, are on the Lord's side? Who prefer the salvation of men above their chiefest joy? Who burn to hide the dishonour of the past in the glory of the future, and aspire to the dignity of being fellow-workers with God? Let them, with one heart and one soul, in the faith of the gospel, in the good will of brethren, in the bowels of Jesus Christ, forthwith pledge themselves to each other, to those apostolical believers beyond the sea, to the heathen who are perishing for lack of vision, that they will unite their efforts to fill the dark places of the land with the light of God's salvation. Should we succeed in the conversion of a single pagan, the acquisition would infinitely repay our expenditure and our toil. For our Lord himself hath pronounced the whole world, in comparison with one soul, to be a thing of naught. But O, my brethren, who shall count the number, or define the extent, or limit the duration of those blessings which our exertions may be instrumental in imparting to the heathen! Who shall stop the river of life in its course through their parched soil! Most transporting thought! that thousands of believers whom we shall never see in the flesh, and tens of thousands who shall come into being when we are gathered unto our fathers, may trace their knowledge of the Saviour to the execution of that plan in virtue of which I address you this evening! and that its magnificent result may never be fully disclosed, till the mystery of Providence be finished, the election of grace brought in, and the shout of final redemption thunder through the temple of God!

SERMON V.*

PARDON OF SINS, &c.

EPHES. i. 7.

"In whom we have redemption through his blood, the forgiveness of sins, according to the riches of his grace."

WHOEVER believe that they have sinned, and that God is just, cannot be indifferent to their condition and their prospects. The perfect development of his righteousness being reserved for a future state, and every question concerning it involving an immortal spirit and an eternal destiny, it would be madness not to inquire what shall be our fate. Reason and conscience, pronounce, with revelation, that "the wages of sin is death." And neither reason nor conscience, neither the works nor the providence of God, can discover the means or warrant the hope of escape. Dost thou doubt? Make fairly the experiment. Retire into thine own bosom, and ask, can God justify the ungodly? Thy reason abashed declines to answer, while the voice of conscience pours accusations into thine ears, and her fingers point to "the wrath to come." Flee from thyself and thy fellow-sinners, whose reason is as dark and whose conscience is as guilty as thine own. Explore the works of the Creator. Thou wilt see order, beauty, magnificence, but not a trace of pardon. Go down now to the abode of those rebel-spirits "who kept not their first estate." Ah! here are only "chains of darkness and vials of wrath." Hasten hence, and consult the angels who surround the throne. Ask them if thou mayst hope for more lenity than the apostates of their own family? Ask them if the Holy One can save thee without prejudice to his glory? The heavenly hosts cannot solve the problem. Silence seals up their lips of love; and thou, thy soul unsatisfied, thy

* Preached in Philadelphia on the Evening of Sabbath, the 31st of May 1801.

doubts redoubled, must return and pass the time of thy sojourning, alternately shivering with the ague and burning with the fever of despair.

On this darkness, which the lights of the creature serve only to deepen, God hath caused the light of the gospel to descend. It hath driven away those forms of horror which stalk around us in reason's and in nature's gloom, and revealed his angel of peace, the Word made flesh. He calls us this day into his sanctuary, not to face his terrors, and to perish at his rebuke, but to embrace his overtures of mercy, and to rejoice in his salvation.

This, then, is the message which we have heard of him, and declare unto you, that to secure an honourable exercise of mercy, God "spared not his own Son, but delivered him up to the death, that he might purge away our transgressions." And we are commanded to announce to you these glad tidings of great joy, that "in him we have redemption through his blood, the forgiveness of sins according to the riches of his grace." Astonishing words! More astonishing truths! Forgiveness of sins; forgiveness through the redemption of the Saviour's blood; forgiveness according to the riches of his grace. These are the sublime subjects of the text; and you see, in their order, the plan of discourse.

Spirit of grace and truth! impart thine influence, that we may speak of them and hear, as belongeth to those who speak and who hear the oracles of God!

I. I am to explain that "forgiveness of sins" which is declared in the text.

To form a correct judgment on this point, we must ponder the condition into which sin has brought us. In his moral government God has inseparably connected sin with punishment. Exclusion from his favour, his communion, his presence: his abhorrence in this world, and the damnation of hell in the next, are its native consequences and its just reward. It is this obligation to punishment which we term guilt. The divine law ties down the person of the sinner to the penalty of his sin. Forgiveness looses the wrathful bond. It dissolves the connection, not between sin and suffering, which is as immutable as the holiness and truth of God, but between sin and the destruction of the sinner. His crimes are consigned to oblivion; and the Lord, instead of entering into judgment with him, acquits him from every charge, pronounces him innocent, and crowns him with blessing. Forgiveness, then, produces a double effect.

1. It removes the curse which, till that moment, abides on the sinner's person.

Justice had issued her sentence; the law had arrested him, and bound him for execution. Forgiveness steps in, takes the death-warrant out of the hand of the law, breaks the seal and cancels the authority of that fatal instrument, strikes off the fetters of the condemned wretch, and bids him to go forth.

2. Forgiveness confers the favour and fellowship of God, and the inheritance of his heavenly kingdom.

Pardon is the great preliminary to advancement. The Lord forgives, that he may bless. A pardoned rebel passes into the family of God's dear children. Accepted in the Beloved, the Spirit of adoption descends upon his heart, and his countenance brightens with the smile of reconciliation. Compassed about with favour as with a shield, he walks in safety and in peace. No weapon that is formed against him shall prosper. The eternal God is his refuge, and underneath are the everlasting arms. Though his transgression may be visited with the rod, and his iniquity with stripes, yet "my loving kindness," saith God, "will I not take from him; nor suffer my faithfulness to fail." And while the Lord is thus his shelter and his shade, his glory and the lifter up of his head, manifesting covenant-mercy in giving that which is good, he is admitted to the divine fellowship. An open door into the holiest is set before him, through which he is commanded and qualified to draw nigh and commune with the living God. Without reluctance, without misgivings, with all holy boldness, it is his duty to "go unto God his exceeding joy." The privilege is most congenial with the principles of the new man. A pacified conscience and a cleansed heart find their element in the presence and enjoyment of God. "O God, thou art my God; early will I seek thee: my soul thirsteth for thee, my flesh longeth for thee in a dry and thirsty land, where no water is; to see thy power and thy glory, so as I have seen thee in the sanctuary. Because thy loving kindness is better than life, my lips shall praise thee. Thus will I bless thee while I live: I will lift up my hands in thy name."

This state of friendship with God is the pledge of his eternal kingdom. "We are no more strangers and foreigners, but fellow-citizens with the saints, and of the household of God." Whom he translates into his family, he appoints to his rest: pardons and adopts them, that they may be forever in the highest heavens, "to the praise of the glory of his grace." Between sonship and the kingdom, his covenant has fixed an indissoluble connection. "If children, then heirs, heirs of God, and fellow-heirs with Christ in glory."

These are indeed glad tidings. Every syllable is accented with transport. "But oh!" cries the desponding spirit, "mock me not with a fallacious hope. I sink under my guilt: I perish, behold, I perish."

Nay, I preach not to you an idle tale. This gospel of forgiveness is faithful and worthy of all acceptation. It is the joint message of mercy and judgment through the lips of truth. The principle on which forgiveness is tendered hushes every tumult, and relieves every doubt. That dread enigma, "how God can be just and justify the ungodly," is unfolded in the text. All forgiveness of sin flows through the blood of Jesus Christ. This is the

II. Part of the discourse. "We have redemption through his blood."

Here occurs a double inquiry. The one involving the doctrine of redemption; the other, the nature of our interest in it.

1. The doctrine of redemption, as taught by the apostle, may be reduced to the following propositions:

First. That sin cannot go unpunished: and, therefore, that a forgiveness which implies its impunity is impossible.

Second. That it is altogether consistent with the divine righteousness to inflict the punishment of sin upon a competent surety, and to pardon sinners in virtue of his atonement.

Third. That no obedience or suffering of any mere creature can atone for sin.

Fourth. That the redemption of the blood of Jesus, as it is the only, so it is the all-sufficient reason of the pardon of sin. May the Spirit of Jesus help us to understand and improve these truths!

First. Sin cannot go unpunished: and, therefore, a forgiveness which implies its impunity is impossible.

The impunity of sin is incompatible with the nature, the government, and the covenant of God.

His nature forbids it. An eternal contradiction to his perfection, it shall not dwell in his presence, but must be marked as that abominable thing which he hateth. And if his very being is set against it, this, in itself, is the most terrible punishment. All other plagues are lost in the abyss of that curse, God is thine enemy. Yes, brethren, his holiness is "a consuming fire, which burns up his enemies round about;" and, therefore, it forbids the impunity of sin.

His government also forbids it. A great God, and a great king, whose glory is the end, and whose will is the law of creation; he must be obeyed, and on him must be the visible dependence of the universe. Sin is the attempt of a creature to throw off his independence. And could he sin with impunity, his independence would be effected. But an independent creature is an atheistical absurdity. The punishment of sin, therefore, results necessarily from the divine supremacy.

It equally results from the divine rectitude. God "sitteth on a throne judging right." But a righteous governor who does not punish crime is a contradiction. It is in giving every one his due, or, in other words, in apportionate condition to character, that righteousness consists. And the perfection of this apportionment is the perfection of righteousness. If, then, God should permit any sin to escape, his righteousness would be imperfect; if every sin, he would have none at all; nor could the idea of righteousness exist in the universe. Sin, therefore, is punished, because its punishment is intrinsically just, and cannot be remitted by a just God. Otherwise it would never be inflicted, or be resolved into a question of mere expediency; and this would annihilate the distinction between right and wrong, and with it every moral attribute of Deity.

Moreover, the protection which the justice of God owes to his innocent creatures, as well as to the honour of his own holiness, requires the coercion of transgressors. That a principle of ingratitude, rebellion, and enmity against him—a principle which defies his wrath, and threatens his throne; which hurls desolation and wretchedness through his world—should go uncontrolled or unchastised, is a thought infinitely shocking. Scripture coincides with these views and this reasoning. The "wrath of God revealed from heaven against the unrighteousness of men," it calls his "judgments."—"As a judge with whom there is no iniquity," he will determine their final state, by recompensing to some eternal rest, and to others eternal tribulation. If he "rain upon sinners snares, fire and brimstone, and a horrible tempest," it is because he is "the righteous Lord who loveth righteousness."

To the consideration of God's general government we must add that of his covenant with man.

The law of morals prescribed to our race is armed with penalty, not only in the nature of things, but by the express declaration of the lawgiver. Coupled, moreover, with a federal transaction, which embraces, on the one hand, the threatening of death, and, on the other, the sweet promise of life, it binds to the fulfilment of their respective stipulations the fidelity both of God and man. But the law is violated: the covenant is broken: the forfeiture is incurred; and fallen man is under a dispensation of wrath flowing from the breach of the covenant of works. His sin is, therefore, under a double obligation to punishment: the one arising from the holiness and rectoral justice of God; the other from that covenant-threatening to which he consented, and which the divine veracity is pledged to execute. Accordingly, the law of God knows nothing of forgiveness. Encircled with terrible glory, she takes her position on Ebal, and with her trumpet, which is "as the voice of the Almighty God when he speaketh," issues her proclamation, "The wages of sin is death!"—"Cursed is every one that continueth not in all things which are written in the book of the law to do them!"

It appears, then, that the perdition of a sinner is inevitable, unless some expedient can be devised which may conciliate his pardon with the holiness, the government, and the truth of God. Blessed be his name! such an expedient is possible. For,

My second proposition is, That it is altogether consistent with the divine righteousness to inflict the punishment of sin upon a competent surety, and to pardon sinners in virtue of his atonement.

By atonement, taken in a large sense, is understood such an obedience as shall fulfil the precept, and such suffering as shall exhaust the penalty, of the divine law; and thus, by satisfying the claims of justice, remove every obstruction to the exercise of mercy.

Atonement proceeds on the principle of substitution. The guilt of men being transferred to an able, a voluntary, and an accepted surety, their responsibility attaches to him, and they are released. So that, by an intervention of an atonement, the righteousness of God may be displayed in the punishment, and his grace in the pardon of sin. Nor is the propriety of such a dispensation liable to just exception. On the contrary, it is susceptible of the clearest proof. For them who, without murmuring or disputing, receive the testimony of God, it is sufficient that his word declares the fact. The Lord Jesus, "his own self, bare our sins in his own body on the tree." Jehovah "hath laid upon him the iniquity of us all; yea, hath made him to be sin for us, who knew no sin; that we might be made the righteousness of God in him."

But in forming our judgment on this point, the nature of justice and the works and providence of God come to our aid.

1st. Justice requires that the law be maintained, and, therefore, that violations of it be punished. And, provided this end be gained, that is, provided "every transgression and disobedience receive a just recompense of reward," justice has no farther demand. The reason why, in all ordinary cases, her stroke lights on the person of the offender, is, that, in all such cases, she has no other way of punishing his offence. It is plain that her quarrel is with sin, and with the sinner solely on account of his sin; but now, on the supposition that his guilt can be separated from his person, so as not to elude the sentence of the law, it is equally plain that her quarrel with him ceases. For the sin which was the cause of it, and to punish which she had arrested him, is, notwithstanding his liberation, in her hands, to be punished to the uttermost. This is the effect of suretiship. The same homage is yielded, the same rights asserted, the same testimony against sin exhibited, the same vengeance executed, in the obedience and suffering of a surety as in the obedience and suffering of the principal. Expiation of sin by a surety is, therefore, most agreeable to the nature of justice.

2d. The part of the divine works with which we are most conversant, our own nature, gives strong confirmation to this doctrine.

The principle of substitution, of the discharge of obligation by a surety, is interwoven with the texture of the human mind and with all the operations of human society. Even those who are most hostile to it, when it appears in the form of imputed sin and imputed righteousness, are constantly and necessarily governed by it. The wisdom and integrity of their agent redound to their advantage, and they must reap the fruits of his folly and his faults. In short, it is the life-spring of intercourse among men; nor could the affairs of the world be carried on one moment without it. Trace up, then, to its source, and pursue through its results, the principle of the substitution of Christ Jesus in the room of his people; and when you find, as upon sober inquiry you will, that it coincides with an essential character of man's moral constitution, you will no longer contemn it as unreasonable, or revile it as unjust.

3d. Upon this dispensation, which is founded in the nature of justice, and has a counterpart in our own frame, the providence of God furnishes an ample comment.

He has always dealt with men through the medium of representation. The fall of our first parent, who, as our surety, transgressed the covenant of his God, "brought death into the world, and all our woe." "In Adam all die:" for "in him all have sinned." In his covenant with Israel, God urged the blessing or the curse which he should bring on their posterity, as motives to deter them from sin, and secure their obedience. He has revealed himself as "a jealous God, visiting the iniquity of the fathers upon the children, unto the third and fourth generation of them that hate him, and showing mercy unto thousands of them that love him, and keep his commandments." In holy baptism parents are the sureties of their infant children. The baptismal vow, (let the truth, O young people, sink down into your hearts!) the baptismal vow is binding upon them, and if they despise it in riper years, especially if they die unbelievers in that Saviour to whom they were dedicated, God will plead with their souls for the profanation of that blood of the covenant of which the symbol has been sprinkled upon them. In the present crisis of human things the vials of his wrath are poured out upon the posterity of those who betrayed his truth, and slew his servants. He gives them blood to drink for the blood of his saints which was shed by their ancestors. Nay, while the sentence is on my lips, thousands of Adam's children, incapable of action, are writhing in agony and sinking in death, the victims of his curse, though not, by any personal agency, the partakers of his crime. The world, then, is full of the imputation of sin. And why shall it not as well be imputed to a representative for expiation, as from a representative for punishment?

From this strong ground we are not to be driven by the plea, that righteousness and sin, being moral and personal qualities and acts, cannot be transferred to a surety. We know it. Neither do the Scriptures teach, nor we maintain, any such transfer. Instead of establishing, it would destroy our doctrine.* We admit that personal acts cannot be transferred, but affirm that they are imputed. Imputation lies in transferring to a surety, not the qualities and acts themselves, but their legal connection. It is a transfer of obligation and of right. The moral principle of this transfer, or, in other words, of the imputation of sin to a surety, enters into every case of representation, whatever be its objects or modifications. And the question, How can sin be expiated by a surety? which stumbles all "the disputers of this world," has the same embarrassments, and the same solution as the question, How can the deed of my representative be sustained in law and equity as my own? It is for these disputers to show why I may not as well suffer as act by representation? Our astonishment in every other instance but that of the kinsman-Redeemer would be, not that the principle of imputation should be admitted but that it should be doubted. As it continually recurs, we lose its diffi-

---

* For if my personal sin could be taken from me, and made the personal sin of another, he must then suffer for himself, and not for me, as I would be personally innocent. He would not be under the imputation of my sin, because I would have none to impute; and I could not enjoy the benefit of his righteousness, because, on the one hand, I would require none; and, on the other, he, as suffering for himself, would have none to offer. So that here would be no representation, neither the substance nor the shadow of a vicarious atonement. Therefore, while my personal demerit must for ever remain my own, the consequences of it are borne by my glorious Surety. It is this which renders the imputation of sin to the Lord Jesus a doctrine so acceptable to the conscience, and so consoling to the heart, of a convinced sinner. And this simple distinction between a transfer of personal acts to a substitute, and the transfer of their legal connection, which is properly imputation, relieves the friends of truth from the embarrassment in which an incautious manner of speaking has sometimes involved them; and blows into air the quibbles and cavils of its enemies.

culty in its utility, and forget that it is mysterious, because it is familiar.

A vicarious atonement being thus consistent with the divine righteousness, the chief obstacle to our hope is surmounted, and the apparent contradiction between the pardon and the punishment of sin vanishes. But our joy is premature. We have discovered that pardon, through an atonement is possible; but an essential point remains to be settled. By whom shall the atonement be made? Here is a new and sad perplexity. In vain we cast our imploring look upon the creatures: not one of them has the love or the power. And this introduces my

Third proposition: which is, that no obedience or suffering of any mere creature can atone for sin.

Conscience, wounded by guilt, groping in the glimmerings of tradition, besotted with ignorance, and abused by imposture, has tried various expedients to propitiate deity. Ablutions, pilgrimages, penances, and a thousand other superstitions, abound in pagan and antichristian nations. Wealth is lavished in offerings of peace, and the body is tortured for the relief of the soul. Lying vanities all. "Will the Lord be pleased with thousands of rams, and ten thousand rivers of oil? Shall I give my first-born for my transgression; the fruit of my body for the sin of my soul?" Ah no! The evil lies infinitely deeper than to be reached by such remedies. That sacrifice which will be to God of a sweet smelling savour, cannot be offered by men, nor by angels, nor by man and angel united. Not by men—for the end of an atonement is to deliver them from that very curse which must be borne in making it. Not by angels—for this would be inconsistent with the truth of God, which denounced the curse upon the human nature. Not by an angel-man—because no combination of created natures can sustain the wrath, or magnify the law, or vindicate the government of God. An overwhelming difficulty, therefore, remains. Where is the sufferer to be found? Who shall yield an obedience to merit heaven for millions, or offer up for their souls the redeeming sacrifice? The mere possibility of relief without a friend to apply it, only doubles our distractions. The light which was dawning upon our darkness recedes, and leaves us to deeper horrors. But hark! it is the voice of the **Deliverer!** "Lo, I come." Who art thou, most gracious? "I, that speak in righteousness, mighty to save!" It is the only begotten Son of God, who comes, clothed with humanity, for the salvation of perishing sinners. Whence my

Fourth proposition is, That the blood of Jesus Christ, as it is the only, so it is the all-sufficient, reason of the pardon of sin.

1st. It is, in itself, of infinite value. Whatever a sacrifice could derive from the person of the sufferer: whatever detestation of sin, or determination to punish it: whatever terror of perdition which it involves: whatever impossibility of its expiation by a creature: whatever consistency of its pardon by a surety, could be testified by the spectacle of a humbled God; all that is to be found in the sacrifice of Jesus; for it is the blood of the only begotten Son. Being really man, when he endured the cross, the curse was executed upon the very nature on which it was denounced. But being unspeakably more than man, even the Father's equal, Jehovah in the flesh, he was able to bear, at once, the whole weight of wrath, and impart to his obedience and suffering a merit and efficacy proportioned to the glory of the Godhead. The submission of the Lord Jesus to fulfil the righteousness and bear the iniquities of his people, reflected infinite lustre upon the divine government. It did what never could have been done by the eternal obedience of all sinless, and the eternal destruction of all sinful, creatures— "magnify the law, and make it honourable." Now, the evil of sin is demonstrated; the threatening of God executed; his truth preserved; his justice vindicated; his government maintained: and what should hinder the release of the wretches for whom these wonders have been wrought? What crime cannot the blood of Jesus atone? What stain can it not efface? How is it not impossible that it should not "cleanse from all sin?" Who shall set the transgressions of man in array against the righteousness of God? Here the conscience may be at peace; for here the divine law is satisfied, and the fires of the curse extinguished. We surely need ask no more. For,

2. Nothing more is required by the holy God.

"The Lord is well pleased for his righteousness' sake; and hath set him forth to be a propitiation through faith in his blood, that he might be just, and the justifier of him that believeth in Jesus." With sinners who are willing thus to accept forgiveness, and to choose life rather than death, he pursues his quarrel no longer, but is "in Christ, reconciling the world unto himself, not imputing their trespasses unto them, but forgiving iniquity, and transgression, and sin."

3d. What the atonement of Jesus is, in itself, and what his Father has expressly declared it to be, millions of sinners have found it to their eternal joy. All "the spirits of just men made perfect," and all believers at this hour upon earth, have "washed their robes, and made them white in the blood of the Lamb." Search the records of the saved, and you will see the names of the most atrocious offenders who were pardoned, and sanctified, and are now with God. Ask them how they escaped the wrath to come, and entered the everlasting rest? With one voice they will exclaim, "He loved us, and washed us from our sins in his own blood!" Ask all the family of grace who shall speedily join the celestial throng how they obtained deliverance from the curse, and access to that terrible God? With equal unanimity they will reply, "We are accepted in the Beloved." There is, therefore, "redemption through his blood."

Let us, then, proceed to our

2. Inquiry, which relates to the interest in this redemption which is implied in the text—We have redemption, says the apostle.

Those who enjoy the dispensation of the gospel have, as sinners, a common interest in the redemption of Jesus: that is, the Father has made a grant of him in the gospel to sinners, as such, for their salvation. I say, to sinners, as such; for the grant of the Saviour is absolutely free. Unshackled with conditions, it is presented to them not as penitent, sensible, contrite, but as guilty, rebellious, vile. This grant invests them with a right to the Lord Jesus, whom they are to receive upon the authority of the divine warrant, with the assured faith that, in thus receiving him, they shall be saved. Do any of you, then, demand where you are to seek forgiveness? The answer is short. You have it in the redemption of the blood of Christ. There it is offered to you. There you must apply. You shall not be sent away empty; for he hath said, "Him that cometh unto me I will in no wise cast out."

Believers, who have fled for refuge to this hope set before them, are in actual possession of redemption. Faith in the blood of Jesus, that faith which is the grace of the Holy Spirit, has made it their own. That which is common to all in the indefinite grant of the gospel, has become, by particular appropriation, their personal inheritance. Theirs it is with its whole train of blessings: theirs are the ordinances: theirs the promises: theirs the gracious covenant: life is theirs: death is theirs: eternity is theirs: the Father, the Son, and the Holy Ghost are theirs—they "shall never come into condemnation:" "neither death, nor life, nor angels, nor principalities, nor powers, nor things present, nor things to come, nor height, nor depth, nor any other creature, shall be able to separate them from the love of God which is in Christ Jesus their Lord.

While our souls rejoice in this plenteous redemption, and the forgiveness which it secures, let us lift up our eyes to the source from whence both proceed. This is the

III. And last part of my discourse. We have redemption and forgiveness according to the riches of Jehovah's grace.

Such is the plan of salvation, that while sinners are delivered from going down to the pit, "the Lord alone shall be exalted." In the pardon of sin, the voice of human pretension must not be heard. Grace, mere grace, the riches of grace, is the burden of our song. The text suggests infinite arguments of this truth.

1. Sin is such an evil, that nothing but the grace of God could have projected its pardon. Sin! ah! my brethren, who can develop the meaning of the horror-smiting term? Canst thou dive into its depths, and display its hidden hells? One sin changed legions of holy spirits into devils. One sin brought perdition on our wretched race. Make thy suit to the benevolence of angels; lay before them, in its true colours, the least of thy provocations, and thy best hope will be as the giving up of the ghost. Not one of them would dream of mercy for thee. It belongs not to creatures to show such forgiveness. Herein he is glorious, herein he is seen to be God, that when he alone has a full view of the sinfulness of sin, he alone can think of its pardon.

2. As nothing less than divine grace could forgive sin, so the purpose of it originated in no exterior cause. Many, whose affections are touched with the love of Christ, entertain forbidding thoughts of the austerity of the Father. This is a great error. Christ purchased not the Father's love. On the contrary, it was the Father's love which appointed and sent the Son to be the Saviour of the world. Grace is its own reason. He loved us,

because he loved us. Here is the original fountain, here the overflowing ocean, from which forgiveness issues. Had it depended upon anything external, no Redeemer had been known, no hope revealed, no sinner saved.

3. The most ineffable effect of the Father's grace, its riches, its infinite expression, is the forgiveness of sin at the expense of the blood of Jesus. Had he given the universe beside, it would have been little, it would have been nothing, in comparison of his Son. With all holy reverence be it spoken, grace can go no farther. Sinners, here is the very heart of God! Here he has uncovered the profound of his compassions. God so "loved the world that he gave his only-begotten Son"—for whom? for rebels; for those who were enemies to him by wicked works. For what? "That whosoever believeth in him might not perish, but might have everlasting life."

4. In the application of forgiveness through the redemption that is in Christ Jesus, grace is exceedingly abundant.

Not only is it beyond our desert and expectation, but far above all that we are able so much as to think. The forgiveness which the gospel reveals, is the forgiveness of God. We can form no conception of the generosity, the extent, the riches of forgiveness, unless we consider the wonderful redemption through which it flows. Grace went every length in giving the Lord Jesus for an atoning sacrifice; and it goes every length in pardoning them that believe in his name.

The doctrine which I have now laid before you, brethren, is not a lofty speculation which you may admire without adopting: it is truth of everlasting moment; truth essential to your happiness; and for which you shall soon, very soon, give an account at the bar of God. I address you as sinners who need forgiveness; who perish without it; and shall never obtain it but through the redemption that is in Christ Jesus. In his great name, therefore, allow me to demand what reception you will give to the gospel of his cross. "Exalted to be a Prince and a Saviour, to give repentance unto Israel, and forgiveness of sins, he waiteth to be gracious;" and tenders to the chief of sinners, without money and without price, all the benefits of his covenant. "Behold," they are his own blessed words, "Behold, I stand at the door, and knock: If any man hear my voice, and open the door, I will come in to him, and sup with him, and he with me." Let no sinner, then, exclude himself from mercy which is offered in the gospel, as directly to him, as if there were not another sinner under heaven: and offered with such marvellous grace, that nothing but his acceptance is wanting to place him forever beyond the reach of the curse. The corrupt heart will invent a thousand pretexts to palliate its neglect of the great salvation, and has even the effrontery to charge its sin upon the holy God. But be it known unto you, that if, after all your means and opportunities of grace, you die in your iniquity, you will be found, at last, to have been your own destroyers; and the real, the guilty cause of your rejecting Christ Jesus, to have been your own voluntary, cherished unbelief. "Ye will not come to him that ye might have life;" for the mouth of the Lord hath spoken it!

Some who have been religiously educated, and who add to a general profession of Christianity all the exterior decencies of life; who are sober, just, humane; active in their temporal vocations; at peace with themselves, and respected by others; may consider as inapplicable to them, remonstrances which imply an impious character and a dangerous state. Supposing their religion to be sufficiently correct, they give to the wind all their anxieties about their present pardon or their future condition: while, at the same time, they are strangers to the power of godliness, nor ever understood the meaning, by enjoying the mercy, of "passing from death unto life." Be not deceived. The salvation of God is not so slight a matter, nor so slightly to be possessed. The Christian name, the charitable opinion of men, the outward privileges of God's people, embellished with the whole train of social morals, fall far short of that "holiness, without which no man shall see the Lord." All this will not prove forgiveness of sin, nor the sanctification of the Holy Ghost. To a hope which shall not become the mock of death, more, my brethren, much more is necessary. You must be divinely convinced of your natural enmity against God. This enmity must be slain, and you reconciled to him by the death of his Son. You must receive, as condemned rebels, a pardon written in his atoning blood. You must be renewed by his Spirit, and conformed to his image; be united with him by that faith which purifies the heart and works by love; be communicants in his death and the power of his resurrection;

and become, in virtue of this union and communion, fruitful branches of the true vine, or—"ye have no life in you."

In some who congratulate themselves on their escape from the bondage of superstition, and who remit religious care to minds incapable of liberal research, this doctrine of forgiveness may perhaps excite only a smile of scorn. Yet with all their contempt for what they call vulgar prejudice, and all their superiority to religious belief, they must allow me one moment to expostulate. We rejoice in the salvation of Christ Jesus: it is our greatest happiness that "we have redemption through his blood, the forgiveness of sins according to the riches of his grace." You affect to pity and despise us, while you reject our Redeemer's cross, and "put him to an open shame." To justify this violence, your own hope ought to be better founded and more animating than ours. Is this the fact? Are you sure that you have committed no offence which, without forgiveness, must ruin you for ever? Are you sure that there is forgiveness with God in any other manner than through the redemption of the Saviour's blood? or that the gospel which reveals it may not prove true at last? Are you sure that your own sins are pardoned? or that you run no hazard of any judgment to come? Can you produce a single instance of pardoned sin except through the obedience and sacrifice of the Lord Jesus Christ? On what, then, do you presume? I shut up this volume of inspiration, and challenge your hope. What is its nature? and where is its warrant? Is it in these heavens? Is it in that deep? Is it inscribed on any page of creation's book, or engraven on the tablets of conscience? Unbeliever! give glory to God, and homage to his truth. Thou knowest that on all these points, on all that awaits thee beyond the grave, thou art tossed from conjecture to conjecture, and thy most flattering expectation is, at best, but dread uncertainty. Upon such slender ground, in the love and indulgence of a thousand lusts, thou art about to take the adventurous leap into a world of everlasting retribution! And, with all this, thou art a man of reason, a philosopher, who never believes but on evidence, nor acts but from conviction, and looks down with disdain upon the Christian faith! God have mercy on thee, poor fanatic! Yet thou canst not altogether stifle thy secret misgivings. There are times when, like Felix, thou tremblest! Guilt, with all thy boastings, makes thee a coward.

Nor wilt thou ever find relief but in the precious blood of Jesus Christ. Be persuaded to try this happiest of all experiments. He is rich in mercy, and ready to forgive even thee. A refusal will cost thee thy soul; and thou wilt perish under that most fearful condemnation which will follow the rejection of eternal life, when it was near, even at the door.

Here, then, we part, and I turn to a voice of anguish which pierces my ear. Who is this that standeth afar off, with his eyes downcast to earth, smiting his breast, and crying, in broken accents, "God be merciful to me a sinner!" What aileth thee? Have the terrors of the Almighty seized upon thy spirit? Are thy sins set in order before thee? And while thou art compelled to sue for pardon, art thou filled with apprehensions lest thy suit be refused? Come to a forgiving God in the name of Jesus, and dismiss thy fears. Let no enormity of transgression be an obstacle to an immediate acceptance of "his unspeakable gift." Sinners entertain most injurious thoughts of forgiving mercy. They measure it by their own contractedness. Be persuaded, brethren, that Jehovah is as far above you in grace as he is in majesty. You profess to believe that there is merit enough in Jesus to save you, but doubt his willingness to apply it to such sinners. This is accursed pride, vailed in the garb of humility. "If you were not such atrocious offenders, you would more easily take courage." That is, if you had less unworthiness, or, which is the same thing, were more worthy. You wish to come with a price in your hands. You are not reconciled to a salvation of which Christ Jesus shall have all the glory. Here is the secret. Men affect to doubt his willingness, but they are not willing. Let them take eternal life as a free gift, and it is theirs. O brethren! never question the superabounding grace of God in Christ. "Come now, and let us reason together, saith the Lord: though your sins be as scarlet, they shall be white as snow; though they be red like crimson, they shall be as wool." This glorious forgiveness is too high to be reached by carnal or merely rational apprehension. The mind will still shrink back from it as more desirable than credible? "Is this the manner of man? Is there any resemblance to it among the creatures? How can it be true? How can it be possible?" No, it is not the manner of man; there is nothing like it among the creatures; and yet it is possible, and yet it is true. Hear the word of Jehovah,

O ye of little faith: "Seek ye the Lord while he may be found, call ye upon him while he is near: Let the wicked forsake his way, and the unrighteous man his thoughts: and let him return unto the Lord, and he will have mercy upon him, and to our God, for he will abundantly pardon."—"Thou hast multiplied sins upon sins," saith God, "and I will multiply pardons upon pardons." Ah! Lord God! I could not pardon with the ten thousandth part of such goodness for my brother that is as mine own soul; and how canst thou pour down such pardons upon me? "Because thou art a man, and I am God. Let not the thankless objection again pass thy lips, nor rise in thy heart."—"For my thoughts are not your thoughts, neither are your ways my ways, saith the Lord. For as the heavens are higher than the earth, so are my ways higher than your ways, and my thoughts than your thoughts." Let the doubting, disconsolate sinner throw himself, with all his guilt and vileness, into the arms of this forgiving mercy. It never yet repulsed any who came in the faith of the Mediator's blood, and it will not begin its repulses with thee. Go without delay; go with all boldness in this blood; and thou shalt find as cordial a welcome as grace can give thee.

This forgiveness of sins in the redemption of Jesus, imposes infinite obligations upon them who have "believed it to the saving of their souls." Whoever disparage the doctrine of sovereignty, it must not be such as owe to it all their present interest in the salvation of God, and all their hope of his eternal glory. But such are we. "By nature the children of wrath even as others; alienated from the life of God through the ignorance that was in us;" rushing madly on in the paths of death; grace, unsought, undesired, met us; opened our eyes to our folly; "hedged up our way with thorns;" turned us back into "the path of righteousness." Our wounded consciences and wearied hearts found healing and rest in Jesus Christ. His precious blood was the remedy of our guilt. How soothing the voice which whispered to our troubled spirits, "Thy faith hath saved thee; go in peace!" Shall we ever forget that we deserved everything the reverse of what we have received? "That our birth and our nativity was of the land of Canaan, our father an Amorite, and our mother a Hittite?"—"That we were cast out in the open field to the loathing of our persons? And that the compassionate Saviour "passed by us, and saw us polluted in our own blood; and said unto us when we were in our blood, Live: yea, said unto us when we were in our blood, Live!" If we have fled "from the wrath to come;" if "we are no more strangers and foreigners, but fellow-citizens with the saints, and of the household of God;" if we "have not received the spirit of bondage again to fear, but the spirit of adoption, whereby we cry, Abba, Father;" all this, and all the "glory which is yet to be revealed in us," are the blessed fruits of forgiveness through the redemption of the blood of Jesus. Sweetly constrained by his love, shall we not judge with the Apostle of the Gentiles, that we must "henceforth live, not unto ourselves, but unto Him that died for us, and rose again?" The sum of our duty and happiness, O believer! is comprised in this precept—"As ye have received Christ Jesus the Lord, so walk ye in him." The blood of sprinkling, kept by faith in the conscience, is the sure preservative from guilt; the holy secret of a comfortable and familiar walk with God. In this privilege let us go "from strength to strength," lifting up our eyes to the "hills from whence cometh our help; showing forth the righteousness and the salvation of Jehovah all the day long:" and waiting for that great consummation, when, all the sorrows of earth's pilgrimage ended, and all its defilements washed away,

> "Heaven lifts her everlasting portals high,
> And bids the pure in heart behold their God!"

SERMON VI.*

LIVING FAITH.

ACTS xv. 9. compared with GAL. v. 6.

" Purifying their hearts by faith—faith which worketh by love."

The church of Christ, " chosen out of the world " to bear his cross and to partake of his holiness, has, from the very nature of her vocation, many obstacles to surmount, and many foes to vanquish. A warfare, on the issue of which are staked her privileges, her consolations, her everlasting hope, opens an ample field for exertion, and ought to concentrate her strength and wisdom. Unhappily, however, controversies about things which do not involve her substantial interests, have at all times interrupted her peace and marred her beauty. Weakness, prejudice, and passion found their way into the little family of the Master himself; and, even after the descent of the Spirit of truth, invaded and violated his sanctuary. Disputes concerning the Mosaic ritual had arisen among Christians to so great a height, and were conducted with so much ardour and so little love, that the power of godliness was in danger of being stifled in a contest about the form, and the Head of the church deemed it necessary to interpose his rebuke. " Whether ye are called Jews or Gentiles, whether ye observe or neglect some formulas of the typical law, are not questions which should kindle your animosities, and exhaust your vigours. A more awful subject claims your inquiries. While you are occupied in vain jangling, the winged moments are hurrying your souls to their eternal state. Are you ready to depart? Is your title to the kingdom clear? Pause, listen, examine. ' In Christ Jesus neither circumcision availeth anything, nor uncircumcision; but a new creature ;' but

---

* Preached before the Society for the Relief of the Destitute Sick, on the evening of Sabbath, the 1st of November 1801, in Bristo Street Meeting House, Edinburgh.

a 'faith of the operation of God;' but a faith which 'purifies the heart, and works by love."

To us, my brethren, not less than to those early professors of the cross, is the heavenly oracle addressed. We, too, have our weaknesses, our prejudices, our passions, which often embark us in foolish and frivolous litigation. We, too, have immortal souls of which the whole world cannot repay the loss, and which are hastening to the bar of God's righteousness. Come, then, let us endeavour to collect our wandering thoughts, to shut out the illusions of external habit, to put a negative on the importunities of sense, and try whether our religion will endure the ordeal of God's word. If our faith is genuine, it "purifies the heart, and works by love." Precious faith, therefore, in its effects upon spiritual character; that faith which draws the line of immutable distinction between a believer and an unbeliever, and without which no man has a right to call himself a Christian, is the subject of our present consideration. And while the treasure is in an earthen vessel, may the excellency of the power be of God!

Before we attempt to analyze the operations of faith, we must obtain correct views of its nature.

Some imagine it to be a general profession of Christianity, and a decent compliance with its ceremonial. They accordingly compliment each other's religion, and are astonished and displeased if we demur at conceding that all are good Christians who have not ranged themselves under the banners of open infidelity.

Others, advancing a step farther, suppose that faith is an assent to the truth of the gospel founded on the investigation of its rational evidence. Without asking what proportion of the multitudes who profess Christianity have either leisure, or means, or talents, for such an investigation, let us test this dogma by plain fact. Among those legions of accursed spirits whom God "has delivered into chains of darkness to be reserved unto judgment," and their miserable associates of the human race who have already "perished from his presence," there is not one who doubts the truth of revelation. Men may be sceptics in this world, but they carry no scepticism with them into the bottomless pit. They have there rational evidence which it is impossible to resist; evidence, shining in the blaze of everlasting burnings, that "every word of God is pure." That faith, then, by which we are saved, must be altogethe different from a conviction, however rational, which is yet compatible with a state of perdition. If any incline to set light by this representation, as taking advantage of our ignorance, and retreating into obscurity which we cannot explore, let him open his eyes on the common occurrences of life. He may see, for there is not even the shadow of concealment, he may see both these good Christians of fashion, and these good Christians of argument, "without God in the world"—He may see them betraying those very tempers, and pursuing those very courses, by which the Bible describes "the workers of iniquity"—He may see them despising, reproaching, persecuting that profession and practice, which, if the scriptures are true, must belong to such as "live godly in Christ Jesus." Of both these classes of pretended Christians the faith is found to be spurious, and at an infinite remove from the faith of God's elect: for in neither of them does it "purify the heart, or work by love." The scriptures teach us better.

As faith, in general, is reliance upon testimony, and respects solely the veracity of the testifier; so that faith, which constitutes a man a believer before God, is a simple and absolute reliance upon his testimony, exhibited in his word, on this solid and single ground, that "he is the God who cannot lie." It was not a process of reasoning which rivetted in Abraham's mind the persuasion that "in his seed all the nations of the earth should be blessed," and procured him the appellation of "the father of the faithful." It was an act of naked trust in the veracity of his covenant-God, not only without, but above and against, the consultations of flesh and blood. Abraham believed God, believed him in hope, against hope; and it "was counted to him for righteousness." It is the same at this hour. "The mouth of the Lord hath spoken it"— must silence every objection, and cut short every debate. And they who do not thus receive the scriptures, cannot give another proof that they believe in God, as a promising God, at all.

The testimony of God which faith respects, comprising the whole revelation of his will, centres particularly in the free grant which he has made of his Son, the Lord Jesus Christ, to sinners of the human race; assuring them, that "whoever believeth on him shall not perish, but shall have everlasting life;" that "he will be a Father unto them, and they shall be his sons and his daughters;"

that he "will dwell in them, and walk in them, and be their God, blessing them," in their precious Redeemer, "with all spiritual and heavenly blessings." Now that faith after which we are inquiring, consists precisely in "receiving and resting upon Christ Jesus for salvation, as he is offered to us in the gospel," that is, in the testimony of his Father.

This faith is not the creature of human power. It is a contradiction to suppose that men can argue themselves, or be argued by others, into a reliance upon the testimony of God. Because this implies a spiritual perception of his eternal veracity: whereas the reason of man is corrupted by sin, and the natural tendency of corrupted reason is to "change the truth of God into a lie." Nothing can rise above its own level, nor pass the limits of its being. It were more rational to expect that men should be born of beasts, or angels of men, than that a principle of life and purity should be engendered by death in a mass of corruption: and carnal men are "dead in trespasses and sin." Cast it, therefore, into the fairest mould, polish and adorn it with your most exquisite skill, that which is born of the flesh will still be flesh; weak, corrupt, abominable; "enmity against the law of God," and, if possible, more rank enmity against the gospel of Jesus Christ. From this source it is vain to look for faith in his blood. We must seek it higher.

It is of divine origin. A gift which "cometh down from the Father of lights:" "By grace are ye saved, through faith, and that not of yourselves, it is the gift of God."

It is of grace—for it is one of those covenant-mercies which were purchased by the Saviour's merit, and are freely bestowed for his sake. It is given us, on the behalf of Christ, to believe on his name.

Of grace—because it is a fruit of the gracious Spirit. As Jehovah, the Sanctifier, he creates and preserves it in the soul. For this reason he is called the Spirit of faith, which is, therefore, of the operation of God."

From this faith there result two glorious effects. Let us consider them, in their turn, as they are stated in the text.

I. It purifies the heart.

Human depravity is a first principle in the oracles of God. From within, out of the heart, proceed those evil thoughts, and evil words, and evil deeds, which defile, disgrace, and destroy the man. And he who refuses to admit the severe application of this doctrine to himself, has not yet arrived at the point from which he must set out in a course of real and consistent piety. He may, indeed, "flatter himself in his own eyes until his iniquity be found to be hateful," but "who shall ascend into the hill of God? or who shall stand in his holy place? He," and he only, "who has clean hands and a pure heart." Now, as it is the grace of faith by which a sinner obtains that purity which qualifies him for the fellowship and kingdom of God, we are to inquire, in what the purity of the heart consists? and what is the influence of faith in producing it?

The heart is a term by which the Scriptures frequently express the faculties and affections of man. As the pollutions of sin have pervaded them all, they all need the purification of grace.

At the head of the perverted tribe stands a guilty conscience. Stern, gloomy, suspicious, it cannot abide the presence of a righteous God, and yet lashes the offender with a whip of scorpions. To render the conscience pure, pardon must intervene, and shelter it from that curse which rouses both its resentments and its terrors. This is effected by the "blood of the covenant, which, speaking better things than the blood of Abel, sprinkles the heart from an evil conscience.

The will is purified, when it is delivered from its rebellion against the authority of God, and cordially submits to his good pleasure. This, too, is from above: for "his people are made willing in the day of his power."

The understanding is purified when its errors are corrected, and the mists of delusion dissipated. When its estimate of sin and holiness, of things carnal and things spiritual, of time and of eternity, corresponds with the sentence of the divine word. This, also, is from above. "The eyes of our understanding are enlightened, that we may know what is the hope of his calling, and what is the riches of the glory of his inheritance in the saints, and what is the exceeding greatness of his power to usward who believe."

In fine, the affections are purified when they are diverted from objects trifling and base, to objects great and dignified. When they cease to be at the command of every hellish suggestion and every vagrant lust—when they add to the crucifixion of those profligate appetites in the gratification of which the ungodly man places his honour, his profit, and his paradise, their delight in a reconciled God as the infinite good—when they aspire to "things above, where Jesus Christ sitteth at God's right hand," breathe after his communion, and are disciplined and chastened as becometh the affections of a breast which the Holy Ghost condescends to make his temple. Such affections are surely from heavenly inspiration: for thus saith God, "I will sprinkle clean water upon you, and you shall be clean; from all your filthiness and from all your idols will I cleanse you. A new heart also will I give you, and a new spirit will I put within you; I will take away the stony heart out of your flesh, and I will give you a heart of flesh."

While the purification of the heart, thus explained from the Scriptures, is the work of the Divine Spirit, it is accomplished by the instrumentality of faith. For he "purifies the heart by faith." Under his blessed direction, the grace of faith possesses a double influence.

1. As a principle of moral suasion,"* it presents to the mind considerations the most forcible and tender for breaking the power of sin, and promoting the reign of holiness. The presence, the majesty, the holiness of God; the sanctity of his law; his everlasting love in the Lord Jesus; the affecting expression of that love in "setting him forth to be a propitiation for sin;" the wonders of his pardoning mercy; the grace of Christ Jesus himself in becoming "sin for them, that they might be made the righteousness of God in him;" the condescension of the Holy Ghost, who deigns to dwell in them as their Sanctifier; the genius of their vocation; the connection of holy obedience with their own peace, their brethren's comfort, and their Master's glory—these, and similar motives which arise from the exercise of precious faith, operate mightily in causing believers to "walk humbly with their God."—"The love of Christ constraineth us," even as a rational inducement, "to live henceforth not unto ourselves, but unto him that died for us, and rose again." And while a graceless man is deterred from the commission of crime, not by a regard to God's

---

* By moral suasion is here meant, not that kind of reasoning which one graceless man may address to the understanding of another, but those persuasives to holiness which the Spirit of God in his word addresses to his grace in the heart. These faith applies and improves.

authority, or by gratitude for his loving-kindness, but by calculations of prudence, or fear of penalty, a Christian, acting like himself, repels temptation with a more generous and filial remonstrance. "How can I do this great wickedness and sin against God!"

But, brethren, I should wrong the Redeemer's truth, and enfeeble the consolations of his people, were I to confine the efficacy of faith in purifying the heart to the influence of motive. I have not mentioned its chief prerogative; for,

2. Faith is that invaluable grace by which we have both union and communion with our Lord Jesus Christ. In the moment of believing, I become, though naturally an accursed branch, "a tree of righteousness, the planting of Jehovah, that he may be glorified:" I am no longer "a root in a dry ground," but am "planted by the rivers of water," even the "water of life which proceedeth out of the throne of God and of the Lamb." I am ingrafted into the true vine, and bring forth fruit in participating of its sap and fatness. I am made a member of the body of Christ, "of his flesh, and of his bones;" so that the spirit which animates his body pervades every fibre of my frame as one of its living members. His vital influence warms my heart. Because he lives, I live: because he is holy, I am holy: because he hath died unto sin, I reckon myself dead unto sin. This is the fruit of union.

Communion with him is, properly speaking, a common interest with him in his covenant perfection. The benefits of this communion flow into the soul in the exercise of faith. Whatever Jesus has done for his people (and their sanctification is the best part of his work), he conveys to them in the promise of the gospel, and that promise is enjoyed in believing. It is by faith that I live upon the great God my Saviour, and make use of him as Jehovah my strength. By faith I am privileged to go with boldness into the holiest of all, and, be it reverently spoken, to press my Father in heaven with reasons as strong why he should sanctify me, as he can address to me why I should endeavour to sanctify myself. Lord, am I not thine? the called of thy grace? redeemed by the blood of thy dear Son? Hast thou not promised? Hast thou not sworn? Hast thou not pledged thy being, that none who come to thee in his name shall be rejected? Is it not for thy praise that my heart be purified, and I made meet for walking "in the light of thy countenance" among "the nations of the saved?" Wilt thou leave me to conflict alone, unaided, unfriended, with my furious corruptions, and my implacable foes? Wilt thou, though intreated "for thy servant David's sake," refuse to work "in me all the good pleasure of thy goodness, and the work of faith with power?" I cannot, "will not let thee go except thou bless me." Such faith is strong; it is omnipotent; it lays hold on the very attributes of the Godhead, and brings prompt and effectual succour into the labouring spirit. This is the reason why it purifies the heart. I know, that to such as have never been brought under the bond of God's covenant, I am speaking unintelligible things. Blessed be his name, that, continuing carnal, ye cannot understand them. If ye could, our hope would be no better than your own. But I speak to some whose burning souls say amen to the doctrine, and rejoice in the consolation; who, in the struggle with corruption and temptation, have "cried unto God with their voice, even unto God with their voice, and he heard their cry, and bowed his heavens, and came down;" gave them deliverance and victory, and shed abroad in their bosoms the serenity of his grace. These are precious demonstrations of his purifying their hearts by faith.

It is obvious that the fruits of faith which have been now enumerated, cannot be exposed to the eye of the worldling. Deposited in the "hidden man of the heart," they are privileges and "joys with which no stranger intermeddles." Shall we thence conclude, that the faith from which they spring is unsusceptible of external proof, and never extends its benign influence beyond the happy individual who possesses it? By no means. This would be an error too gross for any but the theoretical religionist. The text ascribes it to a social effect: For,

II. It does not more certainly purify the heart, than it worketh by love.

Love is the master-principle of all good society. It is the holy bond which connects man with man, and angel with angel, and and angels with men, and all with God. It is itself an emanation from his own purity. For "God is love: and he that dwelleth in love, dwelleth in God, and God in him." Consequently, the new man, whom regenerating grace creates in elected sinners, and whose activities are maintained by faith, must be governed by love. Its first and most natural exercise is toward that God who "hath loved them with an everlasting love, and therefore with loving-kindness hath drawn them." It is the apprehension by faith of Jehovah's love to them in Christ, anticipating them with mercy, forgiving them all trespasses, leading them with covenant-favour, which softens their obduracy, melts them into tenderness, and excites the gracious reaction of love toward their reconciled Father. "We love him," says an apostle who had drunk deeply into the spirit of his Master, "we love him, because he first loved us."

As an enemy to God is, by the very nature of his temper, an enemy to himself and to all other creatures, so one in whose heart the "love of God is shed abroad by the Holy Ghost," not only consults his own true happiness, but is led to consult the happiness of others. "Charity," saith the Apostle Paul, "suffereth long, and is kind; charity envieth not; charity vaunteth not itself; is not puffed up; doth not behave itself unseemly; seeketh not her own; is not easily provoked; thinketh no evil; rejoiceth not in iniquity, but rejoiceth in the truth; beareth all things; believeth all things; hopeth all things; endureth all things." The Scriptures, indeed, mark love to the brethren as the great practical proof of our Christianity. Nothing can be more peremptory than the language of the beloved disciple—"If a man say, I love God, and hateth his brother, he is a liar: for he that loveth not his brother whom he hath seen, how can he love God whom he hath not seen?" On this point, however, there will be little dispute. Men are instinctively led to measure, by their social effects, all pretensions of love to God. The question before us, and which the scriptural decision will be far from uniting the mass of suffrage, is, how faith works by love?

The apostle asserts, that the faith of a Christian, instead of being a merely speculative assent to the abstract truth of the gospel, is an active moral principle, which cannot have its just course without embodying itself in deeds of goodness. The reasons are many and manifest—By faith in Christ Jesus we are justified before God, our natural enmity against him is slain, and his love finds access to our hearts. By faith we embrace the "exceeding great and precious promises," and, in embracing them, "are made partakers of the divine nature;" so that "we are filled with all the fulness of God;" and out of the abundance of the heart, not only does the mouth speak, but the man act; by faith we converse with our Lord Jesus Christ; are conformed to him; "follow him in the regeneration;" and learn to imitate that great example which he left us when he "went about doing good." By faith we obtain the promised Spirit who sanctifies our powers both of mind and body, so that "we yield our members instruments of righteousness unto God." By faith in Christ's blood, which redeems us from the curse of the law, we are also liberated from the vassalage of sin: for "the strength of sin is the law;" and, receiving the law as fulfilled and satisfied by his righteousness, come under its obligation in his covenant, and are enabled to keep it by his grace. Now "the fulfilling of the law is love;" love and kindness to God and our neighbour, in all our social relations: It is, therefore, impossible that faith should not work by love.

All the directions of the book of God for the practice of the moral virtues, consider them as the evolution of the principle of love residing in a heart which has been purified by faith. Our Lord's sermon on the mount, by the perversion of which many have seduced themselves and others into a lying confidence in their own fancied merits, was preached, not to the promiscuous multitude, but to his "disciples," who professed "faith in his name." And the scriptures of the Apostles, especially the Apostle of the Gentiles, follow the same order. They address their instructions to the church of God—to the saints—to such as have "obtained like precious faith with themselves." Not a moral precept escapes from their pen, till they have displayed the riches of redeeming love. But when, like wise master-builders, they have laid a broad and stable foundation in the doctrines of faith, they rear without delay the fair fabric of practical holiness. It is after they have conducted their pupils to the "holiest of all, through the new and living way which Jesus hath opened," that you hear their exhorting voice, "Mortify, therefore, your members which are upon the earth; fornication, uncleanness, inordinate affection, evil concupiscence, and covetousness, which is idolatry. Put off also all these, anger, wrath, malice, blasphemy, filthy communication out of your mouth. Lie not one to another, seeing ye have put off the old man with his deeds. and have put on the new man which is renewed in knowledge after the image of him that created him; where there is neither Greek nor Jew, circumcision nor uncircumcision; barbarian, Scythian, bond nor free; but Christ is all and in all. Put on, therefore, as the elect of God (for this very reason that ye are his elect), holy and beloved, put on bowels of mercies, kindness, humbleness of mind, meekness, long-suffering, forbearing one another, and forgiving one another if any man have a quarrel against any, even as Christ forgave you, so also do ye." And above all these things, above bowels of mercies, above kindness, above humbleness of mind, above meekness, above long-suffering, above forbearance, above forgiveness, above all these things, "put on charity, which is the bond of perfectness." If the Apostles, then, understood their own doctrine; or rather, if the Spirit by whom they spake knows what is in man, we are not to look for real love, *i.e.*, for true morality, from any who are not "the children of God by faith in Christ Jesus." And, on the contrary, this faith is the most prolific source of good actions; because it purges the fountain of all action, and sends forth its vigorous and healthful streams, "purifying the heart, and working by love."

I should be unfaithful, my brethren, to truth and to you, were I to dismiss this subject without employing its aid for repelling an attack which is often made upon the Christian religion; for refuting the calumny which pretended friends have thrown upon its peculiar glory, the doctrine of faith; for correcting the error of those who, separating faith from holiness, have "a name to live and are dead;" and for stimulating believers to evince by their example both the truth of their profession and the power of their faith.

The enemies of the gospel have invented various excuses for their infidelity. At one time, there is a defect of historical document; at another, they cannot surrender their reason to inexplicable mystery. Now, they are stumbled at a mission sanctioned by miracle: then, the proofs of revelation are too abstracted and metaphysical: and presently, they discover that no proof whatever can verify a revelation to a third person. But when they are driven from all these subterfuges: when the Christian apologist has demonstrated that it is not the want of evidence, but of honesty; that it is not an enlightened understanding, but a corrupted heart, which impels them to reject the religion of Jesus, they turn hardily round and impeach its moral influence! They will make it responsible for all the mischiefs and crimes, for all the sorrows, and convulsions, and ruins which have scourged the world since its first propagation.

Before such a charge can be substantiated, the structure of the human mind must be altered, the nature of things reversed, the doctrine of principle and motive abandoned for ever. It is only for the forlorn hope of impiety to engage in an enterprise so mad and desperate. Say, can a religion which commands me to " love my neighbour as myself," generate or foster malignant and murderous passions? Can a religion which assures me that "all liars shall have their part in the lake which burneth with fire and brimstone," encourage a spirit of dissimulation and fraud? Can a religion which requires me to "possess my vessel in sanctification and honour," indulge me in violating the laws of sexual purity, in breaking up the sanctuary of my neighbour's peace, in throwing upon the mercy of scandal's clarion the fair fame of female virtue? Can a religion which forbids me to be "conformed to this world," cherish that infuriate ambition which hurls desolation over the earth, and fertilizes her fields with the blood of men? Can a religion—But I forbear—" From whence come wars and fightings among you? Come they not hence, even from your lusts? Those very lusts from which it is the province of faith to purify the heart? The infidel pleads for his unholy propensions, on the pretext that they are innocent because they are natural: and when a thousand curses to himself and to society follow their indulgence, he charges the consequence upon a religion which enjoins their crucifixion, and which, to give them their career, he trampled under foot. But stop, vain man! Was it the religion of Jesus Christ which, on its first promulgation, "breathed out threatenings and slaughter, shut up the saints in prison, punished them oft in every synagogue, compelled them to blaspheme, and, being exceedingly mad against them, persecuted them even unto strange cities?" Was it the religion of Jesus Christ which, in its subsequent progress, illuminated the city of Rome with the conflagration of a thousand stakes, consuming, by the most excruciating of deaths, a thousand guiltless victims?* Was it the religion of Jesus Christ which, at a later period, when the Tiber overflowed, or the Nile did not overflow; when the earth quaked, or the heavens withheld their rain; when famine or pestilence smote the nations, ordered

* Tacit. Annal. lib. xv. cap. 44.

its opposers to the lions?* Was it in obedience to the religion of Jesus Christ, after the expulsion of pagan idolatry, that the "mother of harlots and abominations of the earth became drunk with the blood of the saints and with the blood of the martyrs?"— Was it the religion of Jesus Christ which, after being rejected with marks of unexampled insult, suggested to the knight-errants of blasphemy the project of regenerating the world by the power of atheistical philosophy? Was it this religion which taught them to blot out the great moral institute of society—the Sabbath of the Lord, to extinguish the best affections of the human heart, to break asunder the strongest ties of human life, and to subvert the basis of human relations by exploding the marriage covenant? This, which instigated them to offer up hecatombs of human sacrifices to every rising and every setting sun; to hew down, with equal indifference, the venerable matron and her hoary lord, the vigorous youth, the blooming maid, the sportive boy, and the prattling babe; and, while they were thus writing the history of their philosophical experiments in the blood of the dead and the tears of the living, to boast the victories of their virtue? But my soul sickens; Ah, no! "The wisdom which cometh from above," that wisdom which the gospel teaches, "is first pure, then peaceable, gentle, and easy to be entreated, full of compassion and of good fruits, without partiality, and without hypocrisy." Such was its imposing aspect in primitive ages. "Give me a man," said a celebrated father of the church, the eloquent Lactantius, "give me a man passionate, slanderous, ungovernable: with a very few words of God I will render him as placid as a lamb. Give me a man greedy, avaricious, penurious: I will give him back to you liberal, and lavishing his gold with a munificent hand. Give me a man who shrinks from pain and death; and he shall presently contemn the stake, the gibbet, the wild beast. Give me one who is libidinous, an adulterer, a debauchee; and you shall see him sober, chaste, temperate. Give me one cruel and blood-thirsty; and that fury of his shall be converted into clemency itself. Give me one addicted to injustice, to folly, to crime; and he shall, without delay, become just, and prudent, and harmless."†

Similar, in proportion to its reception by faith, are still the effects of this blessed gospel. What has exploded those vices which,

* Tertull. Apolog. cap. 40.   † Lact. De falsa Sapientia, lib. iii. cap. 25.

though once practised even by philosophers, cannot now be so much as named? What has softened the manners and refined the intercourse of men? What is it which turns any of them from sin to God, and makes them conscientious, humble, pure, though at the expense of ridicule and scorn from the licentious and the gay? What has espoused the cause of suffering humanity? Who explores the hospital, the dungeon, the darksome retreat of unknown, unpitied anguish? The infidel philosopher? Alas! he amuses himself with dreams of universal benevolence, while the wretch perishes unheeded at his feet, and scruples not to murder the species in detail, that he may promote its happiness in the gross! On his proud list of general benefactors you will look in vain for the name of a Howard; and in their system of conduct your search will be equally fruitless for the traces of his spirit. Christianity claims as her own both the man and his principles. She formed his character, sketched his plans, and inspired his zeal. And might the modesty of goodness be overcome, might the sympathies of the heart assume visible form, might secret and silent philanthropy be called into view, ten thousand Howards would issue, at this moment, from her temples, from the habitations of her sons, from the dreary abodes of sickness and of death. Tell me not of those foul deeds which have been perpetrated in her name. Tell me not that her annals are filled with the exploits of imposture and fanaticism; that her priests and her princes have been ambitious, profligate, and cruel; that they have bared the arm of persecution, and shed innocent blood upon the rack and the scaffold, at the stake and in the field; that they have converted whole nations into hordes of banditti, and led them, under the auspices of the cross, to pillage and massacre their brethren who boasted only the "simple virtues" of pagans and infidels. The question is not what actions her name has been abused to sanctify, but what have accorded with her principles, and are prompted by her spirit? It is no discovery of yesterday that Satan "is transformed into an angel of light;" and, therefore, no great thing if his ministers also be transformed into ministers of righteousness. Ignorance and dishonesty have often borrowed a Christian guise for the more successful practice of knavery and rapine. But when they have violated all the maxims of the Christian religion, when they have contemned her remonstrances and stifled her cries, shall they be permitted to plead her authority? Or shall the scoffer insult her with the charge of being their accomplice and adviser? No! In so far as men do not study "whatsoever things are true, honest, just, pure, lovely, and of good report," they evince not the power of faith, but the power of unbelief; in other words, not the spirit of the gospel, but a spirit directly opposed to it—*i.e.*, the spirit of infidelity. If, then, you think to justify your incredulity by showing a man, who to a profession of Christianity adds a life of crime, the indignant gospel tears the mask from his face, and exposes to your view the features of a brother. Whatever be his profession, we disown his kindred; he acts wickedly, not because he is a Christian, but because he is not a Christian. His crimes conspire with his hypocrisy to prove him an infidel.

Here we must part with some who have cheerfully accompanied us in the detection and reproof of avowed unbelievers. For I am to employ the doctrine of the text for refuting the calumny which pretended friends have thrown upon the peculiar glory of Christianity, the doctrine of faith.

Multitudes—and would to God that none of them were found among the teachers of religion—multitudes, who profess warm zeal for revelation, are yet hostile to all those cardinal truths which alone render it worthy of a struggle. Omitting the mockery of such as call Christ "Lord, Lord," while they rob him of every perfection which qualifies him to be the Saviour of sinners, let me call your attention to those whose enmity is particularly directed against the doctrine which has been preached to you this evening. Nothing, to use their own style, can exceed their veneration for religion in general; but if you venture to speak of the righteousness of the Son of God, "imputed to us, and received by faith alone;" if you insist on the desperate wickedness of the heart, and the necessity of Almighty Power to regenerate and cleanse it; if you rejoice in the blessedness of that union with the Lord Jesus which places you beyond the reach of condemnation, so that "neither death, nor life, nor angels, nor principalities, nor powers, nor things present, nor things to come, nor height, nor depth, nor any other creature, shall be able to separate you from his love," or shut you out of his kingdom, you must expect to pass, with rational Christians, for a weak though perhaps well-meaning enthusiast: nay, you must expect to hear those blessed truths, which are the light of your soul, stigmatized as relaxing the obligations of the moral law, as withdrawing the most cogent motives to obey its precepts, as ministering incentives to all ungodliness. Impossible! Nothing but ignorance of the grace of God in its saving energy could give birth or aliment to such a slander. It proceeds on the supposition that a sinner may be pardoned, and not sanctified; that he may be delivered from penalty, and yet retain an unabated affection for his lusts. Were this the fact—did faith in Christ's blood set him free from the condemning authority of God's law, and yet leave him under the tyranny of sinful habits, there is no doubt that it would encourage him " to work all uncleanness with greediness." But the reverse is true. The blood of Jesus Christ, applied by faith, does not more certainly abolish guilt, than it paralyzes lust. "He is made of God unto us," in a connection which nothing can dissolve, "wisdom, and righteousness, and sanctification."—"Our old man is crucified with him, that the body of sin might be destroyed, that henceforth we should not serve sin." The grace of faith is the leading faculty of that "new man, which after God is created in righteousness and true holiness." Holiness is the proper element of a believer, as sin is the proper element of an unbeliever. And, therefore, although the notion of grace may be abused to licentiousness, the principle never can; for it is that principle from which we learn to "deny ungodliness and worldly lusts, and to live soberly, righteously, and godly, in this present world." To insinuate, then, that the doctrine of free and plenary justification by faith in Christ Jesus tends to licentiousness, is to give the lie direct to the testimony of the Holy Ghost, and to the uniform experience of his people. Whoever cherishes such an opinion, however highly esteemed by himself or by others, is not a Christian; he is "in the gall of bitterness and in the bond of iniquity." But there is no cause of wonder. "The natural man receiveth not the things of the Spirit of God, for they are foolishness unto him." It has been so from the beginning, and will continue so to the end. The objection which he makes, at this hour, to the doctrine of grace, is as stale as it is unfounded. It is the very objection which was combated by the Apostle Paul. "What shall we say then?" exclaimed his adversaries, when he preached justification by faith through the imputed righteousness of the Lord Jesus, and the absolute certainty of being saved from wrath through him in virtue of believing; "What shall we say then? shall we continue in sin that grace may abound?" Or, in modern language, does not this doctrine of yours tempt men to throw the rein upon the neck of their passions, by removing the fear of condemnation, and especially by furnishing them with the pretext, that the more they sin, the more is grace exalted in their pardon, seeing that "where sin hath abounded, grace doth much more abound?" The apostle admits, that the depraved heart is prone to draw such a conclusion, and that it was actually drawn by his enemies, who took occasion from it to represent him as "making void the law." But he repels it with the most indignant reprobation. "God forbid!" The inference is absurd. "How shall we that are dead to sin live any longer therein?" That doctrine, therefore, which wicked men never accuse of leading to licentiousness, is not the doctrine of God's Word. That doctrine, on the contrary, against which, by misrepresenting it, they bring this accusation, is the very doctrine of the apostle. But its true and only effect, which we maintain, which the Scriptures teach, and which all believers experience and exemplify, is, that "sin shall not reign in their mortal body, that they should fulfil it in the lusts thereof."

Of the same nature, and from the same source with the calumny which I have endeavoured to refute, is the practical error of many who, separating faith from holiness, "have a name to live and are dead." The error must be rectified, for it is fatal. Some console themselves with their doctrinal accuracy, while their hearts and conduct are estranged from moral rectitude. They hope that their faith, however inactive, shall save them at last. Others, in the opposite extreme, disregarding faith in our Lord Jesus Christ, trust in their upright intentions and actions. They know little of what Christians call believing, but they are good moral men. Their gospel is the trite and delusive aphorism,

"He can't be wrong whose life is in the right;"
not considering that
'He can't be right, whose faith is in the wrong."

They talk, indeed, on both sides, with much familiarity of "our holy religion," as if its best influences had descended upon themselves. Holy religion it is: but what made it yours? One of you does not pretend to "have received Christ Jesus the Lord;" the other, notwithstanding his profession, has no solicitude to "walk in him:" and both are equally far from the salvation of God. Jesus Christ is "the way, the truth, and the life; no man cometh unto the Father but by him:" no man entertains good thoughts, or performs good works, without being a "partaker of his holiness." Every plant which his heavenly Father hath not planted shall be rooted up. At the great day of his appearance to judge the world in righteousness, no virtue will be approved which did not grow upon his cross, was not consecrated by his blood, and nourished by his spirit. Such virtues, however they may be applauded here, are only brilliant acts of rebellion against him, and will not for one moment reprieve the rebels from the "damnation of hell." Nor let those whose belief does not purify the heart, nor work by love, flatter themselves that their condition is better, or that their doom shall be more tolerable. Whatever judgment shall be measured to others, "they who know their Lord's will, and do it not, shall be beaten with many stripes." Be not deceived. The threatening bears directly upon you. You profess to know God, but in works you deny him. Your inconsistency reproaches his truth, and causes his enemies to blaspheme. You lay stumbling-blocks in the way of the unwary. You multiply the victims of that very infidelity against which you declaim; and, in as far as they have been seduced by your example, their blood shall be required at your hands. For yourselves, if you die without being "renewed in the spirit of your minds," your faith will not save you. The farce of a mock profession will terminate in the tragedy of real and everlasting woe. Oh, then, "while it is called to-day harden not your hearts!" To sinners of every class and character, the forgiveness of God is preached. From his throne in heaven the Saviour speaks this evening. "Unto you, O men, do I call, and my voice is to the sons of men! Hearken unto me, ye stout-hearted, that are far from righteousness: behold, I bring near my righteousness." In him is grace, and peace, and life. Now, therefore, "choose life that ye may live." And may his blessed spirit visit you with his salvation, creating in you that faith which purifies the heart, and works by love!

Finally. Let Christians be admonished by the doctrine of my text to evince, in their behaviour both the truth of their profession and the power of their faith.

They cannot too often or too solemnly repeat the question of their Lord, "What do ye more than others?" It is not enough for them to equal, they must excel their neighbours. They have mercies, motives, means, peculiar to themselves. They have a living principle of righteousness in their own hearts; and in their great Redeemer, they have, as the fountain of their supply, "all the fulness of the Godhead." It is but reasonable that much should be required of them to whom much is given. Let your whole persons, O believers, be temples of God. Set your affections on things above, where Jesus Christ sitteth at his right hand. Remember, that every one who hath the hope of seeing Jesus as he is, "purifieth himself even as he is pure." Walk in love as he hath loved you. Let this amiable grace shed her radiance over your character, and breathe her sweetness into your actions. Compel, by her charms, the homage of the profane. Cleave not to earth, because your treasure is in heaven. Make use of it to exercise the benevolence of the gospel, to glorify your Father who is in heaven, to diffuse comfort and joy among the suffering and disconsolate. "To do good and to communicate, forget not, for with such sacrifices God is well pleased." This evening presents you with an opportunity of showing that faith worketh by love. The society, on whose account I address you, carry in their very name a resistless appeal to the sentiments of men and of Christians. Devoting their labours to "the relief of the destitute sick," they have sought out and succoured, not here and there a solitary individual, but scores, and hundreds, and thousands of them that were "ready to perish." Sickness, though softened by the aids of the healing art, by the sympathy of friends, and by every external accommodation, is no small trial of patience and religion. But to be both sick and destitute is one of the bitterest draughts in the cup of human misery. Far from me be the attempt to harrow your feelings with images of fictitious woe. Recital must draw a vail over a large portion of the truth itself. I barely mention that the mass of sorrow which you are called to alleviate appears in as many forms as there are affinities among men.

Is there in this assembly a father, the sons of whose youth are the stay of his age and the hope of his family? In yonder cell lies a man of grey hairs, crushed by poverty, and tortured by disease. His children are scattered abroad, or have long since descended into the tomb. The sound of "father" never salutes his ears: he is a stranger in his own country: his only companions are want and anguish.

Is there here a wife of youth encircled with domestic joys? or is there one whose heart, though solaced with a thousand outward blessings, calls back the aching remembrance of the loved relation? Behold that daughter of grief. The fever rankles in her veins. She has no partner dearer than her own soul, on whose bosom she may recline her throbbing head. Her name is *Widow*. Desolate, forsaken, helpless, she is stretched on the ground. The wintry blast howls through her habitation, and famine keeps the door.

Is there a mother here, whose eyes fill in the tenderness of bliss, while health paints the cheeks of her little offspring, and they play around her in the gayety of infantine simplicity? I plead for a mother, the toil of whose hands was the bread of her children. The bed of languishing destroys her strength and their sustenance. "The son of her womb" turns pale in her feeble arms, her heart is wrung with double anguish, while unconscious of the source of his pain, he cries for bread, and there is none to give it.

Is there here a man of public spirit who exults in the return of plenty and of peace? Let him think of those who suffer under the stern arrest of hunger and disease. Ah! let him think that this wretchedness belongs to the wife and family of the soldier who has fought the battles of his country. The messenger of peace arrives: the murmur of the crowd swells into ecstacy: their shout echoes through the hills. She raises her drooping head, and hears, not that her friend and helper is at hand, but that herself is a widow and her children fatherless. The blood of her husband and of their father has flowed for the common safety—He shall never return.

Is there a Christian here who knows how to "do good unto all, but especially to them that are of the household of faith?" Among these afflicted who are sinking under their infirmities, and "have not where to lay their heads," are some to whom the celestials minister, and who are "fellow-heirs with Christ in glory." I state the facts; I use no arguments; I leave the result with your consciences, your heart, and your God.

SERMON VII.*

MESSIAH'S THRONE.

HEB. 1. 8.

"But unto the Son, he saith, Thy Throne, O God, is for ever and ever."

In the all-important argument which occupies this epistle, Paul assumes, what the believing Hebrews had already professed, that Jesus of Nazareth is the true Messiah. To prepare them for the consequences of their own principle—a principle involving nothing less than the abolition of their law, the subversion of their state, the ruin of their city, the final extinction of their carnal hopes—he leads them to the doctrine of their Redeemer's person in order to explain the nature of his offices, to evince the value of his spiritual salvation, and to show, in both, the accomplishment of their economy which was "now ready to vanish away." Under no apprehension of betraying the unwary into idolatrous homage, by giving to the Lord Jesus greater glory than is "due unto his name," the apostle sets out with ascribing to him excellence and attributes which belong to no creature. Creatures of most elevated rank are introduced; but it is to display, by contrast, the pre-eminence of Him who is "the brightness of the Father's glory, and the express image of his person." Angels are great in mind and in dignity; but " unto them hath he not put in subjection the world to come." " Unto which of them said he, at any time, Thou art my son?" To which of them " Sit thou at my right hand?" He saith they are spirits, "ministering spirits, sent forth to minister unto them who are the heirs of salvation. But unto the Son," in a style which

* Preached before the London Missionary Society, at their eighth annual meeting, in Tottenham Court Chapel, on the evening of Thursday, 13th May 1802.

annihilates competition and comparison, "unto the Son," he saith, "Thy throne, O God, is for ever and ever."

Brethren, if the majesty of Jesus is the subject which the Holy Ghost selected for the encouragement and consolation of his people, when he was shaking the earth and the heavens, and diffusing his gospel among the nations; can it be otherwise than suitable and precious to us on this occasion? Shall it not expand our views, and warm our hearts, and nerve our arm, in our efforts to exalt his fame? Let me implore, then, the aid of your prayers; but far more importunately the aids of his own Spirit, while I speak of the "things which concern the King:" those great things contained in the text—his personal glory—his sovereign rule.

I. His personal glory shines forth in the name by which he is revealed; a name above every name, thy throne—O God!

To the single eye nothing can be more evident, in the

First place, than that the Holy Ghost here asserts the essential deity of our Lord Jesus Christ. Of his enemies, whom he will make his footstool, some have, indeed, controverted this position, and endeavoured to blot out the text from the catalogue of his witnesses. Instead of "thy throne, O God," they would compel us by a perversion of phraseology, of figure, and of sense, to read, "God is thy throne;" converting the great and dreadful God into a symbol of authority in one of his own creatures. The scriptures, it seems, may utter contradictions or impiety, but the divinity of the Son they shall not attest. The crown, however, which "flourishes on his head," is not to be torn away; nor the anchor of our hope to be wrested from us, by the rude hand of licentious criticism.

I cannot find, in the lively oracles, a single distinctive mark of deity which is not applied, without reserve or limitation, to the only begotten Son. "All things whatsoever the Father hath, are his." Who is that mysterious Word, that was "in the beginning with God?" Who is the "Alpha and Omega, the beginning and the ending, the first and the last, the Almighty?" Who is he that knows what is in man, because he searches the deep and dark recesses of the heart? Who is the Omnipresent, that has promised, "Wherever two or three are gathered together in my name, there am I in the midst of them?" the light of whose countenance is, at the same moment, the joy of heaven and the salvation of the earth? who is encircled by the seraphim on high, and "walks in the midst of the golden candlesticks? who is in this assembly? in all the assemblies of his people? in every worshipping family? in every closet of prayer? in every holy heart? "Whose hands have stretched out the heavens and laid the foundations of the earth?" Who hath replenished them with inhabitants, and garnished them with beauty, having created all things that are in both, "visible and invisible, whether they be thrones, or dominions, or principalities, or powers? By whom do all things consist? Who is "the governor among the nations, having on his vesture and on his thigh a name written, King of kings and Lord of lords?" Whom is it the Father's will that "all men should honour even as they honour himself?" Whom has he commanded his angels to worship? whom to obey? Before whom do the devils tremble? Who is qualified to redeem millions of sinners from the wrath to come, and preserve them, by his grace, to his everlasting kingdom? Who raiseth the dead, "having life in himself, to quicken whom he will," so that at his voice, "all who are in their graves shall come forth;"—"and death and hell" surrender their numerous and forgotten captives? Who shall weigh, in the balance of judgment, the destinies of angels and men? dispose of the thrones of paradise? and bestow eternal life? Shall I submit to the decision of reason? Shall I ask a response from heaven? Shall I summon the devils from their chains of darkness? The response from heaven sounds in my ears; reason approves, and the devils confess—This, O Christians, is none other than the great God our Saviour!

Indeed, my brethren, the doctrine of our Lord's divinity is not, as a fact, more interesting to our faith, than, as a principle, it is essential to our hope. If he were not the true God, he could not be eternal life. When pressed down by guilt and languishing for happiness, I look around for a deliverer such as my conscience and my heart, and the word of God assure me I need, insult not my agony, by directing me to a creature—to a man, a mere man like myself? A creature! a man! My Redeemer owns my person. My immortal spirit is his property. When I come to die, I must commit it into his hands. My soul! my infinitely precious soul committed to a mere man! become the property of a mere man! I would not thus entrust my body to the highest angel who burns in the temple above. It is only the Father of spirits that can have property in spirits, and be their refuge in the hour of transition from the present to the approaching world. In short, my brethren, the divinity of Jesus is, in the system of grace, the sun to which all its parts are subordinate, and all their stations refer—which binds them in sacred concord, and imparts to them their radiance, and life, and vigour. Take from it this central luminary, and the glory is departed—its holy harmonies are broken—the elements rush to chaos—the light of salvation is extinguished for ever!

But it is not the deity of the Son, simply considered, to which the text confines our attention. We are, in the

Second place, to contemplate it as subsisting in a personal union with the human nature.

Long before this epistle was written had he "by himself purged our sins, and sat down at the right hand of the Majesty on high." It is, therefore, as "God manifested in the flesh;" as my own brother, while he is "the express image of the Father's person," as the Mediator of the new covenant, that he is seated on the throne. Of this throne, to which the pretensions of a creature were mad and blasphemous, the majesty is, indeed maintained by his divine power; but the foundation is laid in his mediatorial character. I need not prove to this audience, that all his gracious offices and all his redeeming work originated in the love and the election of his Father. Obedient to that will, which fully accorded with his own, he came down from heaven; tabernacled in our clay; was "a man of sorrows and acquainted with grief;" submitted to the contradictions of sinners, the temptations of the old serpent, and the wrath of an avenging God. In the merit of his obedience which threw a lustre round the divine law; and in the atonement of his death by which "he offered himself a sacrifice without spot unto God, repairing the injuries of man's rebellion, expiating sin through the blood of his cross; and conciliating its pardon with infinite purity, and unalterable truth; summarily, in his performing those conditions on which was suspended all God's mercy to man, and all man's enjoyment of God, in these stupendous works of righteousness are we to look for the cause of his present glory. "He humbled himself and became obedient unto death, even the death of the cross; wherefore God also hath highly exalted him, and given him a name which is above every name; that at the name of Jesus every knee should bow, of things in heaven and things in earth, and things under the earth; and that every tongue should confess that Jesus Christ is Lord, to the glory of God, the Father." Exalted thus "to be a Prince and a Saviour," he fills heaven with his beauty, and obtains from its blest inhabitants, the purest and most reverential praise. "Worthy," cry the mingled voices of his angels and his redeemed, "worthy is the Lamb that was slain, to receive power, and riches, and wisdom, and strength, and honour, and glory, and blessing." "Worthy," again cry his redeemed, in a song which belongs not to the angels, but in which with holy ecstasy, we will join, "worthy art thou, for thou wast slain, and hast redeemed us to God by thy blood."

Delightful, brethren, transcendently delightful were it to dwell upon this theme. But we must refrain; and having taken a transient glance at our Redeemer's personal glory, let us turn to the

II. View which the text exhibits—the view of his sovereign rule—"Thy throne, O God, is for ever and ever."

The mediatorial kingdom of Christ Jesus, directed and upheld by his divinity, is now the object of our contemplation. To advance Jehovah's glory in the salvation of men, is the purpose of its erection. Though earth is the scene and human life the limit, of those great operations by which they are interested in its mercies, and prepared for its consummation; its principles, its provisions, its issues, are eternal. When it rises up before us in all its grandeur of design, collecting and conducting to the heavens of God millions of immortals, in comparison with the least of whom the destruction of the material universe were a thing of naught, whatever the carnal mind calls vast and magnificent shrinks away into nothing.

But it is not so much the nature of Messiah's kingdom on which I am to insist, as its stability, its administration, and the prospects which they open to the church of God.

Messiah's throne is not one of those airy fabrics which are reared by vanity and overthrown by time: it is fixed of old: it is stable and cannot be shaken, for,

(1.) It is the throne of God. He who sitteth on it is the Omnipotent. Universal being is in his hand. Revolution, force, fear, as applied to his kingdom, are words without meaning. Rise up in rebellion, if thou hast courage. Associate with thee the whole mass of infernal power. Begin with the ruin of whatever is fair and good in this little globe—pass from hence to pluck the sun out of his place—and roll the volume of desolation through the starry world—What hast thou done unto him? It is the puny menace of a worm against him whose frown is perdition. "He that sitteth in the heavens shall laugh."

(2.) With the stability which Messiah's Godhead communicates to his throne, let us connect the stability resulting from his Father's covenant.

His throne is founded not merely in strength, but in right. God hath laid the government upon the shoulder of his holy child Jesus, and set him upon Mount Zion as his king for ever. He has promised and sworn, to "build up his throne to all generations;" to "make it endure as the days of heaven;" to "beat down his foes before his face, and plague them that hate him. But my faithfulness," adds he, "and my mercy shall be with him, and in my name shall his horn be exalted. Hath he said it, and will he not do it? Hath he spoken it, and shall it not come to pass?" Whatever disappointments rebuke the visionary projects of men, or the more crafty schemes of Satan, "the counsel of the Lord, *that* shall stand." The blood of sprinkling, which sealed all the promises made to Messiah, and binds down his Father's faithfulness to their accomplishment, witnesses continually in the heavenly sanctuary. "He must," therefore, "reign till he have put all his enemies under his feet." And although the dispensation of his authority shall, upon this event, be changed: and he shall deliver it up, in its present form, to the Father, he shall still remain, in his substantial glory, "a priest upon his throne," to be the eternal bond of our union, and the eternal medium of our fellowship, with the living God.

Seeing that the throne of our King is as immovable as it is exalted, let us "with joy draw water out of that well of salvation" which is opened to us in the

Administration of his kingdom. ere we must consider its general characters, and the means by which it operates.

The general characters which I shall illustrate, are the following:

(1.) Mystery.—He is the unsearchable God, and his government must be like himself. Facts concerning both he has graciously revealed. These we must admit upon the credit of his own testimony; with these we must satisfy our wishes, and limit our inquiry. "To intrude into those things which he hath not seen," because God has not disclosed them, whether they relate to his arrangements for this world or the next, is the arrogance of one "vainly puffed up by his fleshly mind." There are secrets in our Lord's procedure which he will not explain to us in this life, and which may not, perhaps, be explained in the life to come. We cannot tell how he makes evil the minister of good: how he combines physical and moral agencies of different kind and order, in the production of blessings. We cannot so much as conjecture what bearings the system of redemption, in every part of its process, may have upon the relations of the universe; nor even what may be all the connections of providence in the occurrences of this moment, or of the last. "Such knowledge is too wonderful for us: it is high, we cannot attain it." Our Sovereign's way "is in the sea, and his path in the deep waters; and his footsteps are not known." When, therefore, we are surrounded with difficulty; when we cannot unriddle his conduct in particular dispensations, we must remember that he is God; that we are to "walk by faith;" and to trust him as implicitly when we are in "the valley of the shadow of death," as when his candle "shines upon our heads." —We must remember that it is not for us to be admitted into the cabinet of the King of kings; that creatures constituted as we are could not sustain the view of his unvailed agency; that it would confound, and scatter, and annihilate our little intellects. As often, then, as he retires from our observation, blending goodness with majesty, let us lay our hands upon our mouths, and worship. This stateliness of our King can afford us no just ground of uneasiness. On the contrary, it contributes to our tranquillity: For we know,

(2.) That if his administration is mysterious it is also wise.

"Great is our Lord and of great power; his understanding is infinite." That infinite understanding watches over, and arranges, and directs all the affairs of his church and of the world. We are perplexed at every step; embarrassed by opposition; lost in confusion; fretted by disappointment; and ready to conclude in our haste, that all things are against our own good and our Master's honour. But this is our infirmity; it is the dictate of impatience and indiscretion. We forget the "years of the right hand of the Most High." We are slow of heart in learning a lesson which shall soothe our spirits at the expense of our pride. We turn away from the consolation to be derived from believing that though we know not the connections and results of holy providence, our Lord Jesus knows them perfectly. With him there is no irregularity, no chance, no conjecture. Disposed before his eye in the most luminous and exquisite order, the whole series of events occupy the very place and crisis where they are most effectually to subserve the purposes of his love. Not a moment of time is wasted, nor a fragment of action misapplied. What he does we do not indeed know at present, but, as far as we shall be permitted to know hereafter, we shall see that his most inscrutable procedure was guided by consummate wisdom; that our choice was often as foolish as our petulance was provoking; that the success of our own wishes would have been our most painful chastisement, would have diminished our happiness and detracted from his praise. Let us study, therefore, brethren, to subject our ignorance to his knowledge; instead of prescribing, to obey; instead of questioning, to believe: to perform our part without that despondency which betrays a fear that our Lord may neglect his, and tacitly accuses him of a less concern than we feel for the glory of his own name. Let us not shrink from this duty as imposing too rigorous a condition upon our obedience, for a

(3.) Character of Messiah's administration is righteousness. "The sceptre of his kingdom is a right sceptre." If "clouds and darkness are round about him, righteousness and judgment are the habitation of his throne." In the times of old, his redeemed "wandered in the wilderness in a solitary way; but, nevertheless, he led them forth by the right way, that they might go to a city of habitation." He loves his church and the members of it too tenderly to lay upon them any burdens, or expose them to any trials, which are not indispensable to their good. It is right for them to "go through fire and through water," that he may "bring them out into a wealthy place"—right to "endure chastening" that "they may be partakers of his holiness"—right to "have the sentence of death in themselves," that they may "trust in the living God, and that his strength may be perfect in their weakness." It is right that he should "endure with much long-suffering the vessels of wrath fitted to destruction:" that he should permit "iniquity to abound, the love of many to wax cold," and the dangers of his church to accumulate, till the interposition of his arm be necessary and decisive. In the day of final retribution not one mouth shall be opened to complain of injustice. It will be seen that "the Judge of all the earth has done right; that the works of his hands have been verity and judgment," and done every one of them, in "truth and uprightness." Let us, then, think not only respectfully but reverently of his dispensations, repress the voice of murmur, and rebuke the spirit of discontent; wait, in faith and patience, till he become his own interpreter, when "the heavens shall declare his righteousness, and all the people see his glory."

You will anticipate me in enumerating the means which Messiah employs in the administration of his kingdom.

(1.) The gospel, of which himself, as an all-sufficient and condescending Saviour, is the great and affecting theme. Derided by the world, it is, nevertheless, effectual to the salvation of them who believe. "We preach Christ crucified to the Jews a stumbling-block, and to the Greeks foolishness; but to them who are called, both Jews and Greeks, Christ the power of God, and the wisdom of God." The doctrine of the cross connected with evangelical ordinances; the ministry of reconciliation; the holy Sabbath; the sacraments of his covenant: briefly the whole system of instituted worship is the "rod of the Redeemer's strength" by which he subdues sinners to himself; rules even "in the midst of his enemies;" exercises his glorious authority in his church, and exhibits a visible proof to men and angels, that he is King in Zion.

(2.) The efficient means to which the gospel owes its success, and the name of Jesus its praise, is the agency of the Holy Ghost.

Christianity is "the ministration of the Spirit." All real and sanctifying knowledge of the truth and love of God is from his inspiration. It was the last and best promise which the Saviour made to his afflicted disciples at the moment of parting,—" I will send the Comforter, the Spirit of truth; He shall glorify me, for he shall take of mine and shall show it unto you." It is he who "convinces the world of sin, of righteousness, and of judgment" —who infuses resistless vigour into means otherwise weak and useless. "For the weapons of our warfare are not carnal, but mighty through God, God the Spirit, to the pulling down of strongholds." Without his benediction, the ministry of an archangel would never "convert one sinner from the error of his way." But when he descends, with his life-giving influence from God out of heaven, then "foolish things of the world confound the wise, and weak things of the world confound the things which are mighty; and base things of the world, and things which are despised, yea, and things which are not, bring to naught things which are." It is this ministration of the Spirit which renders the preaching of the gospel to "men dead in trespasses and sins a reasonable service." When I am set down in the "valley of vision," and view the bones, "very many and very dry," and am desired to try the effect of my own ability in recalling them to life, I will fold my hands and stand mute in astonishment and despair. But when the Lord God commands me to speak in his name, my closed lips shall be opened; when he calls upon "the breath from the four winds to breathe upon the slain that they may live," I will prophecy without fear—"O ye dry bones, hear the word of the Lord," and, obedient to his voice, they "shall come together, bone to his bone; shall be covered with sinews and flesh;" shall receive new life, and "and stand up upon their feet, an exceeding great army." In this manner, from the graves of nature, and the dry bones of natural men, does the Holy Spirit recruit the "armies of the living God," and make them, collectively and individually, "a name, and a praise, and a glory, to the Captain of their salvation."

3.) Among the instruments which the Lord Jesus employs in the administration of his government, are "the resources of the physical and moral world."

Supreme in heaven and in earth, "upholding all things by the word of his power," the universe is his magazine of means. Nothing which acts or exists, is exempted from promoting in its own place the purposes of his kingdom. Beings rational and irrational; animate and inanimate; the heavens above and the earth below; the obedience of sanctified, and the disobedience of unsanctified, men; all holy spirits; all damned spirits; in one word, every agency, every element, every atom, are but the ministers of his will, and concur in the execution of his designs. And this he will demonstrate to the confusion of his enemies, and the joy of his people, in that "great and terrible day when he shall sit upon the throne of his glory," and dispense ultimate judgment to the quick and the dead.

Upon these hills of holiness, the stability of Messiah's throne, and the perfect administration of his kingdom, let us take our station, and survey the

Prospects which rise up before the church of God.

When I look upon the magnificent scene, I cannot repress the salutation, "Hail thou that art highly favoured!"

She has the prospect of preservation, of increase and of triumph.

(1.) The prospect of preservation.

The long existence of the Christian church would be pronounced, upon common principles, of reasoning impossible. She finds in every man a natural and inveterate enemy. To encounter and overcome the unanimous hostility of the world, she boasts no political stratagem, no disciplined legions, no outward coercion of any kind. Yet her expectation is that she shall live for ever. To mock this hope, and blot out her memorial from under heaven, the most furious efforts of fanaticism, the most ingenious arts of statesmen, the concentrated strength of empires, have been frequently and perseveringly applied. The blood of her sons and her daughters has streamed like water; the smoke of the scaffold and the stake, where they won the crown of martyrdom in the cause of Jesus, has ascended in thick volumes to the skies. The tribes of persecution have sported over her woes, and erected monuments, as they imagined, of her perpetual ruin. But where are her tyrants, and where their empires? the tyrants have long since gone to their own place; their names have descended upon the roll of infamy; their empires have passed like shadows over the rock—they have successively disappeared, and left not a trace behind!

But what became of the church? She rose from her ashes fresh in beauty and in might. Celestial glory beamed around her; she dashed down the monumental marble of her foes, and they who hated her fled before her. She has celebrated the funeral of kings and kingdoms that plotted her destruction; and, with the inscriptions of their pride, has transmitted to posterity the record of their shame. How shall this phenomenon be explained? We are at the present moment, witnesses of the fact; but who can unfold the mystery? This blessed book, the book of truth and life, has made our wonder to cease. "The Lord her God in the midst of her is mighty." His presence is a fountain of health, and his protection a "wall of fire." He has betrothed her, in eternal covenant, to himself. Her living head, in whom she lives, is above, and his quickening Spirit shall never depart from her. Armed with divine virtue, his gospel—secret, silent, unobserved—enters the hearts of men and sets up an everlasting kingdom. It eludes all the vigilance, and baffles all the power, of the adversary. Bars, and bolts, and dungeons are no obstacle to its approach: Bonds, and tortures, and death cannot extinguish its influence. Let no man's heart tremble then, because of fear. Let no man despair, in these days of rebuke and blasphemy, of the Christian cause. The ark is launched, indeed, upon the floods; the tempest sweeps along the deep; the billows break over her on every side. But Jehovah-Jesus has promised to conduct her in safety to the haven of peace. She cannot be lost unless the pilot perish. Why then do the heathen rage, and the people "imagine a vain thing?" Hear, O Zion, the word of thy God, and rejoice for the consolation. "No weapon that is formed against thee shall prosper, and every tongue that shall rise against thee in judgment thou shalt condemn. This is the heritage of the servants of the Lord, and their righteousness is of me saith the Lord."

Mere preservation, however, though a most comfortable, is not the only hope of the church; she has

(2.) The prospect of increase.

Increase—from an effectual blessing upon the means of grace in places where they are already enjoyed: for thus saith the Lord, "I will pour water upon him that is thirsty, and floods upon the dry ground: I will pour my spirit upon thy seed, and my blessing upon thine offspring; and they shall spring up as among the grass, as willows by the water-courses."

Increase—from the diffusion of evangelical truth through pagan lands. "For behold, the darkness shall cover the earth, and gross darkness the people; but the Lord shall arise upon thee, and his glory shall be seen upon thee. And the Gentiles shall come to thy light, and kings to the brightness of thy rising. Lift up thine eyes round about and see: all they gather themselves together, they come to thee: thy sons shall come from far, and thy daughters shall be nursed at thy side. Then thou shalt see, and flow together, and thine heart shall fear, and be enlarged; because the abundance of the sea shall be converted unto thee, the forces of the Gentiles shall come unto thee."

Increase—from the recovery of the rejected Jews to the faith and privileges of God's dear children. "Blindness in part has happened unto Israel;" they have been cut off, for their unbelief, from the olive-tree. Age has followed age, and they remain to this hour, spread over the face of the earth, a fearful and affecting testimony to the truth of God's word. They are without their sanctuary, without their Messiah, without the hope of their believing ancestors. But it shall not be always thus. They are still "beloved for the fathers' sake." When the "fulness of the Gentiles shall come in," they, too, shall be gathered. They shall discover, in our Jesus, the marks of the promised Messiah; and with tenderness proportioned to their former insensibility, shall cling to his cross. Grafted again into their own olive-tree, "All Israel shall be saved." It was "through their fall that salvation came unto us Gentiles." And, "if the casting away of them be the reconciliation of the world, what shall the receiving of them be but life from the dead?" What ecstacy, my brethren! the Gentile and the Jew taking "sweet counsel together, and going to the house of God in company! the path of the swift messenger of grace marked, in every direction, by the "fulness of the blessing of the gospel of Christ—a nation born at once"—the children of Zion exclaiming, "The place is too strait for me: give place to me that I may dwell." The knowledge of Jehovah overspreading the earth "as the waters cover the sea;" and all flesh enjoying the salvation of God!

This faith ushers in a

(3.) Prospect of the Church; the prospect of triumph.

Though often desolate, and "afflicted, tossed with tempest and not comforted," the Lord her God will then "make her an eternal excellency," and repay her sorrows with triumph—

Triumph—in complete victory over the enemies who sought her hurt. "The nation and kingdom," saith the Lord, "that will not serve thee shall perish: yea, those nations shall be utterly wasted." —The sons also of them that afflicted thee shall come bending unto thee; and all they that despised thee shall bow themselves down at the soles of thy feet; and they shall call thee the city of the

Lord, the Zion of the Holy One of Israel." That great enemy of her purity and her peace, who shed the blood of her saints and her prophets, the man of sin " who has exalted himself above all that is called God," shall appear, in the whole horror of his doom as the "son of perdition, whom the Lord shall consume with the spirit of his mouth, and shall destroy with the brightness of his coming." The terrible but joyous event shall be announced by an angel from heaven "crying mightily with a strong voice, Babylon the great is fallen, is fallen!" Alleluia, shall be the response of the church universal, " Salvation, and glory, and honour, and power, unto the Lord our God; for true and righteous are his judgments; for he hath judged the great whore which did corrupt the earth with her fornication, and hath avenged the blood of his servants at her hand!" Then, too, " the accuser of the brethren; that old serpent which is the devil," shall be cast down, "and bound a thousand years that he shall deceive the nations no more." This will introduce the church's.

Triumph—in the prevalence of righteousness and peace throughout the world.

"Her people shall be all righteous." The voice of the blasphemer shall no longer insult her ear. Iniquity as ashamed shall stop its mouth, and hide its head. " All her officers shall be peace, and all her exactors, righteousness. The kings of the earth bringing their glory and honour unto her," shall accomplish the gracious promise. "The mountains shall bring peace to the people, and the little hills by righteousness." Her prince whose throne is for ever and ever, "shall judge among the nations, and shall rebuke many people; and they shall beat their swords into ploughshares, and their spears into pruning hooks: nation shall not lift up sword against nation, neither shall they learn war any more!" Every man shall meet, in every other man, a brother without dissimulation. Fear and the sword shall be far away, " they shall sit every man under his vine, and under his fig-tree, and none shall make them afraid." For thus saith the Lord, " Violence shall no more be heard in thy land, wasting nor destruction within thy borders; but thou shalt call thy walls, Salvation, and thy gates, Praise."

Triumph—in the presence of God, in the communion of his love, and the signal manifestation of his glory."—" Behold, the tabernacle of God shall be with men, and he will dwell with them, and they shall be his people, and God himself shall be with them, and be their God." Then shall be seen "the holy Jerusalem descending out of heaven from God, which shall have no need of the sun, neither of the moon, to shine in it; for the glory of God shall lighten it, and the Lamb shall be the light thereof. And the nations of them which are saved shall walk in the light of it,— and they shall bring the glory and honour of the nation into it; and there shall in no wise enter into it anything that defileth neither whatsoever worketh abomination, or maketh a lie: but they which are written in the Lamb's book of life."

Such, according to the sure word of prophecy, will be the triumphs of Christianity; and to this issue all scriptural efforts to evangelize the heathen contribute their share. That mind is profane, indeed, which repels the sentiment of awe; and hard is the heart which feels no bland emotion—But let us pause—You exult, perhaps, in the view of that happiness which is reserved for the human race; you long for its arrival; and are eager, in your place, to help on the gracious work. It is well. But are there no heathen in this assembly? Are there none who, in the midst of their zeal for foreign missions, forget their own souls; nor consider that they themselves "neglect the great salvation?" Remember, my brethren, that a man may be active in measures which shall subserve the conversion of others, and yet perish in his own iniquity. That very gospel which you desire to send to the heathen, must be the gospel of your salvation; it must turn "you from darkness to light, from the power of Satan unto God;" it must make "you meet for the inheritance of the saints," or it shall fearfully aggravate your condemnation at last. You pray, "Thy kingdom come." But is the "kingdom of God within you?" Is the Lord Jesus "in you, the hope of glory?" Be not deceived. The name of Christian will not save you. Better had it been for you "not to have known the way of righteousness"—better to have been the most idolatrous pagan—better, infinitely better, not to have been born, than to die strangers to the pardon of the Redeemer's blood, and the sanctifying virtue of his Spirit. From his throne on high he calls; calls, my brethren, to you; "Look unto me, and be ye saved, for I am God, and there is none else. Seek ye the Lord while he may be found; call ye upon him while he is near; let the wicked forsake his way, and the unrighteous man his thoughts, and let him return unto the Lord, and he will have mercy upon him; and to our God, for he will abundantly pardon."

On the other hand, such as have "fled for refuge to lay hold on the hope set before them," are commanded to be "joyful in their King." He reigns, O believer, for thee. The stability of his throne is thy safety. The administration of his government is for thy good; and the precious pledge that he "will perfect that which concerneth thee." In all thy troubles and in all thy joy "commit thy way unto him." He will guard the sacred deposit. Fear not that thou shalt "lack any good thing." Fear not that thou shalt be forsaken—fear not that that thou shalt fall beneath the "arm of the oppressor."—"He went through the fires of the pit to save thee; and he will stake all the glories of his crown to keep thee." Sing, then, thou beloved, "Behold, God is my salvation; I will trust, and not be afraid; for the Lord Jehovah is my strength and my song; he also is become my salvation."

And if we have "tasted that he is gracious: if we look back with horror and transport upon the wretchedness and the wrath which we have escaped, with what anxiety shall we not hasten to the aid of our fellow-men, who are "sitting in the region and shadow of death?" What zeal will be too ardent; what labour too persevering; what sacrifice too costly, if, by any means, we may tell them of Jesus, and the resurrection, and the life eternal? Who shall be daunted by difficulties, or deterred by discouragement? If but one pagan should be brought, savingly, by your instrumentality, to the knowledge of God and the kingdom of heaven, will you not, my brethren, have an ample recompense? Is there here a man who would give up all for lost because some favourite hope has been disappointed; or who regrets the worldly substance which he has expended on so divine an enterprise? Shame on thy coward spirit and thine avaricious heart! Do the holy Scriptures, does the experience of ages, does the nature of things, justify the expectation, that we shall carry war into the central regions of delusion and crime, without opposition, without trial? Show me a plan which encounters not fierce resistance from the prince of darkness and his allies in the human heart, and I will show you a plan which never came from the inspiration of God. If missionary effort suffer occasional embarrassment; if impressions on the heathen be less speedy, and powerful, and extensive, than fond wishes have anticipated: if particular parts of the great system of operation be at times disconcerted: if any of the ministers of grace fall a sacrifice to the violence of those whom they go to bless "in the name of the Lord;" these are events which ought to exercise our faith and patience; to wean us from self-sufficiency; to teach us where our strength lies, and where our dependence must be fixed; but not to enfeeble hope, nor relax diligence. Let us not "despise the day of small things." Let us not overlook, as an unimportant matter, the very existence of that missionary spirit which has already awakened Christians in different countries from their long and dishonourable slumbers, and bids fair to produce, in due season, a general movement of the Church upon earth. Let us not for one instant harbour the ungracious thought, that the prayers, and tears, and wrestlings of those who "make mention of the Lord" form no link in that vast chain of events by which he "will establish, and will make Jerusalem a praise in the earth. That dispensation which of all others is most repulsive to flesh and blood, the violent death of faithful missionaries, should animate Christians with new resolution. "Precious in the sight of the Lord is the death of his saints." The cry of martyred blood ascends the heavens; it enters into "the ears of the Lord of Sabaoth. It will give him no rest till he "rain down righteousness" upon the land where it has been shed, and which it has sealed as a future conquest for him who "in his majesty rides prosperously because of truth, and meekness, and righteousness."

For the world, indeed, and perhaps for the Church, many calamities and trials are in store, before the glory of the Lord shall be so revealed, that "all flesh shall see it together."—"I will shake all nations," is the divine declaration—"I will shake all nations, and the desire of all nations shall come." The vials of wrath which are now running, and others which remain to be poured out, must be exhausted. The "supper of the great God" must be prepared, and his "strange work" have its course. Yet the missionary cause must ultimately succeed. It is the cause of God, and shall prevail. The days, O brethren, roll rapidly on, when the shout of the isles shall swell the thunder of the continent: when the Thames and the Danube, when the Tiber and the Rhine, shall call upon Euphrates, the Ganges, and the Nile; and the loud concert shall be joined by the Hudson, the Mississipi, and the Amazon, singing with one heart and one voice, Alleluia! Salvation! The Lord God omnipotent reigneth!

Comfort one another with this faith, and with these words:

Now, "Blessed be the Lord God, the God of Israel, who only doeth wondrous things. And blessed be his glorious name for ever: let the whole earth be filled with his glory! Amen and Amen!"

SERMON VIII.*

CHRISTIAN MOURNING.

1 THESS. 13, 14.

"I would not have you to be ignorant, brethren, concerning them which are asleep; that ye sorrow not even as others which have no hope. For if we believe that Jesus died and rose again, even so them also which sleep in Jesus will God bring with him."

CHRISTIANITY founds her claim to general reception upon doctrines most abasing to human pride, and facts calculated rather to repel than to invite human credulity. Her cardinal doctrine, which all the rest subserve, is the justification of a sinner, his deliverance from the bondage of his sin, and perfect happiness in heaven, through faith in a Saviour who himself fell a victim to his enemies, and expired, as a malefactor, under the infamy of the cross. Nothing more repugnant to their preconceived notions was ever proclaimed in the ears of men. It is the object of their dislike, their derision, and their scorn. "We preach," says the apostle, "we preach Christ crucified; unto the Jews a stumbling-block, and unto the Greeks foolishness!" So it was at the beginning; so it is at the present hour; and so it will remain to the end.

The cardinal fact of Christianity, without which all her other facts lose their importance, is the resurrection from the dead of this same crucified Saviour, as the prelude, the pattern, and the pledge of the resurrection of his followers to eternal life. Against this great fact the "children of disobedience," from the Pharisees of Jerusalem down to the scoffers of New York, have levelled their batteries. One assails its proof; another, its reasonableness; all, its truth. When Paul asserted it before an audience of Athenian philosophers, "some mocked"—a short method of refuting the

---

* Occasioned by the death of Mrs Isabella Graham; and Preached on the Evening of Sabbath, August 14, 1814.

gospel; and likely, from its convenience, to continue in favour and in fashion.

Yet with such doctrines and facts did the religion of Jesus make her way through the world. Against the superstition of the multitude—against the interest, influence, and craft of their priesthood—against the ridicule of wits, the reasoning of sages, the policy of cabinets, and the prowess of armies—against the axe, the cross, and the stake, she extended her conquests from Jordan to the Thames. She gathered her laurels alike upon the snows of Scythia, the green fields of Europe, and the sands of Africa. The altars of impiety crumbled before her march—the glimmer of the schools disappeared in her light—Power felt his arm wither at her glance; and, in a short time, she who went, forlorn and insulted, from the hill of Calvary to the tomb of Joseph, ascended the imperial throne, and waved her banner over the palace of the Cæsars. Her victories were not less benign than decisive. They were victories over all that pollutes, degrades, and ruins man; in behalf of all that purifies, exalts, and saves him. They subdued his understanding to truth, his habits to rectitude, his heart to happiness. In an appeal to that of which they were unexceptional judges, their own experience, Paul thus exclaims to the believers of Thessalonica: "They themselves show of us what manner of entering in we had unto you; and how ye turned to God from idols, to serve the living and true God; and to wait for his Son from heaven, whom he raised from the dead, even Jesus, who delivers us from the wrath to come."

The change from pagan to Christian character; from midnight darkness to light in the Lord, was abundantly visible, and not to be explained but upon the principles of Christianity itself. Yet without detracting from its magnitude, or from the glory of those divine influences which produced it, we may be allowed to question whether we are not prone to look upon the primitive converts as having reached an eminence in knowledge and purity, consistent, under their circumstances, neither with the general laws of our nature, nor with the testimony of holy writ. Falling short of them in zeal, in love, in promptitude of action, in patience of suffering, we regard them as a sort of human angels with whom we may not venture to claim connection. But when emotion yields to thought and reason balances facts, we recover from the fond illusion. We see them to have been men of like passions with ourselves; subject to erroneous conceptions, to rash judgments, to groundless fears, to irregular conduct. Let the Thessalonian Christians be our example. Collected from Jews and Gentiles, they could not rid themselves, at once, of their old prepossessions. Now and then, the Jewish tradition or the pagan feeling would obtrude into the sanctuary of their consolation in Christ. Some of them, led by a then popular opinion, that their Lord was shortly to appear, and tinctured with the doctrine of the Rabbins, mourned over the supposed diminution of happiness to their friends who had died without beholding the glorious advent of the Messiah's reign. Others, through the recurrence of early impressions, the objections of their heathen neighbours, and, it may be, the assiduities of false teachers, seem to have been drawn into doubts concerning the resurrection itself, and, of course, the safety of their friends who had died in faith. The native tendency of such apprehensions was to weigh down their spirits; to check their ardour; to shake their constancy under persecution; and to make them, instead of being "faithful unto the death," begin to think themselves "of all men the most miserable."

To rectify their mistake and establish them under their trial, is the design of the text. And although it was originally addressed to the Thessalonians; yet it is the common property of Christians, and was "written for our learning, that we, through patience and comfort of the Scriptures, might have hope." Let us, then, ponder its import. In general it contains an affectionate counsel, with the reasons thereof, against depression of heart at the death of believing friends.

1. The counsel of the text is, so to cherish the knowledge of the gospel, as that our hearts shall not be depressed by the death of believers; but that there shall be an immeasurable distance between our grief and the grief of unbelievers. "I would not," says Paul, "have you to be ignorant, brethren, concerning them which are asleep; that ye sorrow not even as others which have no hope."

That we may have a correct view of the importance of this counsel, let us briefly develope its leading principle.

Death is, in itself, a most serious and distressful event. It is nature's supreme evil—the abhorrence of God's creation—a monster from whose touch and sight every living thing recoils. So that to shrink from its ravages upon ourselves or upon those whom we love, is not an argument of weakness, but an act of obedience to the first law of being; a tribute to the value of that life which is our Maker's gift.

The disregard which some of old affected to whatever goes by the name of evil; the insensibility of others who yield up their souls to the power of fatalism; and the artificial gayety which has, occasionally, played the comedian about the dying bed of "philosophy, falsely so called," are outrages upon decency and nature. Death destroys both action and enjoyment; mocks at wisdom, strength, and beauty; disarranges our plans; robs us of our treasures; desolates our bosoms; breaks our heartstrings; blasts our hope. Death extinguishes the glow of kindness; abolishes the most tender relations of man; severs him from all that he knows and loves; subjects him to an ordeal which thousands of millions have passed, but none can explain; and which will be as new to the last who gives up the ghost, as it was to murdered Abel; flings him, in fine, without any avail from the experience of others, into a state of untried being. No wonder that nature trembles before it. Reason justifies the fear. Religion never makes light of it; and he who does, instead of ranking with heroes, can hardly deserve to rank with a brute.

Yet it is not the amount of actual suffering inflicted by the loss of those who are dear to us as our own souls that constitutes the chief pain of the privation. Death might "come up into our windows;" might rend from our embraces, and bear away, amidst our unavailing lamentations, all that our tenderest affections cling to here below; and the stroke would fall with comparative lightness, were its effect but temporary. It is from futurity that Grief, like Consolation, derives her power. The tears of separation will the more easily dry up, and be succeeded by the calm of cheerfulness, when we expect to regain what we have lost. But when there is no such expectation; when the treasure ravished from us can neither be restored nor replaced; it is then that nature sickens, and joy descends to the tomb. Ah! who can paint the anguish of the last look! Who can endure, at parting, the distractions of that word, "forever!" Who, that has any thought of hereafter—that but inclines to the belief that man dieth not as a beast dieth, can sustain the rackings of wild uncertainty, unable to surmise whither the beloved one is gone, and to what condition of being?

This was the state of the poor pagans; "others the rest, those that are without," as the apostle terms them. In the death of their friends they had no hope. Not that they were altogether without the notion of the existence of a soul detached from its body, or of happiness in a life to come. Tradition, fortified by the yearnings of nature, had preserved among the vulgar, the poets, and a few sober philosophers, something of distant kin to the truth. But all their conceptions were so obscure, so unwarranted, and therefore so unsatisfying, that they were rather the confused images of a dream, than the clear representations of waking vision. They were sufficient to agitate without convincing; they possessed the torments of anxiety, without the possibility of certainty: and the hope which they fostered, was, for every purpose of consolation and peace, no hope at all.

1. They knew nothing, whatever they might conjecture, of the state of departed man. Whether his soul, his vital and rational principle, survives the body; whether it remains conscious after death; whether, if conscious, it possesses any power of retrospect over earthly scenes; whether it is immortal; whether it enters, in its new mode of being, upon a fixed state of sorrow or joy, of shame or honour. On all these points the heathen were ignorant; although many of them were not quite so unconcerned as numbers who enjoy the pure light of the gospel, and boast of their liberal attainments; but with whom, in that great and terrible day of the Lord, the worst of the pagans would be unwilling to change places.

2. With the resurrection of the body the heathen was absolutely unacquainted. Flesh and blood could not reveal it to them. There are sighings, misgivings, reverential feelings towards the dead, analogies of nature, which eagerly fall in with the doctrine of the resurrection once made known; but which could never lead to the discovery, or even suspicion, of its truth. The apostles who taught it, until God opened the eyes of their hearers, were regarded as fanatics. In respect to the body, therefore Death brought with him into every pagan house, dejection, horror, black despondence.

Under these circumstances, what shall arrest the current of "mourning, and lamentation, and woe?" Where is the voice of the comforter? or what bosom can find room for comfort, which affords no entrance to hope? Oh! it is despair that kills!

Such was paganism bending over the remains of a deceased friend. Such, too, was Judaism, after it had rejected "the Hope of Israel, and the Saviour thereof." Such are still the millions, whether of Gentiles or Jews, who know not God.

And wherein have unbelievers among ourselves the pre-eminence? What have they to gild their evening hour, to bind up their aching head, to soothe their labouring heart? What living hope descends from heaven to smile on the sinking features, whisper peace to the retiring spirit, and announce to the sad surrounding relatives that all is well? There is none! Astonishment, dismay, melancholy boding, are the "portion of their cup." Sit down, ye unhappy, in the desolation of grief. Consolation heard the voice of your weeping: she hastened to your door, but started back affrighted; her commission extends not to your house of mourning; ye have no hope?

But Christians, believers in the Lord Jesus, your condition is widely different, and so must be your carriage. You, too, must resign, many of you have already resigned, some of you very recently, your believing friends to the stroke of death. You must feel, have felt, the pang of separation. You are not forbidden to mourn. The smitten heart will bleed; the workings of nature must have vent. It is right. Tears were not made that they should never be shed; nor the passion of grief implanted only to be stifled. God's gifts to us in the persons of those whom he animates with his love, beautifies with his image, and honours with his communion, are too precious to be relinquished without emotion. It would be a strange way of glorifying him for the best of his earthly blessings, to behave, when they were removed, as if they were not worth one thought. Nor could there be a fouler stain upon the religion of the cross, than a tendency to extinguish affections calculated, in a peculiar manner, to lessen the evils of our miserable world. No! the "grace which bringeth salvation" does not destroy, but restores the man. All that belongs to him, excepting sin and its effects she acknowledges, regulates, exalts. Jesus, the perfection of moral beauty, Jesus himself wept at the tomb of his friend. He has dignified as well as vindicated, by his example, the most sacred of our social feelings. And if we, sharing his sympathy, weep at the tomb of those who are not less his friends than our own, instead of falling beneath the level of profane fortitude, we rise up to the grandeur of fellowship with the "Man of sorrows."

Settle it, therefore, Christian brethren, as a principle not to be shaken, that your religion disclaims alike all kindred with apathy and with frenzy. Mourn you may when the "desire of your eyes" goes down to the dust; but you must not mourn as those "who have no hope." For hope, even the sweetest hope that can lodge in the human breast, is yours. Let your mourning, therefore, be tempered, submissive, holy. Yield not to brooding sadness. Transfer your tears from the cold face of your friend to the feet of your Master, and there compose your souls to serenity and peace. This is evangelical counsel; the counsel of my text. On what grounds it is offered; the reason why it should have a complete ascendancy over our minds, is the

II. Part of discourse.

"For if we believe that Jesus died and rose again, even so them also which sleep in Jesus will God bring with them."

The grounds of our consolation with respect to departed saints are, the nature of their death; their condition in and after it; and the prospect of their glorious resurrection.

1. The very nature of death, as it comes to believers, is a source of satisfaction; an antidote to excessive sorrow. They sleep.

Not that we are to imagine, with some dreaming speculatists, that the souls of the righteous remain unconscious and torpid during the period which elapses between the death and resurrection of their bodies. This cheerless doctrine, desirable to those only whose hearts have never been warmed by the love of Christ, was far enough from the faith and the theology of Paul. He had no cause to congratulate the church, as he does in the twelfth chapter of his epistle to the Hebrews, on her coming "to the spirits of just men made perfect," if, instead of "beholding the face of God in light and glory," they are inert and insensible as a clod. Nor could he who longed to "depart and be with Christ," accounting it the same thing to be "absent from the body, and to be present with the Lord," suppose that all his faculties and affections were to be suspended; and all his opportunities of serving his adorable

Redeemer to be taken away, by death, for scores of centuries together. The Lord have mercy upon them for whom such a prospect has any charms!

The apostle's words have quite another sound in the ears of faith; they are fraught with consolation fragrant as the breath of the morning, refreshing as the dews of heaven. It is true—a delightful truth—that the bodies of the saved, which at death their souls leave in order to be with Jesus, do rest in their graves. But it is chiefly in reference to their happy decease; their safe and comfortable departure, combined as it is with the death of the body, that the scriptures say, They sleep. Blessed assurance! Hear its admonitions.

1st. Death brings no peril to a child of God, and ought to be no more an object of his fear than the approach of sleep at the close of day. I speak not of the physical pangs of dying, which relate to our animal perceptions, and to which our animal part never can nor should be reconciled. I speak of death as affecting our moral being. In this view he is rightly named the "king of terrors;" because, to ungodly men, he is the "wages of sin." It is from guilt that he draws his terrifying power. He announces to the wicked the end of their respite; the filling up of their cup; "a certain fearful looking for of judgment and fiery indignation, which shall devour the adversaries;" and if they be not alarmed, if their faces gather not blackness, and their bosoms horror, it is because they are "hardened by the deceitfulness of sin." Their stupidity will only heighten the surprise and consternation of the eternal world. But Jesus having delivered his people from the wrath to come—delivered them by the blood of his cross—has for them stripped death of his terrors, and given them authority to cry, as he hands them over the threshold of life, "O Death, where is thy sting? the sting of death is sin, and the strength of sin is the law; but thanks be to God who giveth us the victory through our Lord Jesus Christ!" In such a case death deserves not the name. It is but a sleep; sleep in its most heavenly form; sleep in Jesus.

2d. Death is to believers a cessation from their toils and griefs, even as sleep is a repose from fatigue.

"We who are in this tabernacle do groan;" while the day lasts we must bear its burden and its heat. I shall not dwell upon the pains and endurances of a Christian soldier—his fight of faith—his race for the prize—his conflict with flesh and blood; and, what is more, with principalities and powers—his weakness, his weariness, his wounds, his faintings, his falls, his recoveries; in a word, his many and great vicissitudes. The point before us is, the end—it is peace. So saith the Word of our God: "He shall enter into peace; they shall rest in their beds; each one that walketh in his uprightness." To others, death is, emphatically, the beginning of sorrows—to a Christian, the termination. Grief and he have parted. The hour of release is come. He bids adieu to the field of battle. He puts off his harness; and, "knowing that his labour shall not be in vain," he lays his head on the bosom of the Captain of his salvation, and goes quietly to sleep. "Blessed are the dead who die in the Lord, that they may rest from their labours, and their works do follow them." Thus, in the nature of a believer's death there is ample reason why we should not be swallowed up of over much sorrow. He sleeps.

2. His condition in and after death is another spring of our consolation. He sleeps in Jesus. Here we ascertain two momentous truths.

1st. Death, which dissolves every other tie, touches not our union with the Lord Christ. Even then his saints are in him: as much the "members of his body, of his flesh, and of his bones," as when they were serving him in their mortal life. Seest thou that breathless corpse? It was, but a moment ago, the abode of a spirit now glorified with Christ. It was also an abode of the Divine Spirit. "Know ye not," saith Paul, "that your body is the temple of the Holy Ghost?" The human spirit is dead: but shall death, suppose ye, expel the Spirit of God from his own temple? No, he still resides in it, and will keep it for himself. Change it shall. The process of taking it down has already begun. It must descend to dust. It must see corruption. But, notwithstanding, it is the Saviour's property; a part of that whole person which is inseparably one with him. It is an object of his care and love. He does not scruple to call the Church's dead body his own body. This makes their dust precious: and that which he values shall not be worthless in our eyes.

2d. From their sleeping in Jesus, we ascertain that all the rights and privileges which belong to believers in virtue of their union with him, remain to them, after death undiminished and unimpaired. Dead they are, but they are dead in Christ. They are as much comprehended in his covenant; summed up in him as their head; represented by him as their advocate, who has all their claims in his hand for their benefit, as they possibly could be, when, here on earth, they lived by faith, walked by faith, suffered in faith, drew near to God by faith in his blood. Whatever is meant by being in Christ is meant of them now they are dead, and shall be made good to them at his appearing. They "sleep in Jesus."

3d. We derive consolation under the death of Christian friends from the prospect of their glorious resurrection. "If we believe that Jesus died and rose again, even so them also which sleep in Jesus God will bring with him."

Whatever have been the disputes about other doctrines of Christianity, no man can deny that it teaches the resurrection of the body. The very gates of hell, in the shape of that unhallowed philosophy which fritters away its most precious truths into eastern metaphors and Jewish allegories, have not ventured to tamper with the faith of the resurrection. This stands confest a Christian peculiarity. Let us contemplate its nature and proof as displayed in the text.

1st. This clay, which we commit to the grave under that universal sentence,—"Dust thou art, and unto dust thou shalt return,"—will be quickened again, and reassume, even after the slumber of ages, the organization, the lineaments, the expression, of that self-same human being with whom we were conversant upon earth. Otherwise it were a new creation, and not a resurrection: and will be reanimated by that self-same spirit which forsook it at death; otherwise it were a different being altogether, and not the one with whom, under that form, we held sweet communion in this life, and walked to the house of God in company. It has, indeed, been questioned whether Christian friends shall know each other in the world of the risen. But why not? Did not the disciples know the Lord Jesus after his resurrection? Did they not know him at the moment of his ascension? Shall the body which he wore upon earth be the only one recognised in heaven? If Peter and Paul, if James and John, shall not be able to distinguish each other, upon what principle shall they be able to distinguish their Lord? And why should the body be raised at all, if the associations with which its re-appearance is connected are to be broken and lost? It cannot be—But then,

2d. The body will be raised under circumstances, and with properties suited to the new state of being and action on which the saints shall enter. God shall bring them with the Lord Christ.

They shall be found in Christ's train. He will set them on his right hand in the face of heaven. He will present them to his Father, as the "sons whom he was appointed to bring unto glory," saying, "Here am I and the children whom thou hast given me."

They shall be adorned with Christ's likeness. "Beloved! it does not yet appear what we shall be, but we know that when he shall appear we shall be like him, for we shall see him as he is." The change requisite for this exaltation shall pass upon their body without destroying its sameness—as "flesh and blood, it cannot inherit the kingdom of God." But every obstacle shall be surmounted. If "it is sown in corruption, it is raised in incorruption;" if "it is sown in dishonour, it is raised in glory;" if "it is sown in weakness, it is raised in power;" if "it is sown a natural body, it is raised a spiritual body"—fit for the occupations and enjoyments of the heavenly world.

Finally, believers, in their raised bodies, shall be "partakers of Christ's glory" in the judgment of the quick and dead—

Know ye not that "the saints shall judge the world? shall judge angels?" They "overcame by the blood of the Lamb," and "shall sit down with him on his throne, even as he also overcame, and is set down with his Father on his throne."

But how are these transformations to be effected? How? By that same power which "calleth things that be not as though they were." God shall bring his risen ones with Jesus Christ. This is our short answer. I cannot open my ears to the objections of unbelief. We are upon too high ground to stoop to the caviller who marshals his ignorance and imbecility against the knowledge and might of God. Let him puzzle himself with his theories about personal identity—let him talk about one part of the body interred in Asia, another in Africa, and a third in Europe—let him ask as many questions as he can devise about limbs devoured by ravenous animals, and become, by nutrition, part of their bodies; which bodies again have passed, by the same process, into the flesh of other animals; and these, in their turn, consumed by man, and incorporated with the substance of a new human body—let him ask such questions, and ten thousand like them. Has he done? "Dost thou not therefore err, not knowing the Scriptures nor the power of God?" It will be time enough to plead thy difficulties when God shall commit to thee the raising of the dead. For us it is sufficient that he who rears up the living blade from the rotted grain will be at at no loss to rear up an incorruptible from a corrupted body, through what forms and varieties soever it may have passed.

The main question, however, is not what Omnipotence can but what it will perform. That God should raise the dead, if so it please him, will not appear incredible to any sober man. But what proof have we that our faith on this head is not fancy, and that our hope shall not perish? The best of all possible proof.

We have, in the first place, the divine promise. God has engaged to "raise his people up by Jesus, and to present them together with him." Jesus himself has said, "I am the resurrection and the life; he that believeth in me, though he were dead, yet shall he live; and he that liveth and believeth on me shall never die." A thousand scientific demonstrations are not equivalent, as the ground of our confidence, to one word of him "who cannot lie." And so we shall find it in our last extremity.

We have, moreover, the accomplishment, in part, of the promise already. For there are upon the sacred record many instances of resurrection from the dead.

We have, as a sure pledge of its full accomplishment in due season, the resurrection of our Lord Jesus himself. The fact is indisputable, and its consolation full.

(1.) By his resurrection he vanquished Death   He took away whatever gave to Death not only his sting but his empire. Therefore, saith the Scripture, he "abolished death, and brought life and immortality to light through the gospel."

(2.) As the Lord Jesus died, so he rose again, the head and representative of his redeemed. He bought them unto God by his blood; and he came back from the grave to show that the ransom was accepted, and to prosecute the claim which he presented to the throne of God, as he was about offering his soul in their soul's stead: "Father, I will that they also whom thou hast given me be with me where I am, that they may behold my glory."

His resurrection, therefore, is a pledge from the living God to his church, to the universe, that all who die in faith shall rise in glory. Christ is the first fruits; His people the harvest that shall follow; "But every one in his own order, Christ the first fruits; afterwards they that are Christ's at his coming." For this hour of joy and triumph is reserved the fulfilment of his gracious promise: "Thy dead shall live—my dead body shall they raise." He owns them as his body even in their state of death; They shall hear his voice, "Awake and sing, ye that dwell in dust!" They shall answer him from their graves, and shall come forth, the sons and daughters of immortality; resplendent in beauty, worthy of his kingdom. For he shall "change their vile body, that it may be fashioned like unto his own glorious body, according to the working whereby he is able even to subdue all things unto himself." This is Christian consolation; this is Christian hope; hope which all the crowns and treasures of earth are infinitely too poor to purchase or to balance. And it is hope that maketh not ashamed. "For I would not have you to be ignorant, brethren, concerning them which are asleep, that ye sorrow not even as others which have no hope. For if we believe that Jesus died and rose again, even so them also which sleep in Jesus will God bring with him."

In this faith the apostles laboured, and the martyrs bled. Ages have elapsed and it is still the same. It is not a distant wonder; not a brilliant vision; but a solid and present reality, under the power of which at this moment, while the words are on my lips, Christians, in various parts of the world, are closing their eyes to sleep in Jesus. It has come home to our own business and bosoms. It has chosen our houses to be the scene of its miracles. But rarely does it fall to the lot of human eyes to witness so high a display of its value and virtue, as was witnessed in that blessed woman whose entrance into the joy of her Lord has occasioned our assembling this evening.

As we are commanded to be "followers of them who through faith and patience inherit the promises," we should have their example before us, that we may learn to imbibe their spirit, to imitate their graces, and be ready for their reward. With this view permit me to lay before you some brief recollections of our deceased friend.

It is not my intention to relate the history of her life. That will be a proper task for biography. I design merely to state a few leading facts, and to sketch such outlines of character, as may shew to those who knew her not, "what manner of person she was in all holy conversation and godliness." Those who knew her best require no such remembrancer; and will be able, from their own observation, to supply its defects.

Isabella Marshall, known to us as Mrs Graham, received from nature, qualities which, in circumstances favourable to their development, do not allow their possessor to pass through life unnoticed and inefficient.

An intellect strong, prompt, and inquisitive—a temper open, generous, cheerful, ardent—a heart replete with tenderness, and alive to every social affection, and every benevolent impulse—a spirit at once enterprising and persevering. The whole crowned with that rare and inestimable endowment—good sense—were materials which required only skilful management to fit her for adorning and dignifying any female station. With that sort of cultivation which the world most admires, and those opportunities which attend upon rank and fortune, she might have shone in the circles of the great, without forfeiting the esteem of the good. Or had her lot fallen among the literary unbelievers of the continent, she might have figured in the sphere of the Voltaires, the Deffands, and the other *esprits forts* of Paris. She might have been as gay in public, as dismal in private, and as wretched in her end, as any of the most distinguished among them for their wit and their woe. But God had destined her for other scenes and services—scenes from which greatness turns away appalled; and services which all the cohorts of individual wit are unable to perform. She was to be prepared by poverty, bereavement, and grief, to pity and to succour the poor, the bereaved, and the grieving. The sorrows of widowhood were to teach her the heart of the widow—her babes, deprived of their father, to open the springs of her compassion to the fatherless and orphan; and the consolations of God, her "refuge and strength, her very present help in trouble," to make her a daughter of consolation to them who were "walking in the valley of the shadow of death."

To train her betimes for the future dispensations of his providence, the Lord touched the heart of this chosen vessel, in her early youth. The spirit of prayer sanctified her infant lips; and taught her, as far back as her memory could go, to "pour out her heart before God." She had not reached her eleventh year, when she selected a bush in the retirement of the field, and there devoted herself to her God by faith in the Redeemer. The incidents of her education, thoughtless companions, the love of dress, and the dancing-school, as she has herself recorded, chilled for a while the warmth of her piety, and robbed her bosom of its peace. But her gracious Lord revisited her with his mercy, and bound her to himself in an everlasting covenant, which she sealed at his own table about the seventeenth year of her age. Having married, a few years after, Dr John Graham, surgeon to the 60th British regiment, she accompanied him first to Montreal, and shortly after to Fort Niagara. Here, during four years of temporal prosperity, she had no opportunity, even for once, of entering "the habitation of God," or hearing the sound of his gospel. Secluded from the waters of the sanctuary, and all the public means of growth in grace, her religion began to languish, and its leaf to droop. But the root was perennial—it was of "the seed of God which liveth and abideth for ever." The Sabbath was still to her the sign of his covenant. On that day of rest, with her Bible in her hand, she used to wander through the woods, renew her self-dedication, and pour out her prayer for the salvation of her husband and her children. He who "dwelleth not in temples made with hands," heard her cry from the wilds of Niagara, and "strengthened her with strength in her soul."

By one of those vicissitudes which checker military life, the regiment was ordered to the island of Antigua in the West Indies. Here she met with that exquisite enjoyment to which she had been long a stranger—the communion of kindred spirits in the love of Christ: and soon did she need all the soothing and support which it is fitted to administer. For in a very short time the husband of her youth, the object of her most devoted affection, her sole earthly stay, was taken from her by death. The stroke was, indeed, mitigated by the sweet assurance that he slept in Jesus. But a heart like hers, convulsed by a review of the past and anticipation of the future, would have burst with agony, had she not known how to pour out its sorrows into the bosom of her heavenly Father. Trials which beat sense and reason to the ground, raise up the faith of the Christian, and draw her closer to her God. O how divine to have him as the rock of our rest when every earthly reliance is "a broken reed!"

Bowing to his mysterious dispensation, and committing herself to his protection as the "Father of the fatherless, and the Husband of the widow," she returns with her charge to her native land, to contract alliance with penury, and to live by faith for her daily bread. That same grace under whose teaching she "knew how to abound," taught her also how to suffer need. With a dignity which belongs only to them who have treasure in heaven, she descended to her humble cot, employment, and fare. But her humility, according to the Scripture, was the forerunner of her advancement. The light of her virtues shone brightest in her obscurity, and pointed her way to the confidential trust of forming the minds and manners of young females of different ranks in the metropolis of Scotland. Here, respected by the great and beloved by the good; in sacred intimacy with devout and honourable women, and the friendship of men who were in truth "servants of the Most High God," she continued in the successful discharge of her duties till Providence conducted her to our shores. She long had a predilection for America, as a land in which, according to her favourite opinion, the church of Christ is signally to flourish. Here she wished to end her days and leave her children. And we shall remember, with gratitude, that in granting her wish, God cast her lot with ourselves. Twenty-five years ago she opened, in this city, a school for the education of young ladies, the benefits of which have been strongly felt, and will be long felt hereafter, in different and distant parts of our country. Evidently devoted to the welfare of her pupils—attentive to their peculiarities of character—happy in discovering the best avenue of approach to their minds—possessing, in a high degree, the talent of simplifying her instruction and varying its form, she succeeded in that most difficult part of a teacher's work, the inducing youth to take an interest in their own improvement, and to educate themselves by exerting their own faculties.

In governing her little empire, she acted upon those principles which are the basis of all good government on every scale and under every modification—to be reasonable, to be firm, and to be uniform. Her authority was both tempered and strengthened by condescension. It commanded respect while it conciliated affection. Her word was law, but it was the law of kindness. It spoke to the conscience, but it spoke to the heart; and obedience bowed with the knee of love. She did not, however, imagine her work to be perfected in fitting her *elévées* for duties and elegance of life. Never did she forget their immortal nature. Utterly devoid of sectarian narrowness, she laboured to infuse into their minds those vital principles of evangelical piety which form the common distinction of the disciples of Christ, the peculiar glory of the female name, and the surest pledge of domestic bliss. Her voice, her example, her prayers, concurred in recommending that pure and undefiled religion without which no human being shall see the Lord.—Shall we wonder that her scholars should be tenderly attached to such a preceptress? that they should leave her with their tears and their blessing? that they should carry an indelible remembrance of her into the bosom of their families? that the reverence of pupils should ripen with their years into the affection of friends? and that there should be among them, at this day, many a wife "who is a crown to her husband;" and many a mother who is a blessing to her children; and who owes, in a great degree, the felicity of her character to the impressions, the principles, and the habits which she received while under the maternal tuition of Mrs Graham?

Admonished, at length, by the infirmities of age, and importuned by her friends, this venerable matron retired to private life. But it was impossible for her to be idle. Her leisure only gave a new direction to her activity. With no less alacrity than she had displayed in the education of youth, did she now embark in the relief of misery. Her benevolence was unbounded, but it was discreet. There are charities which increase the wretchedness they are designed to diminish; which, from some fatal defect in their application, bribe to iniquity while they are relieving want; and make food, and raiment, and clothing, to warm into life the most poisonous seeds of vice.

But the charities of our departed friend were of another order. They selected the fittest objects—the widow—the fatherless—the orphan—the untaught child—and the ignorant adult. They combined intellectual and moral benefit with the communication of physical comfort. In her house originated the "Society for the Relief of Poor Widows with Small Children." Large, indeed, is this branch of the family of affliction; and largely did it share in her sympathy and succour. When at the head of the noble association just named, she made it her business to see with her own eyes the objects of their care; and to give, by her personal presence and efforts, the strongest impulse to their humane system. From morning till night has she gone from abode to abode of these destitute, who are too commonly unpitied by the great, despised by the proud, and forgotten by the gay. She has gone to sit beside them on their humble seat, hearing their simple and sorrowful story—sharing their homely meal; ascertaining the condition of their children; stirring them up to diligence, to economy, to neatness, to order; putting them into the way of obtaining suitable employment for themselves and suitable places for their children: distributing among them the Word of God, and little tracts calculated to familiarize its first principles to their understanding; cherishing them in sickness; admonishing them in health; instructing, reproving, exhorting, consoling; sanctifying the whole with fervent prayer. Many a sobbing heart and streaming eye is this evening embalming her memory in the house of the widow.

Little, if any, less is the debt due to her from that invaluable charity the "Orphan Asylum." It speaks its own praise, and that praise is hers. Scores of orphans redeemed from filth, from ignorance, from wretchedness, from crime—clothed, fed, instructed—trained, in cleanliness, to habits of industry—early imbued with the knowledge and fear of God; gradually preparing for respectability, usefulness, and happiness—is a spectacle for angels. Their infantine gayety, their healthful sport, their cherub-faces, mark the contrast between their present and former condition; and recall, very tenderly, the scenes in which they used to cluster round their patron-mother, hang on her gracious words, and receive her benediction.

Brethren, I am not dealing in romance, but in sober fact. The night would be too short for a full enumeration of her worthy deeds. Suffice it to say, that they ended but with her life. The Sabbath previous to her last sickness occupied her with a recent institution—"A Sunday School for Ignorant Adults;" and the evening preceding the touch of death, found her at the side of a faithful domestic, administering consolation to his wounded spirit.

Such active benevolence could hardly be detected in company with a niggardly temper. Wishes which cost nothing; pity which expires on the lips. " Be ye warmed and be ye clothed," from a cold heart and an unyielding gripe, never imprinted their disgraceful brand upon Isabella Graham. What she urged upon others she exemplified in herself. She kept a purse for God. Here, in obedience to his command, she deposited " the first fruits of all her increase;" and they were sacred to his service, as, in his providence, he should call for them. No shuffling pretences, no pitiful evasions, when a fair demand was made upon the hallowed store ; and no frigid affectation in determining the quality of the demand. A sense of duty was the prompter, candour the interpreter, and good sense the judge. Her disbursements were proportioned to the value of the object; and were ready at a moment's warning, to the very last farthing.* How pungent a reproof to those ladies of opulence and fashion, who sacrifice so largely to their dissipation or their vanity, that they have nothing left for mouths without food, and limbs without raiment! How far does it throw back into the shade those men of prosperous enterprise and gilded state, who, in the hope of some additional lucre, have thousands and ten thousands at their beck ; but who, when asked for decent contributions to what they themselves acknowledge to be all important, turn away with this hollow excuse, " I cannot afford it!" Above all, how should her example redden the faces of many who profess to belong to Christ; to have received gratuitously from him, what he procured for them at the expense of his own blood, " an inheritance incorruptible, and undefiled, and that fadeth not away ;" and yet in the midst of abundance which *he* has lavished upon them, when the question is about relieving his suffering members, or promoting the glory of his kingdom, are sour, reluctant, mean! Are *these* the *Christians?* Can it be that they have committed their bodies, their souls, their eternal hope, to a Saviour whose thousand promises on this very point of " honouring Him with their substance," have less influence upon their hearts and their hands than the word of any honest man? Remember the deceased, and hang your heads—Remem-

---

* The author knew her, when in moderate circumstances, to give, unsolicited, fifty pounds at once, out of that sacred purse, to a single most worthy purpose.

ber her, and tremble—Remember her, and "bring forth fruits meet for repentance."

In that charity also which far surpasses mere almsgiving, however liberal, the charity of the gospel, our friend was conspicuous. "The love of God shed abroad in her own heart by the Holy Ghost," drew forth her love to his people wherever she found them. Assuredly she had in herself this witness of her having "passed from death unto life," that she "loved the brethren." The epistle written not with ink, "but with the Spirit of the living God; not in tables of stone, but in fleshy tables of the heart; yet read and known of all men:" that is, the Christian temper manifested by a Christian conversation, was to her the best letter of recommendation. Unwavering in her own faith as to the peculiar doctrines of the gospel, she could, nevertheless, extend love without dissimulation, and the very bowels of Christian fellowship, to others, who, whatever might be their mistakes, their infirmities, or their differences in smaller matters, agreed in the great Christian essential of "acceptance in the Beloved." Deeply did she deplore the conceit, the bigotry, and the bitterness of sect. O that her spirit were more prevalent in the churches! that we could labour to abase our "crown of pride;" to offer up, with one consent, upon the altar of evangelical charity, those petty jealousies, animosities, and strifes which are our common reproach; and walk together as children of the same Father, brethren of the same Redeemer, and heirs of the same salvation!

To these admirable traits of character were added great tenderness of conscience and a spirit of prayer. Her religion, not contented to "justify her before men," habitually aimed at pleasing "God who looketh upon the heart." It was not enough for her to persuade herself that a thing *might* be right. Before venturing upon it, she studied to reduce the question of right to a clear certainty. How cautious, and scrupulous, and jealous of herself she was in this matter, they best can tell who saw her in the shade of retirement, as well as in the sunshine of public observation. Perhaps it is not going too far to say, that her least guarded moments would, in others, have been marked for circumspection. At the same time, her vigilance had nothing austere, gloomy, constrained, or censorious: nothing to repress the cheerfulness of social intercourse; or to excite in others, even the thoughtless, a dread of merciless criticism after they should retire. It was sanctified nature moving gracefully in its own element. And with respect to the character and feelings of her neighbours, she was too full of Christian kindness not to "keep her tongue from evil, and her lips from speaking guile."

These virtues and graces were maintained and invigorated by her habit of prayer. With the "new and living way into the holiest by the blood of Jesus," she was intimately familiar. Thither the "Spirit of grace and supplication" daily conducted her; there taught her to pray; and in praying to believe; and in believing to have "fellowship with the Father and with his Son Jesus Christ." She knew her God as the God that heareth prayer; and could attest that "Blessed is she that believeth, for there shall be a performance of those things which were told her from the Lord.

Under such influence her course could not but be correct and her steps well ordered. The "secret of the Lord is with them that fear him; and he will show them his covenant—he will guide them in judgment." Thus he did with his handmaid whom he hath called home. Wherever she was, and in whatever circumstances, she remembered the guide of her youth, who, according to his promise, "never left her nor forsook her; but continued his gracious presence with her when she was "old and grey-headed."

You may perhaps imagine, that with such direction and support, it was impossible she should see trouble. Nay, but "waters of a full cup were wrung out to her!" She often ate the bread of sorrow steeped in wormwood and gall. Her heavenly Father "showed her great and sore adversities; that he might try her as silver is tried, and bring her forth from the furnace purified seven times." It was during these refining processes that she found the worth of being a Christian. Though her way was planted with thorns and watered with her tears, yet the candle of the Lord shone upon her head; and from step to step she had reason to cry, "Hitherto hath Jehovah helped!" In a word, like Enoch, she walked with God; like Abraham, she staggered not at his promise through unbelief; like Jacob, she wrestled with the angel and prevailed; like Moses, endured as seeing him who is invisible; like Paul, finished her course with joy. Blessed were the eyes of the preacher for they saw the victory of her faith; and his ears, for they heard her song of salvation. "You can say with the apostle, 'I know whom I have believed, and am persuaded that he is able to keep that which I have committed unto him!'"—"O yes! but I cannot say the other, 'I have fought a good fight;' I must say, 'I have fought a poor fight, I have run a poor race;' but 'Christ fought for me, Christ ran with me, and through Christ I hope to win.'"—"But you have no fear, no doubts, about your going to be with Christ?"—"Oh no! not a doubt; I am as sure of that as if I were already in my Saviour's arms." It was her final conversation with children of the dust. The next day, "when her flesh and her heart had so far failed" that she was incapable of uttering a sentence, she still proved her God to be the strength of her heart; and knew him to be her portion forever. I said to her, "It is peace." She opened her eyes, smiled, closed them again, bowed her dying head, and breathed out "Peace." It was her last word on this side heaven. The attending spirits caught it from her lips; and brought to her the next day permission to sleep in Jesus.

From this review allow me, brethren, to urge the value of private exertions in promoting general good.

In pursuing his gratifications, man is apt to look upon himself as a being of great importance: in fulfilling his duties, to account himself as nothing. Both are extravagances which it will be his wisdom and happiness to correct. He is neither supreme in worth, nor useless in action. Let him not say, "I am but one: my voice will be drowned in the universal din: my weight is lighter than a feather in the public scale. It is better for me to mind my own affairs, and leave these higher attempts to more competent hands." This is the language, not of reason and modesty, but of sloth, of selfishness, and of pride. The amount of it is, "I cannot do everything, therefore I will do nothing."—But you can do much. Act well your part according to your faculties, your station, and your means. The result will be honourable to yourself, delightful to your friends, and beneficial to the world. I advise not to gigantic aims, to enormous enterprise. The world has seen but one Newton and one Howard. Nothing is required of you but to make the most of the opportunities within your reach. Recall the example of Mrs Graham. Here was a woman; a widow; a stranger in a strange land; without fortune; with no friends but such as her letters of introduction and her worth should acquire; and with a family of daughters dependent upon her for their subsistence. Surely if any one has a clear title of immunity from the obligation to carry her cares beyond the domestic circle, it is this widow; it is this stranger. Yet within a few years this stranger, this widow, with no means but her excellent sense, her benevolent heart, and her persevering will to do good, awakens the charities of a populous city, and gives to them an impulse, a direction, and an efficacy, unknown before! What might not be done by men; by men of talent, of standing, of wealth, of leisure? How speedily, under their well-directed beneficence, might a whole country change its physical, intellectual, and moral aspect; and assume, comparatively speaking, the face of another Eden; a second garden of God? Why then do they not diffuse, thus extensively, the seeds of knowledge, of virtue, and of bliss? I ask not for their pretences; they are as old as the lust of lucre; and are refuted by the example which we have been contemplating; I ask for the true reason, for the inspiring principle, of their conduct. It is this; let them look to it when God shall call them to account for the abuse of their time, their talents, their station, their unrighteous mammon. It is this: They believe not the words of the Lord Jesus, how he said, "It is more blessed to give than to receive." They labour under no want but one; they want the heart! The bountiful God add this to the other gifts which he has bestowed upon them! I turn to the other sex.

That venerable mother in Israel, who has exchanged the service of God on earth for his service in heaven, has left a legacy to her sisters; she has left the example of her faith and patience; she has left her prayers; she has left the monument of her Christian deeds: and by these she "being dead yet speaketh." Matrons! has she left her mantle also? Are there none among you to hear her voice from the tomb, "Go and do thou likewise?" None whom affluence permits, endowments qualify, and piety prompts, to aim at her distinction by treading in her steps? Maidens! Are there none among you, who would wish to array yourselves hereafter in the honours of this virtuous woman? Your hearts have dismissed their wonted warmth and generosity, if they do not throb as the reverend vision rises before you—Then prepare yourselves now, by seeking and serving the God of her youth. You cannot be too early "adorned with the robes of righteousness and the garments of salvation" in which she was wedded, in her morning of life, to Jesus the King of glory. That same grace which threw its radiance around her shall make you also to shine in the beauty of holiness; and the fragrance of those virtues which it shall create, develop, and ennoble, will be "as the smell of a field which the Lord hath blessed."

Yea, let me press upon all who hear me this evening, the transcendent excellence of Christian character, and the victorious power of Christian hope. The former bears the image of God; the latter is as imperishable as his throne. We fasten our eyes with more real respect, and more heart-felt approbation upon the moral majesty displayed in "walking as Christ also walked," than upon all the pomps of the monarch, or decorations of the military hero. More touching to the sense, and more grateful to high heaven, is the soft melancholy with which we look after our departed friend, and the tear which embalms her memory, than the thundering plaudits which rend the air with the name of a conqueror. She has obtained a triumph over that foe who shall break the arm of valour, and strike off the crown of kings. "The fashion of this world passeth away." Old Time approaches towards his last hour. The proudest memorials of human grandeur shall be food for the conflagration to be kindled when "the Lord Jesus shall be revealed from heaven in flaming fire. Then shall he be glorified in his saints, and admired in all of them that believe." There are those, perhaps, in the present assembly, who repute godliness fanaticism; and the sobriety of Christian peace, the gloom of a joyless spirit; but who cannot forbear sighing out, with the prophet of mammon, "Let me die the death of the righteous and let my last end be like his." If they proceed no further, their wish will not be granted. None shall die the death of the righteous, unless by a rare dispensation of mercy, who do not live his life. They only are fit to be with God, who love God and keep his commandments. In that day of transport and of terror which we shall all witness, how many of the thoughtless fair, who now "sport themselves with their own deceivings," would give all the treasures of the east and thrones of the west, to sit with Isabella Graham on the right hand of Jesus Christ! If ye be wise betimes, ye may. "Now is the accepted time; to-day is the day of salvation." The gospel of the Son of God offers you, at this very moment, the forgiveness of your sins, and an inheritance among them that are sanctified. The blessing comes to you as a free gift—Accept it and live. Accept it, and be safe. Accept it, and put away the shudderings of guilt, and the fear of death. Then shall you, too, like our friend, go, in due season, to be with Christ. Your happy spirit shall rejoin hers in the mansions of the saved. God shall bring you in soul and body with her when he makes up his jewels—then shall he gather his elect from the four winds of heaven, shall perfect that which concerneth them, and make them fully and for ever blessed. Be our place among them in that day!

SERMON IX.*

FULL ASSURANCE OF FAITH AND HOPE.

2 TIMOTHY i. 12.

"For I know whom I have believed; and am persuaded that he is able to keep that which I have committed unto him, against that day."

If ever there was an unlikely subject of conversion to the Christian faith, it was Saul of Tarsus. His education, his habits, his prospects, his ardent and active zeal against Christians, his powerful intellect, his pride, his very conscience, all under the influence of wrong impressions, rendered his perseverance in Judaism morally certain, and the idea of his change, in the eyes of thinking men, perfectly chimerical. Satan himself seemed not less likely to become an apostle, than this fierce and intrepid Jew. His active spirit, and his implacable malignity, "breathing out threatenings and slaughter against the disciples of the Lord," would, if permitted to take its course, have "made short work with the dissenters" from the order established at Jerusalem; would have crushed the infant church; and scarcely left materials for one paragraph of the general historian. But the Lord Jesus had other views for his church, and other employment for the persecutor. In the height of his career—in the very act of executing the bloody commission of the high priest—when surrounded by armed men, to enforce his orders—at mid-day—on the public road—near a celebrated city—a burst of glory from the face of Jesus Christ eclipses the brightness of the sun; an invisible power smites him and all his company to the earth; and a voice, the authority of which made him feel that his Creator was speaking,

---

* Preached as part of the ordinary ministrations in Murray Street Church, February 18, 1821, and published in the National Preacher, May 1829.

addressed to him those memorable words,—" Saul, Saul, why persecutest thou me?" The high priest, the Sanhedrim, the nation whose hopes all centre in him, his character, his commission, are forgotten in an instant. Men have no leisure for anything else, when they are conscious that God is speaking. " Who art thou, Lord?" exclaimed the astonished and trembling persecutor: " I am Jesus," answers the heavenly voice, " I am Jesus whom thou persecutest."—" Lord," replies he, every disposition to cavil or tamper being perfectly subdued, " Lord, what wilt thou have me to do?"—" Arise, and go into the city, and it shall be told thee what thou must do." Gentle as a lamb, the high-spirited and ferocious Saul obeys the mandate. Smitten blind by the light which shone around him, he is led by the hand into Damascus: where he remained " three days without sight, and did neither eat nor drink." Under such tutelage as no other man ever enjoyed, he passes through the process of conviction and conversion; experiences the second birth; has a new heart put within him; is instructed in the mysteries of the kingdom; is furnished with all gifts and graces; is taught the service which he is to perform, and the sufferings which he is to endure; and comes forth not a whit behind the chiefest apostles, and straightway preaches Christ in the synagogues, that he is the Son of God. Five and twenty years had he tried the service of Christ, when he penned this epistle to Timothy, proving, by turns, and sometimes all together, the honours, the victories, the disappointments, the pains, the sorrows, of his apostleship. At this very moment he was a martyr to the truth, and suffering unheard-of things for the word of his testimony. Yet he utters no complaint; his tone is firm and cheerful; it is the voice of salvation from the belly of hell. " I am not ashamed," says he, "for I know whom I have believed, and am persuaded that he is able to keep that which I have committed unto him, against that day."

Brethren, there is something in the knowledge of Jesus Christ, and that persuasion of his ability which belongs to his faithful followers, which bears them up over every discouragement, and will at length enable them to elude the great destroyer, and to fly, on the wings of the morning, to the place of their eternal rest. Paul was an example. But he was so, on principles which are common to the household of faith. It was not as an apostle, but as a believer, that he cherished so triumphant a hope, and sung so sweet a song, in the house of his pilgrimage. It will be of advantage to us, if we take a nearer view of Paul's knowledge of the Lord Jesus Christ; and of that perfect confidence, which he entertained, that all should be safe in his hands.

I. The knowledge which Paul had of his Redeemer: "I know whom I have believed."

The apostle's knowledge of Jesus Christ was personal, that is, it was a knowledge of Christ himself, and centred in himself; not merely an acquaintance with his religion. Many people imagine, that to know something about the Christian religion, to be able to explain it, and ready to recommend it, is equivalent with knowing Christ himself. Whencesoever they imbibed such a notion, it was not from their Bible. This makes a very broad difference between the knowledge of Jesus Christ, and every other sort of knowledge; and the Scripture does not deal in vain distinctions. The knowledge and the love which accompany salvation go together, and are coupled by the Scripture to the person of the Saviour. "That I may know him," saith Paul. "Whom, having not seen, ye love," adds Peter. Now here is the parting point with many a decent profession, yet the very point upon which eternal happiness is suspended. Many a demonstration of the Christian verity, and many a splendid panegyric on its excellence, worth, and necessity, have flowed from lips which the fire of God's altar never purified; have been prompted by hearts which were never touched by the love of Christ. Startle not, as if I had preached an unheard of doctrine; but go, if you are not afraid of the experiment, summon the tongues of men and angels to speak the praises of revealed truth; and then stand aghast at discovering, that without charity, that vivifying principle in the world of grace, you are no better than "sounding brass or a tinkling cymbal." In living religion Christ is all. The hearts of his people are, without exception, drawn, in tender affection, to himself. The thought, "that he loved me and gave himself for me," filled, and subdued, and melted the heart of one apostle; and drew from another the gracious declaration, "We love him because he first loved us;" and so do all his sincere followers find the fact to be at the present hour.

Now to both this knowledge and this love of Christ something more is necessary than can be learned from human books, or taught by human speech, or enforced by human example. That which happened unto Paul must happen unto us. God must "reveal his Son in us;" the Holy Spirit must "take of the things which are his, and show them unto us." Is it wonderful that Christ Jesus was so glorious in the eyes of his apostles; and is now so glorious in the eyes of all who have an apostle's hope?

1. Paul was enabled to take an enlarged and decisive view of the glory of the Redeemer's person. He never dreamt that idiot dream of a created Saviour. There was no doubt in his mind, nor is there in the minds of any who tread in his steps, whatever there be in the minds of those who pride themselves in their distinction as philosophical believers, that he who is "the eternal Life" must be the true God—"God over all, blessed for ever." He perceived him to be, and he celebrated him, and taught others to expect him, as the "great God our Saviour." It was, in his judgment a mystery, the great mystery of Godliness—the very pillar and ground of truth, without which the whole fabric of salvation falls to ruins "that God was manifest in the flesh," and so became our Brother, and has made us bone of his bone and flesh of his flesh.

In the person, moreover, of Jesus Christ all the counsels of the Godhead centre. "In him are hidden all the treasures of wisdom and knowledge"—"In him dwelleth all the fulness of the Godhead bodily." If God "reconciles the world unto himself, it is in Christ Jesus." If "the light of his glory shines unto us, it is in the face of Jesus Christ." If he gathers together in one a new family, composed of holy angels and redeemed men, he gathers them in Christ. If every knee is ordered to bow, and every tongue to confess, it is to "Jesus Christ, who has a name which is above every name," and has it expressly for this purpose. In fine, the Father hath committed all judgment to the Son, with this end, that "all men should honour the Son, even as they honour the Father;" and that under the fearful sanction, that whosoever shall refuse so to honour the Son, shall find all his worship rejected: "He that honoureth not the Son, honoureth not the Father who hath sent him."

2. Paul had equally lofty views of the Redeemer's mediatorial work; by whose perfect "obedience many shall be made righ-

teous,"—"who gave himself for us, to redeem us from all iniquity,"—"who is the propitiation through faith in his blood, that God may be just, and the justifier of him that believeth in Jesus,"—"so that we have redemption through his blood, the forgiveness of sins according to the riches of his grace,"—"who has risen again from the dead, and become the first fruits of them that slept,"—"who has gone into heaven, not with the blood of goats and calves, but with his own blood, having obtained eternal redemption for us,"—"who is at the right hand of God, making intercession for us; and is able, therefore, to save unto the uttermost all that come unto God by him."

3. Paul had, further, a view of the glory which Jesus Christ has promised to his followers. For them death hath no sting—over them the grave boasts no victory—nor the second death any power. Their Saviour shall reclaim their dead bodies: "He shall call, and they shall answer him out of the dust." Neither death nor hell shall retain them for an instant. They shall spring up in all the alertness of spiritual and incorruptible bodies—shall be fashioned like unto his own glorious body, and go, in their whole persons, to be for ever with the Lord.

All these things the apostle saw—saw them in the light and with the eyes of that faith which is the evidence of things not seen, and the substance of things hoped for. They left on his soul an impression never to be obliterated: an impression as deep and vivid as the seal of the Holy Ghost—as the image of the living God. Whenever afterward, he speaks of his Redeemer, and of his people's hope in him, his spirit catches fire. O, how unlike the men who are cased in triple ice when they approach the throne of the Son of God! He darts up into the heavens, and when he descends again to the earth, it is to scatter

"Thoughts that breathe and words that burn."

Hear this child of faith and of the skies singing and shouting, and welcoming the decease which was to take him home: "I am now ready to be offered, and the time of my departure is at hand; I have fought a good fight, I have finished my course, I have kept the faith; henceforth there is laid up for me a crown of righteousness, which the Lord, the righteous judge, shall give me at that day; and not to me only, but unto them also that love his appearing."

Throughout his whole representation of the glory, grace, and promises of Christ, it will not fail to be observed, that there is not so much as a hint of any doubt. The Christian religion is not a religion of doubts. Doubting Christians there are, but doubting faith there is none. And it is only when their faith is very low that there is any place for doubt. "O thou of little faith, wherefore didst thou doubt?" The religion of which God is the author cannot be a religion of doubts. He is the immutable Truth. There is no room for conjectures, or mere opinions. It is a dishonour to its glorious Revealer, to say upon a subject of eternal hope, "That is my opinion." Your opinion—and to what more is it entitled than the opinion of another man? But when you speak peremptorily, "This is the truth of God," the ground is entirely changed—then "to the law and the testimony." Accordingly the declaration of Paul has no conjecture about it. He speaks with the confidence of a man intimately acquainted with Jesus Christ: "I know whom I have believed." A gracious boldness, for an example of which you may in vain turn over the ten thousand pages of philosophical Christians. They know nothing of Jesus Christ, the Saviour. They have a great many notions; they sport their several opinions; they are very wise in their own conceit; but about the Lord Jesus, his glory, and his grace, whatever they may prate, they know nothing, and have not the effrontery to pretend that they know anything: for the object of all their philosophy is to strip him of his glory, and to fritter away his grace, till it is not worth a sinner's acceptance. But what says Paul? I know him: there is no uncertainty in the matter; I know him, and am persuaded that he is able to keep what I have committed unto him.

II. We are thus brought to the second point: which is the apostle's confidence that everything is safe in the hands of Jesus Christ.

Here two inquiries challenge our notice: First, what had the apostle committed unto his Saviour? Second, whence arose his assurance that it was perfectly safe in his hands?

1. What was the deposit which Paul had committed to Jesus Christ? It was evidently something personal; something about which, if his hope were deceived, he might be put to shame; some-

thing in which he peculiarly acted as a believer. What was this? What could it be but his immortal soul, his redeemed body, his whole interest in the salvation of God? Men in health and spirits may talk, and do talk, with lightness and gaiety of their own decease, and affect to think it strange that any but a villain should entertain the least apprehension about his appearance before God. But when age, accident, or sickness proclaims their course to be nearly run, and the stock of life to be almost exhausted; when the chill atmosphere of the grave smites them with the last ague, and death's icy hand begins to lay hold upon their frame; when the world, with all its illusions, fades upon the sight, and possesses no more the power of charming; when Eternity rises in all its magnitude—displays its dread realities—draws back the curtain from the judgment-seat—announces the approach of the righteous Judge, and the necessary and speedy appearance before him: O, then lightness and gaiety flee away. They have other thoughts altogether about putting off this body. Nothing but the Christian's hope can sustain their spirits. Then there is seen an emphasis in his words of faith, which was not comprehended before: his brow, glittering in the death-sweat, is encircled with a glory which sheds infinite contempt upon the baubles of earth, and commands them to remove with their impertinence to a respectful distance. O, I have seen a believer preparing to resign his soul into the hands of his dear Redeemer; have seen him make a practical comment upon the declaration of Paul; have seen how infinitely trifling and foolish the world appears when she presumes to draw near him, and to open her absurd lips. The very worldling could not endure it. Then is the moment of the dying conqueror's triumph. He commends his spirit to him that loved him and washed him in his own blood; commits his body to the Resurrection and the Life—commits it "in sure and certain hope" of its being raised again to eternal life: and, as the breath departs from his lips, he shouts, Salvation! and is away, amidst the alleluias of angels, to the "bosom of his Father and his God." What filled him with ecstacy at the arrival of that event which is nature's terror, and from which most of his race shrink and shudder? It was this: "I know whom I have believed, and am persuaded that he is able to keep what I have committed to him against that day." And in what light, think you, does this faith contemplate the Lord Jesus, in trusting him with so precious a deposit? As a creature? a man? a mere man? "frail and peccable?" They who risk themselves in such hands, may; but they must sink down to hell with all the faith they have. A man! a mere man! like myself! I would not thus intrust my body, nor a single member of it, to the mightiest angel that God ever created. O no! no! when a Christian anticipates his departure to the eternal world, he must have other and better security. Heaven is not more distant from earth, than is the ground of his confidence from such a broken reed. And never did you hear, nor will you ever hear in future, Paul's language from the mouth of one who makes such desperate experiments with his immortality. But,

2. Whence arose the apostle's persuasion that all is safe in the hands of Jesus Christ? He knew what the Redeemer is; what he has promised; and what pledges he has given both of his ability and faithfulness.

1st. Who the Redeemer is. The only begotten Son of God, the brightness of the Father's glory, and the express image of his person. The Lord of the invisible world, who was dead and is alive, and lives for evermore, and has the keys of hell and death. His word equally raised the dead and paralyzed the living. He commanded the unclean spirits, and they obeyed him, with fearful deprecations of his power. He trod upon the earth, as upon a province of his government. The submissive elements performed his word. He is now in heaven, at the right hand of God; angels and principalities and powers being made subject to him. He is given to be head over all things to the church, and makes all things work together for good to them that love God, to them that are called according to his purpose. The light of the Divinity is in his eye; the thunder of God's power is in his arm; and he is most worthy of all the confidence which our souls can concentrate.

2d. Paul knew what the Redeemer has promised. Hear—"I give to all my sheep eternal life," and "they shall never perish, neither shall any one pluck them out of my hand."—"He that believeth on me shall never perish, but I will raise him up at the last day."—"Where I am, there shall also my servant be."—"To him that overcometh will I grant to sit with me on my throne, even as I also overcame and am set down with my Father on his throne." Who that shares in these "exceeding great and precious promises," can dispute that Paul had the best reason in the world to believe the " Amen, the faithful and true Witness?"—to believe him without hesitation—to believe him with his whole heart and soul? " Where is doubting then?" Who dares admit even the thought, that the Lord Jesus will break his word? Admit for an instant the thought that God should lie! Where is doubting then, I repeat? It is excluded. By what law? Of works? Nay; but by the law of faith.

3d. The Lord Jesus Christ had given very sufficient pledges of his ability and faithfulness to keep what was committed to him, in what he had done for the apostle; and in what he had done in him; and he was multiplying the reasons of his confidence, by what he was then continuing to do for him.

1. What had Jesus Christ said or done for Paul? The same that he has said or done for all the household of God. He became Paul's surety; obeyed perfectly the law of condemnation; authorized him, in humble faith, to claim and plead that obedience, in the room of his own disobedience. He clothed Paul with righteousness; the righteousness of God; the righteousness of God by faith; directing and enabling him to make it his own, and to present it as such, where it would be properly valued and sure to be accepted—at the bar of infinite Justice. He well knew what place should be assigned to it in the justification of a sinner. He placed it between himself and the righteous God: and glorified it accordingly, as his perfect protection against the stroke of divine justice; as his only and unfailing title to eternal life; as that pure gold, in which the furnace of ultimate trial should not detect a particle of dross, nor a single flaw. Not a syllable would he hear of any works but the works of Jesus Christ, to justify him before God. "That I may be found in him," exclaims he, "not having mine own righteousness which is of the law, but that which is through the faith of Christ, the righteousness which is of God by faith."

This, indeed, is a vital part in the justification of sinful men. Many seem to think that they have no need of anything but pardon. How then can they be justified by a sentence according to law, which enjoins perfect obedience? How can they become entitled to eternal life, which was originally promised to such obedience? What has overturned God's constitution? What has broken the connection, established by himself, between the condition and the reward? Nay, that constitution stands; and sinners, if justified at all, must be justified according to its terms— by obedience, by perfect obedience; but not by such obedience, be it remembered, as you can perform. You are all as an unclean thing, and all your righteousness as filthy rags. This renders the plan of grace so wonderful in our eyes; so infinitely worthy of the wisdom of God. The second Adam, who is the Lord from heaven, has stepped into the first Adam's place, and done what he as our covenant-head ought to have done; he has fulfilled the righteousness of the law. Thence his precious name, Jehovah our righteousness. Of this Paul was very certain: and it was one reason of his committing his eternal interests into the hands of Jesus Christ, with the perfect assurance that they would be safe there. Do you, my dear brethren, follow so blessed an example? Cast away, in your dealings with your Creator, "to the moles and to the bats," everything, everything that can, by any possibility of construction, be reckoned as your own righteousness. The very best of it, trusted in, is no better than a mill-stone about your necks; and when God arises to judgment, will sink you to "bottomless perdition." Lay hold of that one righteousness of Jesus Christ, which is able to cover all who take refuge in it, from martyred Abel down to the last believer who shall cry, "Lord, save me, I perish."

In the next place, Jesus Christ had paid Paul's debt. He owed nothing less than his soul to the violated law of God: and had not his Saviour interposed, the forfeit must have been exacted. But Christ became his security for the amount of that forfeit. He put his own neck under the sword of justice, and redeemed the life of the disciple by the surrender of his own; redeemed it, without his wish or knowledge—redeemed it, while he was yet a blasphemer, and a persecutor, and injurious; that in his case, as a ringleader of rebellion; that in me first—in me as chief—" Jesus Christ might show all long-suffering for a pattern to them who should afterwards believe on him to life everlasting."—" For when the fulness of the time was come, God sent forth his Son, made of a woman, made under the law, to redeem them that were under the law, that we might receive the adoption of sons." Thus, as their representative, sustaining their persons, meeting all the claims which the righteousness of God preferred, answering all accusations against them, facing every adversary, did the beloved One, as their substitute, and for their benefit, lay down his most precious life for the lives of his chosen. The temptations of the evil one, the unbelief and contradiction of sinners, the insolence of his persecutors, and all the degradations of his humbled state; the whole weight of the curse of God, which would have crushed a world of angels; did he endure, the just for the unjust, that he might bring us to God. Then was the law magnified and made honourable—more magnified and made more honourable, than it would have been by the unsinning obedience of all the creatures to all eternity. Then he " by himself purged our sins"—then he paid the price of redemption for an innumerable multitude of prisoners, whom he " bought unto God by his blood;" and having achieved the glorious work, "entered into the holy place, and for ever sat down at the right hand of God, the Majesty on high." There are some who imagine, and who say, "that we know not, nor does it concern us to know, in what manner the sacrifice of Christ is connected with the forgiveness of sins." And grieved I am to find in this number a writer who has done good service to the cause of truth, by stripping the philosophical Christianity of the day of its borrowed plume, and exposing to the abhorrence of every reasonable man all the nakedness of its pretences to learning, to candour, to superior light, and all the unbounded insolence with which it treats the Word of God itself. I allude to Magee on the Atonement, whose words I have quoted above. But our Lord has not left us in the dark on this point, of the justification of a sinner. We thank his blessed name, that we do know precisely, for he has explained to us, as fully as any doctrine in the whole Bible, the connection which his sacrifice has with the remission of our sins. It is because he was "made sin for us," that we are "made the righteousness of God in him;" because he "bare our sins and carried our sorrows," that " by his stripes we are healed." Had not Jesus been our representative, we should have known nothing, and could have known nothing, about the question, whether there is forgiveness with God. But because he took our place, therefore our sins are expiated. Because he bore the penalty due to us, therefore we are freely forgiven for his name's sake, and we rejoice in hope of the glory of God. O believer, cling to this gracious connection between

Christ's suffering and your release, as to the sheet-anchor of your salvation. This and this alone will bear you up, when earth and earthly things are sinking around you. Paul trusted mightily to it. Therefore he was persuaded that there need be no fear of anything committed to the Redeemer's hands.

2. Consider what Jesus Christ had done in the apostle. All that he had done without, had its counterpart within his soul. He had wrought out for him an everlasting salvation, and it was necessary that he should be put in possession of it—had purchased for him a heavenly kingdom, and the next thing was to make him fit for the enjoyment of it. Briefly, he turned Paul into a new man—turned him from darkness unto light; from Satan unto God; from sin unto holiness; changed the relentless persecutor into the suffering lamb; gave to all his affections a holy bias; to all his faculties a heavenly point; to all his pursuits a hallowed direction; filled him with love to Himself and to the souls of men; so that he counted not his life dear unto him, that he might "fulfil the ministry which he had received of the Lord Jesus, to testify the gospel of the grace of God." This was, to Paul himself, the most stupendous miracle in his history. Could he afterwards question whether the Lord Jesus has "power over all flesh;" over all spirit; when he had, within his own bosom, a living demonstration, no more equivocal than the pulsations of his heart, that the word of the Lord Jesus Christ can convert the fiercest enemy into the most tender and faithful friend? And could he be at a loss; could he hesitate a moment, about committing that soul of his, with all its eternal interests, into hands which had done so great things for him and in him?

3. Much as Jesus Christ had done for Paul, he had far more to do for him, ere his work was finished; and was every day giving fresh tokens of his care and love. He was actually in the highest heavens interceding for the apostle. His intercession we may conceive to be an authoritative exhibition of his accepted sacrifice, in behalf of his people. Whatever he had purchased for them, he claims as a matter of right to be conferred upon them in such manner, degree, and season, as the Infinite Wisdom shall determine. Thus he sympathizes with their sorrows: "We have not a high priest who cannot be touched with a feeling of our infirmities." And the secret communications of that sympathy are of infinite value.

He supplies their present wants, both of body and soul. "He who hangs creation on his arm, and feeds it at his board, will not let slip a ransomed child, nor let it starve." It was not a vain lesson that he taught his disciples: "Give us this day our daily bread." Moreover, he holds their souls in life. The riches of glory treasured up in Christ Jesus, are the fund upon which they draw for their succour in every time of need. If their graces languish, he revives and quickens them. If they are scanty, he giveth more grace. If they are hard beset in the spiritual warfare, he throws around them "the shield of his salvation," and in the end makes them "more than conquerors."

Jesus Christ sends down the Holy Spirit to instruct. He compensates the personal absence of the Saviour. The monitions of this heavenly teacher cause the most simple to be wonderful proficients in divine things. They "grow in grace, and in the knowledge of our Lord and Saviour Jesus Christ." He sends him to refresh: He is in them "a well of water springing up to everlasting life." He sends him to invigorate: They are "strengthened with all might by his Spirit in the inner man." He sends him to console: His name is Comforter; and his consolations are neither few nor small. He sends him to prosper them in difficult enterprises: They succeed, "not by might nor by power, but by my Spirit, saith the Lord."

Jesus Christ encircled Paul in his arms in the midst of personal danger. His path lay through snares and treacheries, and deaths unnumbered. If he fought with beasts at Ephesus; if he was in the lion's mouth at Rome; if he was stoned at Lystra; his kind and faithful Lord delivered him from them all. "Fear not, Paul," he had said, "no man shall set upon thee to hurt thee;" and he was true to his promise: and Paul was so sure of it, that he counted confidently on his protection. "The Lord," says he, "shall deliver me from every evil work, and shall preserve me unto his heavenly kingdom."

By all these means Paul's sanctification was improved. He became every day more meet than he was the day before, for an abundant entrance into his Master's kingdom. He accounted nothing done to purpose, while anything remained to be done. Not even his past attainments, great and glorious as they were; not even the career of his services, though the most brilliant among the ranks of the saved, could check his ardour for further attainment, for higher Christian distinction. "I count not myself," says he, "to have apprehended, but this one thing I do, forgetting those things which are behind, and reaching forward to those things that are before, I press toward the mark, for the prize of the high calling of God in Christ Jesus."

Now put all these considerations together, and ask whether Paul's confidence in the ability and grace of the Lord Jesus, to keep what he had committed unto him, till the day of final decision, was weak or chimerical? Whether it was not the most sober conclusion, drawn from the firmest premises? Whether it left any possible room for misgivings and fears? And whether Paul has not exemplified, in his own person, the privilege common to all believers, and the true and proper effect of the religion which they profess?

Let us try if we cannot reap some profitable instruction from this interesting subject.

1. Every real believer has direct and confidential transactions with the Lord Jesus Christ. Like Paul, he has committed all that he is, and all that he has; whatever is most precious for time and for eternity; his body, his soul, his hope, his reversion in heaven, to the hands of his faithful Redeemer. Have you done so, my hearers? Have you done it, professed Christians? Ah, how wide a difference does this make between the formalist and the genuine disciple! Let me ask again, for the question is a vital one: You who name the name of Jesus, who pass for the converts of his grace, and have sworn fealty to his cause, what have you to say? Did you ever give yourselves up formally, fully, irrevocably, to be his property, and at his disposal? When, where, how, did you make the blessed surrender? How do you prove the fact? What obedience do you perform? What self-denials do you endure? What sacrifices, even of the most worthless of your possessions, the trash of this earth, do you offer? Who, of all the numerous retainers of the Christian name, of all the decent professors of godliness, will trust his Redeemer for to-morrow's bread? Who of them would not rather rely on the respectable signer of a bank-note, than upon all the promises of the faithful God? Were it put to the trial, who of them would not grasp the paper, and let go the truth and the oath of a faithful God, who

cannot lie, among the uncertainties of life? And can any man, with such practical feelings, really dupe himself with the persuasion that he trusts the Lord Jesus for the kingdom of the just? That he believes in that most generous sacrifice which Jesus Christ made for him; the blood of his cross? Not a word! Not a single word! He is as absolute an unbeliever in the Captain of our salvation, and as absolute an idolater, in his own way, as any poor wretch that ever threw himself under the wheels of Juggernaut. And that he will find, if death overtake him in his present condition, when the stone which the builders rejected shall grind him to powder. Bear with me, my friends, I may not prophecy smooth things; may not palliate; I must declare the whole truth, on the peril of treason to my heavenly Master. If any of you find it cut deep, "there is balm in Gilead, and a Physician there." I can do nothing but commend you to the Lord, the Healer.

2. Let us remark a peculiar property in the Christian religion, as it exists in the Bible, and in the hearts of those who are thoroughly under its influence; unwavering confidence of spiritual and unseen realities; "I know whom I have believed."

The religion of Jesus Christ is the religion of faith. It acknowledges no conjecture, no surmises, no peradventure. It rests upon the surest of all foundations; that impenetrable rock on which the gates of hell can make not the least impression; the testimony of the living God. It demands the unhesitating consent of our hearts. It contains no provision for doubts. Doubting, in every possible degree, is an implied impeachment of the veracity of its divine Author, and most signally dishonours his glorious name. Every Christian in the world ought to say, as peremptorily as the apostle, "I know whom I have believed;" and to be carried by his faith as fearlessly and triumphantly along as he was, through duties, difficulties, and death itself, perfectly sure that he shall find it all safe at that day. Then why is the fact so different? Why is the world so full of doubts, and fears, and lamentations, even on the part of Christians themselves, that there is scarcely heard any more the "voice of joy and rejoicing in the tabernacles of the righteous?" The fact is indisputable; and allow me to say it is one of those high indecencies which disgrace your profession. It does not become you, Christians, to act and to talk as if your religion were no better than a human speculation, and your Redeemer an adventurer, who may or who may not fulfil the expectations he has raised, as shall hereafter be found convenient. There is not one of you who would not feel himself injured and insulted by the twentieth part of that mistrust in his truth, which he himself is habitually exercising, ('tis well that he does it ignorantly,) towards Jesus Christ.

But still, how is the fact to be explained? Very easily, though not very honourably, for those who furnish evidence of its existence. A neglect to cultivate grace already bestowed, opens the door of the heart to a multitude of those evil doubts. An untender walk; more according to the fashion of this world, than according to the will of God, than your duty, your privileges, your promises, your obligations to redeeming love, exact; grieves the good Spirit of God; mightily shakes your hope; and brings your souls into bondage and terrors. A guilty conscience and a settled peace, or an unbending faith, cannot dwell together in the same bosom. Omissions of known duties; of opportunities of serving and honouring our Master, when fairly put in our way; do naturally and necessarily invite this rebuke. We cannot expect to enjoy the comforts of faith, while the uses for which it was given are unfaithfully overlooked.

But that which is the most common and extensive cause of the criminal state and temper exhibited by the Christian community, in the article of their confidence before God, is walking by sight, and not by faith. Christians are formed for an immortality of action, blessedness, and glory, in a future state and a better world. Earth has no principles from which to draw any conclusions, about the employments or pleasures of heaven. The philosopher and the clown; the men of large or of little acquaintance with human nature; the most refined reason and the most gross, are alike ignorant and foolish on this point. We know nothing at all but what God has been pleased to tell us. And he has told us no more than is absolutely necessary for our present Christian being. "Thus saith the Lord," contains the ground of all our convictions, the elements of all our reasonings, upon the approaching condition of the just. We must take his word for everything; and take it solely because he hath said it. Yet our principal concern in this world is with the invisible realities of the next, and with those affections, principles, and habits, which are linked in with them, by a continuity of existence; which are the great preparatives for them; and are nurtured, and strengthened, by means and influences as much depending upon our faith, as is our interest in the realities themselves.

Now it is perfectly evident, that a life of mere sense, such a life as is common to men who pretend to nothing more than sense can give them, is utterly hostile to the Christian's hope and calling. And yet what do we see, I do not say among those who profess, but among those who, we must hope, experience the faith of God's elect? What, but an incessant contradiction to their heavenly vocation? They believe strongly, when all their sensations go on comfortably. But the instant anything happens to disturb these sensations, their faith and their confidence flag. It is all well so long as they feel comfortably; but the moment anything untoward happens to their bodily perceptions—if they do not feel well—if their health is disordered—if their spirits are depressed—if the east wind affects their nerves; melancholy forebodings invade them; their past experience is all a delusion; their hope vanishes; despair fills their minds: and so the whole of their confidence turns out to be something which depend upon their physical health, or some accidental circumstance. Do you call this believing on the Son of God? Does his faithfulness rest upon the fickleness of your frame? Or is he to be insulted with your doubts, whenever the mechanism of your body is disturbed? Nay, if you ask for better assurance than his words of promise; if that will not fortify you against the ills of life and death; if you have not learned, with the father of the faithful, against hope to believe in hope, not staggering at the promise of God through unbelief, make thorough work of it; cast away his name, his badge, and his livery; take all the comfort that sense can bring you; but do not, whatever else you pretend to, do not set up for a believer in Jesus Christ.

Yet to those who can and do trust the faithful Saviour and his unaltering word, I say, Fear not. Your Lord will perfect that which concerneth you. Your interests are infinitely safe. Your small concerns, as you may account them, are bound up with him in the bundle of everlasting memory; and will no more be forgotten than the concerns of a world. However seemingly worthless your deposit, he will remember it to your unspeakable joy. Give then your fears to the winds. Order all your doubts to be gone. And let the gracious emotion pass from heart to heart, till the shout of confidence shall drown the voice of repining; and the world and the church shall be surprised with the triumph of that song: "I know whom I have believed; and am persuaded that he is able to keep what I have committed to him, until that day." Amen.

SERMON X.*

THE EVANGELICAL MINISTRY EXEMPLIFIED.

ACTS xx. 17-27.

"And from Miletus he sent to Ephesus, and called the elders of the church. And when they were come to him, he said unto them, Ye know from the first day that I came into Asia, after what manner I have been with you at all seasons, serving the Lord with all humility of mind, and with many tears and temptations, which befell me by the lying in wait of the Jews; and how I kept back nothing that was profitable unto you, but have showed you, and have taught you publicly, and from house to house, testifying both to the Jews, and also to the Greeks, repentance toward God, and faith toward our Lord Jesus Christ. And now, behold, I go bound in the spirit unto Jerusalem, not knowing the things that shall befall me there: save that the Holy Ghost witnesseth in every city, saying, that bonds and afflictions abide me. But none of these things move me, neither count I my life dear unto myself, so that I may finish my course with joy, and the ministry which I have received of the Lord Jesus, to testify the gospel of the grace of God. And now, behold, I know that ye all, among whom I have gone preaching the kingdom of God, shall see my face no more. Wherefore I take you to record this day, that I am pure from the blood of all men. For I have not shunned to declare unto you the whole counsel of God."

NEXT to our Lord Jesus Christ, the name of which figures most gloriously in the early stages of the Christian story, is that of the Apostle Paul. The grandeur of his mind, his intellectual and moral magnanimity, his heroic devotion, his patience in suffering; his powerful genius, his decision, his eloquence, his zeal, shine in every page of his writings, raise the admiration and awe the spirits of his readers, and make them feel that they enter into communion with a being of superior order. But it is not that peculiar great-

---

* Preached in Murray Street Church, December 2, 1821, on the occasion of resigning his charge of his congregation.

ness which was inseparable from every act of the man, and excites our veneration while it forbids our rivalship, that creates our deepest interest in his character. Our understandings may be penetrated with light which has no power of warming our hearts. The most profound respect does not necessarily call forth our love. Our affections must be won; they cannot be stormed. To this principle of our nature God has been pleased to pay particular regard, in the first heralds of the cross. However diversified their qualities and attainments; whatever be the zeal of one, the potency of argument in another, the intrepid courage of a third, that which bears the sway in all, is their loveliness. Our hearts are captivated by the same process which subdues our understandings. Nothing, for example, can be more fair and unanswerable, than when Paul closes in his argument with the subtle philosopher; nothing more terrible than when he deals out the thunders of God among the gainsayers: and nothing more exquisitely tender, than his carriage toward the timid and scrupulous disciple. If ever a man knew how to wind his way into the human soul; how to coil around him its most sacred affections; how to explore the secret place of tears, and to put in motion all its kindest sympathies, the Apostle Paul was certainly that man. You know that this has always been with me a favourite theme; that my heart has enlarged, my imagination brightened; and my steps have trodden almost upon fairy ground, when they have been roused and quickened by the name of Paul. But on no occasion does he loom so high, and shine so gloriously, as in the context. All his powers are concentrated; his feelings are condensed into a point; the covering is shoved aside from his breast, and you see, without disguise, the workings of his ingenuous, his upright, his mighty mind. This parting address to the elders of Ephesus, well deserved a place in the holy volume; and deserves it in our best regards, in our most reverential remembrance.

I propose to give you, on this occasion, an analysis of part of the apostle's discourse. You will find it to contain an account of the manner in which he discharged his ministry among the Ephesians, ver. 18-21; his extreme devotedness to the cause in which he was embarked, ver. 22-24; and his presentiment of its being the closing of his ministry, with an affectionate appeal to their consciences, and the ground of that appeal, 25-27.

I. An account of the manner in which he discharged his ministry among the Ephesians, ver. 18-21.

1. He served the Lord with all "humility of mind." The apostles, unlike many of their pretended successors, aimed at no worldly honours, distinctions, nor titles. "Rabbi" is not to be met with in their whole vocabulary. The name of *lords bishops* was utterly unknown to them, nor would they have thought it a meet appellation for the followers of a crucified Master. Whatever be its origin or use, the spirit of the apostles disclaims it, and holds no fellowship with the temper which it is calculated to cherish. Servants of the Lord Jesus Christ, was their highest earthly designation, and rank, and glory. Paul had talents, and powers, and proficiency, which fairly entitle him to a pre-eminence among his brethren; but the only pre-eminence which he courted, was a pre-eminence in dangerous service to the glory of his Master. Let little men sigh after these trifles; it suits their capacities; it is fit for their ambition; but neither an apostle, nor an apostolic man, wishes for any more dignified style, or holy occupation, than to be known in the church as "serving the Lord."

There is a consideration which weighs much with every gracious heart, and is not, cannot be, easily forgotten—the immense distance between the Lord Jesus and his most faithful servants. He, the living God; they, creatures low in the scale of being, when compared with other creatures which "excel in strength, yet obey his commandments, hearkening to the voice of his word."—" The treasure is in earthen vessels, that the excellency of the power might be of God." The angels, who look, with studious anxiety, into the mysteries of redemption by Jesus Christ, would thankfully have accepted the appointment of *ambassadors* of the cross. But God has seen fit to confer that honour upon men of like passions with others; and commanded the angels to be ministering spirits. When we add, that these heralds of his truth were sinners like other men, called by divine grace out of the common condemnation, and sent to tell their fellow-sinners that "there is forgiveness with God," how august the message! how humbling to the messenger! He cannot, or ought not to, forget one single moment, that "by grace he is saved;" and the more profound and lively his sense of this truth, the more completely will he enter into the feelings of Paul, who served the Lord with all humility of mind. Could Paul need a monitor to remind him that he was once a blasphemer, and a persecutor, and injurious; that he obtained mercy because the "grace of our Lord Jesus Christ was exceeding abundant," and obtained it for this end, that in him, first, the Saviour "might show forth all long-suffering to them who should believe on him to life everlasting? He could not open his lips to proclaim the riches of redeeming love, without at the same time exhibiting himself as a monument of that love. No wonder that his service was so strongly tinged with humility. There is nothing, my brethren, which can so humble and elevate a man's soul as a powerful experience of the love of Christ. Nor is anything more unbecoming, more desolating to the holy character—more indicative of communion with the devil, than clerical superciliousness.

Unassuming as were the apostle's manners—innocent as was his conversation—useful as was his whole life, his course was nevertheless a course of trouble. For,

2. His ministry was marked by many tears, and many "temptations, which befell him him by the lying in wait of the Jews."

The tears of an apostle have upon our minds a most melting influence. Our own are disposed to mingle with them upon the bare mention of his. But, after all, what called them forth? You do not hear of his weeping before the Sanhedrim at Jerusalem—before the Roman governor, into whose presence he was brought in chains. No! *there* was a proper scene for a spirit which neither the Sanhedrim, nor the Roman governor, in all his authority, could subdue or bow. He appeared before them less as the criminal than as the judge. His mind rose, his spirit towered, till all before him seemed to be, what indeed they were, comparatively very little men. What then could bring tears, and many tears, from the eyes of a man who could make governors tremble on their bench of justice? The overflowings of his own benevolent heart! When he saw how men slighted their own mercies—how they rejected, some with civil, some with contumelious air, as they do at this hour, the salvation of God, and "put away from them the words of eternal life;" having before him the perils which they encountered, and a full view of the ruin which they could not escape, his whole soul was dissolved in tenderness, and he wept his tears of bitterness over their infatuation. The terror of the Roman government could not extort from his firmness a single drop—the sight of an immortal soul, perishing in its iniquity, and pleased with its delusions, altogether unmanned him, and suffused his cheeks with tears, which in other cases would have been the sign of weakness.

Objections and oppositions were not the only impediments of the apostle's career. Many trials befell him "by the lying in wait of the Jews." That Paul was their countryman, in whom they had prided themselves; that he was among the Pharisees, whom the nation almost idolized; that he had been their ringleader in persecuting the new religion, all passed for nothing. He was now a follower of the crucified Nazarene, and nothing but his blood would assuage their wrath. All the world over, the disciples of the Lord Jesus have been singled out as objects of ultimate violence. It is not to be wondered at in a world under the influence of him who "was a murderer from the beginning." And if their condition is better now, it is because the gospel has triumphed over human madness, and hath put the abettors of wickedness to shame.

Paul trod continually, not amidst vipers and scorpions, but, what is infinitely worse, the snares of hellish men. Every sermon furnished materials for a new conspiracy; every step a track for the bloodhounds. The cowards who shrunk from his eye, would yet venture to stab him from behind. It was only by lying in wait, that the Jews hoped for success. But all this was not to shake the resolution nor alter the conduct of Paul. Such as the grace of our Jesus made him, both the church and her adversaries always found him.

In the midst of these discouragements, nothing could arrest his zeal, nor silence his testimony: "he kept back nothing that was profitable to his Ephesian hearers." Neither the love of fame, nor the hope of gaining a party ever called forth Paul's exertions. His anxiety was to be *useful;* popularity at the expense of duty, had no charms for him. Woe to that preacher who makes his office subservient to the applause of his fellow-men. Whether his hearers approved or disapproved; whether the doctrines coincided with the popular prejudice, or were directly hostile to it, it was the same thing to this wise and gallant apostle. He had to do with " God, who searcheth the hearts;" human opinions dwindled away into their native insignificance, before him "whose judgment is according to truth;" and therefore he kept back nothing that was profitable to those who frequented his ministry. He showed them that truth which admits of no compromise; he had but one doctrine, which he "taught publicly, and from house to house." Be he where he might, in the solemn assembly or in the domestic circle, his instructions were the same. It is the very nature of truth that it should be so. And it equally belongs to imposture to utter things unpleasant in public, and fritter them away in private; or to utter them in private, and suppress them in public. His discourses in the church he followed up with his explanations and applications at home. From house to house the apostle might be tracked upon this line of life.

This passage has been used as furnishing a divine warrant, and proving a divine obligation, to what is termed parochial visitation. Highly important it is no doubt; but men must be careful that they do not convert the sound of words into a divine warrant, and not to require bricks without straw. To prove that apostolic example establishes a precedent for imitation, we must be sure that the circumstances to which it is applied are similar. But this is far from being the case in the present instance. There are two things in which the state of the churches now differs materially from their state in primitive times.

In the first place, they had inspired teachers; who could, therefore, spend the whole week in exhorting, confirming, consoling their converts, without infringing on their preparations for the Lord's day. Our situation is quite different: close and habitual study are necessary for us. And if we cannot get time to attend to it, our ministrations grow uninteresting, and our congregations lean. As for those men who boast of working at the loom all the week, and then acquitting themselves well on the Lord's day, I shall say nothing but that their performances are such as might be expected from the loom; but as far as can well be conceived from the labours of a "workman who rightly divides the word of truth."

In the next place, the primitive churches never permitted themselves to suffer for want of labourers. Their spiritual advancement was, in their eyes, infinitely more valuable than all the pelf which the maintenance of their ministers required. Look over the Acts of the Apostles, and be astonished at the abundance of help which the churches then enjoyed. *Our* economical plan is to make the pastor do the work which was anciently done by three or four, and the very natural consequence follows, the work is *badly* done, or the workman is sacrificed. In our own city, from the accumulation of inhabitants, and their very dispersed residences, if we were to visit as much, or anything like it, as our people are good enough to wish, and unreasonable enough to expect, we should not have an hour left for our proper business; we could make no progress in the knowledge of the scriptures; and not one would be able to preach a sermon worthy a sensible man's hearing. The conclusion is almost self-evident: if congregations will stint themselves in workmen, they must have their work spoiled; and if the work be done at all, they must kill the mind or body of the workman, and sometimes both. Let them not deceive themselves. If they impose hardships which God never commanded, they must expect to go without his blessing.

The burden of Paul's preaching, whether to the Jew or Gentile, was "repentance toward God, and faith toward our Lord Jesus Christ."

That their conceptions and feelings toward God were radically wrong; that these must be altered and purified; and that all their views must centre in our Lord Jesus Christ, as "the way, the truth, and the life," in order to human happiness, his word constantly declares, and the experience of men as constantly confirms. This great truth, "Christ, the wisdom of God and the power of God, flowed alike from the tongue and from the pen of Paul, and was, in fact, "the head and front of his offending," with both Jews and Gentiles. This, however, must be the substance of his testimony. And so it must be still. All who hope to win sinners unto God, and to have them as "crowns of rejoicing" in that day, must, like Paul, "determine to know nothing save Jesus Christ, and him crucified." And cursed with all the curses which are written in this book, be that ministry of which Christ is not the all and in all.

Such is a very feeble outline of the nature of Paul's ministry. O happy, thrice happy, the man who nearly imitates it! We have much reason to blush and be ashamed, when we compare ourselves with this prince of preachers; and have infinite need to address you, my Christian friends, the request of this glorious man of God. "Brethren, pray for us."

II. We are next called to witness Paul's extreme devotedness to the cause in which he was engaged. He was "bound in the spirit to go to Jerusalem." The Holy Ghost put forth a constraining influence upon him to go to that city. He had often heard, and well knew, the voice; had often felt, and well understood, the impression which signified his duty to go to the metropolis of persecution. Of the general nature of the impulse he was well assured. He knew that it came from God, and could not lead him astray. This was sufficient to mark out the course of his obedience. What was to befall him at Jerusalem he could not tell; he only knew that no rest awaited him there. "The Holy Ghost witnessed, that in every city, bonds and afflictions abode him." Go where he would, he was sure that his fidelity would be put to the severest test—sure that whoever found the Christian cause a cause of ease and comfort, it was to be no ease and comfort to him. Well, how does the prospect affect him? He was not such a fanatic as to court pain when he might have avoided it. The school of Baccaria and Voltaire, which teach that the severity of punishment multiplies the offence, was not then known; or, had it been known, would hardly have caught the ear of Paul. He did not dream of fitting himself for the duties of an apostle, by proclaiming war upon the principles of common sense, and the common feelings of human nature. He knew, and never shrinked from the original condition of his Master's service: "Whosoever denieth not himself, and taketh not up his cross, and followeth not after me, cannot be my disciple." Show me the cross, exclaimed this magnanimous man; spread out before me all the self-denials I may be called to endure: be they what they may, I must be a disciple! He did not doubt that his Lord would make up all to him in due season: "for he had respect unto the recompense of the reward."—"None of these things move me; neither count I my life dear unto myself, so that I might finish my course with joy, and the ministry of the Lord Jesus, to testify the gospel of the grace of God."

One of the idlest of human efforts is, the attempt to frighten a man who has deliberately resolved to sacrifice his life, or to succeed in his undertaking. You have lost your hold of him. When you have threatened him with death, you have done your worst, and have no terrors left. It is then that the great commander steps on the scene, and says, "Fear not them that kill the body, and after that have no more that they can do: but I will forewarn you whom ye shall fear: fear him who, after he hath killed, hath power to destroy both soul and body in hell: yea, I say unto you, fear him." Paul entered thoroughly into this feeling: and therefore all appeals to human power and human pains,—to the axe, the gibbet, or the stake, were without effect upon him; for "he endured as seeing him who is invisible." And so, my friends, will it be with us, in proportion as our converse is with eternal realities. Reckon not, when the great trial comes, upon the strength, and courage, and nerves, which have commanded human applause, and secured human expectation. "I cannot argue for Christ," said a female martyr, "but I can burn for him." Her faith was of the same sort with the apostle's; and therefore she did not even count her life dear unto herself, that she might finish her course with joy. My brethren, how could you, the best, the most resolute of you all, abide this test of the apostolic or female martyr? I do not say, that in a life of ease and comfort, which God has vouchsafed to you, you are called to exercise the grace of martyrdom: but I do say, that if, upon your deliberate choice, your preference lean to anything else than our Lord Jesus Christ, you have nothing to expect but that he will cast you out of his kingdom. The apostle was always practical; *i. e.* he never preached Christian duties, or painted Christian trials, without a reference to the possibility of his being called to the performance of the one, or to the endurance of the other. He now felt all the considerations from both press hard upon him. One of his sweet enjoyments arose from the presence and sympathy of his fellow-Christians. He found that this was to be interrupted—to be closed: and that drew from him, in the

III. Place, his presentiment of the present being the last opportunity of converse with his Ephesian friends. "And now, behold, I know that ye all, among whom I have gone preaching the kingdom of God, shall see my face no more!"

There is a relation, and a tenderness of relation, produced between a people and the instrument of their spiritual blessings, which nothing on earth can equal: something which identifies him with all their affections, and which they cannot easily transfer:

something which creates a soothing pillow for him in every bosom: and for which every exchange is little better than a pillow of thorns. On this subject it is impossible for me to enlarge: could I summon up apathy enough, your own feelings would not endure it. Let me, therefore, rather invite you away from this touching theme to Paul's appeal to the consciences of his hearers. Thus runs its terrible but affectionate language: "Wherefore I take you to record this day, that I am pure from the blood of all men: for I have not shunned to declare unto you the whole counsel of God." There is a most awful trust committed by the Lord Jesus to his ministering servants. It is nothing less than the "blood of men." O that they felt this trust more than they sometimes do! You would not see the pulpit converted into a stage for the display of human ingenuity, or perverted to the display of human vanity. These things are lighter than a feather, and lose all their importance in the eyes of a man who remembers that he has an account to settle with God for "blood;" and that he knows not the moment when his account may be demanded. It is observable, and ought to sink deep into your hearts, and especially into the heart of every preacher of the gospel, that Paul accounted himself pure from the blood of men, because he had not concealed from them any part of God's truth. He knew not that policy by which some pulpits have been disgraced, of deferring the declaration of the whole truth to a more convenient season. As if the native enmity of the heart were to be softened by delay—as if it could be reduced by anything but by the truth itself—as if men ever found their audiences more tractable by this kind of forbearance; or were themselves more instrumental in bringing sinners to God: or had the answer of a good conscience more complete in their own bosoms. God, my friends, knows infinitely better than we, what truths are suited to our circumstances, and has revealed them in his book; and accursed be that prudence which suggests the propriety of suppressing any one of them. If there is one trait of a faithful minister more obvious than another, it is this, that he is not afraid nor ashamed to say what God has said before him in his Word.

Here, my beloved friends, is a breathing place for every honest messenger of God's truth: may I be permitted to say that I feel it to be so myself? When the ministry of Paul is the subject, blushes and tears become the sense which I cannot but perceive of the immense disparity. But in this particular, I can stand even in the presence of God, and can say, that in so far as he has been pleased to enlighten me, I have never shunned to declare his whole counsel. You know that, in this matter, I have not "sought glory of men;" have not made their applause, not even your applause, how respectable soever, my object; have never concealed a truth, however unpopular; nor ever asked if it were acceptable or not. It has always been enough for me to have the Word of God on my side. And when that has been clear, you cannot forget how frequently, nay, how habitually, you have been turned over to his tribunal. On this ground I do stand in this awful day of my life. Bear witness against me if I have not told you the truth. Very feebly, I own; very imperfectly, I do confess: but corruptly, never. And, O, my friends, remember that you have a heavy account to render, an account for blood, for your "own blood." I call heaven and earth, and your own consciences, to witness against you this day, that if you perish, "your blood will be upon your own heads, I am clean." With this cheering, but melancholy assurance, I close my ministry among you. Yet let me say, are there any of you to whom that ministry has been sanctified? Bless the Father of mercies; and do not waste your anxieties upon the worthless instrument. "Look unto Jesus, the author and finisher of your faith, to complete in you all the good pleasure of his goodness," till he bring you to his kingdom, shouting, "grace, grace!"

Are there none here, and those whom we respect and love for their amiable and social qualities, yet who never knew what it is to love the Lord Jesus Christ? To whom his truth, proclaimed day after day, has been like water poured into a sieve—all "spilled on the ground, and not gathered up." Let me say to you, my friends, perhaps it is the last time, the day of your reckoning cometh; and you will find that the things so lightly esteemed by you, are not forgotten by your God. Who of you would escape going down to the pit? Who would not? Then hear, and hear it again, and hear it as for eternity: "There is forgiveness with God!" The doors of his mercy are not closed! The very chief of sinners may yet find acceptance with him through his dear Son. "Whosoever will, let him take of the water of life freely; yes, freely;" with all the welcome of God's authority, and all the riches of God's bounty, "freely, so iniquity shall not be his ruin."

It may be expected that on this occasion I should deliver my thoughts concerning the person who is to take my place, and concerning your own part in the selection. How unfit I am for the discharge of these duties, I abundantly feel; and particularly how much easier it is to tell you what you should not do, than what you should. Yet, such as I have, give I unto you; and in that name which you should never hear quoted with lightness or irreverence—the name of Jesus.

I trust you will not choose a *vain* man, who occupies the pulpit more to display himself, than to profit you. Of all the melancholy things seen among men, this is perhaps the most melancholy; a poor sinful being complimenting himself upon the discharge of his office, while the ministering angels look upon him with a mixture of dislike, of shame, and of horror; and while his Judge, before whom he is shortly to appear, regards him with a frown, of which the interpretation is, " Ill done! thou bad and faithless servant; enter thou not into the joy of thy Lord!"

2. Do not choose a *showy* man. Many of these men there are who have only *outside*. You will be as sick of him at last, as you were enamoured of him at first. You will speedily find that he cannot instruct nor edify you; and will be heartily tired of seeing him show himself.

3. Do not choose a man who always preaches upon insulated texts. I care not how powerful or eloquent he may be in handling them. The effect of his power and eloquence will be, to banish a taste for the Word of God, and to substitute the preacher in its place. You have been accustomed to hear that word preached to you in its connection. Never permit that practice to drop. Foreign churches call it *lecturing;* and when done with discretion, I can assure you, that while it is of all exercises the most difficult for the preacher, it is, in the same proportion, the most profitable for you. It has this peculiar advantage, that in going through a book of Scripture, it spreads out before you all sorts of character, and all forms of opinion; and gives the preacher an opportunity of striking every kind of evil and of error, without subjecting him to the invidious suspicion of aiming his discourses at individuals.

4. Do not choose a man of *dubious* principles. The truth of God was given to be *proclaimed;* not suppressed. It is a " city set on a hill;" a light which must shine, and not be smothered under a

bushel. When I hear of a man's preaching for years together in such a manner that his most attentive and intelligent hearers are unable to conjecture what his sentiments are upon the cardinal truths of revelation, I cannot avoid pronouncing him a traitor. His business is to preach Christ; and not to treat the gospel as if it were a bundle of mere negations: and see his hearers sink down, one after another, in death, uninstructed, unwarned, unprepared, through his negligence: and himself following them with all the "deep damnation" of their blood upon his soul. O! it is inconceivably fearful!

5. Above all things, it is devoutly to be hoped that you will never invite to the "care of your souls," one who cares nothing about them. I mean more particularly, for I would not be misunderstood, a man who belongs to those who miscall themselves "rational Christians." Against these men I have ever warned you, as the enemies of our Lord Jesus Christ, and all that is valuable in his religion, and peculiar in his salvation. I know well that this congregation is considered by them as the very focus of what they term bigotry; and I do rejoice that thus far I and you have been counted worthy to suffer shame for his name. Long may it continue so! This pulpit, this church, were destined to the glory of the Lord Jesus. Let them never be polluted by a foot, nor profaned by a tongue, which are not moved by his honour.

I cannot better describe the character of a profitable ministry than it is done to my hand in a work too little known, "The Directory for Public Worship," under the head "Of the Preaching of the Word."

"Ordinarily, the subject of his sermon is to be some text of Scripture, holding forth some principle or head of religion, or suitable to some special occasion; or he may go on in some chapter, psalm, or book of the Holy Scripture, as he shall see fit.

"Let the introduction to his text be brief and perspicuous, drawn from the text itself, or context, or some parallel place, or general sentence of Scripture.

"If the text be a long one, (as in histories or parables it sometimes must be,) let him give a brief sum of it; if short, a paraphrase thereof, if need be: in both, looking diligently to the scope of the text, and pointing at the chief heads and grounds of doctrine which he is to raise from it.

"In analysing and dividing his text, he is to regard more the order of matter than of words: and neither to burden the memory of the hearers in the beginning with too many members of division, nor to trouble their minds with obscure terms of art.

"In raising doctrines from the text, his care ought to be, *First*, That the matter be the truth of God. *Secondly*, That it be a truth contained in or grounded on that text, that the hearers may discern how God teacheth it from thence. *Thirdly*, That he chiefly insist upon those doctrines which are principally intended, and make most for the edification of the hearers.

"The doctrine is to be expressed in plain terms; or if anything in it need explication, it is to be opened, and the consequence also from the text cleared. The parallel places of Scripture confirming the doctrine are rather to be plain and pertinent than many, and (if need be) somewhat insisted upon, and applied to the purpose in hand.

"The arguments or reasons are to be solid, and, as much as may be, convincing. The illustrations, of what kind soever, ought to be full of light, and such as may convey the truth into the hearer's heart with spiritual delight.

"If any doubt, obvious from Scripture, reason, or prejudice of the hearers, seem to arise, it is very requisite to remove it, by reconciling the seeming differences, answering the reasons, and discovering and taking away the causes of prejudice and mistake. Otherwise it is not fit to detain the hearers with propounding or answering vain or wicked cavils, which as they are endless, so the propounding and answering of them doth more hinder than promote edification.

"He is not to rest in general doctrine, although ever so much cleared and confirmed, but to bring it home to special use, by application to his hearers; which, although it prove a work of great difficulty to himself, requiring much prudence, zeal, and meditation, and to the natural and corrupt man will be very unpleasant: yet he is to endeavour to perform it in such a manner that his auditors may feel the Word of God to be quick and powerful, and a discerner of the thoughts and intents of the heart; and that, if any unbeliever or ignorant person be present, he may have the secrets of his heart made manifest, and give glory to God.

"In the use of instruction or information in the knowledge of some truth, which is a consequence from his doctrine, he may (when convenient) confirm it by a few firm arguments from the text in hand, and other places of Scripture, or from the nature of that commonplace in divinity, whereof that truth is a branch.

"In confutation of false doctrines, he is neither to raise an old heresy from the grave, nor to mention a blasphemous opinion unnecessarily; but if the people be in danger of an error, he is to confute it soundly, and endeavour to satisfy their judgments and consciences against all objections.

"In exhorting to duties, he is, as he seeth cause, to teach also the means that help to the performance of them.

"In dehortation, reprehension, and public admonition, (which require special wisdom,) let him, as there shall be cause, not only discover the nature and greatness of the sin, with the misery attending it, but also show the danger his hearers are in to be overtaken and surprised by it, together with the remedies and best way to avoid it.

"In applying comfort whether general against all temptations, or particular against some special troubles or terrors, he is carefully to answer such objections as a troubled heart and afflicted spirit may suggest to the contrary.

"But the servant of Christ, whatever his method be, is to perform his whole ministry.

"Painfully, not doing the work of the Lord negligently.

"Plainly, that the weakest may understand; delivering the truth not in the enticing words of man's widom, but in demonstration of the Spirit and of power, lest the cross of Christ should be made of none effect; abstaining also from an unprofitable use of unknown tongues, strange phrases, and cadences of sounds and words; sparingly citing sentences of ecclesiastical or human writers, ancient or modern, be they ever so elegant.

"Faithfully, looking at the honour of Christ, the conversion, edification, and salvation of the people, not as his own gain or glory; keeping nothing back which may promote these holy ends; giving to every one his own portion, and bearing indifferent respect unto all, without neglecting the meanest, or sparing the greatest, in their sins.

"Wisely, framing all his doctrines, exhortations, and especially his reproofs, in such a manner as may be most likely to prevail:

showing all due respect to each man's person and place, and not mixing his own passion or bitterness.

"Gravely, as becometh the Word of God; shunning all such gesture, voice, and expression, as may occasion the corruption of men to despise him and his ministry.

"With loving affection, that the people may see all coming from his godly zeal, and hearty desire to do them good. And,

"As taught of God, and persuaded in his own heart, that all that he teacheth is the truth of Christ; and walking before his flock as an example to them in it; earnestly, both in private and public, recommending his labours to the blessing of God, and watchfully looking to himself, and the flock whereof the Lord hath made him overseer: so shall the doctrine of truth be preserved uncorrupt, many souls be converted and built up, and himself receive manifold comforts of his labours even in this life, and afterward the crown of glory laid up for him in the world to come."

After all, be it never forgotten, that it is the Lord Jesus himself who must send you a pastor after his own heart. The ministry of the word is his ascension-gift; and if there is one thing more than another for which he will be inquired of by his church, this is the important thing. Then look up to him for the Holy Spirit, as the "spirit of grace and supplication." Pray for the effusion of his heavenly grace. Pray in secret, in private, and in public; in your closets, in your families, in your social meetings, after such form as you may find most suitable to your circumstances; be instant in your entreaties to the throne of grace, and give the Hearer of prayer no rest, till he hear you from his holy heaven, and grant you the hallowed desires of your hearts.

And now, my dear friends, the moment of so much trembling anxiety, of which you and I have turned away from the sight; the moment of severance is come. Yet in the midst of those agitations which it excites, there are two considerations which comfort and soothe my spirit—

1. I leave you in peace.

During the whole course of my ministration among you, it is my happiness to be conscious that there has been no strife between us. Never has there been any misunderstanding between my people and myself. Harmony unbroken has marked my intercourse with them all. Between officers and private Christians and myself, not a shadow of collision has ever occurred. I part with you without one unkind feeling. Many infirmities have you borne with: and for the affectionate regards of so many years' continuance, I return this day, all that is in my power, the thanks of a grateful heart, which assuredly do not proceed from feigned lips. Now, my beloved friends, for a recompense of the same, go on cultivating the unity of the Spirit in the bond of peace. Take care that the election of a new pastor do not become a source of contention and heart-burnings. "Pray for the peace of your Jerusalem. They shall prosper that love her. Peace be within thy walls and prosperity within thy palaces. For my brethren and companions' sakes, I will now say, Peace be within thee. Because of the house of the Lord our God, I will seek thy good." "And may the God of peace, that brought again from the dead our Lord Jesus Christ, that great Shepherd of the sheep, through the blood of the everlasting covenant, make you perfect to do his will, stablish, strengthen, settle you."

2. The second consolatory thought is, that the Lord Jesus is the living head, the centre of union, to all his people.

Their souls are bound up with him in the same bundle of life. Nothing, my Christian friends, can ever part us from him. "What shall separate us from the love of Christ? shall tribulation, or distress, or persecution, or famine, or nakedness, or peril, or sword? (As it is written, For thy sake we are killed all the day long; we are accounted as sheep for the slaughter.) Nay, in all these things we are more than conquerors, through him that loved us. For I am persuaded that neither death, nor life, nor angels, nor principalities, nor powers, nor things present, nor things to come; nor height, nor depth, nor any other creature, shall be able to separate us from the love of God, which is in Christ Jesus our Lord."

Well, then, though far asunder, we shall be still united: we remove not one hair's breadth from the mercy-seat. There I shall meet you, and remember you. There do you also remember me. We may be abundantly happy in the light of his countenance. Ever bear in mind that the Disposer of our lot is the Saviour of our souls.

A word to the young people of my charge shall finish my discourse. My dear young friends, you are the hope of the Church;

"your fathers, where are they? and the prophets, do they live for ever?" Older Christians must be gathered to their rest, and you must occupy their places. That terrible deposit, the truth of God, must come into your hands. Ask your souls, how will you receive it? The Lord Jesus has powerful claims on you. You were early dedicated to his name, and cast upon his providence. This hand has poured out upon most of you the symbol consecration to the fear, the love, and the service of God. The oath of his covenant is on your souls. Have your consciences felt the power of its obligation? My ministry, which for more than eleven years I have discharged among you, is at an end; but not so the consequences. The good Lord knows with what fidelity and what success my labours have been attended. The hour is not far distant when I must deliver up my account, and you must deliver up yours. O, to deliver them up with joy! Thou blessed and heavenly Judge, shall I stand before thy seat, charged with any of their blood? Shall they stand before it charged with their own? Shall all the offers of thy mercy, all the pathos of thy sufferings, all thine inimitable patience, and all thy marvellous love, have been preached to them in vain? Shall there be any here who does not more certainly turn his back upon the closed doors of this house of prayer, than he does upon the last lingering offer of thy salvation? The thought is too overwhelming. Pardon me, my friends.—I can no more.

SERMON XI.

SALVATION BY GRACE.

EPHESIANS ii. 8.

"By grace are ye saved, through faith, and that not of yourselves: it is the gift of God."

The apostle Paul was largely indebted to redeeming love; and, like all other debtors to that love, he was so far from being ashamed of the debt, that he thankfully owned the obligation it laid upon him, and exulted in it, as his happiness, his honour, his glory. Fully convinced, that in opposing the gospel of Jesus he ignorantly courted ruin, and rushed with mad precipitation upon the thick bosses of Jehovah's buckler, he gratefully commemorates that undeserved, unexpected, undesired grace, which came down from the highest heavens—arrested him in his career of impiety—unmasked him to himself—revealed to him the Saviour. This grace is the affecting and dignified theme which melts his heart; which elevates his powers, and tunes his tongue to praise. Whenever he mentions the endearing subject, his whole soul dissolves in tenderness; the emotions which heave his holy bosom he communicates in

"Thoughts that breathe, and words that burn."

"'Tis a faithful saying; it is worthy of all acceptation, that Christ Jesus came into the world to save sinners. I know, by experience, the cheering truth; for he saved me, who am the chief of sinners." Viewing now, from his rock of safety, the darkness, the danger, the death, which environ the unconverted, he sighs for their misery, and ardently covets the honour of being made instrumental in warning them "to flee from the wrath to come." Far as his voice can be heard; wide as his labours can extend; distant as his writings may reach; he proclaims to perishing men the deadly disease under which they labour, and the remedy which is provided by the covenant, and is offered by the gospel of peace. His invaluable epistles are a comment upon the prophetic declaration,—"O Israel thou hast destroyed thyself; but in me is thy help." For all the evils which sin has introduced, he directs us to grace, reigning grace, as the sovereign antidote. To abase pride, to confound presumption, to guard against the vortex of error which has sunk into perdition millions who were caught in its whirl, he solemnly assures us that our own deeds and dispositions, however important or holy we may imagine them, have not the least influence, directly or indirectly, in procuring our acceptance with God. "By the works of the law shall no flesh be justified; for by the law is the knowledge of sin." But, to kill despair and quicken hope, he accompanies this alarming doctrine with the reviving intelligence that the "righteousness of God without the law is manifested," and that "Christ is the end of the law for righteousness to every one that believeth." Deeply impressed with the magnitude of this truth, and thoroughly aware of the deceitfulness and power of a legal propensity by which men are inclined to connect with the work of the Saviour some work of their own, he cautions us against the danger of yielding to its suggestions; he not only urges the caution by the weight of his apostolic authority, but by arguments the most pointed and forceful, he demonstrates that if ever we be saved, our salvation must be of free grace. This precious doctrine the preceding parts of the epistle before us exhibit in a variety of lights; but nowhere is it asserted in terms more downright and unequivocal than in the words of our text,—"By grace are ye saved, through faith, and that not of yourselves: it is the gift of God."

To facilitate the discussion of this subject, it may be proper to state the meaning of the words, grace, salvation, faith. Grace evidently denotes free favour. It is often confounded with mercy, but it conveys an idea more strong and impressive. Mercy is kindness shown to the miserable: grace is mercy shown to the worthless.

Salvation contemplates its objects as labouring under evil, and exposed to danger. The salvation of the gospel contemplates its objects as sinners; as ruined by their own transgression; as condemned by the sentence of a righteous law, and liable to the tremendous penalty which the sentence includes. Faith, in its general acceptation, is reliance upon testimony. The faith of a Christian—that faith from which he obtains the honourable denomination of a believer—is the cordial reception of the record which God hath given of his Son, upon the credit of his own veracity. The doctrine, then, of our text is briefly this, that we receive, by faith of divine operation, the salvation which is provided by grace.

You will not deem a few minutes unprofitably spent in meditating upon the blessing which is here exhibited; upon the source from which it originates; and upon the instrument by which we are instated in the possession of it.

I. The blessing is "salvation:" a blessing of large and joyous extent; implying deliverance from guilt—reconciliation with God, the restoration of our nature, and a right, an unalienable right, to eternal life.

1. Salvation confers deliverance from guilt. The punishment to which our fallen nature is liable, is commonly styled the penalty of the law—is death, in the widest signification of the word and is the just award of sin, "for the wages of sin is death." With this death Adam was threatened in case of disobedience, when God enjoined abstinence from the tree of the knowledge of good and evil, as the pledge of his fidelity. Now since he stood in a federative character, and neither the precept nor its sanction was confined to the person of Adam, but embraced in him those who should spring from him, it follows, that "all his posterity, descending from him by ordinary generation, sinned in him, and fell with him, in his first transgression." So saith the Scripture: "In Adam all die.—By one man sin entered into the world, and death by sin, and so death passed upon all men, for that all have sinned; and by one offence judgment is come upon all men to condemnation." Therefore, our deplorable condition is, that "we are by nature children of wrath." Born under a broken law, eternal justice attaches our persons, and binds us over to all the evils which the curse of that law contains. And till we become the sons of God by faith in Christ Jesus, the actions of every day augment our guilt, and in the same proportion our woe. But the

salvation of the gospel delivers from the curse. It dissolves for ever our connection with the law as a rule of life: it dissolves this connection by bestowing upon us a justifying righteousness,—a righteousness in which we are complete,—a righteousness which Jehovah himself will pronounce unblemished,—a righteousness not wrought out indeed by ourselves, but by our surety. Our rejoicing is, that Messiah " has magnified the law, and made it honourable," and, therefore, that " Jehovah is well pleased for his righteousness' sake." The Father " made him to be sin for us, that we might be made the righteousness of God in him:" and in accomplishing this work, the amazing work, which was given him to do, he has redeemed from the curse of the law, and " forever perfected them who are sanctified."

God is angry with men, not because they are finite, but because they are wicked. It is sin which renders them the objects of his abhorrence. If, then, a righteousness which provides at once for the safety of the criminal and for the glory of the Lawgiver,—which pays to justice her full demand,—which repairs the indignity done to the law, blots out every aspersion upon God's character, and vindicates the rights of his government; if such a righteousness can be imparted to the sinner, and can be pleaded by him, his guilt is removed, and with it must be removed the Lord's holy displeasure. The gospel-salvation, therefore, in procuring for sinners a justifying righteousness, procures.

2. Reconciliation with an offended God.

The necessity of such a reconciliation has been felt by the consciences, and owned by the practice of men in every age. This invaluable blessing was typified by all the expiatory sacrifices, and by all the sacerdotal employment of the Levitical economy. This enviable blessing, Christ, the apostle and high priest of our profession—Christ, the author of eternal redemption, has obtained: he " has made peace by the blood of his cross:" he has " made reconciliation for iniquity ;" " and God was in Christ, reconciling the world to himself, not imputing their trespasses unto them." It is in Christ, that the Father considers the heirs of salvation. Accounting the work of Christ as theirs, and the satisfaction of Christ as theirs, he says of them, "they are all fair, there is no spot in them." This benefit of the covenant, sealed upon the heart by the Spirit of promise, delivers from the terrors and the misgivings of an unappeased conscience, and fills with that divine peace which passeth all understanding. By virtue of this reconciliation, we can view with composure the high demands of the violated law; we can look forward with confidence to the tribunal of our Judge. The Judge is our friend, who has blotted out with his own blood, the black and heavy accusation which was marked against us. Thus reconciled, we, "who were once afar off, are brought nigh unto God, and joy in him, through our Lord Jesus Christ, by whom we have received the atonement."

This doctrine of justification and acceptance, by which Christ is declared to do everything, and we to do nothing, is reprobated by many as encouraging sloth, and promoting immorality. Were it possible, indeed, to be freed from the condemnation of sin, and yet to remain under its power, there can be no doubt that men would be induced to "commit all uncleanness with greediness;" and the doctrine which should assert a deliverance of this kind, would unquestionably lead to licentiousness, and would be supremely execrable: but let it not be forgotten, that with freedom from guilt and reconciliation to God, is inseparably connected, in the

3d Place, The restoration of our nature.

God can be pleased with nothing but excellence; and there is no moral excellence but what resembles himself. The restoration, then, of our nature, termed in Scripture the being "born again,"—the being "renewed in the spirit of our minds,"—the being "created anew in Christ Jesus,"—consists in the recovery, by Christ the moral excellence (the divine image), which we have lost (lost in Adam). What that excellence (what that image) is, we can be at no loss to determine, when unerring truth has declared that the "new man is, after God, created in knowledge, righteousness, and true holiness." In knowledge, that we may discern the true end of our being; the true source of our happiness; the true value of things temporal and things eternal. In righteousness; not that righteousness which justifies the sinner. This is widely different from the righteousness which forms in believers a part of their Father's image. The latter is purchased by the former; the one, that by which we are justified; is a righteousness imputed; the other is a righteousness implanted. The one is a righteousness without us; the other is a righteousness within us. The one is absolutely perfect; the other is not, cannot be, perfect, till that which is in part is done away. It is, properly speaking, a "rectitude of nature;" a rectitude which expresses and exerts itself in sanctified acts, and sanctified habits: and these acts and habits are what the apostle terms "true holiness." Let it not then be wondered at, that they who live under the influence of the belief, that there is, that there can be, "no condemnation to them who are in Christ Jesus," are most afraid of sin, and most "adorn in all things the doctrine of God their Saviour." This fact (and let men argue as they please, it is a stubborn fact which no ingenuity can explain away), this fact is an inexplicable riddle to the worldling: but the easy solution of it is, that they have another nature; and holiness is as much the element of the new creature, as sin is the element of the old. The name Jesus, was given to the Mediator because he "saves his people from their sins." "Sin," says the apostle, "sin shall not have dominion over you, for ye are not under the law, but under grace: and he that is born of God sinneth not, because his seed abideth in him, and he cannot sin, because he is born of God."

Heaven is the proper abode of innocence and holiness. It is the abode which Christ hath prepared for them who love him. They, therefore, who are delivered by his righteousness from the guilt of sin, whom he has reconciled to God, and whose nature the Spirit of truth has renovated and restored, must enjoy,

4. As a part of their salvation, a sure title to everlasting life.

For these (favoured ones) there is reserved in heaven, an "inheritance incorruptible, undefiled, and that fadeth not away." This is the record of God, that "he hath given to us eternal life; and this life is in his Son. He, therefore, who hath the Son, hath eternal life." Eternal life! how big the expression! Eternal life! Who can *tell*, who can *think*, its glories? If it is desirable to be forever free from fears and fightings; from sin, and pain, and sorrow—If it be a comfort to have all the graces of the Divine Spirit, which at best can but bud in this cold and frozen clime; to expand in their native soil; to shed the fragrance, and bloom in the beauty of Paradise—If it be pleasant to mingle in familiar society with holy angels and holy men; to admire with them the countless wonders of creation and providence; and the superior wonders of redeeming love—If it be delightful to be honoured with the unclouded communion of a triune Jehovah; to have pure streams from the fountain of uncreated joy flowing perpetually

o

into the gladdened soul; If these things can constitute bliss, blessed is the son of adoption; blessed is the heir of Christ; he has eternal life, and eternal life comprehends them all!

If you enquire whence proceeded a salvation so great, so invaluable, so divine? The answer, which brings us directly to the

II. Branch of our subject, is, that it flows from grace, free grace! So saith our apostle, "By grace are ye saved." This is the invariable doctrine of the Bible. "Not unto us, O Lord, not unto us, but to thy name give glory."—"Not for your sakes do I this, O house of Israel, be it known unto you, saith the Lord God, but for my holy name's sake;" so that "salvation is of the Lord," and therefore it is by grace; yes, it is all of grace. It is grace in its origin; grace in its execution; grace in its application.

1. The origin of salvation is vainly ascribed to any other cause than free grace.

There is not, in the oracles of God, a point ascertained with more precision, nor corroborated with testimonies more frequent and irrefragable, than this, that electing love is the fountain of salvation. "I will have mercy," says Jehovah to Moses, "I will have mercy on whom I will have mercy:" whence our apostle draws the solid and undeniable inference, "So, then, it is not of him that willeth, nor of him that runneth, but of God that showeth mercy." It were easy to accumulate the proofs of this doctrine: but we need go no farther than the first chapter of the epistle from which our text is taken. There we are told, in language which all the efforts of violent criticism cannot torture into any other meaning, that God has chosen us in Christ "before the foundation of the world: having predestinated us to the adoption of children, by Jesus Christ, according to the good pleasure of his will." 'Tis true, many who are too proud to be indebted for their eternal salvation to the free favour of God, insist that the election by which he distinguishes sinner from sinner, is grounded upon good disposition, upon faith and holiness foreseen in the objects of that election. But if men be allowed to interpolate divine revelation, and to add to the oracles of Jehovah the figments of their own invention, we may lay aside our Bibles. The fashionable tenet which was just now mentioned, some may deem an ingenious interpretation of the apostle; but sober inquiry will say, **that instead of explaining it contradicts** him. The apostle asserts that God hath chosen us in Christ, that we should be holy; or which is the same thing, we are holy because he hath chosen us. But the doctrine against which I contend is exactly the reverse, viz. that he has chosen us because we are holy. Upon whatever principle the election proceed, it will hardly be denied that God chooses men to salvation, and that by Jesus Christ. But if good dispositions, if faith and holiness foreseen, are the cause of election, then sinners are saved before the Lord chooses them: for faith and holiness undoubtedly constitute salvation; and where, upon this plan, where is the obligation to grace? The same plan requires, as a previous qualification for receiving Christ, the very thing which is the effect of receiving him; for it is the office of Jesus to save his people from their sins, *i. e.* beyond controversy to make them holy. Moreover, the apostle roundly affirms that "whatsoever is not of faith is sin," and that "they who are in the flesh cannot please God." But how a man can become holy by accumulating sin, is a point which deserves better elucidation than it has yet received. Salvation, then, originates in grace; and not only so, but,

2. It is grace in its execution.

The meritorious executor of the new covenant is the Lord Jesus. And what but grace, large, unbounded grace, could have prompted him to become "a man of sorrows, and acquainted with grief?" To obey perfectly, as the covenant head of his people, all the precepts of the righteous law? To endure as their substitute, the tremendous evils which are included in its penalty? Infinitely happy and glorious in himself, he needed neither our services, nor ourselves; he might have left us to perish in our wilful apostasy, and his justice would have shone in our eternal destruction. Thus he treated the angels who kept not their first estate. But while in the exercise of sovereignty he passed by the angelic nature, in the exercise of the same sovereignty "he took on him the seed of Abraham, and made his soul an offering for sin. The universal Lord, he can suffer no compulsion: and those for whom he interfered had nothing to merit his condescension. They were not innocent creatures in distress; but thankless, wanton rebels against the God of their mercies; in their crime, without excuse; in their characters, supremely vile. It was, then, free love; it was his voluntary act by which he entered into covenant with his Father;

when, before all worlds, the "counsel of peace was between them both." In virtue of that counsel, "Lo, I come," said he, "to do thy will, O God." In virtue of that counsel, he "laid down his life for the sheep."—"No man took it from him; but he had power to lay it down, and he had power to take it again; this commandment had he received from his Father." Well, therefore, might our apostle remind the Corinthians of the "grace of our Lord Jesus Christ, who though he was rich, yet for our sakes he became poor, that we through his poverty might be rich."

Nor does the grace which reigns in the origin and purchase of salvation, exceed the grace which, in the

3d. Place, we find to characterize its application.

By the application of salvation, I mean, that preternatural and supernatural work of the Holy Spirit, by which he creates in (elect) sinners, the temper, and bestows on them the privileges, of God's dear children—privileges which were bought and secured by the unblemished obedience, and the vicarious suffering, of their Elder Brother. Without deep reflection upon the nature of things, or the experience of every believer, the least veneration for the oracles of God is enough to convince all who are not blinded by the god of this world, that the work of the Holy Spirit, of which we are speaking, is entirely of grace. It is grace in its commencement; grace in its progress; grace in its completion.

To the commencement of this work, may be referred all benefits of redemption, which, however different in their natural order, take place, in fact, at one and the same moment. We can barely mention some of them. One of them is justification; and we are "justified freely by his grace, through the redemption that is in Christ Jesus. Another, is the infusion of spiritual life. "When I passed by thee," they are the words of Jehovah, "when I passed by thee, and saw thee polluted in thine own blood, behold, thy time was a time of love: and I said unto thee, when thou wast in thy blood, Live: yea, I said unto thee, when thou wast in thy blood, Live." With these we may connect "regeneration, pardon, and adoption."—"Not by works of righteousness which we have done, but according to his mercy he saved us, by the washing of regeneration, even the renewing of the Holy Ghost."—"I, even I, am he that blotteth out thy transgression for mine own sake"— and in Christ we have "forgiveness of sins, according to the riches of his grace"—and we were "predestinated unto the adoption of children, according to the good pleasure of his will." And if salvation begin with grace, it must proceed by grace. The apostle tells us that when we are united to Christ, we are made new creatures; one of the first ideas that will occur to the mind when reflecting upon the wants of a living creature, is, that it cannot thrive unless it be properly fed. And as the new creature is of heavenly birth and spiritual kind, what food is adapted to its nature, but that which is supplied by the gracious Spirit? It is not the Lord's method to furnish his people with a stock of grace, and then leave it entirely to their good management. Were this the case, like witless prodigals, they would soon squander away not only the earnest of their inheritance, but the inheritance itself. No, he deals with them more tenderly and wisely. It is in spiritual, as in temporal life. The food which sustains our nature to-day, was not intended to serve us to-morrow; and therefore it is our duty to be no less mindful of our souls than of our bodies, when we offer up our petition for our daily bread. "The branch cannot bear fruit except it abide in the vine." It is the fulness of Christ from which we receive "grace for grace." The advocate whom he hath promised —the Lord, the sanctifier, dwells in his people as a well of living waters. He purifies their affections; he encourages their hope; he nerves their exertion. From the effect of his mighty working, he is denominated the "Spirit of grace;" and for the same reason, progress in those holy tempers of which he is the immediate author, is called "growth in grace."

Equally free, equally unmerited, is the completion of our salvation. "He who begins the good work, performs it until the day of Jesus Christ."—"He hath given to us eternal life." The inheritance of believers is an inheritance already purchased. The full price was paid by their surety, and it is kept, by the faithfulness of God, till they become of age, when they shall enter with exceeding joy, into "the kingdom prepared for them before the foundation of the world."

As the great salvation is, in all its parts, the offspring of gratuitous bounty, so the manner in which we acquire a property in its benefits, corresponds to its nature. Which leads us to consider, in the

III. Place, the mean or instrument by which salvation becomes ours. This is faith. "By grace are ye saved, through faith." Genuine faith, as has been remarked already, is a cordial assent to the testimony of God, and a firm reliance upon his new covenant faithfulness. It views him as a promising God, and as a God who performs what he promises. Thus "Abraham believed God, and it was counted to him for righteousness." The love of God proposes Christ Jesus as the "propitiation for sin;" as the peacemaker between God and man; as the only foundation of our hope and confidence. We are told that "God so loved the world, that he gave his only-begotten Son, that whosoever believeth in him should not perish, but have everlasting life." The offer of his salvation is made in style the most tender and terms the most unlimited: "Hearken to me, ye stouthearted, that are far from righteousness. Behold, I bring near my righteousness." Eternal Truth has sworn that no sinner, be his character what it may, if he flee to this righteousness, shall ever be rejected. "Him that cometh to me," saith the Redeemer, I will in no wise cast out." "Amen," says the believing soul, with her eye fixed on the exceeding great and precious promises, "it is enough: these are all my salvation, and all my desire. I wish for no other, no better security. Christ is offered to sinners freely and indiscriminately. Here is my ample warrant to receive him: I am a sinner: I appropriate to myself the general offer: I take Jesus to be my Saviour and portion, and God to be, in him, my covenant God. Henceforward I am not my own, but bought with a price; I am bound to serve God with my body and with my spirit, which are his." In thus receiving the divine testimony respecting the Redeemer, we set to our seal that God is true. And that he may mark with an indelible stain the pride of all human glory, the apostle takes care to inform us that even this faith by which we embrace the Saviour does not originate in our will; is not effected by our power: "Ye are saved through faith, and that not of yourselves, it is, the gift of God. The Scripture is decisive on this head. "It is given us to believe in Christ." It is God who "deals the measure of faith." It is he who fulfils in his people "the work of faith with power."

The subject we have been considering affords matter for copious and interesting meditation. We shall very briefly improve it, for correcting a very common but destructive error; for inviting the nner to lay hold on eternal life; and for quickening the believer in his way to glory.

1. We may correct, from what has been said, a common but destructive error. Multitudes who would gladly break down the hedge of distinction which God has planted around his chosen, and reduce them to a level with the carnal world, are fond of the notion that the faith which constitutes a Christian is but a rational assent to the truth of the gospel—a notion, my brethren, which will ruin eternally the man who dies under its influence. An assent to historical fact and to rational proof is an exercise of the mind which belongs to us as intellectual beings. It is an essential property of a reasonable creature. Destroy this property, and you destroy his very nature. But it is by no means necessarily connected with good moral qualities. And who does not know that it is moral state and character which distinguish the believer from the world? Intellectual powers necessarily belong to us: but the faith of a Christian is not born with him, nor is he born with powers which can produce it: if he were, it could not be a faith of God's operation. A speculative and a saving faith are, therefore, specifically different. The difference, and an important one it is, lies here: the one is the fruit of arguments addressed to the understanding merely, and may be possessed, in a very high degree, by the devil himself. The other is the proper effect of the sovereign and almighty agency of the Spirit of truth, not only upon the understanding, but upon the heart and upon the will. And it is the more needful to be decided in this matter, because men, as long as they indulge the idea that they are able to believe at their pleasure, will slumber in security, and dream of bliss, but will not, cannot be solicitous about salvation by grace. But a free —an absolutely free salvation is the substance of the gospel. While, therefore, we may properly improve our subject for alarming the fears of men by showing them their utter inability to help themselves, we must not forget to improve it.

2. For encouraging their hope, by inviting them to lay hold on eternal life, through the medium of a gracious salvation. Hear it, and rejoice, ye sons and daughters of Adam: Grace reigns! Her throne is erected on the blood of the atonement, and she proclaims to dying mortals life and pardon, acceptance, peace, and glory. Her wide commission extends to the most worthless and vile

Before the tribunal of God, all are guilty: and, therefore, before the throne of grace all are on a level. At this throne, by which we are introduced to the favour of Jehovah, there is no respect of persons. Grace makes not the smallest difference between the rigid pharisee and the rapacious publican; between the severe moralist and the abandoned libertine. If she did, she would cease to be grace. Be persuaded, then, wretched sinners, to come to the living God through Jesus Christ. Every difficulty which guilt and defilement can create is completely removed: for grace reigns. Say not, "I have sinned too long and too heinously to be forgiven. I dare not; it would be presumption, to hope for acceptance with a holy God." The answer to every objection is, Grace reigns! Grace has made ample provision for all your wants. She has provided righteousness for the guilty; purity for the filthy; faith for the unbelieving; repentance for the impenitent; strength for the feeble. The more worthless and impoverished thou art, the fitter subject art thou for the operation of grace. All the mercies of the new covenant, all that Christ purchased and we can want, she offers without money and without price. While she addresses you in the name of Jesus, listen to her voice, yield to her entreaties. Children of pride, bow the knee to this amiable sovereign! Prisoners of death, touch her friendly sceptre and live! Whosoever will, let him take of the water of life freely. "I," says Jesus, "I am the resurrection and the life: he that believeth on me, though he were dead, yet shall he live."

Lastly. Let us improve our subject for quickening the believer in his way to glory.

Is salvation by grace? then let boasting lips be for ever silent. What have we, O Christian, that we have not received? Everything bad in us is our own: everything good is the gift of divine bounty. And why did the Lord fix his love upon us, when he has passed others in their iniquity? Were we in any respect better than they? Oh no! We all belonged to the same lump of perdition. Sovereignty, adorable sovereignty, made us vessels of honour. Even so, Father, for so it seemed good in thy sight. Surely, then, it becomes us to be clothed with humility, and gratefully to own our obligations to that love of God which called us from darkness into his marvellous light.

Is the progress of salvation by grace? Why, then, believers, should our hands be weak or our souls cast down? In every trial, in every danger, our unfailing consolation is, that grace reigns. We are authorized to come boldly to our Father's throne, and to ask at once, with the affection and the confidence of children, for all the benefits which we need. Our Jesus, our brother, has all things at his command. "For it hath pleased the Father that in him should all fulness dwell." As the administrator of the new covenant, he is the treasurer of heaven; and he has promised his people to send down his Spirit, to unlock his storehouse, and unlock their hearts, and pour them full of blessings!

Is salvation completed by grace? Who, then, or what shall hinder the holy warriors that fight under Immanuel's banners from arriving in triumph at the heavenly Canaan? Did Jesus ransom them by his blood? Did he quicken them by his Spirit? Did he purify them by his grace? Has he given them the pledge of the promised inheritance? And shall they not persevere? Absurd idea! They shall! Kept by the power of God, they shall go from strength to strength, till every one of them appear before him in Zion. "Let us gird up, therefore, the loins of our faith, and run with patience the race set before us!" Let us look forward, with exultation, to the blissful period when the mystery of God shall be finished. Then the Redeemer shall complete the temple of mercy which was built on his blood, and reared by his Spirit; and every stone of the sacred pile shall bear the motto of redemption; a motto engraved by the finger of God, and emblazoned by the light of heaven, "To the praise of the glory of his grace!"

LECTURE.

PSALM XXIII.

"1. The Lord is my shepherd; I shall not want.

"2. He maketh me to lie down in green pastures: he leadeth me beside the still waters.

"3. He restoreth my soul: he leadeth me in the paths of righteousness for his name's sake.

"4. Yea though I walk through the valley of the shadow of death, I will fear no evil: for thou art with me; thy rod and thy staff they comfort me.

"5. Thou preparest a table before me in the presence of mine enemies: thou anointest my head with oil; my cup runneth over.

"6. Surely goodness and mercy shall follow me all the days of my life: and I will dwell in the house of the Lord for ever."

THE pastoral life, which is one of the most ancient and simple forms of society, and has furnished the groundwork of this psalm, was prevalent and honourable among the eastern nations. Flocks and herds were their chief possessions, and the character of a shepherd was not beneath the dignity of their patriarchs and princes. An occupation so innocent and useful, so familiar with their habits, and so friendly to reflection, had a natural influence upon their thoughts and language. It supplied the poet with beautiful images, the moralist with insinuating lessons, and the scripture itself with materials for sacred allegory. Of the last, there cannot be a more apposite example than the psalm which we are now to consider. Under the easy and elegant figure of a shepherd's care over his flock, it represents the love of God toward his chosen. He is their shepherd, and they are "the people of his pasture, and the sheep of his hand." "The Lord," said the psalmist, in verse 1, "the Lord is my shepherd."

There is no difficulty in ascertaining the person here intended; for the description agrees to no other than our Lord Jesus Christ, who is at once Jehovah and the Shepherd promised to the fathers. He has ever delighted in this character, which, from the beginning, has supported the faith of his church, and animated her worship. The testimony which Jacob, with his dying breath left to the Shepherd of Israel, she has perpetuated and improved. "Give ear, O Shepherd of Israel, thou that leadest Joseph like a flock. Feed thy people with thy rod, the flock of thine heritage which dwell solitarily in the wood." With these petitions concurs the promise, "He shall feed his flock like a shepherd: he shall gather the lambs with his arm, and carry them in his bosom, and shall gently lead those that are with young." It was also predicted, that in discharging his engagement, he should become a sacrifice for the benefit and in the room of his flock. "Awake, O sword, against my Shepherd, and against the man that is my fellow, saith the Lord of hosts; Smite the Shepherd, and the sheep shall be scattered, and I will turn mine hand upon the little ones." He owned the relation, and confirmed the oracle, when he "laid down his life for the sheep." The name and office descended with him into the grave; and that same "resurrection from the dead," which declared him to be "the Son of God with power," declared him also to be the "great Shepherd of the sheep." We know him, at this hour, "as the Shepherd and Bishop of our souls;" and recognize our fellowship with his servant David, breathing the same sentiment in the same words, the Lord is my shepherd.

Here is obviously a claim of personal interest in the Lord Jesus. For the faith of his people is not a cold assent to abstract propositions. "The substance of things hoped for and the evidence of things not seen," it appropriates to itself a common good, and applies general promises to particular use. We shall reap little advantage from "the redemption that is in Christ Jesus," if he be not to us individually, whatever he is to his people at large. *My* shepherd, my *own* shepherd, are words of life as well as of assurance. And when I can utter them believingly, my bosom swells with joy, and all my soul is on my lips. It is thus that the psalmist, mingling with the Redeemer's flock, takes refuge in his protection, exults in his favour, and reposes upon his truth. The choice was wise and happy: for as it terminated upon the Creator and not upon the creature, it incurred no danger of disappointment. "My shepherd," saith David, "is Jehovah." Ancient believers were better instructed than to be ignorant of Messiah's divinity. Their good "confession" was not dishonoured by the dream of a created Saviour, nor the atheism of a secondary God. They did not perceive the impossibility, so plain to modern refiners, of conciliating essential godhead with covenant-office. On the contrary, they saw, as all true believers now see, that without the former, there could be no place for the latter. He who is not divine, cannot be their shepherd. The force of their reasoning, their consolation, their life, depend upon this principle, "My shepherd is Jehovah." Hence the psalmist infers, "I shall not want." The argument is short, but firm. It is the argument of a man who knows his God. Less than the all-sufficient can neither fill our capacities, nor accomplish our desire. We should soon exhaust the highest angels, and find them to be, like every other creature, when embraced as our portion, a broken cistern, and a lying vanity. "The portion of Jacob is not like them." His attribute is infinity. The father and fountain of all being and blessedness, when he condescends to bind himself to men by covenant relation, and to sanction his promise with his oath, they have obtained the last security for their happiness. As impossible is it for him not to give that which is good, as it is impossible for him to lie. Not everything, indeed, which would gratify their wishes, often impatient, and ill-directed, but everything seasonable and proper, everything conducive to their benefit, everything which they themselves would ask, were they perfectly free from error, shall they receive at his hand. "For the Lord God is a sun and shield: the Lord will give grace and glory; no good thing will he withhold from them that walk uprightly." This David believed, and he reasons accordingly: "The Lord is my shepherd; I shall not want."

An illustration of the position contained in this introductory verse, and of its effect upon a gracious mind, occupies the rest of the psalm, and divides it into two corresponding parts—the first, (verses 2, 3, 4, and 5,) unfolds the nature of Christ's pastoral office; and the second, (verse 6,) is the psalmist's tribute of faith and gratitude.

I. The pastoral office of Christ is represented to consist in making provision for his flock, in its direction and defence.

1. The good Shepherd porvides for his flock. Verse 2. "He

maketh me to lie down in green pastures: he leadeth me beside the still waters."

A flock of sheep feeding securely in rich pastures and by the cooling stream, is a pleasing spectacle in any country. But under the sultry skies, and amidst the burning sands, of the East, it awakened exquisite emotion, and was a lively emblem of temporal and spiritual felicity. Most significantly does it depict the condition of believers. The world around them is a land of deserts and of drought, which yields nothing to " satisfy the longing soul." Sooner shall the body be nourished by whirlwinds and the dust, than the spirit with things of mere time and sense. But from this land of deserts and of drought, does the gracious Shepherd lead his flock to green pastures, and gentle waters ; that is, he provides enjoyments for them as suitable to their nature and circumstances, as the best of pasture and of water are to the literal sheep. Let us, therefore, inquire what these enjoyments are, and where they are to be found.

In general, they are the mercies of the new covenant, established in his hands as in the hands of a mediator. He delivers his people, by faith in his blood, from the inquietudes of an evil conscience; puts them beyond the reach of the curse, "for there is no condemnation to them who are in Christ Jesus; and rescues them from the bondage of sin and Satan. He reveals to them his excellence, admits them into his friendship, "sheds his love abroad in their hearts, introduces them to his Father as their reconciled God, intercedes for them within the vail, supports them by his grace, gives them " an inheritance among them that are sanctified," and is Himself their all.

Now these are enjoyments adapted to the nature of an immortal soul, and commensurate with its faculties. Here " the meek eat and are satisfied." The void in the bosom is filled up. They have found the "pearl of great price," and are enriched for ever. Secured in the possession of everlasting good, they may say, " Return to thy rest, O my soul, for the Lord hath dealt bountifully with thee." Till the pastures of God wither, and the river of life fail, they cannot want: and it is their own fault, if " the peace of God, which passeth all understanding, do not keep their hearts and minds through Christ Jesus."

These spiritual blessings are dispensed in the Church; for she is the "Church of the living God," without whose pale there is no revealed way of salvation. He has committed to her, as a sacred deposit, his word and ordinances, by which sinners are convinced, converted, and made heirs according to "hope of eternal life."

The original of all saving truth is in the person of Jesus Christ; and the exact transcript of it, in his word. "His word is truth," and truth is the food of the soul. All its principles, and precepts, and promises, are designed to convey supplies of grace out of the fulness of our Lord Jesus. Even the scandal of the cross, and the sublimer doctrines of religion, are adapted to the taste of the new man, and promote his growth. And as they all have a practical use, not one of them, however odious to carnal wisdom, can be taken from the Bible without depriving believers of a means by which they receive from God out of heaven both the bread of life and the water of life. Hence the testimonies of the psalmist and the prophet: "How sweet are thy words unto my taste! yea, sweeter than honey to my mouth. Thy words were found and I did eat them; and thy word was unto me the joy and rejoicing of my heart." And hence, too, the reverence of believers for the holy scripture. It is the language and the voice of their God and Father, " speaking peace to his saints," which is " better to them than thousands of gold and silver." His sentence is creation; and when it has gone forth to bless them through the medium of his word, neither earth nor hell shall hinder them from "rejoicing with joy unspeakable and full of glory."

With the word of God we are to connect his ordinances, comprehending the whole system of instituted worship. They bear the image and superscription of the Lord our lawgiver, and are instruments by which he both maintains his authority, and imparts his grace. To these ends, beside the devotion of the closet and family, the public homage of the church on his own day, the holy sacraments, the ministry of reconciliation, all contribute. In preaching the word, and in the other functions of their calling, the under-shepherds obey the commandment of the Chief Shepherd, " Feed my sheep—feed my lambs." Precious as are the divine truths in themselves, and at all times, they are clothed with less majesty, and, ordinarily, accompanied with less power, in the exercises of private religion, than in the service of the sanctuary. For "the Lord loveth the gates of Zion more than all the dwellings of Jacob." Next to the Holy Spirit, the ministry of the Word is our Redeemer's principal ascension-gift; a standing pledge to the church, and proof to the world, that he is now "in the presence of God for us." Accordingly, he puts a distinguished honour upon this ordinance; for "the preaching of the cross," which is "to them that perish, foolishness," is "to them who are saved, the power of God." This explains the attachment of true Christians to the house of God. Many resort thither from the impulse of habit, of fashion, of curiosity, or, it may be, of less reputable motives; but "they see his power and his glory." There are the "goings of their God, their King: and there he abundantly blesses Zion's provision, satisfies her poor with bread, and clothes her priests with salvation, so that her saints shout aloud for joy." "Happy is the people that is in such a case: yea, happy is that people whose God is Jehovah."

2. The good Shepherd exercises a vigilant superintendence over the steps of his flock. Verse 3. "He restoreth my soul: he leadeth me in the paths of righteousness for his name's sake."

This branch of his office includes the double grace of recovering his people from their errors, and shaping the course of their renewed obedience.

1st. Recovery from their errors. "He restoreth my soul."

Sheep are proverbially prone to wander; and the farther they proceed, the more are they bewildered, and the more unlikely to return. Alas! the resemblance is but too exact. To exchange obedience for transgression, that is, to exchange peace for anguish, is superlative folly: but such folly has existed, does exist, and may be ours. Christians, although "renewed in the spirit of their mind," carry about with them, in the remnant of corruption, a principle of "departure from the living God." Take away, or suspend the influence of his grace, and the work is done: the most enlightened and tried believer goes astray the next moment. The examples proposed in Scripture for our humiliation and warning, are not of obscure and dubious professors, but of men eminent for their faith, and eminently favoured of God. How far the regenerated may go, it is not for us to conjecture, and it would be madness to try. That they shall not finally perish, is one of the plainest promises of the Bible. But between the circumspection of grace and the damnation of hell, there is ample room for sinning and for chastisement. To lose your comfort it is not necessary that you should lose your soul. Even within the boundaries of pardon, there are a thousand deviations from duty sufficient to mar your peace, and bring you under the rod. No inconsistency can be traced between the Lord's forgiving his people, and his taking vengeance of their inventions. How many afflicted have borne witness to these truths! How do our hearts smite us for our aberrations from the straight path of God's commandments! And how sad is the condition of those who, duped by the deceitfulness of sin, have "left their first love," and gone away after vanity! Lost attainment, forfeited joy, withering graces, barrenness, leanness, lameness, and a long train of kindred miseries, follow the steps of disobedience. If the *end* be not *destruction*, it is because "the issues from death belong unto the Lord our God." The eye of the Shepherd is continually upon the track of his wandering sheep; and in the critical moment when they are ready to be torn or dashed in pieces, he interposes for their help, takes them up in his arms, and carries them back to his pasture and his fold.

The manner in which he conducts this interposition may be concisely stated in the three following particulars:

(1.) He comes upon them, for the most part, by surprise. In a course of backsliding, and often in the very acts of provocation, when nothing is farther from their thoughts than his presence and reproof, he speaks to their consciences. "What dost thou here?" with a voice which recalls the memory of a thousand mercies, and awakens them from their slumbers. Their eyes open, and the dream is at an end. The seducing vision has fled, and the realities around them are realities of guilt and horror. They stand before him abashed and petrified, unable either to escape or to apologize.

(2.) He communes with them about the nature and aggravation of their sin. His former kindnesses come into remembrance, and are contrasted with their ungenerous requittal. His forgotten love, his injured sacrifice, his grieved Spirit; their own experience, and profession, and vows, rise up, and present each a separate accusation. Ah! who can tell the amazement which then seizes them? the bitterness of their self-reproach? the depth of their self-abhorrence? "O, my God," is their contrite moan, "O, my God, I am ashamed, and blush to lift up my face to thee, my God." Hapless prodigal! "Hast thou not procured this unto thyself, in that thou hast forsaken the Lord thy God when he led thee by the way?" Sin with impunity we cannot. Our remorse and compunction belong to the discipline of our Father's house: for he hath said, that "if his children forsake his law, and walk not in his judgments; if they break his statutes, and keep not his commandments; then will he visit their transgression with the rod, and their iniquity with stripes: Nevertheless, his loving-kindness will he not utterly take from them, nor suffer his faithfulness to fail." These chastenings, therefore, of the Lord, though painful, are in mercy, that we may not "be condemned with the world." Their degree and continuance are regulated by his wisdom; but whenever they have accomplished their purpose, when they have vindicated the purity of the gospel, have turned the sweets of iniquity into wormwood and gall, have shed new charms over the beauty of holiness, the way is prepared for binding up the broken heart; and then,

(3.) The good Shepherd "restores peace to his mourners." For he leads them, by faith, to a renewed application of his blood for pardon: and he pardons most freely. "I am pacified," saith he, "I am pacified towards thee for all that thou hast done." This, O this melts the heart. Such patience! such compassion! such forgiveness! All the springs of contrition are opened at once; "Rivers of waters run down their eyes;" they throw away with disgust the idols which they had laid in their bosom, and "turning their feet unto the divine testimonies," say, "Behold, we come unto thee, for thou art the Lord our God." They now regain the "fellowship of their Saviour's death, and crucify the flesh with the affections and lusts." Their languid graces revive; "precious faith," and all the other powers of the new man resume the sway and their "smell is as the smell of a field which the Lord hath blessed."—"I will heal," saith he, "I will heal their backsliding, I will love them freely: for mine anger is turned away from them." "I will be as the dew unto Israel: he shall grow as the lily, and cast forth his roots as Lebanon."—"His branches shall spread, and his beauty shall be as the olive-tree, and his smell as Lebanon." The blessed influence extends through them to their fellow-believers and their fellow-men: "they that dwell under his shadow shall return; they shall revive as the corn, and grow as the vine; the scent thereof shall be as the vine of Lebanon." Jesus had, from the beginning, "prayed for them, that their faith should not fail;"

and now that "they are converted," they are qualified, by the varieties of Christian experience, to "strengthen their brethren."

Thus he restoreth their souls, and when restored, does "not turn away from them to do them good." For,

2d. He conducts them in the course of their future obedience. "He leadeth me in the paths of righteousness for his name's sake."

Here we must satisfy an inquiry embracing the nature of that course which the restored of the Lord pursue; his interference to preserve them in it; and the reason of his interference.

(1.) The nature of their course is indicated by the phrase, "paths of righteousness."

Right, righteous, righteousness, are terms borrowed from sensible objects, and express the combined ideas of a rule perfectly exact, and of correspondence with the rule. Whatever coincides with it is straight, or right; whatever does not coincide with it, is crooked. Transferred to moral subjects, this figurative language marks the distinction between good and bad, whether in doctrine or practice. Accordingly we consider the law of God as the rule or standard to which every principle and action must be referred. All its precepts are righteous; conformity with them is righteousness; and, consequently, "paths of righteousness" signify that habitual and actual holiness which they prescribe both for the heart and life. But, then, we must remember that the divine law as regulating Christian obedience, is, in a very peculiar sense, the law of Christ. For, as the representative of his people, he has, on the one hand, divested it of its covenant-form by fulfilling its injunctions in the righteousness of his life, and extinguishing its penalty in the sacrifice of his death, so that it neither justifies nor condemns them. And, on the other, he has given them, as the test and measure of their sanctification, this very law, to keep which they are both required by his authority, and constrained by his love. Thus connected, its precepts ascertain and promote evangelical purity, and are transcendently "paths of righteousness."

In the first place: like a path literally straight, they lie directly before us, and cannot be missed without perversion of the will. "The wayfaring men, though fools, shall not err therein;" and though "a scorner seek wisdom and find it not, yet knowledge is easy to him that understandeth."

Unlike the circuitous paths of sin, they contain no deception.

When the sinner takes one step he cannot see the next. Gayety dances around him; Flattery whispers in his ear; Promise enumerates joys at hand: and thus, by little and little, he is seduced into a labyrinth where he is bewildered and lost. The smiling scenery is blasted; Promise has proved a liar; Flattery fills her tongue with imprecation; and Gayety is transformed into a fiend at the threshold of hell! Not so the paths of righteousness; Light from above shines on them, and our view reaches even to their termination. "Mark the perfect man, and behold the upright: for the end of that man is peace."

Secondly. As a straight or right line is the shortest distance between two points, so the obedience of faith is the shortest road to comfort. "They who turn aside after their crooked ways, only weary themselves with vanity; till at length, their days consumed, and their mercies gone, "God leads them forth with the workers of iniquity." But "wisdom's ways are ways of pleasantness, and all her paths are peace." Here is no painful retrospect. Lost time, and wasted powers, shall never reproach the service of God. They belong to the folly of sinners and the wages of sin; while every act of holy obedience brings present satisfaction, and gains upon ultimate hope. This, my brother, is no illusion: no empty boast to cover a damning conscience and a tortured heart. It is the sobriety of bliss, sealed in the experience of millions besides the psalmist. "Thou hast put gladness in my heart, more than in the time that their corn and their wine increased." Gladness, which grows large with use, and more exquisite with age. "Adding to their faith, virtue; and to virtue, knowledge; and to knowledge, temperance; and to temperance, patience; and to patience, godliness; and to godliness, brotherly-kindness; and to brotherly-kindness, charity;" believers are "neither barren nor unfruitful" now, and at last shall have "an entrance ministered unto them abundantly, into the everlasting kingdom of their Lord and Saviour Jesus Christ."

(2.) They owe their preservation in these paths of righteousness to the interference of their Redeemer. "He leadeth me," saith David. He leadeth us, say all who, like David, have known his restoring grace. The metaphor is taken from the custom of the eastern shepherd, who did not drive, but lead his flock; going before them, and calling them after him. Applied to our Lord

Jesus and his redeemed, it instructs us in many precious truths: for instance—That all our practical holiness lies in imitating him, "who hath left us an example that we should follow his steps."—That the most self-denying duties should be attempted with cheerfulness, as they have been sanctified by the experience, and are softened by the sympathy, of our Elder Brother. "Though he were a son, yet learned he obedience by the things which he suffered." He has not left a thorn in our path which did not pierce his own blessed foot: not one, of which his blood will not counteract the poison, and heal the wound—That in all the opposition which his people have to encounter, he is the first to perceive the foe, and to sustain the onset; for "their King shall pass before them, and the Lord on the head of them; that he enlarges their hearts to run the way of his commandments:" his love constraining them, both as a motive and a principle, to "live not unto themselves, but unto him that died for them and rose again;" a constraint which liberates their will, so that they "walk at liberty," and without which they would infallibly revert back into bondage. Summarily, they know nothing, perform nothing, and are nothing, but in their Leader's might. He is the "Lord their strength, who guides them with his counsel," as a pledge that he will "afterward receive them to glory."

(3.) The reason of this, his interference to keep his people in the paths of righteousness, is assigned in the last clause of the third verse—It is "for his name's sake."

The name of Jesus includes all the excellencies of his person, offices, and work. To display them in the redemption of sinners, and to acquire the glory which had been promised to its accomplishment, was the end of his incarnation, his sorrows, and his death. "For the joy that was set before him, he endured the cross, despising the shame; and because he humbled himself, and became obedient unto death, even the death of the cross; therefore God also hath highly exalted him, and given him a name which is above every name." Whatever grace, love, truth, wisdom, power, belongs to the Lord Jesus as the "Captain of salvation," it is comprehended in that name for the sake of which he leads believers in the paths of righteousness. Its lustre shines forth in his regard for them.

As the "first-born among many brethren," of whom he is not

ashamed; and for whom he "is entered as the forerunner within the vail."

As "the high priest of their profession," through whose blood they "have boldness to enter into the holiest;" and who, being their "advocate with the Father, ever liveth to make intercession for them."

As the author and pattern of their perfection; drawing more and more strongly the lines of their resemblance to himself; evincing his omnipotence in the transformation of their minds; and exhibiting to holy angels and spiritual men, the rudiments of that beauty which is to receive its finish "when he shall come to be glorified in his saints, and to be admired in all them that believe."

The praise thus derived to his name bears directly upon the consolation of his people in two important points.

First, it shows the safety of their state.

By leading them in the paths of righteousness, he connects their preservation with his own glory. And the question, whether they may fall into complete and final apostacy? is answered by another, whether the Son of God shall tarnish the honour of his own name? In virtue of his covenant-engagement, he must either keep them, or deny himself: and, therefore, not one of them, no, not the feeblest of them all, can perish without the ruin of his glory. The alternative is awful, but sure; and while it stands on the heavenly record, let no heart faint, nor any joints be loosed. Here is the refuge of the church of God; here the assurance of her children's peace.

Secondly. The name of Jesus, for the sake of which he leads his people in the paths of righteousness, furnishes them with argument before the throne of grace. "Me," may the tempted and disconsolate say, "me he might overlook and contemn, but will he contemn or overlook his own name?" No, thou afflicted: the charge of indifference toward his name, or those who trust in it, shall never be attached to God thy Saviour. To repose such confidence in his name as couples it with thine eternal salvation, is that boldness of the gospel which never went ashamed from the mercy-seat. This was well understood by the "elders who obtained a good report through faith." Let us plead in their spirit and language, "For thy name's sake, O Lord, pardon mine iniquity for it is great." If we die when suing for the mercy of the covenant, or be deserted while our eyes are toward thee for guidance in the paths of righteousness, the seekers of thy face will be discouraged: thine enemies will triumph, "and what wilt thou do to thy great name?" We are, indeed, most criminal and vile: "but there is forgiveness with thee that thou mayest be feared." Our appeal is to the proffers and promises of thy word. "Do not abhor us, for thy name's sake; Do not disgrace the throne of thy glory; remember, break not thy covenant with us."

But the shepherd's care does not end with the direction of his flock: he supports and defends it also, both under the pressure of calamity, and in the enjoyment of privilege. The proof of this point is in verses four and five, which describe the

3d Part of his office. "Yea, though I walk through the valley of the shadow of death, I will fear no evil, for thou art with me: thy rod and thy staff they comfort me. Thou preparest a table before me in the presence of mine enemies; thou anointest my head with oil; my cup runneth over."

The psalmist shows the support and protection which believers may expect from their Redeemer, in the most grievous calamity. For, having put an extreme case in relation to himself, he declares his security, and then assigns the reason of it.

The case, which is extreme, he puts in these words: "Yea, though I walk through the valley of the shadow of death."

That we may rightly understand the whole passage, we must fix the meaning of the expression, "valley of the shadow of death." It does not signify *dying:* for it is not the valley of *death,* but of the *shadow* of death; and the shadow of an object cannot be the same thing with the object itself. The psalmist speaks of *walking* through this valley: which is a scriptural term for a habit of action, or a course of suffering. But death is neither the one nor the other; it is a *single* event. Accordingly the scriptures use the similitude we are now considering in a quite different sense. Two or three examples will suffice: Psalm xliv. 19. "Thou hast sore broken us in the place of dragons, and covered us with the shadow of death." Psalm cvii. 10-14. "Such as sit in darkness, and in the shadow of death, being bound in affliction and iron; because they rebelled against the words of God, and contemned the counsel of the Most High: therefore he brought down their heart with labour; they fell down, and there was none to help. Then they cried unto the Lord in their trouble, and he saved them out of their distresses. He brought them out of darkness and the shadow of death, and brake their bands in sunder." Jer. ii. 6, 7. "The Lord—led us through the wilderness, through a land of deserts and of pits, through a land of drought and of the shadow of death, through a land that no man passeth through, and where no man dwelt; and I brought you into a plentiful country," &c. As a shadow bears to the mind an obscure image of the appearance and proportions of its object, together with the idea of its being present or near: and as darkness is gloomy, and death dreadful, the "valley of the shadow of death," is a scene of great and uncommon distress—of such trials as overpower the soul; throw it into amazement; break its purposes; fill it with alarm and horror like that which invades trembling nature at the approach of the "king of terrors." This condition may arise from one or both of the following causes:

(1.) Temporal calamity. Acute and lingering disease; strokes upon family, or fortune, or fame; the rod of oppression; the rage of persecution, when men of blood hunt for the precious life; have taught thousands of whom the world was not worthy, what is meant by walking in the valley of the shadow of death.

(2.) A similar effect may be produced by spiritual conflict, whether it be with the "plague of the heart," or with "the accuser of the brethren." The apostle Paul had experience of the former, when "the law in his members, warring against the law of his mind, and bringing him into captivity to the law of sin which was in his members," forced from him that *exceeding great and bitter cry*, "O wretched man that I am! who shall deliver me from the body of this death;" and of the latter, where "there was given to him a thorn in the flesh, the messenger of Satan to buffet him:" with respect to both, most, if not all believers, are sooner or later, his "companions in tribulation." They often go in the bitterness of their souls through the power of "sin that dwelleth in them," and often are summoned to the field in the "whole armour of God." The name of our foes is "legion; for they are many." In what manner they act upon our spirits, it were idle to conjecture; but their existence and operations being matter of clear revelation and sober experience, it were still more idle to dispute. "The fiery darts of the wicked," are well known to those who "fight the good fight of faith." And when he is permitted to assail them by ministering fuel to their corruptions; by obscuring their graces; by distracting their minds with blasphemous suggestions; the most resolute among them are liable to faint, and are sometimes driven to such extremities, that their "souls choose strangling and death, rather than life."

From the necessity of thus walking through the valley of the shadow of death, God has not promised an exemption to any of his "dear children;" and they ought not to "think it strange concerning the fiery trial which is to try them, as though some strange thing happened to them. For they are called "to deny themselves, to take up their cross, and follow their Lord;" and are warned from the beginning, that they "must through much tribulation enter into his kingdom." The doctrine is as old as that of redemption, and is exemplified in the history of all the redeemed. In the verse before us, David considers it a very probable case, that he might himself shortly walk through the valley of the shadow of death. With his eye fastened on the prospect, he stands firm and collected, in the persuasion that he shall come off without ultimate loss. "I will fear no evil." Not to fear evils against which we are unprotected, savours more of stupidity than of courage. But there is often safety without security : for as there may be great danger where there is no apprehension, so there may be much apprehension where there is no danger. This frequently happens even to the "Israel of God," who, judging by delusive rules and " according to the outward appearance, are afraid where no fear is." But the psalmist, who at this time saw his objects in a true light, and measured them by a correct standard, was as free from dread as from danger. "The good man," saith he "can have no cause to shrink back from tribulation. Horrible as is that valley of the shadow of death which lies across my path, I will not turn aside to avoid it. Deaf to the report of inward feeling and outward circumstance, I will hold on my way, and fear no evil." But was the psalmist a madman? Had he learned to contemn the counsels of reason, and to stifle the emotions of nature? Did he court woe in the work of useless mortification? Or had religious discipline soured him to life, and wrought him up to the frenzy, that the agonies of body and mind are beneath a wise man's care? None of all these. He resolves his confidence into a principle which humbles the pride of the world, and is unapproached by the maxims of philosophy; and that is, the presence and guardianship of his Redeemer. "I will fear no evil, for thou art with me; thy rod and thy staff they comfort me." Behold the source of Christian magnanimity! Behold the charm which controls the mischief, and lightens the gloom of the shadow of death! "I will never leave thee nor forsake thee," is one of the "gracious words which have proceeded out of his mouth," and which shall not fail, though earth and heaven be sacrificed to its accomplishment. Thou art with me! My trials pass under thine eye, are apportioned by thy wisdom, and softened by thy love. Thy hand ministers help in the season of need: and it is thine to cause all things to work together for my good.

The rod and staff, by which the shepherd assisted his flock and kept off the beasts of prey, are emblems of those means which indicate the presence of Jesus: comfort his people, and awe their enemies; especially his word, his providence, and his Spirit, all which conspire in their preservation and support. Encouraged by such company, and backed by such aid, the language of David is both natural and modest: while it expresses a pre-eminence which believers will ever have over carnal men. In a world of sin we must look for sorrow; but without the faith of Jesus we shall look in vain for consolation. Peace of conscience and the repose of the heart; the light of God's countenance and an imperishable hope, belong not to the wicked, even in their best estate. And when they are to enter the valley of the shadow of death, their idols broken and their glories gone, who, ah, who would step into their place?. But out of that dreary vale there issues a voice: "I will fear no evil for thou art with me." The voice is Christian, and Christ is there! His gracious presence compensates the keenest suffering. Who has not heard of the wonders which it has wrought? It calmed the spirit of Daniel in the den of lions: it called forth the song of Paul and Silas from the dungeons of Philippi: it has borne ten thousand of the faithful above persecution and the persecutor: and at this hour, after the lapse of ages, it instructs ten thousand more to "glory in tribulation;" so that "they may boldly say, the Lord is my helper, and I will not fear what man shall do unto me." Encircled thus with mercy, and "walking by faith," they "endure as seeing him who is invisible." Patience has her perfect work, and they "go in the strength of the Lord

God," waiting till their deliverance come, and "the shadow of death be turned into the morning."

This happy reverse, which repays sharp affliction with sweet enjoyment, is not uncommon in the life of faith. The psalmist has noticed it in verse 5, where he introduces his Redeemer under the new emblem of a most hospitable friend.

Verse 5. "Thou preparest a table before me in the presence of mine enemies; thou anointest my head with oil: my cup runneth over."

These words, in very simple and impressive figure, celebrate,

(1.) The bounty of the Lord Jesus. "Thou preparest a table before me."

The allusion is to that hospitality of the East, which entertained even strangers with the fattest of the flock, with wine and oil, and with the most precious fruits of the earth. And these kind offices were the more grateful, as travellers had often no other accommodation than what was furnished by private munificence. But to invited guests, and on festive occasions, the preparations, according to rank and condition, were most liberal and sumptuous. Now believers are "strangers and pilgrims" who pass through this world, a land of wilderness and drought, in search of "a better country, that is, a heavenly." Exposed to fatigue, alarm, and conflict, they would faint without the refreshments provided for them by their Lord and Master. There are intervals in which he "deals bountifully with them." Taking them by the hand, he leads them from the valley of the shadow of death into his "banqueting house, and his banner over them is love." Instead of that awful reserve which they might anticipate in the "King of glory," he treats them with the most gracious familiarity. "Eat, O friends; drink, yea, drink abundantly, O beloved." Here their spirits are recruited, and their toils forgotten. They "delight themselves in the abundance of peace," and have the best of all proof that it is not "vain to serve God." Thus does he bestow upon his Church collectively, and upon her members individually, periods of prosperity and joy. When the one is favoured with "quietness and assurance," in the possession of his truth and ordinances, and the other flourish under the "light of his countenance," he has "prepared a table before them."

(2.) The circumstances which attend this privilege enhance its own value and the glory of its author. "Thou hast prepared a table before me," saith the text, "in the presence of mine enemies."

Like David, every believer is compassed with those who seek his life. And when to him, as to David, the Lord has "given rest round about from all his enemies," they are made the reluctant witnesses of his comfort. It greatly heightens our mercies to know, not only that they are from the hand of our Redeemer, but that he maintains us in the possession of them, against both earth and hell. This truth, which we are never to forget, should be asserted with more than ordinary zeal, when "many deceivers are entered into the world." We hear much of the philosophical character of the day: "that the ages of intolerant bigotry are succeeded by an age of liberal forbearance; that the rights of conscience are too well understood and established to be in danger hereafter; and, therefore, that the reign of persecution is over." But let no Christian be thrown off his guard by these "good words and fair speeches, which deceive the hearts of the simple." That we may, at present, worship our God without molestation of person or property, is true: and it is an inestimable privilege. But let us refer it to the right cause, and not array a philosophy "falsely so called," in honours which are due to our Redeemer alone. Enmity against his cross and followers, as implacable and active as ever, is limited by that sovereign control which makes "the wrath of man to praise him, and restrains the remainder of wrath." Let that control be taken off, and the next hour thousands will arise to "mingle your blood with your sacrifices." No! we ascribe nothing, for we owe nothing, to the mitigated spirit of the world. But we owe everything, and therefore ascribe everything, to the grace of our Lord Jesus. We thank Him, and not the liberality of the times, that our gospel-table is spread, and we surround it "without fear." The foe stands by and burns with rage, that he must look on but may not disturb. Under his eye, and within his reach, we safely break our bread and pour out our wine. Blessed Jesus! We adore thee for thy protection! Thou alone "hast prepared a table before us in the presence of our enemies!"

(3.) This bounty of our Lord is likewise accompanied with marks of singular condescension. "Thou anointest my head with oil."

Here, again, we must recur to a custom prevalent in the East—

the custom of anointing the head with scented oil. In those hot climates this was a most agreeable service, refreshing to the guest, and perfuming the apartment; while it was performed, if not by the hands of the " good man of the house," at least by his direction. Anointing the head with oil is, therefore, an emblem of happiness arising from the kindest offices of friendship. Scriptural usage applies it to the Holy Spirit, who is, emphatically, "the oil of gladness" wherewith the Saviour himself was anointed, and with which he anoints the heads of his people. In other words, the Holy Spirit, who rested without measure upon the Lord Jesus, and, by this measureless communication of all divine gifts and graces, constituted him the Christ, the Anointed, rests likewise upon all the members of his mystical body; communicating to them, out of his fulness, a suitable measure of gifts and grace. For they "have an unction from the Holy One," on account of which God calls them his Anointed, his Christs,* and by the efficacy of which they become Christians. This David knew and has expressed: this all believers know and experience. The Holy Spirit, as the " Spirit of the Son," God " sends forth into their hearts, crying, Abba, Father." He, therefore, dwells in them as the "spirit of grace and supplication," and the immediate efficient of all their spiritual character and joy. "Receiving of that which is Christ's, and showing it unto them," he mortifies their corruptions, quickens their graces, enlightens their darkness, dispels their fears. His name is Comforter; and when he descends upon them in his exhilarating power, solacing them with his love, beautifying them with his salvation, and breathing around them his fragrant grace, they have all that is signified by the emblem of the text: their heads are " anointed with fresh oil."

(4.) To conclude his animated description, "My cup," saith David, "runneth over."

Wine distributed in a cup, by the master of the house, among his guests, closed a Jewish entertainment: and hence, both in Scriptural and common language, an overflowing cup is the symbol of complete satisfaction, or, as the subject requires, of consummate

---

* 1 Chron. xvi. 22. Psalm cv. 15. The word in Hebrew משיחו equivalent to the Greek Χριστος (Christ), and, like it, signifying *Anointed*, is applied primarily to the Redeemer, and secondarily to believers, on account of their union with him, and participation of his Spirit.

woe. There can be no dispute about its meaning in the present instance. It proclaims the "blessedness of the man whom God hath chosen and caused to approach unto him. This, their communion with him in the Lord Jesus; this defence against their enemies; this participation of the Holy Ghost, fills up their souls. "Jehovah is the portion of their cup:" they know it, they rejoice in it, and they ask no more.

Such "marvellous loving-kindness" from the "Hope of Israel," may find, but cannot leave, a hard and unbelieving heart. The psalmist, therefore, follows the enumeration of his mercies with the tribute of his faith and gratitude, which is in verse 6, and composes the

II. Part of the psalm.

"Surely goodness and mercy shall follow me all the days of my life; and I will dwell in the house of the Lord for ever."

1. The tribute of his faith. "Surely goodness and mercy shall follow me all the days of my life."

That this is an exercise of faith, and not an expression of mere feeling, is plain from the confidence with which he anticipates futurity: thus answering to the apostle's forecited definition: "Now faith is the substance of things hoped for, the evidence of things not seen." Let us, then, consider what this exercise of faith contains, and upon what it is founded.

(1.) It contains a testimony to the propriety of the Lord's dispensations.

The psalmist had visited the "green pastures" and "still waters:" he next surveyed the "valley of the shadow of death," under the impression that he might shortly "walk through it:" he afterwards turns his eye from the "ten thousands that set themselves against him round about," to the "table prepared before him in their presence;" and gives his judgment. "It is all right," saith he. "It is just as it ought to be. I have nothing to diminish, to add, nor to alter. My soul owns it as 'goodness and mercy' throughout."

(2.) It contains an act of implicit trust, that whatever might be his own unworthiness, this "goodness and mercy" should never be withdrawn. "It shall follow me," saith he, "in all my wanderings: it shall tread in my very steps, and not leave me a moment till my warfare be over: it shall follow me all the days of my life." This is strong persuasion, but it rests on a strong foundation. Our God and Saviour, who "keepeth the covenant and mercy to them that love him," will neither disown his people nor break his word. Admit the possibility of his casting them off; that his gifts and his calling are" not "without repentance," and you cut the sinews of their rejoicing. No more must words of confidence be heard from their lips. I will walk through the valley of the shadow of death, and fear no evil! is a vain boast, because I have no assurance that the Lord will be with me. Nor is it any relief to tell me that I shall have his presence, provided I be faithful in my obedience. Without his presence to secure my fidelity, I am put upon the performance of an impossible condition. A very little acquaintance with myself, will teach me that if it in the least depended on my own strength, my claim to the continuance of the Lord's goodness and mercy, though ever so valid the present hour, would be forfeited the next. But this is not, and never can be, the case. My Redeemer is "Jehovah who changes not," and therefore, I am neither consumed, nor forsaken. All this is practical truth, which the psalmist has recorded as his own experience; and which is substantially the experience of other believers. "The Lord," saith he, "who is my Shepherd, actually makes me to lie down in green pastures; he actually restores my soul, and leadeth me in the paths of righteousness; he actually is with me in the valley of the shadow of death, and has prepared a table before me in the presence of my enemies." Here is no room for cold and wavering speculation: for here is nothing but plain fact as the fulfilment of covenant-promise. The psalmist declares what he had seen, and heard, and felt. He had, therefore, in his own bosom, a comment upon his Lord's veracity, and a pledge of future bounty, more solid and satisfying than a thousand arguments, though from the mouth of an angel. He placed his foot upon the rock of eternal truth; and "as he believed, so he spake."—"Surely!" exclaims he, "it is not vague opinion, nor fluctuating hope; it is sweet reality, it is blessed certainty."—" Surely goodness and mercy shall follow me all the days of my life!" O that our souls knew more of the precious exercise! how would it silence our murmurs, and hush our tumults, and swell our joy! Happy psalmist! may I learn with thee to weigh all things in the balance of the sanctuary;

and to sing, with thee, of goodness and mercy which have followed, and shall follow me, all the days of my life!

2. As none who have ventured their souls upon the Lord's promise make an evil report of his ways; and as their only return for his benefits is devotion to his fear, the psalmist, who speaks their mind, has added the tribute of his gratitude to that of his faith. "I will dwell in the house of the Lord for ever." The same resolution, with a slight variety of phrase, occurs in Psalm lxi. verse 4. "I will abide in thy tabernacle for ever:" and they both express the most unreserved and hearty dedication to the service of God. Particularly,

(1.) A deliberate choice, on the part of Christians, of the interests of God's glory and of God's Church as their own most valuable interests.

Nothing less can be signified by "the house of the Lord" as the object of their affections. They approach him not with the dry compliment of occasional visitors, but with the dispositions of those who mean to be constantly under his eye and obedient to his will. They "cast in their lot" with his people; they join themselves unto his family; they live in his house, and everything belonging to it is dear to their hearts.

(2.) Waiting upon God in all the ordinances of instituted worship.

To know him, and not to worship him, is a contradiction. To pretend to worship him, and not wait upon him in his ordinances, is to stand self-convicted of slandering his wisdom and slighting his grace. In Christians such conduct is impossible. They "love the habitation of his house, and the place where his honour dwelleth:" thither they repair, that they "may behold his beauty and inquire in his temple;" may hear from his own lips, and find in his own appointments, solutions of difficulties which would otherwise dishearten and distract them; may be "satisfied with the goodness of his house," and with the communion of that "lovingkindness which is better than life."

(3.) An open confession of his name.

There is nothing in the service of God to create a blush; and a heart renewed by his grace is too honest to play the hypocrite. Worldlings often show a fair face to religion, while their souls overflow with enmity against it, and they secretly plot its ruin.

But to pretend affection for the world, while the "hidden man of the heart" cleaves unto God, is repugnant to every principle of the Christian calling. And such a deception would be not less impracticable than absurd. A living Christian can no more refrain from giving indications of his life, than light can refrain from shining in the dark. Carnal men quickly discern and avoid those who "run not with them to the same excess of riot," and are seldom backward to "speak evil of them." So that if we take up our abode in the house of the Lord, it cannot be long a secret to the world; nor do we wish it to be so. We pursue different objects in a different manner: we "come out from among them, and are separate," as belongeth to "the sons and daughters of the Lord Almighty." And having learned to "esteem the reproach of Christ greater riches than the treasures in Egypt," we can have neither reason nor inclination to conceal, that "we had rather be door-keepers in the house of our God for a single day, than to dwell a thousand in the tents of sin."

(4.) As this devotion to the Lord Jesus is voluntary and open, so it is irreversible. I will dwell, saith David, in the house of the Lord for ever; or as he has interpreted his own words "all the days of my life."

Christians make no experiments with their religion; and it is incredible they should. Having "passed from death unto life," how can they waste a moment in considering which is preferable? Their choice being for eternity, and necessarily including the remainder of their days in time, they "are not of them who draw back unto perdition, but of them that believe to the saving of the soul." Consequently, there can be "no place for repentance." For who would exchange the favour of God for his displeasure? his blessing for his curse? his kingdom for the bottomless pit? Of those who walk "according to the course of this world," thousands have expired with curses on their folly. But among all who "have made the Lord their trust," not one has recalled his choice, nor regretted that he was too early, too closely, or too long attached to the house of God. A believer's condition affords present enjoyment, and a happy presage of his end."—"My soul," cries he, "has regained her rest. Here I am satisfied, and here will I remain. 'While I live, will I praise the Lord;' and when I am to 'finish my course,' I will expect in glory the consummation of what is begun in grace. For both worlds, it is my resolution and my hope, to "dwell in the house of the Lord for ever."

Out of this review of the psalm, there arises a question deeply interesting to him who speaks, and to them who hear. "What acquaintance have I with its truth, and what share in its consolations? The latter spring out of the former, and are inseparable from it. To aim at their separation, as many do, is the wicked and vain attempt to "put asunder what God has joined." Be it written on the tables of our hearts, "as with a pen of iron, and with the point of a diamond," that none who are strangers to the grace of the gospel, have any right to its comforts. Through any other channel, all pretensions to them are false, for all enjoyment of them is impossible. Take heed, professor of religion, that thou "sport not thyself with thine own deceivings." It is easy to say Lord, Lord; to yield verbal assent to the doctrine of this psalm concerning the mutual relation of Jesus and his people; to preserve such a "form of godliness" as shall obtain credit among thy fellow-mortals; but without something more, and something better, thou shalt not "see God." That religion which shall survive the grave, and go with thee into the eternal world, results from union to Jesus, as the Lord thy Life. It is not enough that he is the "Shepherd of the sheep;" he must be thy Shepherd, and thou one of his flock—not enough that he saves sinners; he must save thee, even thee in particular, "with an everlasting salvation"—not enough that he supplies the wants of the saved; he must enable thee to live by faith upon him for thine own soul, and to receive out of his fulness "grace and mercy to help in the time of need." Whoever stops short of this, stops short of life. His services are rejected, because his person is under condemnation. Till Christ be "formed in him the hope of glory," not only is he shut out from the blessings described in this psalm, but all his penitence, devotions, virtues, are of no avail. He wants the original principle of all genuine virtue and all acceptable obedience, which is laid in the "renewing of the Holy Ghost." His hope is the hope of the hypocrite, which shall perish, and "the wrath of God abideth on him."

Yet the condition of unregenerated men, though dreadful, is not desperate. Lost they are; but "the Son of man came to seek and to save that which was lost," and is now "exalted to the right hand of God to be a Prince and a Saviour, for to give repentance and forgiveness of sins." In the days of his flesh he "was not sent but to the lost sheep of the house of Israel;" but, at parting with his apostles, he informed them, "other sheep I have, which are not of this fold: them also I must bring, and they shall hear my voice; and there shall be one fold and one shepherd." He has been gathering them, ever since, "out of every kindred, and tongue, and people, and nation:" they have crowded, by thousands, into his fold: they are pressing into it at this very hour, *and yet there is room:* there is room, O perishing man, for thee. The very circumstance of thy being forlorn and destitute, instead of keeping thee from the Saviour, should impel thee to flee to him as thy refuge from the approaching tempest. Art thou criminal and base? "Are thine iniquities increased over thine head, and thy trespass grown up unto the heavens?" This only renders the salvation of Jesus the more indispensable, and his grace in proffering it the more alluring. His work is with sinners, the chief of sinners; his delight, to pluck them as "brands out of the burning;" and therefore, O guilty man, his overtures are to thee. Exclude not thyself from his kingdom by voluntary unbelief; seeing that he is able, and hath promised, "to save them to the uttermost that come unto God by him."

"Christians, who alone have a right to claim, and a taste to relish, the consolations of this psalm, should improve it to "their furtherance and joy of faith." No sweeter song can they sing "in the house of their pilgrimage." Their Redeemer, whom it celebrates, is rich, and mighty, and bountiful, and vigilant, and gracious. They are "complete in him;" they "have all and abound." Be satisfied, then, O believer, with thy portion! Let not an emotion of discontent stir in thy bosom! "Be not envious at the foolish, when thou seest the prosperity of the wicked." Thou hast a better inheritance, and better company, and all thy concerns shall come to a better issue, than theirs. Repress every hard thought of thy munificent Shepherd. Believe his truth; believe it against the objections of sense and the calumnies of Satan; believe it without staggering, and thine eyes shall see his salvation. Whatever be the judgment of thine own ignorance and of the world's malice, he is leading thee by "a right way;" and this thou shalt confess, with wonder and praise, when he shall have brought thee to thy "city of habitation!" Go on, then, in his strength; set up thy banners in his name, and inscribe them with this triumphant motto: "The Lord is my Shepherd, I shall not want."

LECTURE.

PSALM VIII.

"1. O Lord, our Lord, how excellent is thy name in all the earth! who hast set thy glory above the heavens.

"2. Out of the mouth of babes and sucklings hast thou ordained strength because of thine enemies, that thou mightest still the enemy and the avenger.

"3. When I consider thy heavens, the work of thy fingers; the moon and the stars, which thou hast ordained;

"4. What is man, that thou art mindful of him; and the son of man, that thou visitest him?

"5. For thou hast made him a little lower than the angels, and hast crowned him with glory and honour.

"6. Thou madest him to have dominion over the works of thy hands; thou hast put all things under his feet:

"7. All sheep and oxen, yea, and the beasts of the field;

"8. The fowl of the air, the fish of the sea, and whatsoever passeth through the paths of the seas.

"O Lord, our Lord, how excellent is thy name in all the earth!"

On what occasion this psalm was penned, interpreters are not agreed, nor is it material for us to know. It seems probable, however, that it was composed by David, before God called him from the cottage to the crown, and whilst, in the exercise of the pastoral employment, he watched his flocks by the light of the moon. But whether this is really the case or not, it is of high moment that we should rightly understand and duly improve its important instructions. A little reflection discovers that the redemption by Christ Jesus is the endearing theme to which our attention is invited. For we shall find, in the course of our discussion, that, after proposing in general terms the illustration of God's glory in the victories of the gospel, it informs us, particularly, of the instruments who were to carry on the wondrous plan—ascends to the original source of the blessing—tells us how it should be purchased for men—and what provision is made for its security and success to the end of the world.

The mind of pious David was deeply affected by this interesting view. How did his heart burn within him while he mused on the endearing topic! How did his spirit exult when he saw with prophetic eye the honour of his Redeemer spreading to the east and to the west, to the north and to the south! Dazzled with the brightness, and overwhelmed with the immensity of the prospect, he loses himself, and, as the mouth of those millions who should flock to the Shiloh, exclaims, in the language of admiring gratitude,

1. "O Lord, our Lord, how excellent is thy name in all the earth; who hast set thy glory above the heavens!"

By the "name" of God we are to understand, in general, anything which he makes known of himself; and, therefore, we find that his different attributes are called, in different parts of Scripture, his name. Here, and in some other passages, it signifies the divine glory, or the assemblage of the divine perfections as they shine in the dispensation of grace.

That the psalmist is not speaking of the divine perfections as they are displayed in the works of nature, is manifest; because it is Jehovah, whose name he says is "excellent in all the earth,"—*i. e.*, in all the habitable parts of the earth, where there are rational beings to know, to feel, to celebrate its excellence. Now, though nature teaches that there is a God, and teaches something, too, of his character, yet nature teaches neither the name nor the whole character of Israel's God. We are not to suppose that the psalmist means to exclude any part of the divine character from a share in this excellence; and how could Jehovah's character appear excellent where it was not known? We are also to reflect that when the Scriptures mention the knowledge of God's name as a ground of reverence, fear, trust, delight, &c., they always refer to a knowledge derived from revelation. Farther; excellence is a high degree of good, and cannot but attract love. But the apostle Paul declares that "the carnal mind is enmity against God," and, therefore, cannot love him, nor deem his perfections excellent. Now if unrenewed men are unable to love God, even with the help of revelation, they certainly cannot learn to love him, without it, from the works of nature. If they think they can, it is a proof of their ignorance and self-deceit. The God whom they love is a

God of their own making. Nature and philosophy discover nothing of Jehovah, but as an absolute God. They may, and if they do him justice they will, represent him as clothed in majesty: but it is the majesty of terror. A flame goeth before him—the whirlwinds play around him—his voice is thunder, his look, the lightning's flash. It is only in Christ Jesus that God reconciles the world to himself; it is in him alone that all the divine perfections appear excellent; and it is in the view of the universal preaching of the gospel that the psalmist could with any propriety say, "O Lord, our Lord, how excellent is thy name in all the earth."

To the earth, however, the praise of God's excellent name is not confined, for he "has set his glory above the heavens." Not in the heavens: an expression which might lead us to think of the glory of creation and providence as exhibited in the heavenly bodies: but above the heavens, far beyond the reach of mortal observation. That by this phrase is meant the highest heavens, that glorious place which Christ has prepared for his people, and in which, with the angels, they adore redeeming love, will be abundantly clear if we attend to another of a similar kind. In the 113th Psalm, we read thus, "From the rising of the sun unto the going down of the same, the Lord's name is to be praised." "The Lord is high above all nations, and his glory above the heavens." The parallel passage in Malachi i. 11, "From the rising of the sun unto the going down of the same, my name shall be great among the Gentiles" makes it plain that the glory mentioned in the psalm just quoted, is the glory of God in the salvation of men; and this is the glory which is there said to be "above the heavens." And the words which we are considering, present to our view the august and solemn scene formed by the church militant and the church triumphant, joining in one general chorus of praise to the Father of mercies. We may therefore rest satisfied, that the immediate and only object of this verse is to extol the grace of God in sending his Son to redeem sinners. Well may we wonder at the immensity of such love: and our wonder will be increased if we follow the psalmist. He not only bids us admire the salvation itself, but tells us,

II. What instruments should be employed in carrying on the amazing plan, as in

Verse 2. "Out of the mouth of babes and sucklings hast thou ordained strength because of thine enemies, that thou mightest still the enemy and the avenger."

That the words we are now considering are prophetical, we are not allowed to doubt, for so they were viewed by Him who could not mistake the meaning of scripture. We are told, by the evangelist Matthew (ch. xxi.) that when our Lord, according to an ancient oracle, made his public entry into Jerusalem, the multitude, actuated, it would seem, by a divine impulse, cried out, "Hosanna to the son of David; blessed be he that cometh in the name of the Lord; Hosanna in the highest!" When he passed to his house of prayer, authoritatively purged it from impious intruders, and performed, in the sight of admiring crowds, some of his most benevolent miracles, the sacred ardour flowed in every breast, and even the children who were sporting in the temple caught the cry, "Hosanna to the son of David!" On this occasion, the blind, envious, unprincipled Pharisees, nettled at one of the most delightful and sublime scenes that can interest a reasonable nature, asked, in the spirit of discontented petulance, "Hearest thou what these say?"—"Yea," replied the Saviour, quoting the very words of David, "Yea: have ye never read, Out of the mouth of babes and sucklings thou hast perfected praise?" This circumstance clearly shows that the passage before us refers to the times of the gospel; and if it received an accomplishment in the fact just related, it was more abundantly accomplished in the ministry of the first preachers of the gospel. These were characterized by the spirit of prophecy as babes. "Whom shall he teach knowledge? and whom shall he make to understand doctrine?"—"Them that are weaned from the milk, and drawn from the breasts." (Isaiah, xxviii. 9.) They were termed babes by Christ himself: for when he upbraided with ignorance and hardness of heart "those cities wherein most of his mighty works were done, he answered," the historian tells us, "and said, I thank thee, O Father, Lord of heaven and earth, that thou hast hid these things from the wise and prudent, and hast revealed them unto babes." This passage, with the correspondent one in Luke, makes it manifest that the disciples are intended: for that evangelist informs us, that these words were spoken when "the seventy returned again with joy, saying, Lord, even the devils are subject unto us through thy name." (Luke x. 17.)

The disciples of Christ, though adult in years, were babes in knowledge and improvement: plain, simple men, unfurnished with that erudition to which the affluent had access. With respect to the great work also, in which they were to be employed, they were as feeble in themselves, and as unfit for it, as babes are for performing the duties of active life. To the world likewise, they appeared contemptible in their birth, in their connections, in their fortune, in everything about them. And the project of reforming mankind, in their hands, carnal wisdom, which would think such a task proper for statesmen only and philosophers, would pronounce as silly as the charge of an empire committed to an infant. And yet, "from the mouth of these babes and sucklings," (let proud philosophy take a lesson from the fact,) God, the psalmist assures us, "ordained strength: such strength, as shook to its centre the kingdom of darkness, and made Satan fall as lightning from heaven. The great Mediator, during and especially after his own ministry, crowned with abundant success the preaching of his word. The apostles went forth in the name of Jesus; Jehovah's arm was nerved in their cause; and, by the might of that arm, "worm Jacob thrashed the mountains, and beat them small as chaff." In thus ordaining strength, God "perfected praise:" for the weakness of the instruments, compared with the miraculous effects they produced, showed to all who were not "given up to the lusts of their own hearts, that the excellency of the powers was of him."

The strength of which we are speaking, God, the psalmist informs us, ordained "because of his enemies: that he might still the enemy and the avenger."

"Enemies," in the former part of this clause, seems to comprehend all who were unfriendly to the cause of Christ, whether secretly or openly. Enemy and avenger perhaps refer chiefly to Satan; for these characters unquestionably are his: or if not to him solely, to Satan and the persecutor. If this distinction be not admitted, if the whole clause be considered as a general description of the foes of the Redeemer, the truth which it inculcates will yet remain the same; viz. that these foes were so strong as to yield to nothing less than almighty power; or as the psalmist expresses it, that such power was necessary to enable the disciples " to still the enemy and the avenger." And did they still him? Yes. Their preaching silenced the heathen oracles—they refuted the arguments —they detected the sophistry—they stopped the mouths of their adversaries. The Jews, we are told, "could not resist the Spirit and wisdom by which Stephen spake." And of the disputes which Paul had with his antagonists, the issue frequently was that they replied with reproach and persecution, the sure tokens of a baffled cause. In the triumphs which the apostles and fellow-labourers gained, they found their Lord faithful to his promise, that "he would give them a mouth and wisdom, which all their adversaries should not be able to gainsay nor resist." In fact, nothing else could have supported them: for no sooner was the trumpet of the everlasting gospel blown, than hell, alarmed, mustered its legions: earth joined the conspiracy: and the resistance, to human ability, must have been invincible. But the sword of the apostles (the Word of God, the doctrines of the cross) was of heavenly temper: it shivered the weapons, it mowed down the ranks, of their enemies; and they became "more than conquerors through him that loved them." If we are duly affected with a sense of the precious favours that flow from the gospel of peace, and of the divine wisdom and energy employed in propagating them among men, we will be prepared for attending the psalmist whilst, in the

III. Place, he directs us to the original source of these blessings. This is the good pleasure, the free grace of God, as we are taught in verses 3 and 4.

"When I consider thy heavens, the work of thy fingers; the moon and the stars which thou hast ordained; what is man that thou art mindful of him? and the son of man, that thou visitest him?"

I remark, in passing, that it is from his omitting the sun, while he speaks of the other heavenly bodies, that David is thought to have composed this psalm when he watched his flocks at night.

Difference of sentiment appears in the answers which have been given to the question, who are meant by "man, and the son of man?" That these words cannot relate to mankind in their state of innocence, is perfectly clear. The word here rendered man, conveys an idea of frailty and misery; neither of which belonged to our first parents before the fall: besides, there would be neither propriety nor sense in denominating them the "son of man;" for there was then no son of man in existence—and, to add no more, the psalmist is lost in wonder, at God's being mindful of man, and visiting him. But it is no wonder at all, that God should notice, and kindly visit, innocent man. Nothing which he saw fit to create, while it continues as he created it, does he judge below his attention. It is moral deformity alone that renders a creature odious and loathsome in the sight of a holy God.

On the other hand, men, valuable for their erudition, and venerable for their piety, have supposed that the words *man* and *the son of man*, or at least the latter, refer to the Redeemer in his state of humiliation. We know that he is frequently, though not exclusively, styled "the Son of man." We know, likewise, that he speaks of himself in terms of the lowest abasement. " I am a worm, and no man; a reproach of men, and despised of the people." But, with all deference to the respectable authority of those who think that Christ is meant in the verses before us, I hope I shall be pardoned for deviating a little from their opinion. What striking proof did Jehovah give that he was mindful of the person here mentioned, and visited him? The psalmist tells us in the very next words, it was by making his Son "a little lower than the angels." But, according to the hypothesis to which I object, Christ was already in a state of humiliation; so that God could not express his being mindful of him, and visit him by bringing him into that state. And where was the wonder that God the Father should thus visit the humbled Saviour? He was, even in his lowest humiliation, the Son of Jehovah's love. Divine faithfulness was pledged to the suffering Redeemer; and is it any wonder that God should keep his word?

I therefore conclude that the psalmist has his eye upon mankind in their lost, their wretched condition. When I look, says he, at thy heavens; when I contemplate the immensity of thy works; when I consider the boundless theatre on which thy glory is displayed; that thou needest neither us nor our services; that we would hardly be missed were we blotted from the page of existence; particularly when I consider our guilt and vileness, I cannot but exclaim, what is man, insignificant, worthless man! what is he? what has he to attract thy notice? Nothing at all. That thou shouldst be mindful of him, and visit him with thy salvation, is of sovereign grace! Well might the psalmist be astonished! well may we be astonished! and our astonishment will rise if we accompany him while he tells us, in the

IV. Place, how the great salvation was provided for men; it was by the humiliation and exaltation of the Son of God in the character of our Redeemer. This is what the psalmist means when he says, verse 5,

" For thou hast made him a little lower than the angels, and hast crowned him with glory and honour."

We commonly hear those words interpreted of man as he came originally from the hands of his Creator. But this interpretation proceeds from a negligent view of the subject. No criticism can torture the psalmist's expression into such a meaning, and make it consistent with the rest of the psalm, and the rest of the scripture.

The verse plainly tells us, how the Most High testified that he was mindful of man, and with what honour and favour he visited him. But the very idea of being mindful of him and visiting him, supposes that he was created before, for it is not easy to see how one can visit a nonentity.

Farther, the Apostle Paul, in the second chapter of his epistle to the Hebrews, cites this passage to prove the divine glory of the Lord Christ: but if it relates to man, the apostle would argue very strangely, in asserting that Christ was above the angels, because man was below them.

The phraseology, however, both of the psalmist and of the apostle puts the matter beyond doubt and forbids reply. The word which we translate made lower, has not the smallest reference to creation, but signifies in both the original languages, to lessen, to diminish, to bring from a superior to an inferior station: and the word which we render little, refers, not to degrees of dignity, but to length of time.

Now, if the glory of Christ suffered a diminution by his being made (as the margin very properly reads) for a little while lower than the angels; the inference is strictly logical, that prior to this event he was above them, and therefore was God. In this view the words are not at all applicable to man; for when was he higher than the angels? In any other, the apostle's quotation is impertinent, and his argument ridiculous.

The only difficulty which can remain, is, that the psalmist should introduce the Redeemer so abruptly, by the relative "him," without any previous notice of the person whom he meant. But this difficulty will vanish, if we allow ourselves to reflect that this psalm was composed in the hours of retirement—that it is a devout effusion of gratitude to God. Surely the psalmist knew whom he meant, and as surely God could be at no loss to understand him —nor will this circumstance prejudice the general use of the psalm, for we must farther reflect not only that the manner in which the sacred penman speaks precludes uncertainty about the person to whom he alludes, but that the faith of ancient believers pointed perpetually to a promised Saviour, like the needle to the pole— that they were so frequently engaged in meditating upon his character and offices, as not to be taken by surprise when he was suddenly mentioned without any formal intimation. In truth they knew much more of their Redeemer, and thought much oftener upon him, than we are willing to believe—they knew much more of him, and thought much oftener on him, than many who are inclined to pride themselves on their superior light.

When, therefore, the psalmist says, "thou hast made him for a little while lower than the angels," nothing else can be intended than God's sending his own Son to assume our nature, to sojourn in our earth, and to submit to all that train of afflictions which are comprehended under the term of his "humiliation." But this scene of suffering was of short duration: for having "finished the work which was given him to do,"—having, by his obedience and death, made "reconciliation for iniquity, and brought in everlasting righteousness;" he rose from the dead, he ascended up into heaven, "he sat down at the right hand of the majesty on high;" or, as the psalmist expresses it, he was "crowned with glory and honour."

That Jehovah should be at such vast expense to rescue perishing men from everlasting ruin, is a thought too big for our little souls; but the fact is as certain as the thought is transporting: and to complete our consolation, the inspired psalmist not only assures us of the reality, and tells us how the blessing was procured for men, but informs us,

V. What provision is made that it shall not be lost, but

shall be continued and experienced in the world till the end of time.

The provision of which I speak, is the supreme and uncontrollable authority of the Lord Jesus; an authority which he constantly exerts for the benefit of his church, so that "all things shall work together for good to them that love God, to them that are called according to his purpose."

Of this authority we have a description in the 6th, 7th, and 8th verses. "Thou madest him to have dominion over the works of thy hands: thou hast put all things under his feet. All sheep and oxen; yea, and the beasts of the field: the fowl of the air and the fish of the sea, and whatsoever passeth through the paths of the seas."

No argument is necessary to show that the whole of this passage belongs to the same person: and the beginning of it is expressly applied to Christ by the Apostle Paul, 1 Cor. xv. 27, and Ephes. i. 22. In the latter, after declaring that God the Father had exalted Christ "far above all principality and power, and every name that is named, not only in this world, but also in that which is to come," he sums up his description of the Redeemer's authority, in the general expression of the psalmist, "and hath put all things under his feet." The very same application is made in the epistle to the Hebrews, where the apostle proves from the fact, that the psalmist could not mean the dominion which man exercises over the creatures: "for," says he, "we see not yet all things put under him:" yet, after so long a time, after all his advantages, and improvement, and labour, we see not yet all things put under him: "but we see Jesus, who was made a little lower than the angels—crowned with glory and honour."

It is perfectly clear that all the works of God, are not now, and never were, and never will be, under our government: but to our Redeemer is "given all power in heaven and earth." His unlimited rule extends to even the meanest thing that swims in the waters, creeps on the earth, or flies in the air. But by his command, even the beasts of the field shall espouse his quarrel: the veriest reptile shall be to his enemies a messenger of wrath!

After this brief, but comprehensive and delightful view of the dominion of the Messiah, David concludes the psalm as he had begun, by expressing his reverence, gratitude, and admiration:

and all who are governed by the same spirit, will cordially join his note of praise—" O Lord, our Lord, how excellent is thy name in all the earth!"

Let us dwell upon a few of the practical reflections which this psalm suggests.

1. The brightest and most endearing illustration of the divine glory, is in the scheme of redemption.

'Tis true God has sketched, if I may so speak, the outlines of his character upon his works. They all unite in proclaiming,—

"The hand that made us is divine."

But 'tis equally true that our understandings are darkened, and our wills corrupted; so that of ourselves, we can neither perceive Jehovah's character as we ought, nor love it if we could. The misfortune, however, is that multitudes, and of those too who are called philosophers, think they can derive from the works of creation all the knowledge of God which they need: and thus we hear them talk of rising from nature up to nature's God; and at the same time they totally disregard, as below their notice, his revealed will. But it is an eternal truth that the God of nature is the God of grace: and he who never saw his glory shining in the face of Jesus Christ, never yet saw it aright in the system of nature. To assert the contrary, would be to assert, that a man who is stark blind at noon-day, can see clearly at twilight. Give philosophy every advantage, and she can teach nothing but some abstract general attributes of the deity; his goodness, his justice, &c. Whatever matter they may afford for sublime speculation to the reasoning mind, they can impart no peace to the sinner. In vain is it told to him that God is the Father of mercies, and pours down his blessings upon his children. He sees that the blessings of providence fall alike upon the evil and the good; so that, notwithstanding these tender mercies, he may perish eternally. Philosophy is mute at questions like these: " Wherewithal shall I come before the Lord, and bow myself before the Most High God? How shall justice be exalted, and the sinner sheltered from wrath? She never yet enabled, and never will enable, any one to use the language, " My Lord and my God." The gospel of Jesus can alone satisfy our doubts, and fill us with joy and peace in believing. Let us never then hear of putting our hope in God out of Jesus

Christ. We have nothing to do with an absolute God. Every attribute of his nature thunders into the bosom of guilt ten thousand terrors. It is our Emmanuel alone who hath opened a new and living way to the Father, and in him alone we have boldness and confidence in approaching the throne of grace. I would not be understood to discredit philosophy: but let her keep her proper place, the place of a handmaid. Let not her votaries strip the Son of God of his honours to decorate this idol of their vows.

2. When the love of God is shed abroad in the heart, the lips will show forth his praise. This part of the Christian temper is beautifully illustrated by the example of David. What are his psalms but the holy breathings of his devout soul? "Be not deceived: out of the abundance of the heart the mouth speaketh." Impudent are that man's pretensions to piety, from whose closet and family the incense of prayer and praise never ascends— equally impudent are their pretensions, who can see, with coolness, the Saviour slighted; who can hear, without an indignant emotion, his name reviled. If God is our Father, we cannot be indifferent to his glory: if Jesus is our Redeemer and Friend, every blow aimed at him will be as a sword within our own bones.

3. Since God has thought proper to "ordain strength out of the mouth of babes and sucklings," let us improve the fact for instruction, for admonition, for consolation. Let us improve it for instructing ourselves in the ways of divine providence. In every age, God has conducted, and protected, and prospered his church, by means which carnal wisdom would pronounce utterly insufficient for the mighty task. When the gospel was about to be published to the world, did he call in the aid of philosophers and kings? Quite the reverse! Rather than employ them he wrought miracles. He committed the amazing trust to men, most of whom were in every respect contemptible, and whose undertaking could appear little else than the wild reverie of a delirium. Yet, through Christ strengthening them, they triumphed over all opposition. The history, too, of later periods, has recorded more than one example in which the plainest truths of the gospel, told in the plainest manner, have entirely confounded the acutest reasoner. This is exactly the apostle's doctrine. "Ye see your calling, brethren, how that not many wise men after the flesh, not many mighty, not many

noble, are called: but God hath chosen the foolish things of the world to confound the wise; and God hath chosen the weak things of the world to confound the things which are mighty; and base things of the world, and things which are despised, hath God chosen, yea, and things which are not, to bring to naught things that are: that no flesh should glory in his presence." In a word, God has not only chosen such instruments to gather in his elect, but has commonly the greatest number of his children among people of a similar description. Let us therefore improve the fact for admonition.

That Christians should be abused, and mocked by those who are open enemies to their Lord, is nothing strange: it is no more than they expected. But sooner or later, the great Redeemer will have with such persons a very solemn reckoning. This admonition, however, is not intended for them alone. There are many, with shame, with grief, with indignation be it spoken, there are many who profess the name of Jesus, and yet do not blush to vilify those who love him in sincerity. What more common than to hear the truly pious, especially those who are in the humbler walks of life, branded as hypocrites, enthusiasts, the fanatic rabble, and the like: and this too often by those from whom we had a right to look for other and for better things? Is it not enough, that they are careless about the important concerns which relate to God, eternity, heaven, and hell: but must they condemn as superstitious fools, all who are not willing to be as indifferent as themselves? Is it not enough, that they can see no beauty in the exalted Saviour—that they feel not the value of his righteousness, and think they need no supplies from his fulness: but must they reproach as idiots all to whom he is altogether lovely, and who desire nothing so anxiously as to "live a life of faith upon the Son of God?" Whatever persons who act thus may think of their own characters, they are the most implacable enemies of Christ. He hath said that he considers as done to himself, every indignity done to the least of his brethren: and he hath said, "that whosoever shall offend one of the little ones that believe in him, it were better for him that a millstone were hanged about his neck, and that he were drowned in the depths of the sea." Such conduct, however, shall not materially injure the weakest believers—it shall end in disappointment and shame for it fights against God, who has determined "to ordain strength out of the mouth of babes and sucklings." We may, therefore, improve the fact for their consolation.

Our Lord has told his followers that in the world they shall have tribulation: and one of the bitterest ingredients in their cup of sorrow, is the hatred and insult of professed friends. But let them remember that their mean appearance in the eyes of men, and the obloquy which is heaped upon them, are no barriers to the grace of the Saviour, and cannot depreciate them in his esteem. Let them remember that he has promised to put "their tears into his bottle, to write them in his book:" and that in due time he will raise their voices, though now feeble as the voice of babes and sucklings, to sing the high praises of their redeeming God; when the mirth of the scorner shall be turned into horror and howling, and his name be covered with deathless infamy.

4. Whilst we magnify that rich grace which provided a redemption for man, let us admire the stupendous method by which it was accomplished. Lost in wonder, let us stand still and see this great sight, the incarnation of the Son of God! Behold! the Creator of the ends of the earth becomes an infant of days—humbles himself to death, even the death of the cross; and descends to the silent tomb! O death, how great was thy triumph in that awful hour! and had the triumph been perpetual, where were our hopes of heaven? But let every heart rejoice that it was not possible our Surety should be kept the prisoner of the grave. God had sworn that his Holy One should see no corruption. He therefore burst the bars of death; and having thus proved himself to be the Son of God, he ascended, a complete conqueror, into the highest heavens. Brethren, if the Lord Jesus so loved sinners of our race—if for them he emptied himself of his glory—if for them he became "a man of sorrows and acquainted with grief"—if for them his blood streamed on Calvary—if the sufferings he endured for them, extorted from him that expiring cry which pierced the heavens, shook the earth, and rent the caverns of the tomb—if for them he bowed to the dust of death—if for them he spoiled principalities and powers, and reassumed the splendours of his former state—if to them he offers, freely, the "redemption purchased by his blood;" the least return we can make, is to devote ourselves wholly to this celestial friend. Let every faculty of our souls, every member of our bodies every action of our lives, be inscribed with this motto,

R

"Holiness to the Lord!" It is his own command, "My son, give me thine heart." We may cheerfully obey; for no guilt, no unworthiness, no vileness, can equal the multitude of his compassions. He is able to "save to the uttermost all that come unto God by him;" and he hath promised that "them who come to him, he will in no wise cast out." Let such as either openly or practically deny his divine glory, and the necessity and virtue of his atoning blood, solemnly reflect, that if they do not find, by happy experience, that he is almighty to save; their certain, their fearful, their irretrievable ruin will furnish a tremendous proof that he is almighty to destroy.

Finally, "Let the children of Zion be joyful in their King." Christians, it is a delightful truth, that Jesus the Saviour lives, Jesus the Saviour reigns; and lives and reigns for you. Let hope, then, lift up her fainting head—Let faith stretch her pinions, wing her flight to the third heavens, and view the Redeemer enthroned in all the glory of incarnate Deity. Invested with infinite power, he is able and faithful to "keep what you have committed to him." "Looking, therefore, unto Jesus, the author and finisher of our faith, let us lay aside every weight and the sin that doth most easily beset us, and let us run with patience the race set before us." Let us pray for the influences of his good Spirit, that we may continually grow in grace, till the arrival of that happy hour when "there shall be ministered unto us abundantly an entrance into his kingdom." Then we shall join with saints and angels in singing the high praises of God our Saviour; and this shall be the heavenly anthem: "To him that loved us, and washed us from our sins in his own blood, and hath made us kings and priests unto God and his Father; to him be glory and dominion for ever and ever. Amen.

LECTURE.

MATTHEW XXVII. 1—5.

"1. When the morning was come, all the chief priests and elders of the people took counsel against Jesus to put him to death.

"2. And when they had bound him, they led him away, and delivered him to Pontius Pilate the governor.

"3. Then Judas, which had betrayed him, when he saw that he was condemned, repented himself, and brought again the thirty pieces of silver to the chief priests and elders,

"4. Saying, I have sinned in that I have betrayed the innocent blood. And they said, What is that to us? see thou to that.

"5. And he cast down the pieces of silver in the temple and departed, and went and hanged himself."

The deed is done! Treason has accomplished his work. The Son of man is in the hands of sinners. He has been arraigned at their bar, convicted of blasphemy, sentenced to death; and, as if that were too little, reviled, ridiculed, abandoned to the coarsest effusions of malignity, and the most vulgar insolence. All this in the presence and by the hands of ministers of religion! of ministers assembled in solemn council, acting in the name of God, and professing to guard the interests of his truth, and to maintain the purity of his worship! Of all the forms of depravity, there is none so desperate and execrable as that which reigns in wicked ecclesiastics. No heart is so hard, so pitiless, so entirely estranged from all "compunctious visitings;" no conscience so seared; no spirit so fertile, refined, persevering in barbarity; no thirst for blood so insatiable; no vengeance so cool, so cruel, so devilish, as are to be found in a priest who has sold himself to work iniquity. Whatever it is, it was permitted to take its full sweep, to put forth its whole force, against our Lord Jesus Christ. "He had done no sin, neither was guile found in his mouth." But this was the "hour of sinners, and the power of darkness." "The dunnest smoke of hell" enwrapped their minds; the foulest spirit of the pit swayed their measures; and the malice of the devil and of the priesthood, expended all its treasures upon Him "who was fairer than the sons of men." Why, O Saviour, was all this shame and sorrow poured into thy cup? Why was thine Almighty power held in abeyance? Where were thy distracting thunders, and thine obedient lightnings? Where those twelve legions of angels, any one of whom could have blasted these conspirators into death? Where the divinity of that eye which in a moment could have looked them into hell? Ah, "How then should the scriptures have been fulfilled that thus it must be!" If the Lord Jesus Christ had exercised his power, he would have hurled instant confusion and perdition among the rebels; and appeared in all his glory as the sinless One. But where, then, would have been the sacrifice for our sins? What the hope of our souls? All thanks be to thee, thou patient Son of God, that thou didst not refuse " the cup which thy heavenly Father gave thee to drink!" The glory of the divine government was to be maintained and vindicated, and his people to be redeemed by the blood of his covenant: therefore, "when he was reviled, he reviled not again; when he suffered, he reproached not; but committed himself to him that judgeth righteously; and went as a lamb to the slaughter; and as a sheep before her shearers is dumb, so he opened not his mouth."

Let us trace the sequel.

The Roman governor had taken away from the Jews the power of inflicting capital punishment. This explains the circumstance mentioned in verse 1. That "when the morning was come, all the chief priests and elders of the people took counsel against Jesus to put him to death." Of their inclination there can be no doubt; they had already declared him to be "guilty of death;" and had nothing but their mercy stood in the way, they had executed their sentence upon the spot. But considerations of prudence interposed to check the course of malice. Had they ventured to take into their own hands the execution of their own sentence, it would have been such an act of rebellion as might have brought down upon their heads the whole weight of the Roman governor's resentment. It is wisely ordered, in the providence of God, that personal fear often restrains those who are lost to every sense of righteousness and humanity. Here is one of the principal guards which he has placed over the order and peace of civil society. Villains, who are not deterred by the atrocity of their designs, and who make no account of the misery which would follow their success, are often kept within bounds by the fear of consequences to themselves. They do not commit crimes from pure disinterestedness. They wish to see the issue and enjoy the fruits. The certainty, or even probability, of losing their own lives, is a mighty damper on their courage. Accordingly, the result of the counsel which the chief priests and elders of the people held, was to deliver Jesus up to the Roman governor; not doubting that their own influence, aided by such representations as it would cost them no trouble to make, would succeed in destroying their victim, with perfect safety to themselves. In all this there was nothing to be seen but human wickedness, and the ordinary principle of human nature. Who thinks of questioning whether the Jews followed the bent of their own corrupted will? Who thinks of any apology for their sin? Yet there was an invisible hand overruling and guiding their free and criminal actions to the very point which divine pre-ordination had fixed, and divine prescience had declared. The "Messiah was to be cut off" by a death unknown to the Jews. Crucifixion was exclusively a Roman punishment. Yet the Messiah could die in no other way. For this the prophetic spirit had pointed out. It is minutely described, because it could not be named; as the Jews had not a term to express it in their whole language. Thus saith the Messiah himself, in the twenty-second Psalm: "They pierced my hands and my feet." For this purpose was the empire of the world given to the Romans. Following only their own ambition, they, in the progress of their conquest, annexed Judea to their provinces, established their laws, abolished the Jewish right of life and death, and substituted the Roman in its stead. Here was proof that the Messiah had come; because "the sceptre was departed from Judah, and the lawgiver from between his feet." Thus all circumstances, brought about by men's pursuing their own devices, conspired to accomplish the purposes, and fulfil the promises of God. Thus all were rendered subservient to the kingdom, the salvation, and the glory of our Lord Jesus Christ. It is no otherwise at the present hour. The nations rage—the kingdoms are moved—revolution after revolution shakes the earth—plans of aggrandizement are formed for perishing worms—alliances, called holy, are framed for their security—daring spirits break the peace of the world—crimes and horrors multiply. What, brethren, is to be the end? Why, "God standeth in the congregation of the mighty: He sitteth upon the flood; He sitteth King for ever." The potentates, the revolutionists, and the multitude of the world, are doing nothing but "what his hand and counsel determined beforehand to be done." And while he avenges with blood his dreadful quarrel with bloody men, he is "judging with righteousness for the meek of the earth," and causing all things to converge to that centre of his providence, to that magnificent consummation, in which that Jesus who stood as a malefactor before Pontius Pilate, shall appear in his glory, "as the Prince of the kings of the earth, having on his head many crowns."

Before the completion of this tragedy, in which the chief priests and Pilate were conspicuous actors, the traitor Judas, terrified by the view of his crime which then bursts upon his mind, hastens to the chief priests and makes a voluntary confession: "I have sinned, in that I have betrayed the innocent blood." His Master's uniform goodness and grace stand unclouded before him; his own ingratitude and baseness crowd upon his soul; the wages of treason have lost their charm: shame, remorse, despair, rack his bosom; and he swells his crime by rushing, unbidden, into the presence of his Judge.

Let us recover ourselves from the terror of this frightful spectacle, and look into the lessons which it preaches to us.

I. The sins of men often lead to results which they do not anticipate.

Judas appears to have flattered himself that no eventual harm would arise from his treason. He had often seen, and perfectly knew the power of Jesus Christ. He could not imagine that he would suffer himself to become a victim to his enemies. With infinite ease he could extricate himself and baffle their designs, as he had done before, and thus give a new display of his own superiority, and acquire fresh reputation among the wondering millions, while himself would enjoy his ill-gotten gold. Thus he seems to have reasoned; and if you ask me why he did not reason in the same manner as to himself, when he was negotiating the fall of his Master, I answer, because sinners against God are universally but half reasoners. They are sharp-sighted and ingenious in espying out every circumstance which may extenuate or conceal their sin, and always blind to some things which may lead to their detection or punishment, or may conduct their sin to uncomfortable issues. It was the "condemnation" of our Lord Jesus Christ which Judas had not expected, and which awakened him to a fruitless repentance.

Let men, therefore, when they are about committing any known sin, pause a moment and reflect,

1. That they know not the natural connections of that sin.

They can form no idea of the crime and consequences to which it is nearly or remotely allied. They cannot even guess at the length of the chain with which they propose to entangle themselves, nor how deep a hold they take of hell when they adventure. They know not to what a mine of miseries to their persons, to their fame, to their friends, to the church of God, to the world, to the present race, to generations yet unborn, that sin may be the spring, and which shall explode at their touch.

2. They know nothing of the secret providence of God respecting that particular sin.

You promise yourselves pleasure, honour, profit; you cannot see that it will produce any disastrous effects. If they should be naturally connected with it, you flatter yourselves that something shall intervene between you and them to ward off their mischief and leave you in the enjoyment of all their advantages. Perhaps you have already had some hairbreadth escapes. Are there none here whose consciences bear witness that they have been delivered, as if by a miracle, from their best grounded fears? God gives many infallible proofs that he is gracious and long-suffering. Do not abuse his goodness. Do not presume upon impunity; imagine not yourselves to be exceptions from his rule of dealing with sinners. The very next offence may be your ruin in both worlds. Your hands may even now be weaving the net for your own feet. God may arrest you in a moment when you think not; when you suppose yourself to be perfectly secure from his visitation; and let the example of Judas warn you that it is no trifling thing to "fall into the hands of the living God."

3. We see exhibited in meridian light the accursedness of that maxim, that "the end sanctifies the means."

Was there ever equal benefit to the world, to the universe, to that which redounded from the death of our Lord Jesus Christ? Prophecies fulfilled—God glorified—hell vanquished—sin expiated—sinners saved—angels instructed—the intelligent universe edified, were its immediate and progressive fruits. Did all this diminish the sin or the punishment of Judas the traitor? Was his horror the less? the wrath of God more mitigated? his place of torment the more tolerable? You easily accede to the reprobation of Judas. But hold! "Thou that judgest another, condemnest thou not thyself?" No good to be effected could justify Judas in his sin. But do you never, in infinitely smaller matters, set up for your own justification the very principle which you have rejected in his? What means the defence, found in the mouths of celebrated moralists, for an imitation of the devil in one of his worst attributes—the practice of telling deliberate lies? Is not evil to be prevented, or good to be effected, the very pith and marrow of that defence? I blush when I think that such a doctrine has crept into our seminaries of learning to corrupt our youth. What reconciles men's consciences to perjuries in the custom-house, and the daily frauds which are glossed over by false pretences, but the consideration of their paltry gain? I pursue not the subject. "Let the stricken deer go weep." But be it remembered that the maxim, "Let us do evil that good may come," by whomsoever adopted, in whatever case or to whatever extent, is the maxim of those "whose damnation is just."

4. Observe the hardening power of sin.

Judas comes to the chief priests with his ill-gotten wealth in his hand, and acknowledges in most pathetic terms his unprovoked treachery: "I have sinned, in that I have betrayed the innocent blood!" Does not the confession chill their blood? Does it not instantly stop their proceedings, or at least compel them to pause, and inquire whether they were not about shedding "the innocent blood?" No such thing. With cool malignity they deride alike the majesty of justice and the misery of the traitor. "What is that to us, see thou to that!" What is that to you? the ministers of law! the professional maintainers of truth! the protectors of innocence! the commissioned agents of a righteous God? Is it nothing to you that the very wretch who had delivered his Master into your hands hastens to you with horrible compunction, declares your prisoner guiltless, and wishes to restore the hire of his own infamy? Can you get rid of your share in the crime by throwing all the responsibility upon the distracted traitor? "See thou to that!" Shocking infatuation! But these men had trained their minds by long practice to familiarity with sin. They had neglected, resisted, slandered, persecuted the truth. They had exercised themselves in all the arts which envy, guile, and hatred can suggest, to entrap the Just One. Being constantly foiled, they become intriguers for blood, and seize with avidity the opportunity which the bad faith of a disciple afforded, of glutting their vengeance. Jesus is in their hands; it is enough; they have gone too far to recede; the ultimate crime caps the climax of their iniquity!

O ye who tamper and trifle with the truth of God, look well to your feet! You are upon a declivity which grows steeper the farther you advance. There is an intimate connection between falsehood in principle and criminality in action. God may in righteous judgment give you up to your delusions, till, "hardened by the deceitfulness of sin," you shall advance from crime to crime, and at last reach that point where you will hold fellowship with the murderers of the Prince of life, and plunge yourself into bottomless perdition.

5. The power of a guilty conscience, when fully aroused.

During the whole time Judas was seeking an opportunity of perpetrating his treason; and until he had completed the execrable deed, and had seen it terminate in his Lord's condemnation, the soul of the traitor was callous; his moral sensibility was stupified; with the pleasure of covetousness he was contemplating "the wages of unrighteousness:" but his career was over, his work finished; God had abandoned him; his conscience awakens from its stupor; his crime is set before his eyes in its unalloyed horrors. Racked with remorse and despair, he throws down the abhorred gold, and departs in agony, unpitied and distracted. Unhappy man! Thy repentance, such as it is, comes too late. It availeth not to arrest the hand of violence against thy Master, nor to save thyself. The furies are pursuing "thee to thine own place," where thou shalt know the full meaning of thy Master's words, "It were good for that man if he had never been born." He retires to his house; he seeks relief by self-destruction; nature sinks under the insupportable load; throes of agony stifle his breath and dissolve his frame; "all his bowels gush out," and he dies accursed of God, and "an abhorrence to all flesh!"

It is not in order to produce a mere stage effect—to agitate the stronger passions of our nature for the sake of agitating them—that this odious and terrifying spectacle is set before you. Many, too many, of those within my hearing at present have a fearful interest in the story of Judas. They are living in the love and the practice of sin. Their consciences were once tender, and did not fail to admonish them upon the recurrence of their aberrations from the path of known duty. Its admonitions have been disregarded, they grew fainter and fainter, and perhaps have ceased to trouble them. They go on in their sinful course, undisturbed by painful reflections; they hear with indifference, it may be with a smile of contempt, the remonstrances of God's word, the warnings of his providence, the threatenings of his laws. All these pass by them "as the idle wind which they regard not," and they confirm themselves in the persuasion that "they shall have peace though they walk after the imaginations of their own evil hearts." Hear, then, once more, ye despisers, a little plain truth: it may be the last time before some of you "go to your long account."

You have within your bosoms and carry about with you, just such a faculty, with the same sleepless observation, the same power of recollection and reproach, the same capacity of inexpressible horror, as that which inflicted its punishment upon Judas Iscariot. If, then, you are resolved to persevere in your rebellion against God, why then you must go on, and, if you can, abide the consequences. The day of reckoning will come; it is at hand; it is very near; when all restraints shall be removed from off thy conscience, and all its sensibilities sharpened, and thou shalt feel what it is to grapple with its might and its vengeance. *Now* thy communion is with the *matter* of thy sin, which fills thee with intoxicating joys; *then*, when the vision of truth shall make thee sober, it shall be with the *guilt* of thy sin. Then conscience arises in his majesty to do the work of God's vicegerent. The moment he begins, the stoutest heart trembles. With a precision there is no evading: a determination which can neither be repelled nor postponed; severe integrity which no promises can bribe, and no pleadings mollify, he sets thy sins in order before thy face; not an aggravation nor a circumstance forgotten; excuses and apologies are at an end; every mask is stripped off; the laughter of fools yields no relief; thou must look upon thy sins as disembodied spirits look at them; as the ministering angels who have been their witnesses always looked at them; as they are seen in the light of Jehovah's countenance. Thou art now where thou canst not shuffle; under the power of that eye which penetrates thy being, and annihilates the consideration of everything but itself and thy own crimes. Profaned Sabbaths; the despised Bible; the neglected sanctuary; lost opportunities; abused mercies; ridiculed convictions; crowd in upon thy mind. As they pass by thee in slow and solemn procession, the hand of each presses thine heart like a millstone. Each one utters in a tone of coming vengeance, "Let me sit heavy on thy soul to-morrow!" Thus circumstanced, conscience overcomes the love of life, and what is often more than life, of reputation. It rips up and discloses sins which had not been suspected, and would never have been known. To be disgraced or honoured before men cannot command a thought. Equally unable to endure or escape its terrors, he sinks into despair. What aileth thee, thou man of boasting? Is this the son of successful sin? This the gay and gallant youth who laughed at the simplicity of his serious friends, at the fables of the Bible, and the croakings of a faithful ministry? What is become of thy courage? Where is the pleasantry with which thou usedest to sport with that bug-bear, conscience? Ah, he has no reply! He has other employment than to attend to his pitiable figure in the eyes of men. He has "fallen into the hands of the living God!" It is the hour of the Lord's vengeance! He has nothing but the shriek of despair. The mountains and the rocks flee from the face of his Judge. What shall he do? His profit lost; pleasures lost; fame lost; soul lost; God himself hath nothing to do but to punish him. Oh, may some of you say, oh that one from the world of spirits, that some good angel, would interpose to show to men their peril, and reclaim them from their folly? what are you wishing? They have more than apparitions of the dead; more than an angel voice; more than if he were to rend asunder the curtains of death, and to make visible the secrets of the eternal world. More sure than all this, more close and powerful is the warning of God's word. In accents more terrible than the thunder that shakes the heavens;

more gentle than the dew-drop upon the springing herb; more tender than a mother's love, does he remonstrate with the rashness of sinners. Hear ye " despisers, and wonder and perish!"—" Look unto me and be saved all the ends of the earth!"—" As I live, saith Jehovah, I have no pleasure in the death of the sinner."— " How shall I give thee up, Ephraim? How shall I deliver thee, Judah? How shall I make thee as Admah? How shall I set thee as Zeboim?"—" Mine heart is turned within me, my repentings are kindled together." Now is the day of the divine forbearance! Now does God wait to be gracious. Now he pleads forcibly, plainly, loudly. Then "To-day, if ye will hear his voice, harden not your hearts." Do you shudder at such an interview as has been exhibited with your own consciences? We proclaim the only method of escape, by having sprinkled upon them the precious blood of Christ, that they may be purged from dead works to serve the living God.

SERMON XII.

MINISTERIAL FIDELITY ILLUSTRATED AND VINDICATED.

JOHN xviii. 23.

"If I have spoken evil, bear witness of the evil: but if well, why smitest thou me?"

ALL men, of all sects, agree that the treatment of our Lord Jesus Christ, immediately before the close of his course, exhibited the very highest injustice, and the most cool and consummate depravity. When a criminal is arrested and put upon his plea for life and death, there is something within a man which involuntarily softens down his feelings into those of tenderness. Nor can there be a greater insult offered to the common sympathies of our nature, nor one which would be more speedily and roughly resented, than any gratuitous indignity: anything which tends to render his situation more painful. In the case, however, of our Lord and Saviour, all the courtesies of life, and all the kindlier attentions of humanity, were denied, with a barbarity which shocks us in the recital. Not one kind action was performed, not one generous sentiment expressed, during the whole of his trial. He seemed to be interdicted from the common rights, even of those who were destined to public execution. The sanhedrim forgot their majesty, and the high priest his dignity, when Jesus of Nazareth stood before them—forgot themselves so far as to permit vulgar insolence to inflict personal violence upon their prisoner without provocation, and in circumstances which entitled him to protection. On an interrogation about "his disciples and his doctrine," Jesus referred the high priest to those who had attended his ministry; and a more fair or respectful reference could not have been required. The only notice taken of it, was a blow from "one of the officers who stood by," with a question after the blow, "Answerest thou the high priest so?" Jesus, who knew perfectly well what was due to a court of justice, and those who were arraigned before it, meekly replied, "If I have spoken evil, bear witness of the evil: but if well, why smitest thou me?"

I have chosen to discourse on these words, because they convey a general instruction, both to the official witnesses for truth, and to those who hear their testimony. The one are taught to deliver their message firmly and courageously; and the other to refrain from hasty and especially from passionate judgments.

I. The duty of official witnesses to the truth. It is to speak *well*. And my first remark is,

1. That they have a high and responsible duty to perform, which cannot be slighted or evaded.

God is carrying on in our world the most important design that he was ever pleased to unfold to the contemplation of the universe, the manifestation of his own glory in the salvation of sinful men. A salvation in which his only begotten Son, our Lord Jesus Christ, acts the principal part, and forms the great point of re-union both to his own infinite perfections, and the adoration of all holy beings in his empire. Is is the object of their study, and the theme of their praise. The minutest portion of its development, such as the repentance of one sinner, puts all heaven in commotion, and creates a new allotment of the services of those who are destined to be ministering spirits. The visible execution of this design he has seen proper to commit to the hands of men—men of like passions with others—involved in the same ruin, redeemed by the same means, and heirs of the same inheritance, with all those who shall see the King in his beauty. The treasure is indeed put into earthen vessels, that the excellency of the power may be of God. But though they are earthen vessels, made of dust and returning to the dust, they are raised to the dignity of " fellow-workers with God." They have his commission in their hands—his promises to animate, and his Spirit to help them. Who that rightly considers the employment would not tremble to undertake it? Who that undertakes it, with a due sense of his own insufficiency, and an humble trust in the support of that God whose he is and whom he serves, will not feel himself infinitely above the fears, the favours, the frowns, the applauses, of fellow-worms, and all the petty calculations which find a place in the minds of those who can stoop to be the servants of men?

Commensurate with this mighty trust is the responsibility attached to it. Life for life, blood for blood, in the case of all who perish through carelessness or unfaithfulness, is a terrible alternative; but yet that to which the ministers of God are subjected. "Son of man," is the divine mandate to Ezekiel, "Son of man, I have made thee a watchman unto the house of Israel: therefore hear the word at my mouth, and give them warning from me. When I say unto the wicked, Thou shalt surely die; and thou givest him not warning, nor speakest to warn the wicked man from his wicked way, to save his life; the same wicked man shall die in his iniquity; but his blood will I require at thy hand." There is, you perceive, no room left for discretion. The man has a message to deliver, and it must be delivered, as it was given to him, on the peril of his soul. God has taken the issue of his truth into his own hands; how it shall be received, and what the end shall be, is not for us to inquire. The aids of human prudence, and all the expedients of human wisdom, are but the efforts of human impertinence to direct his infinite wisdom, or to assist his almighty power. We have but one concern to mind, and that is, that we be found faithful. Now as all God's messages to sinful men are messages of the Infinite Sovereign to his deluded subjects, who have revolted far away from their allegiance, my next remark is, that

2. In discharging his duty, the minister of God will come into habitual collision with the predilection, the opinions, the habits of many who hear him.

It seems to be an established point with some who profess Christianity, that they have a right to entertain and publish what opinions they please. The first part of this proposition is, with respect to human control, above contradiction. But do they not often forget that the jurisdiction of divine authority spreads itself as much over the province of thinking as over the province of acting? that the world of spirits is as really a part of the divine government as the world of matter, only much larger, more comprehensive, and more important? We may then ask, who gave them a right to think contrary to the thoughts of God their Maker? to think what he has forbidden them to think? to cherish in their bosoms direct rebellion against him? and to imagine that all shall pass off unnoticed? In so far as God has revealed himself, he has not only decided what is truth, *i. e.* what is to rule the inward parts, but he has enjoined his servants to declare it. "He that hath my word, let him speak my word faithfully."—"What is the chaff to the wheat? saith the Lord." And as thoughts are much more numerous than actions, as they are equally efficients of character in the sight of God, and reach over an immense field of agency, which actions can never touch, they furnish precisely the ground in which truth must have her most desperate conflicts with error; and on which man feels his pride great, and his responsibility little or nothing. To maintain here the truth of God, and to expose every deviation from it, are among the highest of the high duties which the man of God has to perform. It is here that the transgressor is to be convinced, humbled, converted, and made to sit in his right mind, clothed, and at the feet of Jesus. It is here that the fidelity of those who profess to be teachers of the gospel is chiefly tried; and that the true disciple of Jesus Christ is to keep his ground, unmoved, unshaken, though he stand alone, the single witness for his Saviour, among a faithless and perverse generation. He must encounter, as his Lord did before him, the contradiction of sinners; and the worst and most obstinate of all contradictions, that of philosophical sinners, who claim a bolder privilege than any others to make free with the Word of God, to contradict its language, to fritter away its sense, and to expunge everything which does not accord with the dictates of their corrupt, and falsely called, enlightened reason.

They who are the objects of evangelical instruction and remonstrances, are also distinguished by their habits of transgression. God commands one thing, and they practice another. The moral law, in all the extent of its obligation, as a spiritual law, lies across their path. They are vastly fond of moral preaching, but that is, when it shuts out the salvation and the Saviour of God's providing; when it opens to them some avenue, something which lets in a glimpse of hope that they may be saved by works of righteousness that they have done. And to quote the words of one who was much abused for preaching the gospel of the grace of God, "O that men were as fond of doing good works, as of being saved by them!" But to urge upon them such moral conduct as the law of

God requires, and the Spirit of God suggests, is at once to put them at variance with the world that lieth under the power of the evil one; is to call them to come out from among them, and be separate, and touch not the unclean thing: and the promise of God himself, that he will be a Father unto them, and they shall be his sons and his daughters, falls lighter than a feather upon their ear.

It cannot be but that this contrariety between the commands of God and the practices of men, must produce a strong, though very possibly a smothered hostility, against the plain declarations of the one, and denunciations of the other. Sinners do not love to be told that the end of these things is death. They love, under a Christian garb, to be soothed, and flattered, and be assured that all shall be well at last. And though conscience side with the truth, they will rather side with the flatterer, and agree to count as an enemy him that tells them the truth. Their feelings are like those of the king of Israel, who hated Micaiah the son of Imla, because he never prophesied good to him, but always evil. Micaiah was a prophet of Jehovah; and Ahab a prince of pre-eminent wickedness who sold himself to work iniquity. There was therefore no room to "prophesy good to him," for there was nothing good about him: and it was the work of the prophet to "withstand him to the face." The case was not much different with the apostle of the Gentiles. For a while the Gentile converts were enthusiastically attached to Paul. "They received him as an angel of God, even as Christ Jesus." So great was their affection, that "if it had been possible, they would have plucked out their own eyes, and have given them to him. But after false and smooth-tongued teachers had crept in among them, and had gained their ear, all this blessedness disappeared: and the faithful apostle was suspected, traduced, treated as an enemy. It is doubtless no easy matter to declare the whole counsel of God when your doctrine must sear, and scathe, at every step, men highly useful in the community, men of amiable and generous tempers, men with whom you are in the habit of personal intimacy, and who may be in many respects your kindest and most valuable friends. I speak not of invidious personalities, nor of discourses so constructed as to be aimed at individuals; than which nothing can be more mean and cowardly, nor more unworthy of a minister of the cross. But in stating and urging general truths, in describing characters as they appear in real life, and of which the originals meet you by thousands in every crowd, principles, affections, habits, must be touched in a manner that will be very sore to some, and those whom you think not, in every assembly that can be collected. And the more plainly and faithfully you perform your duty, the more frequently will this recur. But blows often repeated, however unintentionally as to the individuals, excite first pain, next irritation, and then alienation. It is not in human nature, where the conscience has not become callous, and is not driven to Jesus Christ, to endure patiently those flagellations which it is the business of truth to inflict upon every form of error and ill conduct. Even zealous friendship at length gives way, and is succeeded by dislike, if not by hatred. These things are exceedingly distressing, especially to minds of a softer mould : and they beset a man with more dangerous snares than can be laid by open hostility. The appeals which they make to kindness, to tenderness, to gratitude, though altogether misplaced, will go much farther to stagger resolution, and to undermine fidelity, than the most vehement direct attacks. Against an avowed adversary, it is comparatively easy to hold your position. The mind braces itself up, and the very principle of resistance furnishes both resource and energy. But against the gentle, the friendly, the humane, it is very hard to keep up a warfare, and very natural to relax what may be thought the harder features of truth. Yet this must be done: done steadily, done without respect of persons, by him who, in the language of the text, "speaks well." His anxiety must be, and is, not to commend himself to men's notions, to their prejudices, to their wishes, but to their "consciences in the sight of God;" and to acquit himself, not as one that pleaseth men, but God who searcheth the hearts. Infinitely more valuable in his eyes, than all the applauses of perishing judges, is his ability to say to his hearers, "I take you to witness, that I am pure from the blood of all men." And more deep and lasting is the respect given to such a declaration, backed by the testimony of conscience, than by the loudest peals of popular applause.

Such is the duty and such the present recompense of them who "speak well." Let us now turn to the

II. Point of consideration, the duty of those who hear, to refrain from hasty and intemperate judgments. "If I have spoken evil, bear witness of the evil: but if well, why smitest thou me?"

The earth scarcely furnishes a more interesting spectacle than an assemblage of sinful men met together in the presence and for the purpose of worshipping God. The glorious majesty of their King—the contrast between his infinite holiness and their unworthiness—his wonderful condescension in treating with them at all—the nature of their employment in the house of prayer—the homage which they are to render to him as the universal Sovereign—their sins to be confessed—their complaints to be poured out before him; their wants, their weaknesses, their perils, to be spread before his gracious notice—that exhibition of his doctrine—that correction of their errors—those rebukes for their faults; that instruction in righteousness for which his Word is profitable and is intended to convey; the tremendous consequences which hang upon them; what calmness, what tenderness, what a subdued spirit, what candour, what docility, do they not require and imply? Surely we have a right to expect a disposition like that of the centurion's friends, when Peter as a minister of grace visited them. "Now therefore we are all here present before God, to hear all things that are commanded thee of God."

But the depravity of men abusing their great privileges, the frequent recurrence of divine worship, has perverted this majestic scene to quite other ends, has almost driven the thought of God out of their minds, and to account the assembling of themselves together to be little else than a means of their own gratification. To entering within themselves and there instituting a fair self-examination they are utter strangers; but are either fond admirers, or listless hearers, or fastidious critics and imperious judges. Yet every one expects that his particular humour shall be pleased. The consequence is exactly what might have been anticipated. No man who intends to be faithful, can possibly perform an exercise without displeasing somebody.

When the pulpit arraigns prevailing sin, calls it by its own name, and points the divine denunciations against it, some, whom the remarks of the preacher happen to strike, immediately take fire. They cannot deny the truth, but think "there was no necessity for being so particular." They even imagine that he must have received some information concerning them, and that he has been exposing them to the whole congregation. The affair becomes personal; the hearer is not profited, and the preacher is abused.

In the meantime he was perfectly innocent of the design imputed to him, and his angry auditor does not suspect or wish to conceal the fact that the supposed informer has never been out of his own bosom. And although, "in drawing his bow at a venture," the speaker may not exactly hit an individual, yet his shaft may fly farther, and do severe execution among a class, whom some present reckon among their friends; and forthwith the feelings of friendship are kindled, and a man deems it necessary to be highly indignant because his friends are touched. Their offences may be very flagrant, the general description very just, and the censure indisputably scriptural, yet the zeal of friendship cannot be satisfied without lighting, if possible, a fire of high, flaming resentment against the preacher. It is indeed setting a high value upon his friendship to suppose that it shall stop the mouth of truth, and screen the most notorious sinners from reprehension, because they are *his* friends. If he could arrest the arm of Justice, and protect them from the notice and curse of his Maker, his jealousy would be of some moment. Till then it is as foolish as it is impotent.

Sometimes sins of great atrocity in civil transactions become very frequent in the community, and from the numbers who are involved in them, are scarcely thought to be a reproach. Their turpitude is merged in their frequency, and men begin to think they may sin with impunity, when they can sin without disgrace. If then a minister of the gospel lay hold of these fashionable transgressors; If he bring them to the bar of God, and show them that in his sight numbers are no apology for crime, and from his hand cannot effect an escape; if he dispute the Christianity of all who, under whatever pretext, live in the commission of deeds which they know to be contrary to the commandments of God, and insist that they must be new men in heart, and lead lives of new obedience, before they can make the least claim to the possession of eternal life, why then the provocation assumes a different shape. They who smart under the fair application of the rod, discover that the preacher has travelled out of the limits of his commission; that he injures himself and his cause by meddling with things which do not belong to him; "Let him," is their practical language, "let him confine himself to the doctrines and duties of Christianity, and not thrust himself into concerns which are out of his sphere, and where nobody thanks him for his intrusion." What storms of wrath have men excited in this way, when, for example, they have ventured to touch the sinful party politics of the day, or to bring the power of truth to bear upon a favourite political sinner! How impatient is a party-man under the rebuke of his iniquities! How strenuously does he argue against the impertinence of Christianity interposing to check his most flagrant transgressions, or even against the divine law itself undertaking to control his excesses, and to dictate his moral course! Of all this you are yourselves sufficient witnesses.

On the other hand, when a man teaches boldly the doctrines of the Gospel; when he presses them home upon the conscience; when he exposes to just detestation those "damnable heresies" which subvert the whole "gospel of the grace of God," and people the regions of despair with the victims of their seduction, how loud is the cry against his "bigotry," his "uncharitableness," his "unchristian temper," his "pride," his "ferocity," his "damning spirit," and the other amiable attributes in which rational Christianity is ever ready to array him.

All these forms of treating the minister of religion are very common, and they fall to his lot nearly in proportion to his honesty. And what are they but "smiting" him for "speaking" well? He has set men at variance with their own conscience, and they try to make themselves amends by reviling him, and casting out his name as evil. But the facts remain as they are. Doctrines of devils will be doctrines of devils still, though all the friends and servants of the devil fret and rave. Sinful habits will be sinful habits still, and as much exposed to the righteous judgment of God, though a whole world of sinners conspire to excuse them and to uphold one another, and rend the air with their clamours against him that reproveth in the gate. God's holy truth is still his holy truth, though it be rejected and scorned by the wretched unbelievers whom it was revealed to save, and involves as terrible a responsibility on their part. Considering these things, the hearers of the gospel are not to form rash and hasty judgments. It is unwise, unfair, and may be ruinous. When their consciences get a prick —when their notions or opinions are condemned—when their practices are severely arraigned, they are not forthwith to fly into a passion, to flout at the preacher's doctrine, to resent it as a personal insult, and to heap injurious epithets upon him. This refutes nothing, establishes nothing but your own unreasonableness and obstinacy. If you think that he "has spoken evil," the Lord Jesus Christ has prescribed the proper course, "Bear witness of the evil."

The Word of God is the universal and infallible standard of truth, by which every opinion, principle, and practice, must be tried; and according to which it must stand or fall. The testimony by which you are to show that a preacher of righteousness has spoken evil, is the contrariety of his doctrine to the divine word. Bring his declarations most freely to this ordeal. Lay your finger upon any part of what God is pleased to teach, and demonstrate to the preacher, and to all the world if you please, that he has contradicted the teachings of inspiration. When you shall have proved that he has not spoken "as becometh the oracles of God," you will convict him, to some purpose, of having "spoken evil." You will be yourselves more established in the faith of the gospel; you will edify your brethren; will do good service to the Christian cause; will bid fair to correct the mistake of the man himself, leading him to sounder views, promoting his own growth in grace, and subserving his usefulness in the church of God. I submit to yourselves, my brethren, a much more rational, dignified, honourable, and profitable proceeding, than the common method of growing angry, and indulging in ill-natured and bitter remarks. You may possibly discover that what you reject as false or resent as improper, may turn out, upon investigation, to be the very truth of God. And you may have been all the while revenging a supposed affront upon your Maker himself. And this may draw after it serious consequences to your everlasting welfare. For you must remember that when the preacher has laid before you the truth of God, he has delivered his message; and he has delivered his soul. Not a drop of your blood shall be found in his skirts, in that day of reckoning. The moment he has done, responsibility ceases with him, and it passes over to you. Take heed, then, that in your displeasure against him, you be not found fighting against God. I would recommend the same course to you, when you happen to be much pleased. Do not take it for granted that everything agreeable is therefore safe. Apply the touch-stone; ask your counsel at the mouth of the Lord as he has spoken in your Bible. Peradventure this pleasing thing may be only the craft and sleight of deceivers. You may have been drinking poison for the pure water of the river of life; and may correct your error in time to save your own soul, and to testify against the evil speech and the evil speaker.

In the next place, sit down and commune with your own heart, open your eyes upon the scenes that are passing around you: and inquire whether that with which you are disgusted may not only be true, but *seasonable* truth.

It is freely conceded, that there may be much unprofitable preaching where there is no error. Every syllable may be scriptural truth, and yet the effect be positively bad. Truth it is, but not the truth suited to the time and place. It is pitiable to think of the mischiefs which proceed from the want of a little ministerial prudence. But these are cases which excite contempt rather than animosity. They lower respect for a man's understanding, and seldom expose him to hatred and reproach. What mankind perceive to be absurd, they generally account harmless. But it is different where they are vexed, and show themselves to feel very sore. It is truth; the refuting or condemning present error; reproving some present sin; detecting some gross self-deception; reproving some lawless affection; making men feel criminal while they resolve to adhere to their crimes that rouse the malevolent tempers. Their consciences are disturbed, while their lusts are exposed; and they endeavour to pacify the one and to screen the other, by quarrelling with the doctrine, or the preacher who has been unceremonious enough to interrupt their repose, or embitter their gratifications. When the fire of divine truth has been well directed, it is the wounded that cry out. As surely as there is any tender spot, any vulnerable point, they who are conscious of its being theirs, shrink and wince, as the surgeon-touch approaches the disordered place, and he begins to apply the medical knife. So then it may and often does happen, that the doctrine which gives most pain, and causes most displeasure, to some hearers, is not only truth, but the very truth which the occasion calls for. The preacher would have been faithless had he concealed it or softened it down. He might have pleased a part of his audience, and have fallen at the same moment under the displeasure of God. And while he was puffed up with the praises of his fellow-worms, he might for the same deed, be transfixed with the spear of the Almighty. Nay, my friends, we cannot afford to purchase your favour upon such terms—the price is too enormous. Our souls are infinitely too precious to be so wantonly and so cheaply thrown away.

Before then any of you begin to smite the man who has discomposed you, seriously inquire whether his stroke was not only well-deserved, but well-timed. He may have been doing nothing but his duty: may have been performing a work of real benevolence, of Christian charity, towards you: resembling the skilful physician, who, disregarding the cries, the threats, or the anguish of his patient, is intent upon one thing, performing his operation well. O remember that the wounds of a friend are faithful, but the kisses of an enemy deceitful. That he wounds you for your good; such smiting will not break your head: it will rather be a precious oil, both healing by its virtue, and refreshing by its fragrance.

I may, in drawing to a close, be permitted to remark,

1. That a spirit of criticism, especially of captious criticism, is one of the worst possible frames of mind in which a hearer of the gospel can place himself. God is dishonoured, his awful majesty affronted, his truth accounted suspicious, the soul is not edified, the church not unfrequently scandalized, her most faithful ministers persecuted, by its prevalence. One would be almost tempted to imagine that some persons attend the church as a very convenient place for getting angry. Like restive steeds who are always on the look-out for something to be frightened at, they seem to be constantly on the watch for something which may discompose and irritate them. If there be any such present, let me affectionately warn them that they are themselves the greatest enemies of their own salvation. The gospel has done and is doing them no good: the Sabbath is employed to draw tighter around them the cords of their spiritual bondage; and the great means which God has provided for breaking their thraldom and setting them at liberty, are rendered fruitless by their own fault. How much better to take your seats in his house, humbly, reverentially, disposed to submit the pride of your heart and your understanding to his high authority, inquiring "what the Lord saith unto his servants." This is the way of waiting at wisdom's doors, and in which you may expect to receive blessings from the Lord, and righteousness from the God of your salvation.

2. How little reason ministers of the gospel have to shrink from

the duty in order to avoid the rash and passionate judgments of their hearers.

Like Paul, they are to declare as far as they know it, the whole counsel of God; if, like him, they hope to be pure from the blood of all men. Their only concern in this matter is to see that they speak the truth of God, and speak it seasonably, and properly: about all the rest, as regards themselves, they are to be perfectly indifferent. They have spoken well; and the gainsaying, and abuse, and slander, of men of corrupt minds, reprobate concerning the faith, ought to be, in their eyes, lighter than vanity. It is a small thing, says faithful Paul, for me to be judged of you, or of man's judgment; he that judgeth me is the Lord Of all his hasty critics who cannot endure sound doctrine, there is not one who will take our Lord's advice, and "bear witness of the evil." Well, then, let them pursue their own course. They have done with the minister, when he, as a man of God, has finished his message. But they have not done with the consequences of his ministration. The question is now between God and their souls, and an awful question it is; as they will find it to be when he shall summon them to his bar, and deal with them in righteousness; when all the small excuses which pass current on earth, will be utterly annihilated, for slighting and rebelling against his living oracles. When they shall call in vain to the rocks and mountains to hide them from the face of Him that sitteth upon the throne, and the rocks and mountains shall flee away and leave them naked to his eye, then shall the preacher of righteousness lift up his head with joy, and have an inconceivable recompense in that approving voice and those cheering words of his righteous Judge, "Well done, good and faithful servant, enter thou into the joy of your Lord."

SERMON XIII.

THE CHRISTIAN WARFARE.

1 TIM. vi. 2.

"Fight the good fight of faith."

Whoever has read the records of truth, must frequently have remarked that the life of a Christian is almost always mentioned in metaphorical terms. This fact is so far from being a blemish in divine revelation, that it is a shining beauty in itself, and an invaluable blessing to us. We are so immersed in sense, that it is impossible for us to speak without speaking more or less figuratively, and equally impossible to feel the propriety of any discourse which does not abound with allusions to sensible objects. Even that language which we employ in expressing our thoughts on immaterial things, is borrowed from the material world. As this disposition appears to result inevitably from the connection between soul and body, and the influence which external objects have upon both, it must remain while our present circumstances remain. And the most honourable end to which we can direct it is to make it subservient to our knowledge and experience of eternal realities. We are happy in having before us an example which we may safely follow, for this is the use which God himself has designed to make of it. He graciously adapts himself to our frailty, and addresses us in language calculated to rouse attention and animate exertion. He summons all nature to our aid. He represents the duties, the difficulties, the dangers, the delights of our heavenly calling, by figures which tend to make the deepest impression; which tend at once to chase away sloth and enkindle ardour, to humble our pride and exalt his grace. He holds up our progress unto his kingdom of glory under the ideas of a journey, a pilgrimage, a race, a wrestling, and as in our text, a warfare—a warfare too of the most formidable kind—a warfare in which courage, firmness, fortitude, diligence, patience, and perseverance must be kept in continual and vigorous exercise. But while our Lord shows us the hardships, he shows us also the advantages of his service, and the means he has provided for our safety, our comfort, our success. Let us, therefore, in the order which the text points out, view the Christian life as a fight, as a good fight, and as the good fight of faith.

I. Let us consider the Christian life as a fight.

Yes, believer, you are surrounded with foes whom you cannot shun. You must vanquish them, or they will destroy you. Inaction will cost you dear. Put on, then, the whole armour of God. Gird yourselves for the battle. And that you may feel the necessity of "quitting yourselves like men," come, let us climb the heights of Zion, and reconnoitre our enemies. Skilfully are their encampments formed, and strongly intrenched. A triple league is combined against you; a league consisting of the powers of darkness, the world, and the corruptions of your own hearts.

1. The powers of darkness.

Every day's experience furnishes a practical proof of the enmity which subsists between the seed of the woman and the seed of the serpent. Satan and his host of apostate angels, actuated by the same spirit which lost them heaven and hurled them into hell, are constantly and indefatigably employed in scattering misery through the works, and attempting to subvert the government, of God. Their rage is particularly excited against the honour of Christ and the triumphs of his grace. Whenever the Holy Spirit commences his saving operations in the souls of men, and the Redeemer with his almighty arm shakes to its centre the kingdom of destruction, all the legions of hell are roused into action. They combine their joint and furious efforts to render ineffectual a work that shall infallibly succeed. And though they well know this, yet so implacable is their spite against the Lord Christ, that if they cannot counteract the power nor arrest the progress of his grace, they will exert all their strength in disturbing the peace and tormenting the hearts of the objects of his love. Nor, when the soul is united to the Mediator and safe for eternity, do they either lessen their malice or remit their activity. The moment, therefore, that a sinner flies to Jesus Christ, he proclaims war against all the fiends of darkness;

and if he once draw the sword, he must throw away the scabbard. As Christ has no concord with Belial, he will not allow it in his followers. They must enter into no reconciliation, no truce, no parley with their enemies, but are bound, are sworn to maintain a sore and perpetual conflict. That in this conflict they receive many a wound, and many a fall, and are forced to utter many a groan, Christians can well attest, and no wonder that this often happens, for

(1.) Their adversaries are very powerful.

Intelligences of a superior order possess abilities and powers considerably greater than those of an inferior nature. Unincumbered, too, with bodies, they enjoy no small advantage over those whose movements are impeded by a load of gross and corruptible matter. Their agency in the material world—a notorious fact proves to be very astonishing. Their influence upon the persons and the minds of men is neither less extensive nor less undeniable; and did not the restraining providence of God tie up their hands, we should fearfully experience their strength. These reflections are supported by the authority of Scripture. The devil is there compared to a roaring lion—to a strong man armed—to a great dragon vomiting a flood of waters. He is called the prince of the power of the air. We are said to wrestle not with flesh and blood, but with principalities and powers, and believers are commanded to put on the whole armour of God. All these things indicate enemies formidable and powerful.

(2.) They are not only powerful but numerous.

"My name is Legion," said the hellish tribe which had seized the poor demoniac; "my name is Legion, for we are many." Think you, then, that the Christian can proceed in his way to Zion without fierce opposition? Quite the reverse. He no sooner takes a step in the heavenly journey, than he is attacked by a host of enemies, who unite their forces in the attack. He must dispute every inch of his ground till he reach his Father's house. Often must he travel with a sad and heavy heart, while his foes beset him on every side, and lay siege to every avenue of his soul. Ah, Christian, you would soon fall a prey to their teeth, was not your "help laid on One who is mighty to save."

(3.) They are as malicious as they are numerous.

It is the very essence of malignity to commit injury without the smallest prospect of advantage. This is the precise case of the devil and his angels. They hate the Lord Jesus, and let slip no opportunity of testifying their hatred. But as they cannot mount up into heaven, and vent their malice against his blessed person, they endeavour to strike at himself by vexing those who bear his image. Although they know that they cannot destroy the children of God while their Redeemer lives, yet they do not desist. Although they are sensible that they are preparing for themselves a more terrible condemnation, they still persevere. Although they were foiled by the Captain of salvation, and are foiled by those who fight under his banners, they still renew the combat. Do not dream, then, Christians, of peace, while you are on this side heaven. Your adversaries will press you with the utmost virulence in every part where they find you vulnerable. They showed no quarter to your Lord, and they will be far from showing any to you.

(4.) In addition to their malice, they possess great knowledge and equal art.

Not to mention that evil spirits are naturally capable of grasping, in one view, more objects than we can imagine, the practice of near six thousand years must have furnished them with a large stock of experience. Veterans in rebellion against God, and trained to the ruin of man, they cannot but be expert in deeds of wickedness. The Scripture, therefore, speaks of "the depths of Satan"— of "the snare of the devil"—and the apostle Paul says, "we are not ignorant of his devices." They are indeed devices which are neither understood nor suspected without illumination from on high. Satan is well acquainted with the tempers and circumstances of mankind, and can tell, often more exactly than themselves, "the sin that doth most easily beset them." He accordingly adapts himself to the taste of those whom he tempts, and plans his stratagems so as to render them most effectual. "Be sober," then, Christians, "be vigilant," that your understandings be not blinded by the craft, that your feet be not caught in the snare, of your enemies; but in all cases let your appeal for instruction be to the "law and to the testimony;" and your recourse for aid to Him, who hath all power in heaven and in earth.

(5.) These adversaries of God's people are indefatigable.

Never was chemist more indefatigable in scrutinizing the composition and qualities of bodies, than is Satan in studying the human heart. Never was an active and able general more assiduous in striving to vanquish his antagonist, either by superior force or by surprise, or by drawing him into an ambuscade, or by overreaching him in any other military manœuvre, than is Satan in attempting to gain the victory over the children of light. With an eagle's eye he watches all their motions. If the sons of God present themselves before him, Satan never fails to present himself along with them. If they go to the house of prayer, Satan goes too; and when he is there he is never idle, however many of the hearers may be. Whence comes it to pass that such a multitude of memories, which are very faithful and retentive in the affairs of life, grow so very treacherous as soon as people enter a place of public worship, that they can scarcely carry away a single truth which concerns their eternal peace? It is because that arch-thief steals away the word from their hearts, and most of the hearers permit him to steal it very quietly. Why are the minds of those who truly seek the Lord often more distracted with vain, wandering, blasphemous thoughts, while they wait upon God in his ordinances, than at other times? It is because Satan is then most busy in trying to keep them from contemplating the person and feeding upon the fulness of their Saviour. He does not stop here. When Christians retire to their secret devotions, Satan is at their heels; and what chamber so close as to shut out the fiend? If they quit their solitude, and mingle with the society of their friends, Satan is sure to make one of the party. Ah! believers, you cannot sufficiently know the importance of your Lord's command to watch, nor the necessity of observing it. The devil sets his gins in every spot, and if you are so happy as to avoid one that is designed for you now, you cannot take the next step ere he will fix another. If the good hand of God prevent you from falling into the pit, which he has prepared for you here, he will speedily dig one yonder. If you escape both the net and the pit, he will plant your path with thorns, and render painful every step you take. One would suppose that opposition like this is enough to shake the most courageous faith; but formidable as it is, it is only a part of that which he has to encounter. He finds

2. A host of enemies in the world.

By the world, in Scripture, we are sometimes to understand the men of the world, and sometimes the things of the world. In both these senses the world is a mortal enemy to the peace of the Christian, and to his comfortable progress in the divine life.

(1.) The men of the world are decided and uniform enemies to the Christian.

It is long since One who could not err told us, "In the world ye shall have tribulation." His first followers experienced the truth of this information in its most tremendous extent. Like their brethren of old, (for the righteous have always resembled each other as well in their fate as in their character,) "they had trial of cruel mockings and scourgings; yea, moreover, of bonds and imprisonments. They were stoned, they were sawn asunder, were tempted, were slain with the sword: they wandered about in sheepskins and goatskins, being destitute, afflicted, tormented." These, and every other species of torture which malignity can invent, or barbarity execute, they endured for their faithfulness to Christ and his gospel. The history, too, of later ages, and men from whose profession and knowledge we might have expected other conduct, records many a horrid tale of the sufferings of those who held fast the testimony of Jesus.

But though God, in his kind providence, has wrested from the hand of persecutors the murdering sword and the blazing faggot, so that his people no longer bleed on the scaffold nor fry at the stake, yet we must not imagine that the carnal world and they are on better terms than formerly. Since the first promise was given to Adam, "He that was after the flesh has persecuted him that was after the spirit," he does so yet, and will continue to do so while the devil has a particle of empire upon earth. It cannot be otherwise; for the righteous and the wicked differ so widely in their characters, in their motives of action, in their joys and sorrows, in their interests, in their objects, and in their prospects, that an agreement between them is simply impossible. The Scripture is decisive on this point. "The carnal mind," says Paul, "is enmity against God," and, therefore, cannot love anything that looks like him. The case of some whom Christ calls to follow him exactly tallies with the case of Abraham. How often has it happened that God singles out from a graceless family one of its members to be an heir of eternal life. He speaks in the powerful application of his word "Get thee out from thy country, and from thy kindred, and from thy father's house." But mark the consequence. No sooner does the Holy Spirit arrest the attention of this chosen vessel, embitter to him the pleasures of sin, and excite a serious concern for his immortal soul, than his impious relatives use every exertion to stifle in their birth those blessed convictions, which they affect to esteem a disease or a madness. Authority, entreaty, stratagem, threats, are alternately employed. Every principle of human action is artfully plied with arguments calculated to make the deepest impression; and nothing is omitted which promises either to soothe or frighten the soul from Christ. They who have been thus tried know it to be a sore persecution. But they are not alone. All who profess Christ must be persecuted in some shape or other; for they "who will live godly in Christ Jesus shall suffer persecution." In no age have they been exempted. But to some will appear unaccountably strange what I am going to assert, that, notwithstanding the high panegyrics which we constantly hear on the rapid progress that mankind are making in a noble and happy liberality in religious sentiment, there never has been, since the expulsion of Adam from paradise, a period in which a certain species at least of persecution was exercised, with more bitterness and rancour against the people of God, than at this moment. Many, indeed, will swell with indignation at what they may deem a groundless calumny, and exclaim, is it possible that the fair character of our polite, our liberal, our philosophic day, is stained with persecution? You may startle, but it is a truth; and the most noisy pretenders to enlightened philosophy are the most active in the unworthy pursuit. What is their boasted liberality? If a judgment might be formed from their conduct, one would imagine that it consists in freedom from the influence of principle and the restraints of decency. Look around you. Is it not a fact that everything serious and sacred is ridiculed with the most shameless effrontery by multitudes of those who affect to be the genteeler world? Is it not a fact that the doctrines of God's holy Word are the mirth of the licentious, and that they who wish to regulate their hearts and lives by its salutary precepts become the mockery of the profane? Nay, is not the infection so general and so deep, that even the young, whose purest happiness and most exalted honour lie in consecrating their powers to the Lord Jesus, are so ashamed of their glory, so glory in their shame, as to commence their career of liberal philosophy by opening their mouths against the heavens? If any begin to "remember their Creator in the days of their youth," and are not willing to go to hell with the crowd, what do their gay acquaintances think and say of them? They laugh at and despise them as poor, weak, melancholy, crazy fools. Yes, young Christians, you in particular must expect to be the scoff of impiety; you must endure the mortification to be branded with the opprobrious epithets of madmen, enthusiasts, hypocrites, and the like; nay, to "be the song of the drunkard." I know you will find it hard to bear; you will feel the force of the psalmist's petition to be kept from the strife of tongues. But be not disheartened, young believer, your Lord met with no better treatment; and "if they have called the Master of the house Beelzebub, how much more they of his household?" Oh! see that you add not to the number of those unhappy mortals, who, though they gave their names to Christ, can hear him reviled, and never utter a syllable for his honour; who shrink at the sneer of malice; whose faith is blown away by the breath of profanity: who barter their souls and heaven for a jest.

But the Christian's danger does not arise from those only who are open infidels. His graceless connections, who are more sober in their principles, and more decent in their practice, are no contemptible snare. A pleasant temper and engaging manners, especially if joined with polished education, with opulence and honours, steal upon the affections, throw the heart off its guard, and not only render it liable to be surprised by other temptations, but insensibly draw it into forbidden paths. This enemy to your peace advances under a form so sweet and smiling, that it is hardly possible either to suspect her treachery or resist her persuasions. Here you have need of continued watchfulness, great self-denial, much of that wisdom which cometh from above, and unfailing supplies of strength from Christ your head.

2. The Christian is not only opposed by the men, he is trammelled also by the things of the world.

Immersed in sense, and imperfect in his graces, the most experienced saint requires to be often reminded that here he has no continuing city, but is a pilgrim and a stranger. We are more prone to nothing than to misplace our blessings. When God showers down upon us the bounties of his providence, we too frequently give them that affection which belongs exclusively to the

Lord Christ. Every new comfort is apt to twist a new cord round our hearts; and they tie themselves so firmly that nothing but almighty grace can loosen the knot. Divine is the lesson, and they alone who are divinely taught will practise it, to abound in this world's goods, and yet to set their affections on things above. Far different is the effect which prosperity has on the multitude of those who enjoy it. It is recorded of Israel, that when the Lord "slew them then they sought him." But no sooner did he visit them with peace and plenty, than "Jeshurun waxed fat and kicked." Instead of raising higher his hymn of gratitude, he "tempted and provoked the most high God, and turned aside like a deceitful bow." Prosperity has detected many a rotten professor; and it becomes the affluent not to forget what our Lord has said of the deceitfulness of riches, especially since he has so solemnly declared that "it is easier for a camel to go through the eye of a needle, than for a rich man," or as he himself explains it, "them who trust in riches, to enter into the kingdom of heaven." Often do we see his curse fearfully verified. "Woe unto you, ye rich, for ye have received your consolation." Mistake me not, brethren. I mean not to rail against wealth as a thing evil in itself, nor to insinuate that the enjoyment of it is a crime. All the creatures of God are good; and if he has distinguished you by opening his liberal hand and poured plenty into your dwellings, these gifts of his bounty are to be received with thankfulness and improved with care. But that they expose you to dangerous temptations, that they have actually proved a fatal snare to many, you must acknowledge; and if you belong to Christ, it will not be difficult to convince you that you need more watchfulness and more grace than others, and that there is much necessity for this divine caution, "If riches increase, set not your hearts upon them."

The same may be said of the honours of the world. Hurried with the business of office, surrounded by the irreligious, and flattered by the obsequiousness of those who court their favour, men of high station are in circumstances very unfavourable to warm and humble piety. And although it may be thought superfluous to enlarge on this topic, as there appear to be but few of the Lord's people who fill places of earthly dignity and power, yet it is not superfluous to entreat them to guard against an anxiety for a situation that will lay them open to the hazard of many sinful compliances—that will cool their ardour in pressing forward toward the mark, the prize of their high-calling in Christ Jesus—and be to them hereafter a fruitful source of bitter regret. Whilst the old leaven remains, they will sometimes feel the workings of a temper which "loves the praise of men more than the praise of God;" and as they are required to "run with patience the race set before them," they should listen to the voice from heaven, commanding them "to lay aside every weight," and not incur the guilt of disobedience by tying new ones about their necks

If riches—if honours are hostile to the travellers who are marching to Zion, surely carnal pleasure cannot be their friend. The desire of ease and sensual gratification is so interwoven with man's present frame, that he seldom makes a resistance so feeble and ineffectual as when attacked in this quarter. Never does he commit such egregious blunders, as when he undertakes to value the enjoyments of sense. Viewing objects through a false and jaundiced medium, he must inevitably pronounce a false and pernicious judgment; whilst unhallowed propensities giving him frequently no time for reasoning or reflection, urge him into rash and destructive actions. We cannot advance far in the ways of Christ, without knowing the painful struggle which is necessary to withstand the allurements of pleasure. Let those who profess the religion of Jesus fix it in their minds as a most important truth, that we must employ continued vigilance and prayer if we would escape her entanglements. To those particularly who are in the bloom of life I address myself. Flee from her blandishments. Her cords are silken, but they are strong, and draw to ruin. Taste not the mixture of her cup; 'tis sweet, indeed, but fraught with death. Trust not her innocent and enchanting appearance: it is the cloak of treachery; and whilst you listen to her syren tongue, and are fascinated with her bewitching smiles, she is aiming at your bosoms a mortal blow.

What think you now, brethren, of the Christian life? Is it not a life of toil, of hardships, of peril? Is the representation now given of it widely different from that which your experience has realized? Has the profession of the gospel cost you no fightings, no fears, no trouble? Then, brethren, deceive not yourselves, you have serious reason to doubt your relation to the Lord Jesus; and this alarming idea will be confirmed when I tell you that you have not yet heard the whole of those trials which fall to the lot of a believer. He finds a

Third class of terrible enemies in the corruptions of his own heart.

A Christian is a singular phenomenon—he has within him two moral principles directly contrary to each other, both in their nature and in their operations. They must, therefore, and do keep up an unceasing conflict. "The flesh," says Paul, "lusteth against the spirit, and the spirit against the flesh, and these two are contrary the one to the other, so that ye cannot do the things that ye would." On this text, the daily experience of God's people is the best commentator. Every rising and setting sun furnishes them with some new proof, that though implanted grace, when succoured from on high, overcomes, it cannot extirpate corruption. Their old man is indeed crucified, but he still lives. He is dying, 'tis true, but he dies a lingering death; and, in struggling for life, he will make many violent exertions before he expires. Followers of Jesus, you can easily enter into my meaning. However the apostle's language may have puzzled speculative men who decided concerning their own hearts, you comprehend him without difficulty when he says, "I see another law in my members, warring against the law of my mind, and bringing me into captivity to the law of sin and death which is in my members." You know the truth of that humiliating declaration: "The heart of man is deceitful above all things, and desperately wicked." You know what it is to groan under the workings of pride, ingratitude, insensibility, impurity, unbelief, and all the other evil affections which are expressed by the term of indwelling sin. You know that there is in your souls, notwithstanding all the goodness and all the love of your Redeemer, such a propensity to depart from the living God, that were not the everlasting arms continually underneath you, your feet would soon slide into the paths, would sink in the mire, of the grossest sin. Distressing situation! To be surrounded with foes thirsting for our blood is painful enough, but to harbour in our own bosoms traitors who are leagued with these foes, is beyond measure afflicting. How sweetly and serenely would the Christian's days glide on were it not for the power of inward corruptions. These are the combustible materials which the fiery darts of the devil kindle into a blaze. Since the fall none except our blessed Lord was ever without them Him, it is true, Satan tempted and the world allured. But the world allured, and Satan tempted, in vain. Happily for us, he could say, "The prince of this world cometh and hath nothing in me."

After the view which we have taken of the Christian's danger, one who has never tasted the consolations of the gospel will be ready to ask, "Where, then, is the blessedness of which you speak? If such are the enemies, such the snares, such the sorrows of those who are travelling to Zion, what do you mean by telling us, that wisdom's ways are ways of pleasantness, and all her paths peace?" This objection will be fully obviated when we come to consider the other parts of our subject in a subsequent discourse. In the meantime, your attention is called to the practical improvement of the doctrine which has been exhibited.

1. Are the powers of darkness, the world, and the natural principles of the heart, combined to oppose the Christian's growth in grace, and prevent his arrival at heaven? Let us hence learn the "vileness of sin." Obedience to the law, and resemblance to God, are at once the happiness and the glory of rational creatures. All created intelligences came from the hand of God, shining in beauty, and perfect in bliss. Love to their kind benefactor was their highest principle, and their love to everything else was proportioned to the likeness which it bore to their heavenly Father. This is still their duty, and would be their temper, had there not been a dreadful revolution in the moral world. How inexpressibly hateful must that be which is diametrically opposed to holiness, and justice, and goodness, and truth, and every perfection of Deity! How inexpressibly hateful must that be, which prompts a reasonable being to cherish malignity against the God in whom he lives, and moves, and breathes! How can one show greater malignity against a parent, than by venting spite against his children for his sake? How can one give a more pointed proof of enmity against God than by tormenting his ransomed ones? It is because they resemble him, that men and devils view them with a malicious eye: and the more they resemble him, the more furiously will the malice of their enemies be exerted. Now what has introduced this horrible confusion? What has thus defaced the beauty of God's creation? What has reversed the lovely order which originally

prevailed? It is nothing but sin! And shall we think it a trifle? "O do not that abominable thing which I hate," says Jehovah: and shall any of us indulge ourselves in the commission of it? Ye "who make a mock of sin," pause, reflect, tremble! It made the devil; it kindled hell; and unless your opinions respecting it be essentially altered, it will plunge you into that lake of fire, and keep you there for ever.

2. Let us remark the plain manner in which God deals with men. He calls us to his service, but tells us at the same time, that he calls us to suffering. "If any man," says the Saviour, "if any man will come after me, let him deny himself, and take up his cross daily and follow me." He promises to his faithful followers a rich inheritance in the heavenly Canaan: he promises them also supplies of grace from his abundant fulness to maintain them while they are here: but he informs them likewise that the path to glory lies through difficulty and danger. He holds up to their hope an unfading crown; but he lets them know that it is the crown of victory, and therefore that they must fight for it. Whatever then be the hardships which distress them, they cannot reproach their Lord with deceiving them. Ere they advance a step towards the New Jerusalem, he shows them without disguise what they must expect, and thus addresses them: "Behold! I have told you before!" Far different is the manner in which the devil treats his servants. He promises them pleasure and profit, but says not that he neither intends nor is able to perform his word: nor that Almighty God may blast in a moment their most flattering prospects. He presents the rose but he covers the thorn—he strews their way with flowers, but never hints that it leads to the bottomless pit. Deluded men! who listen to his suggestions. Recollect that he is the father of lies. Recollect that these sinful pleasures which you may enjoy for a season, will not, cannot, compensate for everlasting burnings. Fly to the Captain of salvation, and you shall be safe.

3. Learn the value of the Christian's inheritance. God does not sport with his people: surely, then, it must be a glorious reward which awaits them beyond the grave, when their God, who loves them with more than a father's tenderness, thinks it a sufficient recompense for all their trials. Were it not unspeakably great, and infinitely desirable, it would not be worth so much sorrow and

suffering. O ye careless ones, who neglect Jesus and the benefits of his purchase, stand still, and ask yourselves, Is there not a reality in religion? May not the scripture be true in declaring that "it shall be well with the righteous, and ill with the wicked?" Indeed the question merits your most serious attention. An immortal soul is the depending stake: an error here ruins you eternally.

4. Learn the necessity of watchfulness, and the danger of sporting with temptation. Is all your vigilance sometimes too little to guard you against the wiles of your enemies, and all your strength too feeble to secure you against their power? How then will you stand when you neither watch nor fight? A slothful Christian is a sentinel sleeping on his post! A slothful Christian is a mariner slumbering in a storm! A slothful Christian is a sheep composing itself to rest in the sight of hungry wolves! But what shall we say of those who, besides being negligent, throw themselves into the way of their adversaries? "Avoid all appearance of evil," is the divine command. But if they will disobey, they must abide the consequences. If they will take coals in their bosoms, they must expect to be burnt! If they will stray into the enemy's ground, they must expect to be caught! If they will run into the mouth of the lion, they must expect to be worried: and no thanks to them that he does not worry them to death: thanks to the great Shepherd who gives "to all his sheep eternal life, so that they shall never perish, neither shall any pluck them out of his hand." Christians, watch and pray, that ye enter not into temptation. "Put on the whole armour of God. Quit yourselves like men: be strong." But while you are thus active and cautious, remember,

Finally, the insufficiency of your own strength.

What are the weapons of your warfare? Do you intrench yourselves behind your good frame? Alas! one puff of temptation will blow away this ideal refuge. Do you trust to your own firmness? Satan laughs at the shaking of this pointless spear. To leave Satan out of the question, what are your resolutions when opposed to inward depravity? Mere chaff before the whirlwind. He is a raw Christian who is not sensible of this. No! believers! you must neither lean to your own understanding, nor confide in your own ability. You must "be strong in the Lord, and in the power of his might." You must "run with patience the race set before you, looking unto Jesus, the author and finisher of your faith." His grace alone is sufficient for you. With his heaven in your eye, and his word in your hearts, go up " from the wilderness, leaning upon your Beloved."

SERMON XIV.

THE CHRISTIAN WARFARE.

1 TIM. vi. 12.

"Fight the good fight of faith."

WHEN men engage in any arduous enterprise, we naturally conclude that they have in view some object, which, upon plausible grounds, they deem an equivalent for their labour and self-denial. To renounce our ease and comfort; to plunge into difficulty; cheerfully to endure fatigue of body and anxiety of mind; to submit to varied suffering without the prospect of remuneration of any kind; is conduct from which nature shrinks; is a sacrifice which neither reason nor religion requires us to make. Not less ignorant than malicious are the calumnies which many think themselves entitled to heap upon the religion of Jesus, because it enjoins mortification to the world; that is, the corrupt world; and assures the Christian that he must maintain with his foes, while on earth, a painful and perpetual conflict. How preposterous is the judgment of carnal men! They contemplate with blind admiration the warrior, who, impelled by a passion for military glory, or fired by the enthusiasm of freedom, rushes to the field of blood, courts the post of danger, and, in the grim face of death, shakes his martial steel. What does he hope to gain by these heroic exertions? His ambition centres perhaps in the plume of victory. He sighs for fame: "a fancied life in others' breath;" the empty plaudits of a fickle multitude. Or should he fall, his high reward is to have his name enrolled in the historian's volume, and his memory embalmed with the eulogies of the brave. Give him his due; call his passion noble if you please—recapitulate his services—celebrate his achievements—and hold up his example to animate the rising patriot.

But here we must stop. Pause—remember that these objects, for the attainment of which, the shout of acclamation rends the air, are confined to this world—remember that these coveted glories are fading, fleeting, momentary — not one of them can pass the verge of time: not one of them can cross the threshold of that dark house appropriated for all the living; no respect is paid to them beyond the grave; and, oh! how killing the thought, that the man who has won the applause of his fellow-men may have lost his own soul, and be excluded for ever from the kingdoms of God! Shall we then lavish praises on a son of earth who sheathes his sword in a mortal cause; and shall we dart the glance of scorn on the Christian soldier who fights for the crown of immortal life? Shall we extol the valour of him who coolly meets a man like himself; and shall we despise as a coward him who faces undaunted not only earth but hell? Shall we say that any earthly foe is to be named in comparison with those enemies against whom the Christian wages war? For you will recollect, that in the last discourse on this subject we showed that the powers of darkness who constantly oppose him are strong; are numerous; are malicious; are skilful; are indefatigable. We saw that the men of the world are his uniform and decided foes. We saw that the riches and honours of the world have a dangerous tendency to warp his judgment and pervert his heart, and that the pleasures of the world spread on every side their fatal snares. We saw, finally, that his own corruptions often rage with violence and reduce him to great extremities.

To encounter such a terrible combination of adversaries not only demands more than human boldness, but demands also great encouragement; but here the Christian is not left destitute. His Lord not only requires them, as we saw in the first place, to fight, but,

II. From the advantages which this warfare has over all others, it is termed with peculiar propriety a good fight. And why may the Christian be said to "fight a good fight?" The answer is obvious; he fights in a good cause; he fights upon good support; he fights in good company; and shall be infallibly victorious.

1. He fights in a good cause; the cause of God.

Sin made sad divisions in the family of heaven. It rent from the honour and bliss of the divine presence, and from every hope of pardon, those sons of pride who rose in rebellion against their Creator. The iniquity of every succeeding day has widened the breach between the persevering and apostate angels and multiplied the grounds of Jehovah's quarrel. It is both our shame and our misery that we so basely forget the duty which we owe to our Benefactor, as to desert his laws, to league ourselves with hell, and become a party in those plots of wickedness in which the fiends of darkness are ever busy. Can anything be more degrading and reproachful than to lift up our heel against the God "who fed us all our lives long?" Can there be a more vile prostitution of our souls, or bodies, and all the blessings which mark our lot, than to employ them as materials and instruments in abetting the devil to carry on his works of treachery? Yet this is the hateful character, this the devilish pursuit, of all whose hearts are not renewed by the spirit of Christ. And shall not the Christian exult that divine grace has opened his eyes to see the filthy drudgery of his former life, and enabled him to abandon the cause and camp of Satan, to renew his allegiance to his rightful Lord, and thankfully to take up his station behind Emmanuel's banner? In rectitude there is something which gives a divine firmness to resolution; which smooths the rough features of difficulty; and even in the midst of danger sheds through the untrembling soul a heavenly calm. If, therefore, to be engaged on the side of all that is honourable and glorious; if to be engaged on the side of truth, and righteousness, and purity, and faithfulness, and love, and all the excellencies which constitute the happiness of Jehovah himself, can alleviate suffering, can originate comfort, can repay self-denial, the Christian's warfare has an unrivalled title to be called a good fight. And the title will shine, if possible, more fair, when we consider, not only that he fights in a good cause, but,

2. That he fights upon good support.

By support I mean the promises of the covenant, the supplies of grace, and all that rich variety of wisdom which our spiritual Joshua has made for the wants of his church. The wisdom of our leader, the affection of our brother, neither requires nor permits us to war upon our own charges. Great is the variety of trouble which we must encounter in our march, but it is not greater than the variety of comfort. In this Bible, this magazine of our military stores, there is everything necessary for our laborious expedition. To fit us for resisting and defeating the foes who always hover about us, here is the "whole armour of God." Here is the "girdle of truth" to strengthen our loins. Here is the "breastplate of iron" to cover our hearts. Here is the "preparation of the gospel of peace" to secure our feet from burning sands, and the thorns and spikes which our adversaries may plant in our path. Here is faith's impenetrable "shield to receive and extinguish the fiery darts of the wicked. Here is the "helmet of salvation" to defend our heads, and here the "sword of the Spirit," whose divinely-tempered edge not all the host of hell could ever withstand. When we are obliged to pass, though shrouded in darkness, between the craggy precipice and the wily snare, here is the torch of celestial fire to show us at once our danger and escape. It is this lamp of heaven which David tells us was "a light to his feet." When worn out with fatigue, here is "the water of life" to recruit our spirits. Here is the food with which our Redeemer covers our table in the wilderness—food of every kind, from milk to strong meat, suited to all ages and all degrees of strength, and set before us in all the vast profusion which a God can furnish. The weary traveller who has passed through an inhospitable wild, and is exhausted by the scorching sun, does not more relish the cool refreshing stream, the fragrance of the opening flower, or the luxuriant fruit, than does the Christian that divine repast which his Lord has prepared for him. None but they who have been filled with the fatness of God's house can conceive the rapture of the believer's soul when his faith is enabled to grasp the promises of the covenant, and to press from them unutterable sweetness. It is when the great Dispenser of new covenant bliss "satisfieth their mouths with good things" that "their youth is renewed like the eagle's." When he makes them "sit down under his shadow with great delight"—when his fruit is sweet to their taste—when his Holy Spirit descends in the dew of his sacred influences, and gladdens their dejected hearts—these moments of love, these droppings of his myrrh, repay a thousandfold their sorrow and their suffering. This, indeed, is not their common privilege. They "walk by faith and not by sight," and therefore their brethren who dare not lay claim to such distinguished honour, and whose trembling knees totter while they follow in the footsteps of the flock, should not be discouraged. Christ looks with peculiar tenderness upon these lambs; and if in sovereignty he does not think proper to feast them so highly as others, yet he holds around them his almighty arm, and keeps from them the roaring lion and the ravenous wolf. He puts them into his bosom, and carries them, they know not how, through difficulty and danger, sets them in a plain path, and enables them to run with cheerfulness the way of his commandments. Nor let those stronger disciples, whom the King has dignified with peculiar marks of his favour, indulge a slothful temper. It is after these seasons of joy that they may look for some of the rudest attacks of their enemies. The combat is still before them, and many a terrible wound may they receive ere it be ended. But shrink not, O Christian! shrink not from the conflict; wounded you may be, but not mortally. No blow can be so fatal as to be incurable by the balm of Gilead. The great Physician of souls, whose judgment never errs, whose skill never fails, hastes to the relief of his people, pours into their painful wounds his sovereign balsam, and not only applies but blesses his own prescription. Thus we see that the believer's hardest trials are softened with a consolation and a joy with which a stranger to his life can never intermeddle. There is not within these walls a child of God, (and I hope there are a goodly number,) who will not join issue in the bold assertion. Try the experiment if you please. Watch the Christian in his most afflicted hours. When beset with his spiritual enemies, his agonizing soul is almost overwhelmed, ask him, in this moment of anguish, to part with his Redeemer—promise, as the reward of compliance, all the sensual delights that can enter into a voluptuary's heaven. Know, vain man, that he would spurn thy most splendid offer—he would cleave more closely to the cross, and tread thy baubles in the dirt; and indeed it cannot be otherwise, for the circumstances of the Christian and the carnal man are exactly the reverse of each other. In few of the wicked is the cry of conscience so completely stifled as not to fill the soul occasionally with serious alarm. The hopelessness of the sinner's cause cannot but imbitter his joy, and give to all his griefs their most corroding venom: whilst the enjoyment of the Christian, cheered with the goodness of his cause, carry with them an unutterable relish, and soften all the pains of his pilgrimage. Surely, then, he has every reason to pity those who affect to pity him, and to triumph in the reflection that he fights a good fight.

But 3. The Christian fights a good fight because he fights in good company.

Agreeable society prevents despondence, lightens toil, and inspires courage. Let the believer then look around him, and see how many excellent ones of the earth, even in this day of coldness when multitudes have left their first love, are seeking with him "a better country, a city which hath foundations, whose builder and maker is God." Let faith's keen eye glance over the field of action, and view the bright, the numerous bands that appear on the Lord's side. View them, believer, pressing towards "the mark, the prize of their high calling of God in Christ Jesus." View them, and refrain, if thou canst, from congratulating thyself at being enrolled in the list, and sharing the labours of the blissful throng. View them, and say, does not a holy emulation burn in thy bosom? Does not the animating sight impart fresh vigour, and stimulate thee to strain every nerve in order to keep pace with those soldiers of Christ? But these are not your only companions: the angels of God are never absent. "Are they not all ministering spirits, sent forth to minister unto them who shall be the heirs of salvation?" This has been their delightful employment from the commencement of the gospel to the present hour. It is true, they do not now, as in former times, visibly interfere for the people of God, but their agency is not the less real nor effectual. It is as much a promise of the covenant as any other: "He shall give his angels charge concerning thee, to keep thee in all thy ways; and in their hands they shall bear thee up, lest thou dash thy foot against a stone." From a thousand evils which we never suspect, do these heavenly friends protect our souls. About thee, O Christian, these armies of heaven have many conflicts with the hosts of hell—conflicts which thou never shalt know till thy warfare be ended, and the hallelujahs of eternal victory fill the temple above. What a thought is this? That Jehovah shall despatch, to support our faltering steps, the shining messengers of his will! and let the grateful soul swell with emotions too big for utterance, when we reflect that not only the angels, but the Lord of angels, the Angel of the covenant, is at our side. Those lips which knew no guile, have said, "I will never leave thee nor forsake thee." This is the marrow of our consolation. Who shall vie in dignity with the favoured ones that walk in company with Jehovah-Jesus? Who shall harm the child of blessing that marches towards Zion with his arm locked in the arm of his Redeeming God? Ye glittering toys of earth, where is your brightness, where your worth, when ye come in competition with an honour and a happiness like this? Let these glow-worms of the night sink into their native obscurity, when the Sun of Righteousness beams around us the splendours of his glory. Triumph, believer, in the grace and goodness of your Lord. And ye who have no interest in his salvation, take care how ye meddle with these beloved Jacobs. In unchanging faithfulness, God has drawn around his chosen, a sacred circle. Stand back, thou profane! Touch not, with an unhallowed hand, these monuments of mercy. It is the command of him, whose frown is worse than hell, "Do my prophets no harm;" and all his saints are as dear to him as his prophets; he "who touches them, touches the apple of his eye." Indignant thunders murmur over your heads, and the vengeful lightning is impatient to chastise your temerity. Who then dare say that the Christian does not fight a good fight? What will the scorner have to reply, when to the precious privileges that have been already mentioned, we add,

4. That the believer fights a good fight, because victory is sure.

There is not, my believing friends, a promise in the whole Bible, (and it is full of promises) which does not belong to you. There is not in the Bible a promise which does not, either directly or indirectly, insure to you strength to overcome your enemies. Many of them are express to this very purpose; what words are these? "No weapon formed against thee shall prosper."—" Thy enemies shall all be found liars unto thee." What though they tell you that the difficulties in the way are insurmountable? You have nothing to do with difficulties: your inquiry is, What saith the Lord? Your reply must be, "Get thee behind me, Satan! The God who hath commanded, will support: the God who hath promised, will perform. I know I am unable of myself to emerge from my trouble; but I know also that the "Lord will provide." He hath said, "Fear not, for I am with thee; be not dismayed, for I am thy God: I will help thee, yea, I will uphold thee by the right hand of my righteousness." Are not these promises sealed with the blood of your Redeemer? And who dares question his veracity? Is it not he who "is a liar, and the father of lies?" Is not the arm of Omnipotence bared to execute what immutable truth engaged? And who are these spiritual Philistines that defy not the armies, but the Son of the living God? Are they not the creatures of his hand? Did he not foil them on the cross? Did he not, at his resurrection and ascension, chain them as captives to his chariot-wheels, and make a show of them openly? And shall they be too strong for him now when he is "set down at the right hand of the majesty on high?" Absurd idea! Face, then, the fiercest of your foes, and let this be your song of battle, "In the name of our God we will set up our banners." But while you rejoice in the advantages of your Lord's service, see that you keep things in their proper connection: break not that harmony which he has established: and to preserve this harmony, you will find it of high moment to be under the practical influence of the principle inculcated in the

III. Part of our subject, which assures us that the Christian's warfare is not only a good fight, but the good fight of faith.

It is this important grace which gives life and vigour to all the rest. Not that it has any merit in itself; but it is the instrument by which the Holy Spirit applies the benefits of redemption. It is faith which keeps us close to Christ, and receives continually supplies from his fulness; and what cannot this faith effect? What difficulties can she not endure? What temptation not trample under foot? What corruption not subdue? Look over the long list of worthies whose names shine in the annals of redemption, and see what faith has done. As she has the same object, and the same support, she has done nothing but what she can yet do. She is as able as ever to "stop the mouths of lions; to quench the violence of fire; to escape the edge of the sword; to make you valiant in fight; to turn to flight the armies of the aliens," and to perform all those other deeds of wonder, which few, very few amongst us, would think of imitating. Ye faint-hearted Christians, why do ye stare astonishment when ye read the achievements of Old Testament saints? These were men; you are but dwarfs—in the divine life. Blush that they outstripped you so far. Look up to the cloud of witnesses who bore testimony to the faithfulness of a promising God, and who have now "received the end of their faith, even the salvation of their souls." Set their example before you, and "go ye and do likewise." In marching to the battle, let faith lead the other graces, while she follows the Redeemer, and thus tread in the "footsteps of them who, through faith and patience, are now inheriting the promises."

In improving the subject on which our thoughts have been employed, let me exhort believers to be of good courage. Arduous is the work, but glorious is the cause, and unspeakably great the encouragement. And when you equip yourselves for the combat, see that every part of your armour, from your helmet to your sandals, be instamped with the name of Christ. No weapon which does not come from his armoury, and bear the impress of his name, will in the least intimidate your daring foes. It is this name (for they well remember it since the defeat of Calvary), it is this name which strikes dismay into their hearts and confusion into their ranks. And to banish every fear, be careful to recollect that you fight not only in the name, but under the eye, and with the aid, of your Lord. Young Christian, here is encouragement for you. You have just put on the harness of your celestial warfare. You are just beginning a career of glory, in which you may lay your account with meeting opposition the most determined and unremitted. You are in that stage of your life in which your own corruptions are most powerful and active; in which the allurements of a depraved world are most fascinating; in which the smiles and the frowns of men most deeply affect the mind. You, above all others, are marked out to feel the malice of wicked men, and of those evil spirits by whom they are governed. But fear not, you fight under an invincible Leader. Jesus, the Author and Finisher of your faith; Jesus, who has all power in heaven, in earth, and in hell too, goes before you. He lifts above the necks of them who hate you his glittering sword, which shivers all hostile armour, and mows down the thickest ranks of his and your enemies. Be assured he will strike the blow of your deliverance at the very moment when you most need it. Gird up, then, the loins of your faith. "Run with patience the race set before you." Look constantly unto Jesus; for though you can do nothing of yourself, yet "through Christ strengthening you, you can do all things." Remember that his faithfulness is pledged to bear you through. "He will perfect that which concerneth you." He will make you not only a conqueror, but more than a conqueror; and when your warfare is finished, he will receive you to himself; his own hand shall twine about your brows the wreath of victory, and it shall bloom for ever in all the glories of Paradise.

Old Christian, here is encouragement for you. Since you gave your heart to the Redeemer you have had many a bitter hour, and endured many a terrible conflict for his sake. But sure I am that you do not repent your choice. All your afflictions have been amply compensated by his love and his presence. He promised you at first that he would dwell in you, and walk in you, and walk round you, and be your God. Has he not been as good as his word? Is it not because you have obtained help of him that you continue to this day? And will he forsake you now? He will not, he cannot. If he was the God of your youth, he will be the God of your declining years. He has said even to "old age, I am he; and even to hoary hairs, I will carry you." How comforting the thought that when your heart and your flesh fail, "this God is the strength of your heart and your portion for ever." Courage, then, old friend! A few more sighs, a few more sorrows, a few more sufferings, and all shall be well for ever. Now is your salvation nearer than when you believed; now are you approaching the borders of your promised inheritance. Lift up your eyes and view the heavenly Canaan. 'Tis true you cannot enter till you have passed through the swellings of Jordan, but your Lord hath promised, when thou "passest through the waters I will be with thee, and through the rivers they shall not overflow thee." 'Tis true you must grapple with the "king of terrors." Hastily he advances upon you. But startle not at his grisly appearance. It is the mimicry of danger—the mock terror of an enfeebled, a harmless foe. It is, too, your concluding struggle, "for the last enemy that shall be destroyed is death." When you have vanquished this enemy (and vanquish him you shall), you will understand, far better than you can now, the meaning of these triumphant words, "The ransomed of the Lord shall return, and come to Zion with songs and everlasting joy upon their heads; they shall obtain joy and gladness, and sorrow and mourning shall flee away."

To them who are unacquainted with the Christian's life I have nothing to say. You, my brethren, are fighting; but did you ever take the pains to ask yourselves in what cause? A cause beyond description degrading and hopeless. You are fighting with the devil, and for the devil, and against the God of your mercies, and against your own happiness. You are treasuring up to yourselves wrath against the day of wrath, and if you are resolved to remain on the devil's side, you must share at last the devil's fate. You are engaged against infinite odds; there is not any hope that you shall succeed. It is a dreadful thing to "fall into the hands of the living God;" and if he spared not the angels that sinned, he certainly will not spare you. We invite you to a warfare better in itself and better in its end. Come, cast in your lot with us, and "fight the good fight of faith." Besides the consolation of a righteous cause and divine support, you will have the best of company. The saints will be your friends, angels will be your friends, a triune God will be your friend, heaven your eternal home, and a crown of life your rich reward.

SERMON XV.

NATURE AND NECESSITY OF REGENERATION.

JOHN iii. 5.

"Verily, verily, I say unto you, Except a man be born of water and of the Spirit, he cannot enter into the kingdom of God."

In the preceding part of the chapter, our Lord had inculcated upon Nicodemus the absolute necessity of a new birth, in order to a sinful man's even perceiving the kingdom of God. The candid Pharisee, to whom such a doctrine appeared as uncouth, incredible, and absurd, as it does at this day to many who call themselves enlightened Christians, expressed his astonishment, as if the Redeemer had uttered a physical contradiction: "How can a man be born when he is old? can he enter a second time into his mother's womb and be born?" Without stopping to notice the grossness of his conceptions, our Lord Jesus, with the majesty of "a teacher sent from God," repeats his assertion with a slight variation in the form, which might lead Nicodemus to some general idea of his meaning: "Verily, verily, I say unto you, Except a man be born of water and of the Spirit, he cannot enter into the kingdom of God."

The "kingdom of God" means that gracious establishment in our world of which he is the author, which derives all its principles and efficiency from him, of which the design is to destroy the works of the devil and bring back, with increased beauty, the order originally set up; in a word, to make such a display of his righteousness, truth, grace, and love, in and towards our rebel world, as should command the admiration of all holy beings, and be an eternal exhibition, in all places of his dominion, of the perfection of his government.

no other "became him for whom are all things and by whom are all things, in bringing many sons unto glory," and that it is infinitely impossible they should be deceived in trusting it. "I know," says an assured believer—"I know whom I have believed, and am persuaded that he is able to keep that which I have committed unto him against that day." They see that sin is folly, and the wages of sin death—that the cup of sinful gratification, in which they formerly took pleasure, is charged with poison, and was actually working their destruction. They see that wisdom's ways are ways of pleasantness, and her paths the only ones "that lead to glory and to God." They see, in an inverted order and proportion, the things of time and sense, and the things which are eternal; in one word, they see what they never saw before—"the kingdom of God!"

2. When a man enters into the kingdom of God, he exists by a new medium.

This new medium is the Spirit of God in his gracious influence. He is universally the "Spirit of life." In him we live, and move, and have our being. All the created life in the universe is from him. But he dispenses it agreeably to the nature of the constitution under which he acts. The vegetable, animal, and intellectual worlds have their lives such as the Spirit of God gives them for the purposes they are intended to answer. It is no otherwise in the world of grace, the kingdom of God. There too, "it is the Spirit that quickeneth, and that which is born of the Spirit is spirit." He bestows and maintains a life answerable to the part which the saved sinner has to perform, the affections he is to cherish, the blessedness he is to enjoy, the glory which awaits him. As one who is made alive unto God, not a faculty of the new man is unfolded, not a function exercised, not a motion performed, but by the Spirit of God. His very faith, the elementary principle of his life, is from the Holy Spirit; so that "he lives by the Spirit, he walks by the Spirit, he is led by the Spirit." By the Spirit the Christian mortifies the deeds of the body; he brings forth fruit unto God; he cultivates his love, enjoys his fellowship, is "spiritually minded." All this is manifestly a new life, infinitely removed from any merely intellectual attainment, however refined or exalted. A life for which earth has no atmosphere, and which can exist nowhere but in "the kingdom of God."

3. He who is born again lives by new "means."

These are, the word, the ordinances, and the grace of our Lord Jesus Christ. No sooner is the babe of grace born into the kingdom of God, than he cries for the "sincere milk of the word." The speculations of men, and their discoveries, even of truth, however elegant or lofty, are at best but "dry breasts;" they afford no nutriment to his soul, nor can satisfy the cravings of his appetite; and in every after stage of his existence, it is the bread of God which came down from heaven—it is the meat which endureth to everlasting life—that can either fulfil his desires, or refresh and invigorate his frame. Then the word of God is found of him, and he eats it, and it is unto him "the joy and the rejoicing of his heart." The "judgments of the Lord are," to his taste, "sweeter than the honey and the honey-comb." In the ordinances of Christ he finds those green pastures and those gently flowing waters which delighted the psalmist and equally delight him. These ordinances are thus precious and powerful, because they are channels through which the Redeemer's grace pours into his heart. Christ himself is his life. "His flesh is meat indeed, and his blood is drink indeed." His words are verified in a believer's experience. "He that eateth me, even he shall live by me. So that the life which he now lives in the flesh is by the faith of the Son of God." Thus fed and nourished, and filled with the fulness of God, he "grows in grace and in the knowledge of our Lord and Saviour Jesus Christ," until that which is perfect is come, and he is admitted into his presence with exceeding joy.

4. In consequence of his "new birth," his faculties acquire a new development.

The eyes of his understanding are enlightened, so that he perceives what is "the hope of the calling of God, and what the riches of the glory of his inheritance in the saints." As a "natural man he received not the things of the Spirit of God, because they were foolishness unto him." But being "born of the Spirit," he has "spiritual discernment, so that what things were "foolishness" to him appear to be "the wisdom of God," and "the power of God to his salvation."

His will, which before was all enmity, is now made pliant and ductile to the will of God. It is the rule and reason of his duties and of his submission. Show a Christian that what he is called to do or to endure is agreeable to the will of his heavenly Father, and you do infinitely more to nerve his resolution or to calm his spirit—to render him courageous, inflexible, persevering, or to soften or subdue his soul—to repress every rising murmur and bend his mind into meek and cordial acquiescence—than by a thousand arguments drawn from the necessity of the case, from the dignity of virtue, from the fitness of things, from the good of the universe, or any of those sterile topics which ignorance addresses to vanity. It is the will of God! forms a short summary of a regenerated man's ethics, and disposes of all the objections of flesh and blood, and sinful appetite, and earthly decencies, interests, and passions, with a celerity somewhat proportioned to the majesty of Him who has spoken. In short, " to do the will of God from the heart" is the perfection after which the new man habitually aspires.

The *affections* also undergo a renovation. Once they were "set on things on the earth;" the love of this present world occupied and filled their hearts with the lust of the flesh, the lust of the eye, and the pride of life." But being born again, they are taught to " set their affections on things above, where Jesus Christ sitteth at the right hand of God." Disregard and despise the good gifts of God's providence they do not, they cannot. They are the only people on earth who know how to assign them their proper places; to use them according to the intention of the blessed Giver, and to be unfeignedly thankful for them. Gratitude to God is a conspicuous feature on the face of the new man; it forms a family likeness, by which the members are identified. " Be ye thankful" is a precept which none but a Christian obeys. But when the question is concerning their supreme and ultimate preference, the soul of a believer fastens upon other objects, and he values the things of this transitory life, whatever they may be, quite as low as, when viewed in their proper relations of the gift of God, he values them highly. " What things were gain to me, those I counted loss for Christ; yea, doubtless, and I count all things but loss for the excellency of the knowledge of Christ Jesus, my Lord." The principle of love, which has its perfect reign in the kingdom of God, and binds together the society of holy beings, is "shed abroad in his heart." He loves the Lord Jesus, the Redeemer, tenderly, intensely, fervently. He joins, without a qualification, in that sacred curse of the apostle, " If any man love not the Lord Jesus Christ, let him be Anathema Maran-atha. He loves the God and Father of our Lord Jesus Christ as the original fountain of all saving mercies, and can, from his inmost soul, re-echo that benediction of Peter, " Blessed be the God and Father of our Lord Jesus Christ, who of his abundant mercy hath begotten us again unto a living hope, by the resurrection of Jesus Christ from the dead." He loves that Holy Spirit, the Comforter, the Advocate, who comes as the representative of the risen Saviour, to dwell in them, to abide with them forever, as the Spirit of holiness, as the Spirit of grace and supplication, to make the petitions of their breast a counterpart of the intercessions within the vail. An argument drawn from the "love of the Spirit" touches every spring of ingenuous emotion within him. How can he but love, with his purest affections, that gracious Friend, who was deputed by his glorified Lord to woo him and win him to blessedness and God; to take possession of him in the Conqueror's name; to put the seal of heaven upon his forehead; to subdue and finally to slay all the enemies of his own peace and of his Master's glory, and in the mean time as " the Holy Spirit of promise," to be in him " the earnest of the purchased possession," and to "seal him up until the day of redemption."

Finally, he loves the children of God. " By this we know that we love God, when we love the children of God. Every one that loveth him that begat, loveth him that is begotten of him." Formerly they were no more to him than kindred, business, or the common offices of humanity made them. Now there is a feeling of brotherhood, a community of interests, and instincts. He has a fellowship with them which is founded upon their " fellowship with the Father and with his Son Jesus Christ." All the children of God are like him. They are renewed after his image; and one of the first effects of the Holy Spirit's agency is to draw the lines of that image deep and indelible. It has tints which speak the beauty and colouring of the skies. It is accompanied with the rudiments of that language which sounds barbarian in uncircumcised ears, but which is common and peculiar to renewed men, and is spoken perfectly and alone at the court of the great King. "Their speech bewrayeth them," and marks a dignity, for which, were it possible, the monarchs of the world would do well and wisely to barter their crowns and kingdoms. They may be obscure and contemptible to outward view. Lazarus lies at your palace-door, perhaps hated and disregarded. But he has a life-guard of a celestial Prince. Ministering spirits are in attendance, and wait for the signal to convey him away to the regions of light. You may perhaps see him there one day, when a drop of water to cool your tongue will be of more value to you than all that earthly grandeur which now pampers pride, and, it may be, shuts you out from the kingdom of God. But that "love of the brethren," of which I speak, depends not upon external things. It looks to the image of God, which can send forth the rays of its glory through the poverty, and meanness, and misery, of earthly beings. It is not ashamed of those rags of which God himself is not ashamed, and which comport with a heavenly inheritance. O ye, who bear the image of the heavenly as ye have borne that of the earthly Adam, whatever be your condition here, I will call you my brothers, my sisters, by a dearer tie than ever bound flesh and blood together —the tie of the Saviour's grace, of which the whole beauty and strength shall be reserved for our rapturous discovery in the kingdom of our Father!

Lastly, The regenerated sinner has new relations and tastes, preferences, pleasures, and pursuits, adapted to and growing out of his new state of existence.

1. He has new relations.

To God the Father. In his natural state, his relations were those of a rebellious creature under sentence of death. Now he is "reconciled to God by the death of his Son." The sentence which was passed against him is reversed, and he stands adjudged to life, by a sentence which there is no power in the universe to cancel. "Who shall lay anything to the charge of God's elect?" "It is God that justifieth!" His relations as a rebel are replaced by those of a dear child, and God is become to him a gracious and loving Father.

To God the Son, who has redeemed him by his blood and subdued him by his grace to the obedience of the faith. He is accepted in the Beloved, who makes intercession for him; who is gone up on high to prepare a place for him, and shall show him, at last, among that ransomed family, of which he shines in the honours of the first-born.

To God the Holy Ghost. No longer to him the Spirit of the curse but of blessings manifold, who is now his companion, his guide, his protector—who shows him the path of life, and will be with him to the end, crowning him with ultimate and complete victory over all adversaries, and introducing him at last into the presence of the blessed One with exceeding joy.

To the divine law. Armed no longer with destructive penalty, but commissioned to be his preceptor, to guide his feet into the way of peace, that his path, being the path of the just, shall shine brighter and brighter unto the perfect day.

To the providence of God, which shall permit no ill to befall him—nothing which shall endanger his substantial interests—nothing which shall not promote his sanctification—working an increase of grace—producing the peaceable fruits of righteousness, and causing all things to co-operate for his final and perfect good.

To the holy angels, with whom he is united into a new family under Christ the Head, who love him for the sake of his Elder Brother, and always behold the face of his Father in heaven, waiting to do him good, and glad to be employed at his command in acts of kindness to him as the heir of salvation.

2. Regenerated men have new tastes, preferences, and pleasures. For those things which were once their delight they have lost their relish. "They that are Christ's have crucified the flesh with its affections and lusts." They taste that the Lord is gracious. They prefer the company and condition of fellow-heirs. Like Moses, they had "rather suffer affliction with the people of God, than enjoy the pleasures of sin for a season; esteeming the reproach of Christ greater riches than the treasures of Egypt."—"The Lord puts gladness into their hearts more than in the time when corn and wine," the best sensual joys, abound to the men of sin.

3. Regenerated men have entirely new pursuits.

Like other Gentiles they once walked in the vanity of their minds—committing iniquity with greediness—minding only the things of time and sense—neglecting, despising, hating whatsoever looked farther than the sphere of their purblind vision, and aimed at an inheritance beyond the grave. Now that their eyes are opened, and their hearts changed, they cast their glance back with shame and horror, upon the practices and the perdition they have escaped.

God hath called them into the fellowship of his Son Jesus Christ, and they " no longer run to the same excess of riot."— " They have chosen the better part, which shall not be taken from them." They have cast in their lot with the strangers and pilgrims, who, though *in* the world, are not *of* it, but are marching through it to the place of their destination, to the land of the shining ones. " They seek a better country " than earth, " even a heavenly: therefore God is not ashamed to be called their God, for he hath prepared for them a city." With their eyes fastened on that city—" the peace of God keeping their hearts and minds " —and with the hope of seeing Jesus as he is, strong in their bosoms, they press toward the prize of their high calling, till, every duty fulfilled, every obstacle surmounted, every enemy vanquished, they are welcomed by the shout of the holy ones, into the presence of their Father.

Recollecting and comparing the remarks which have been made on the change, commonly called regeneration, or more scripturally, the " being born again," you may form something like a just idea of those who "enter into the kingdom of God—in other words, of true Christians. They are brought into a world where they see and discern spiritual objects in a spiritual light. They exist by a new medium— the Spirit of God. Their life is maintained by new means—the divine word and ordinances. Their faculties undergo a new development—understanding, affections, will, all are directed to new and holy things ; particularly a sanctified charity, exerting itself in love to God and man, rules in their hearts—and, finally, they have new relations, tastes, preferences, pleasures, and pursuits —all marking a complete and radical change in the ruling principles of the soul.

This description of the new man rests not upon human fancy, but on the divine testimony : every part and portion of it being supported by clear scriptural authority, and comes to your consciences with "'Thus saith the Lord." I have not said that every believer is at all times an example of this character, in the whole variety, extent, and power of its graces ; nor that he may not fall short, now in one and then in another. But I say that these graces, of their own nature, belong to that new life which the Holy Ghost implants in the new birth—that they are elements which enter into the composition of that new character which is more or less unfolded here, and shall be seen in all its proportions and perfections in the future life—I say that they all of them belong substantially to every one who "enters the kingdom of God." That he will study to be a living proof of their presence and prevalence—and that in fact they are expanded, the seed of God which contains them being gradually developed, in size, strength, and beauty, as the several circumstances of his lot render their proper exercise necessary. We are now to enquire,

II. Into the absolute necessity of such a change before a man can enter into the kingdom of God. It arises,

1. From the divine determination. Without it, says the Redeemer, "he cannot enter into the kingdom of God." Be your religious connections ever so pure—your external privileges ever so great—your outward profession ever so decided—your moral conduct among men ever so exemplary—the question still remains, have you been "born again?" Without this all other advantages are nothing; all other recommendations are of no avail; "except a man be born"—lay it well to your hearts that there be no fatal mistake—"except a man be born of water and of the Spirit, he cannot enter into the kingdom of God." Our Lord Jesus Christ, who is the eternal Truth, has settled this point beyond the possibility of reconsideration. Never hope that it may be reversed; that it may be revised; that some favourable judgment may be passed, which shall admit you at last, however unqualified; for, in the

2. Place, this necessity arises from the "very nature of the case." For this purpose was the Son of God manifested, that he might destroy the works of the devil. Now the devil's principal work in our world is the apostasy and corruption of man. It is in the human soul that his abominable triumph is to be seen and felt. There he has effaced the glorious image of his Creator, and has drawn his own hideous likeness in its place. There he has entered in as a foul usurper; he makes the heart the citadel of his rebellion; and marshals under his command all the faculties and affections, to resist the authority of his rightful Sovereign. Can a man thus forsworn to his allegiance, thus allied to the prince of darkness, thus sharing with him in all the tempers and principles of his revolt; can a man thus circumstanced, suppose ye, be admitted

into that kingdom which is set up for the annihilation of Satan's power, and supposes a renunciation of his cause, and a desertion of his standard, in every one who joins himself to Messiah the Prince, and becomes a loyal subject of the King of kings? Must not the thieves be expelled, and their den purified by celestial ablution—be converted into a temple of the living God? Must not the faculties be restored to their original use, and ability imparted to perform the duties and to relish the pleasures of this new and sacred state? And as the kingdom of God here is preparatory to his kingdom hereafter, or rather is but a part of that same dispensation, shall any who are not qualified for the kingdom of glory be acknowledged as the real subjects of his grace? "Shall any thing that defileth, or that worketh abomination" find a place, do ye imagine, in the regions of the just? And shall a sinner, laden with guilt, steeped in pollution, his heart filled with enmity against the Holy One, and himself, at best, whatever be his appearance in the eyes of men, but an accomplice in the treasons of the pit; shall such an one find his way into the number of those "whom the Lord knoweth to be his," and claim his place in the ante-chamber of the King's palace? The bosom of every sanctified one, of all who shall see the King in his glory, swells with abhorrence. The faces even of those who are yet strangers to the commonwealth of Israel, redden with shame at the impudence of the expectation; and every unseared conscience is appalled at the blasphemy. No, no, the thing is impossible! "Ye must be born again." All the principles, affections, tastes, and habits, of your natural state, must be changed; a revolution, internal, holy, complete, must be effected, or you bid an eternal adieu to the "kingdom of God." It is a terrifying thought, a fearful utterance to be proclaimed in the ears of professed Christians, yet an utterance of imperious necessity, except ye be thus changed, except ye be washed, justified, sanctified by the name of the Lord Jesus, and by the Spirit of our God, ye never see his kingdom—not a soul of you.

Allow me then, with all plainness and fidelity, to press this point, and to ask you, who pass in the world as Christians, do you know from experience, what is this new birth, this transition from death unto life, without which the gates of the kingdom of God are barred against you here, and will be so forever hereafter? Do you know anything about it? I do not mean what you can say about it. There are many who have been well instructed by man, on this as on other peculiar doctrines of the gospel, and who can make long, luminous, and eloquent dissertations on their abstract truth; yet never knew their grace, nor felt their power, nor set their foot in the "kingdom of God." My friends, this is not enough. You may have abundance of intellectual light—as much speculative wisdom as the most distinguished spirit of the pit—you may believe the truths of this Bible upon conclusive external evidence—you may be exemplary in your moral deportment toward your fellow-creatures—participate in all the outward privileges of the Christian church—be accounted a believer of high degree before mortal tribunals, and yet the renewing spirit of God has had nothing to do with you. "The world," says the beloved John, "knoweth us not." Is not the Christian character a riddle and a mystery, containing something which you cannot unravel? When he speaks of the blood of Jesus Christ "cleansing the conscience from dead works to serve the living God—of that peace which passeth all understanding—of setting his affections on things above—of looking for the blessed hope, the appearing of the great God our Saviour"—does he not speak a foreign language? Are you not sensible there is something here which you do not understand? which has no counterpart in your soul? It is dreadfully ominous. There is every ground to fear that when God shall judge the secrets of men by Jesus Christ, you may prove destitute of the only thing which can entitle or qualify you to enter his heavenly kingdom—all your knowledge, gifts, profession, and privileges notwithstanding.

And is it so indeed? Must we admit the overwhelming thought, that many whom we knew in the flesh, whom we loved for their amiable properties, whom we hailed as brethren in the common salvation, must at last sink down before our faces in bottomless perdition? Shall any pass from their seats in this sanctuary into the place of despair? O what a sweet relief to the foreboding heart, that still there is hope! It has not yet come to the dreadful extremity. O then, what shall we do to be saved? Who utters that agonizing cry? The way is but one, and it is short. "Believe on the Lord Jesus Christ and thou shalt be saved."—"The mouth of the Lord hath spoken it." There is no peradventure in the case. Thou shalt be saved! O had I but that precious faith, this unbelief would not weigh me down, like a mill-stone of death. Go to "Jesus, the author and finisher of faith," who has it to give, and who gives it freely. Go to him with your stony heart, with your death "in trespasses and sins,' and plead with him for the quickening Spirit. Never quit him till you get an answer of peace; throw yourself at his feet, and lie there where sinner never yet perished, till he be gracious unto you. He hath said, "Him that cometh unto me, I will in no wise cast out."

A word to the children of God, and I have done. Beloved, now are we the sons of God. Born of his Spirit, and introduced into his kingdom, "What manner of persons ought we to be in all holy conversation and godliness?" Exemplify the beauties, breathe the tempers, speak the language, cherish the loftiness, of the kingdom. It is not for those who are of such high descent and such infinite expectations, to stoop to those toys which the children of earth mistake for riches, nor to defile themselves with the pollutions which they miscall pleasures. Keep unspotted that white robe in which you were clothed on the day of your new birth, the day of your espousals, and of the gladness of your heart. Know ye that the very angels of God can tell you, as the heirs of the kingdom, only by your "walking as Christ also walked?" It is the light of the divine image shining out in its brightness that renders your names visible in the catalogue of God's elect. Ponder much your obligations to the grace of the Lord Jesus, who loved you with an everlasting love—so loved you as to give himself an offering for you. The bitterness of Gethsemane and the anguish of Calvary, the rage of hell and the curse of God, could not shake his loving purpose, nor make him flinch from his resolution to save you. From the sentence of God's righteous law and the danger of eternal death—from the filth and power of your depravity—the service, the communion, and the recompense of the devil—he hath called you to a rank above the angels, and to all the blessedness of the kingdom of God. Oh! "We will remember thy love more than wine."—" To him that loved us, and washed us from our sins in his own blood, and hath made us kings and priests unto his God and Father; to him," with all affections, "be glory and honour, dominion and power, for ever and ever, amen."

SERMON XVI.

WORKS OF THE FLESH AND SPIRIT DISTINGUISHED.

JOHN iii. 6.

"That which is born of the flesh is flesh; and that which is born of the Spirit is spirit."

The doctrine of the new birth, which the Prophet of the Church has declared to be the original of all spiritual character, and all heavenly hope, and without which, he has decided most peremptorily, a man "cannot enter into the kingdom of God," sounds most uncouth in the ears of corrupted reason. It is so entirely out of the way of human wisdom—it contains a fact so utterly anomalous, or rather so repugnant to the known constitution of either physical or moral nature, that even "masters in Israel" have pronounced the plain meaning of the terms in which it is proposed, to be absurd and fanatical, and have had recourse to a monstrous figure in order to make our Redeemer's language intelligible, and vindicate him from the charge of Puritanism. Men, to whom "the things of the Spirit of God," in their obvious construction, are foolishness, love to take refuge in this system of figuring; and when they have so strained and altered the phraseology of the Bible as not to leave standing a syllable which savours of its sense, or from which you could by any possibility guess at its propositions, they please themselves with having made it speak a rational Christianity, when they have only destroyed every character which can alarm the guilty or give peace to the alarmed. Thus it has fared with the doctrine of regeneration. The words of our Lord are so very simple and plain, that it requires some effort of ingenuity to mistake them. Yet they have not been able to escape. Criticism has laid her foul hands upon them, and, by the aid of that machine called a figure, had at one time diluted them into baptism of water by the hands of a regularly ordained priest, and at another has made them typical of outward reformation, though always in such a form as to bespeak something clearly within the power of corrupted man, and effectually to exclude the similitude of a birth. But it is so palpable as to need no proof that our Lord designates every effect produced by the agency of man flesh, and the effects produced by the agency of the Spirit of God spirit—that these effects are essentially contrasted—that they allow of no mixture, no concurrence, in the formation of the new birth—that they are, and necessarily must be, as different and opposite as flesh and spirit are—that alter, modify, refine, as much as you will, that which proceeds from the flesh, it is flesh still and nothing else, partaking exclusively of the nature of its author—so alter, modify, debase, if you can, that which proceeds from the Spirit of God, it is spirit still and nothing else, partaking exclusively of the nature of its blessed Author. He therefore denies that in this new birth there can be any copartnership, co-operation, or concern whatever, of the power of man with the power of the Holy Spirit. They who become the subjects of it "are born, not of flesh, nor of blood, nor of the will of man, but of God."

Our unrenewed nature, with all its propensities and habits, acts and inclinations, the Scripture emphatically terms flesh; using it as equivalent with our "old man"—with the "body of sin," which is to be put off, to be crucified, to be destroyed, but never to be amended. There is not such an idea to be found in the whole Bible, nor any thing which contains a shadow of it, as that of reforming the works of the devil. The Lord performs his gracious work by creating a "new man in Christ Jesus," not by repairing the "old man." Yet it is a common and ruinous error for a sinner to imagine that, if he cannot do all that is requisite to insure the kingdom of heaven, he can do much. If he cannot completely renew his heart, and make himself meet for the inheritance of the saints in light, he can do a great deal—or if not a great deal, can do something towards forwarding this desirable work. So that the Spirit of God, though he may have a large or even principal share in the glory, shall not have it all; but he shall himself receive due credit for improving the opportunities he had. Without taking up your time in exposing the ignorance and arrogance of such a pretension, I shall briefly observe, that it finds its way into the heart of every unconverted man, and has wound its insidious coil so firmly around many hearers of the gospel, that nothing short of a divine deliverer can set them at liberty.

To counteract so pernicious but natural a mistake is the manifest design of the text. Hear it, professed disciple, and let it stir thee up to a rigorous examination of thy exercise and attainments: "That which is born of the flesh is flesh; and that which is born of the Spirit is spirit."

Let me entreat you to accompany me through a short inquiry into those religious phenomena which, however specious, may rise no higher than corrupt nature, and wherein the work of the Spirit of God is to be distinguished from them.

I. Those religious phenomena to which corrupted nature is equal. "That which is born of the flesh is flesh."

1. Early impressions of serious things in a religious community.

Where a reverence of the gospel is established—where it pervades all the social habits, and especially where our own friends are under its influence—nothing is more natural or certain than that, under such circumstances, the religious feeling should become characteristic, and that many persons should imagine themselves to be true Christians, who know of no other power operating upon their minds than the power of imitation. How far this may be carried it is impossible to tell, but it is lamentable to think how deep and how extensive are the delusions which accompany it, and how immensely difficult is the recovery of persons involved in it. They were brought up in the profession of the Christian religion— it may be in the very exact and austere performance of religious duties. Their parents, their ancestors, were all most exemplary in the same way, and who, if not themselves, should have a claim to the Christian character? I shall not admonish my hearers that there is no such thing as prescription in Christianity for a man's personal interest in its privileges. Unhappily, the argument is very short, very plain, and brings us directly to the conclusion of the text.

We happen to have known some who had no other religion than

an hereditary religion, and who were reported as religiously inclined, but whose course soon proved how untrue was this opinion respecting them. We have seen numbers of them gradually throwing off their religious inclinations, and becoming perfectly content with the reputation of honest men. This reputation, indeed, they keep up, and it is highly honourable in them to do so; but for any resemblance to our Lord Jesus Christ—for any evidence that they pay the least regard to his authority or his glory—for any that they ever think of him—you might as well, to use a comparison of the ancients, you might as well look for a knot in a bulrush. I speak of all those who have been religiously educated, and have turned their backs upon that holy name which they were early taught to fear. I bring into my remonstrance millions of facts, and, what is infinitely more terrible, millions of immortal souls, that have sunk down to hell with all the benefit of a traditionary faith. If you will not hear me, hear them who have perished, and who can testify, by the most tremendous of all experience, that the religion of the father will not save the son; and that all in which they trusted was nothing more than the doings of the flesh, which never brought them out of the condemned world, nor ever enabled them to see the kingdom of God.

2. There are not a few among the men of more inquisitive minds, who hold the previous class of religionists in sufficient contempt. To inherit their faith as they would a tract of land or a bag of money; to be taught religion as they were taught their alphabet: or to join the cry and follow in the course of the multitude around them—appears to them ignoble and base, a sort of swindling for reputation upon the credit of more honest men. Christianity, they are told upon the highest of all authority, is a "reasonable service." and they cannot conceive how any man, who consults his reasonable nature, can make an intelligent profession of a religion of which he has not examined the proofs; and he finds no difficulty in explaining the apostacy of those whom change of climate, of company, or the habits of society, have introduced into a scene where their former principles and profession, if not disreputable, were at least of no advantage. For themselves they are satisfied upon mature examination, that revelation is true, and furnishes the only solid ground of present peace and future blessedness. Demonstration is always the same; conviction founded upon it never alters; and

consequently, go where they will, they carry their religion with them. Christianity is never insulted, nor Christians put to the blush, by their infidelity.

We are not now to learn that belief arising from personal research and conviction, is in matters of reasoning of a much higher order than any persuasion induced by the authority or example of others. And as there is no necessity, so we have no inclination, to disparage the rational evidence for Christianity, and the conviction growing out of it. We maintain, on the contrary, that genuine conviction of revealed truth is the most rational thing imaginable; and that they who reject it, labour under disordered intellects. But it is still a most serious inquiry, whether the *merely* rational belief in the truth of the scriptures, such as has been described, has any connection with the salvation of the soul; or involves in the least degree the favour of God; or rises any higher than what our Lord calls the flesh; *i. e.* whether it any more secures than can be attained by mere carnal reason, or is experienced by the "carnal mind, which is enmity against God."

In his dispensations towards sinners, the Most High deals with t em as with rational creatures, in whom their reason, though d praved, is not destroyed. He has therefore fortified his revelation by every sort of moral proof; so that his servants may always be "able to give a reason of the hope that is in them;" that every attack upon their faith and hope may be successfully repelled, and unbelievers left without excuse. But who does not see, that in order to accomplish its purpose, this must proceed upon principles common to the friends and the enemies of his Gospel; upon principles strictly within the reach of the unsanctified mind! Accordingly, a man by the use of his natural though corrupted reason, may easily arrive at the conclusion that the Bible is the Word of God; nay, that every particular doctrine therein revealed, not excluding the very doctrines on which the salvation of the soul depends, are undeniably his word, and may be quite as sound in his speculative opinions as the believer who stands highest in the records of life. All this is nothing more than drawing fair conclusions from simple and well-established premises; and were this enough to constitute a true Christian, the best logician would certainly be the soundest believer. But what is the fact? Are the most humble, tender, spiritual Christians to be found in the ranks of these men of reason? Does their religion ever stand in the way of those tempers and passions, which, the Scripture being judge, shut them out of the "kingdom of God?" Do we not see them to be as careless of their immortal souls, and of the things that accompany salvation, as if going to heaven were a matter of course? or let men live as they please, there were no possible risk of being refused an entrance? Do we not often see them reproaching, reviling, persecuting, those who do not choose to be cast at last among "the devil and his angels," for the sake of company? Do they not deal as freely in that courtly vocabulary which finds no more respectful epithets for those who "give all diligence to make their calling and election sure, than "enthusiasts," "fanatics," "priest-ridden," "hypocrites," as the veriest infidel in the land? Do they not all the while retain their *religion*, profess to be undoubted believers, and inveigh loudly against those spiritual ruffians who would snatch away from us our faith and hope? What shall we now say to these things, with the proofs of which the whole face of the community is overspread? Shall we say that these men are, in a scriptural sense, Christians? that they have any mark about them of the "new creation?" that you could so much as suspect them to be "God's workmanship, created in Christ Jesus unto good works?" The question is almost a libel upon human understanding, corrupted as it is? No, my friends, the utmost which this Christianity can pretend to, is a persuasion of the *fact* that the scripture is the Word of God, and every one of its doctrines a part of his testimony, But between believing that they *are* his word, and believing "the testimony of God," there is as wide a difference as between being in the kingdom of God and being out of it. Apostacy does not prevent clear perceptions of abstract truth. The wickedest man upon earth may have his head filled with right notions. Suppose ye that the devil doubts of the divine original of Scripture, or that he is not well versed in their sense? It is his puny disciples *here*, who, swelled with the pride of their philosophical character, murder and mangle it in a way of which Satan himself would be ashamed. There is, therefore, nothing in all we have been considering, that may not be the fruit of depraved principle—nothing that at all requires a better or holier parentage. It may be, it often is, "born of the flesh," and as worthless and unholy as the source from which it springs—"it is flesh."

3. Some men's affections are much engaged in religious things—they undergo strong excitement, and these pass for evidence of a divine change.

In drawing this conclusion, has due allowance been made for the excitement of the preacher; for the energy, the pathos, the eloquence, of his manner? Have you not known some hearers of the word to be awed into seriousness, softened into tenderness, melted into tears? to experience these effects repeatedly, and yet manifest to the entire conviction of every observer, that they were only for the moment—a shower upon a rock; copious while the cloud poured, and instantly dried off. Has due allowance been made for the *occasion*, often of itself so touching as to subdue the feelings of the heart? for the time of life, or for the natural temperament, which, in minds of gentler mould, is extremely susceptible of soft impressions? for the power of sympathy, which the strongest nerve cannot always resist? and which bears down alike him who came to pray, and him who came to scoff? What multitudes of conversions, as they have been hastily called, has our day seen, which were to be referred to groanings, and screechings, and fallings, and faintings, and other extravagancies of a heated imagination, which have yet been extolled as the work of the Spirit of God, and which have left behind them nothing but that animal lassitude which follows a fit of great excitement, or it may be something worse? To this general remark upon the effects of high-wrought feeling, ministers of the gospel ought to pay some attention. When God bestows a peculiar talent, he intends that it shall be employed, and the employment is generally obvious. The power of strong reasoning—of rousing the secure—of comforting the afflicted—of animating exhortation—of pathetic persuasion, he has distributed as it pleased him; to some after this manner, to another after that. Employ what he has given you for the glory of the Giver. Reason—rouse—comfort—exhort—persuade, as he hath enabled you; he will take care that his own gifts, properly used, shall do no harm. But never attempt, by unhallowed means, to stir up artificial emotions. Violent intonations, vehement utterances, furious gesticulations, irreverent boldness, you may put off for zeal, but you must not father your absurdities, nor its effects, upon the Spirit of God. Sooner or later he will bring you into disgrace, and show the spiritual children whom you think you have "begotten in the gospel," to be indeed born "after your own image." There is nothing in all this commotion of the affections, nor all the religion which is ascribed to it, that the flesh may not produce. Bear in mind the parable of the stony-ground hearers, and the pungent lamentation over ancient failures. "O Ephraim, what shall I do unto thee? O Judah, what shall I do unto thee? For your goodness is as the morning cloud; and as the early dew it goeth away."

4. Among the professors of Christianity, are some who lay a stress upon their works and their zeal.

It is quite an aphorism in religion, that "faith without works is dead, being alone:" and when the world is so full of lip-service, of Pharisees who "say and do not," it is some relief to find any who "do as well as say;" and it seems harsh to question any thing in the shape of practical piety. We might, however freely admit the amount of what is done, and yet tax the age, much as its liberality has been celebrated, with great niggardliness in promoting the kingdom of Jesus Christ. It is by the contributions of poor people, swelling the mass by their number, that those mighty operations which are now shaking the nations, have been chiefly commenced and carried on. To hear wealthy men, wearing the Christian name, pleading their inability to do what the twentieth part of their means, in the hands of those whose hearts lie in the right place, would do without difficulty, without complaint, without touching on a single earthly comfort, does not give a very high idea of prevailing bounty; and the complacency with which they talk of the wonderful occurrences of the day, looks very like a petition to the poor for a scrap of reputation. But passing this: allowing as much credit as is claimed on the score of alms and other good works; are there no donations to pious and charitable purposes given but from a motive which the Searcher of hearts approves, and will reward? This question, it is true, lies between the donor and his God. But to him, it is awfully serious. How much is done from mere constitutional generosity? How much from the influence of example? How much from the force of importunity? How much from sectarian pride? How much from sheer vanity? all of which is set down to the credit of religion; but not a farthing of which will be allowed as such in that day when the Son of man shall appear in his glory, to give to every one according to his works! In this great inquiry, the *quantity* will be of no account; the widow's mite will not outweigh the rich man's treasures, if the motive of both be alike reprehensible: and neither will be of any value, where evangelical charity was wanting. You "may give all your goods to feed the poor," or to do the community any other service, yet without that heavenly grace, charity, you will be nothing. How many splendid monuments are at this hour in existence of so false and delusive a liberality? It is very true, that few churches are now built, or hospitals founded, or colleges endowed, by the death-bed legacies of men, who seek to compensate in the last moment by such acts of equivocal piety, whole lives of iniquity and rapine, and to bribe the keeper of purgatory by the tender of gold which they cannot retain; but there are other, cheaper, more Christian-like forms of deception, where the light of truth has driven popery with her monks, penalties, pardons, and the whole rabble of her imposture from all respect in the public opinion.

We live at a time when the zeal for diffusing Bibles and for sending missionaries swallows up almost every other species of religious zeal, and when mere men of the world—judges, generals, politicians—are among the foremost in seconding and sometimes in leading the popular enthusiasm. It is good—it is glorious—it is the doing of the Lord. The silver is his—the gold is his—and he is pressing it into Messiah's service. But do none of those who are engaged in this holy work lay upon it an unscriptural stress? Is there not a righteousness fabricated from it of no firmer texture, nor valuable material, than the giving a Bible to a pauper or a dollar to an Indian mission? Do not many deceive their souls with a notion that to be a member of a Bible society is nearly if not quite equivalent to entering the kingdom of God? And, though the idea is too gross to be formally avowed, is there not a fancy lurking about the heart, that a five-dollar bill is about enough to purchase the kingdom of heaven? If we should judge from the reluctance with which some men part with a little money for a purpose confessedly the most noble that is prosecuted upon earth, our conclusion would not be far from the fact. It will be well if individuals, who are trusting to such performances as these, do not at last meet with that fatal and final repulse: "I know you not;

depart from me, ye workers of iniquity!" All such things can be explained without the supposition of a particle of preternatural grace. They may all at best proceed from the workings of a corrupted principle; they can be no better nor purer than their source, " for that which is born of the flesh is flesh."

This train of reflection might be carried out into a long detail; but I forbear, and call your attention to notice by what, in the

II. Place, a real work of the Spirit of God may be distinguished from every work of the flesh. "That which is born of the Spirit is spirit."

1. Where the Spirit of God performs his gracious work, he introduces into the soul a new principle altogether. This he has himself called a new man—a new creature—a being created anew in Christ Jesus. It is more than an improvement of our old faculties or affections. It partakes of the nature of its blessed Author. It is spirit—all spirit—nothing but spirit. It can receive no aliment from the flesh. It is supported by its immediate intercourse with the eternal Spirit. It brings into a fellowship, of which "flesh" has no manner of conception, with the living God. It is hidden—a sacred secret—hidden with the Lord Jesus Christ —with Christ in God—as perfectly impervious to the observation and inexplicable to the understanding of carnal men, as are the thoughts and affections of Christ himself. "The world knoweth us not because it knew him not." When you can find out Jesus Christ, you can find out a Christian, but not till then. He is utterly out of your world, the scene of your investigation. He is, as a Christian, where your researches never penetrated, and never can penetrate. I undertake not to explain his interior and spiritual life. I have no language that can describe him, nor have strangers to his peculiarities any ideas to comprehend him. But I bless the Lord my Saviour, that when the simple proposition is announced, "that which is born of the Spirit is spirit," there are some within these walls whose yearning hearts fly into his meaning, and can attest the fact. They have just as good evidence of its existence as they have of their own—their consciousness. I cannot impart this evidence to the mind of another man; but to me it is paramount to all others. "The Spirit of God also witnesses with their spirits that they are the children of God;" giving such percep-

tions and consciousness of the fact as set all disputation at defiance. These indeed are favoured moments even to the most favoured disciples. But there are other things, other consciousnesses, which, in the midst of general doubt, and under the blackness of temptations, show infallibly the operation of the Spirit of grace, a new life, a new principle, and order of living, for,

2. That which is born of the Spirit believes the testimony of God.

It was suggested above, that to believe that the Bible is the testimony of God, and to believe the testimony itself, makes all the difference of being in the kingdom of God and being out of it—all the difference between being real believers in Christ Jesus and believers in name only—between having the form of godliness and its power also. This is a peculiarity common to all that have been "born of the Spirit." It is the idiom of their character, which the men of mere rational conviction can never learn. A plain Christian believes every jot and tittle of divine revelation because God hath said it, and looks no farther for the ground of his faith. Arguments from miracles, from prophecy, and the whole stock of moral proofs, external and internal, have, properly speaking, nothing to do in forming his persuasion. He has higher, holier, more perfect ground, on which to build his faith, than the most conclusive reasoner the world ever saw is able to furnish. He "believes the witness of God" because it is his witness. He has got up to the fountain-head of truth—the most victorious evidence that can shed its light into the created mind. When he perceives the authority of the ever-blessed God in its glory and majesty, no mathematician was ever half so sure of a demonstration in Euclid as he is of the truth of that portion of the word of grace thus divinely attested. This explains at once why Christians, though without any learning—though extremely limited in their capacities of attaining it—are yet so firm in their faith, and are not to be circumvented by those who "speak lies in hypocrisy," nor by the "craftiness of those who lie in wait to deceive." They may catch in their toils, as we see every day, the witty, the wise, the disputer, the reasoner, of this world, but they lay not their sacrilegious hands upon God's elect. He has given them by the regenerating Spirit an understanding to know him that is truth, and has made them so one with him "as to be in him that is true, even in his Son Jesus Christ." This Jesus Christ is the true God, therefore he is the eternal life. Nor is there any power in hell or out of it to move them from that ground. Seest thou that man? He walks by faith, not by sight. He is one of those guileless souls who cannot argue for Christ, but he can burn for him; and, while the flames are consuming his body, can commit it to the Lord Jesus, with infinite confidence of its being raised up in glory to an incorruptible inheritance. How came he by his faith? Does it rest upon your reasoning, or anything of the sort? Upon your reasoning?—a poor, feeble, blundering creature like himself! Why, he would not burn one of his fingers for a string of your syllogisms long enough to belt the earth; and a rare fool would he be if he should. Other influence has been at work. The "Spirit of faith" has touched his heart. He has revealed Christ Jesus in him the hope of glory, and made his "faith to be the evidence of things not seen, the substance of things hoped for." —"Through" this "faith the elders obtained a good report," and the same faith must possess, and fill, and rule, in every bosom that entertains a Scriptural expectation of seeing God.

3. That which is born of the Spirit cherishes the highest esteem of our Lord Jesus Christ. "He shall glorify me," said the Saviour, "for he shall take of mine and shall show it unto you."

There are people, with great professions of religion, that take much pains to hinder the world from thinking too highly of Jesus Christ. They even try to degrade him below his own angels; and if that were not enough, can feed their vanity by a comparison between him and themselves, in which they have quite the advantage. A ringleader in one of these sects did not scruple thus to qualify his commendation, that "Jesus Christ was a very good man, but no philosopher." He claimed to be a philosopher himself, and who then was the more important personage, in his eyes, is manifest enough. (Such blasphemy, which treats our Lord Jesus Christ with less respect than does the devil himself, never came from the Holy Spirit, nor fouled the mouths of any who were born of him.) The scriptures, on the contrary, magnify him with every form of elevated and high-wrought expression. There he has a name which is above every name. He is seated at the right hand of God. He sends forth the angels to do his will, and glorious as they are, they are commanded to worship him even when he was an incarnate babe. He sits arbiter of the fate of men and devils The great empire of the grave is under his control. The generations of the dead come forth at his bidding, and not one of them shall escape his righteous doom. In short, every name proper to the true God; every term by which the attributes of Deity can be expressed; the whole stock of human language is exhausted to heap up epithets of glory upon Jesus Christ. There are things with which the soul of a believer is in perfect accord. They delight him, even to rapture. Nothing good and glorious is too good and glorious for his gracious Redeemer. Has he loved me and given himself for me? Do I owe my place among the ransomed of the Lord to his unmerited, unutterable grace? Come, fellow-citizens of the saints, ye household of salvation, strike all your harps at once! Come, ye holy ones on earth, and ye holy ones in heaven, tune up your sweetest anthems! Lift up your grateful hands, and crown him Lord of all! Thus a Christian feels towards his Redeemer. It is that which is born of the Spirit, breathing the air and enjoying the elasticity of the spiritual world.

4. That which is born of the Spirit makes incessant use of the Spiritual Saviour.

He has said, "without me ye can do nothing;" and so a Christian finds it. His attachment to his Redeemer, is not to make a parade on a gala day, and have done with it; it is necessary for his habitual walk. The blood of Christ, which has washed away his sins—the merits of Christ, from which he gets his title to eternal life, must every hour exert their virtue upon his soul. He cannot go to the throne of grace without the blood of sacrifice; and the interceding priest—can perform none of his duties, endure none of his trials, face none of his foes, but in the strength of his heavenly leader—"but through Christ strengthening him he can do all things." This man is a Christian, born of the Spirit; all his characteristics are spiritual, and with him "Christ is all and in all."

Now, friends and brethren, who and what are ye? To whom do you belong, and whither are ye going? Search and look: for upon the decision of these questions hangs your eternity; and you may be just upon the brink. Do not deceive yourselves. A Christian is not of earthly materials or manufacture. Flesh and blood, with all its powers, attainments, and persuasions, can do nothing for you. The Spirit of God must do the work; he must open your eyes, must renew your hearts, must lead you to Jesus, must do everything; for if you are his, you are "his workmanship created in Christ Jesus unto good works, which God hath before prepared that ye should walk in them." But "if any man have not the Spirit of Christ, he is none of his;" and whatever may be his security, his hope, or his presumption, will be disowned in that day, when one word of approbation will be worth more than a thousand worlds.

SERMON XVII.

TRUE HONOUR.

JOHN v. 44.

"How can ye believe, which receive honour one of another, and seek not the honour that cometh from God only?"

Next to a being perfectly holy, there is nothing so indefatigable as a mind given to wickedness. Let the life of Jesus Christ supply the proof. From the beginning to the end of his public course, he encountered the contradiction of sinners; walked among their snares; and sustained, in every shape, ceaseless conflict with their hatred and hostility. That they were invariably foiled, exposed, disgraced, did not in the least deter them from repeating the same hopeless experiment. In fact, having all shared in their turn, the same fate, the ignominy of their defeat was too much divided to be a reproach. The Pharisee could not point at the Sadducees, nor these at the Herodians, because the finger of scorn could be pointed back again. There was no public opinion which they regarded, to frown them into decency. It came to be a practical maxim with them, that to be defeated and silenced by Jesus Christ was no disgrace; and they were too closely united in the brotherhood of guilt to suffer any abatement of their rancour. (The professing world affords, so far as I know, but one parallel of their malevolence and persecution; and that is to be found among the self-styled rational and philosophical Christians.) They seized the occasion of his curing the impotent man on the Sabbath-day to accuse him as a breaker of God's laws; and when he vindicated himself on this principle, "My Father worketh hitherto and I work," they heightened their accusation into a charge of blasphemy, and "sought the more to kill him, because he had not only broken the Sabbath, but said that God was his Father, making himself equal with God." What wrongs and insults did the Lord Jesus endure at the hands of these ancient Unitarians! (Wrongs and insults to be surpassed only by those from the heirs of their unbelief, the modern Unitarians.) Their imputation of blasphemy he repels, by claiming such prerogatives, powers, and honours, as are proper to God only; and winds up his defence, by giving these hypocrites a sensible proof that he was all what they deemed it blasphemy in him to pretend to be; gave them this sensible proof by breaking open the recesses of their hearts, bringing into light their secret principles of action, and proving to their faces the base and abominable motives of their conduct. The applause of men lay at the bottom of their zeal for God, and effectually excluded all love for him, and all faith in his testimony. "How can ye believe who receive honour one of another, and seek not the honour which cometh from God only."

This rebuke to pharisaical pride, and explanation of pharisaical unbelief, contains a principle of universal application; the "inconsistency of receiving honour from men, with the faith of our Lord Jesus Christ." They are such eternal opposites, that they cannot live in the same heart. Whoever cleaves to the one must let the other go. We cannot, indeed, determine the existence in this matter of a corrupt propensity with the precision of our Lord Jesus Christ, nor could any of his apostles; because we have not, nor had they, like him, the faculty of searching the heart. But availing ourselves of his declarations, and pursuing the path which his spirit has marked out for us in the Word, we shall, by his grace, be enabled to assist others in the important and difficult work of searching their own hearts. Let us therefore, try to fix by this rule, the reigning principles of men "who receive honour one of another;" and why they produce an "impediment, amounting to an absolute impossibility, of believing on our Lord Jesus Christ?"

I. What are the reigning principles of men who receive honour one of another?

"A good name," saith the Scripture, "is rather to be chosen than great riches." He who has once discarded it from the number of his inestimable things—who is at no pains to keep it up—who would as soon commit an act from which his character is sure to lose as one from which it is as sure to gain, has found his place among the off-scourings of human nature, and is one of the most dangerous enemies to human peace. It is a false indulgence, a pernicious liberty, which permits a man to go at large who has forgotten to blush. We should sadly mistake the Redeemer's meaning, if we supposed that he intends to untie the bands of civil society, or those ruffian hands which would gladly engage in the detestable work. His own people guard their characters with the utmost vigilance, and are the foremost to cultivate "whatsoever things are of good report." To have therefore a good name—to be well reported of for good works—to enjoy the praises of other men, for upright principles and worthy deeds, is no obstacle to our faith; it is its natural consequence.

But the Scriptures, while they set its just value upon a fair fame in the eyes of men, never purpose it as the end, or as the recompense of actions substantially correct. They refer every thing to the authority of God as its reason, and to its approbation as its reward. Their design throughout is to bring us back to the God from whom we have deeply revolted; to break the power of all meaner influences and motives; to elevate our views to him, the only source of duty, honour, and happiness; making him the centre of all our affections, as he is of all holy intelligences; and turning all our thoughts to "him first, him midst, him last, him without end."

The character of the Pharisees was precisely the reverse of this: and so is the character of all who, like them, "receive honour one of another." Good things they did, many of them—good things for number and kind, which far outstrip the deeds of some who think that they sufficiently prove their faith by their works. The Pharisee, who thanked God that he "was not like other men, extortioners, adulterers, unjust, nor even like the poor sinner of a publican that stood beside him, who fasted twice in the week, who gave tithes of all that he possessed," leaves far behind him in the race both of negative and positive virtues, many a gallant and many a grave professor of Christianity. O could we bring them to but the half of the Pharisee's liberality, there should never be any lack of means for religious purposes. Yet he who "knew waht was in man," has planted his anathema upon the Pharisee's glory, and has told us most explicitly, that "except our righteousness shall exceed the righteousness of the Scribes and Pharisees, we shall in no case enter into the kingdom of heaven." Why, what was it that spoiled so fair a show? What made so rich a stockholder a bankrupt in the wealth of the skies, and exhibited him to the eyes of holy angels and men, a more wretched pauper than the beggar whose rags were his wardrobe, and his seat a dunghill? This: he "loved the praise of men more than the praise of God." All his devotions were performed, all his virtues displayed, all his distinctions sought, for the ostentation of human notice, and the breath of human applause. "God was not in all his thoughts"—that which he coveted, he obtained—he got "his reward, and lost his soul."—"So shall my heavenly Father do also unto you," if your "inward parts," like his, are found to be "very rottenness." Let us take this dreadful character, enlightened as it is with the curse of God, and carry it round among the religious community, to see if it warns none to fear an equally terrible fate.

Let us see whether its brand of reprobation is not upon many a profession which cries "Lord, Lord," with the air of a disciple, and confidently calculates upon a triumphant issue.

A marked revolution has taken place within a few years in the public sentiment. Most of us can remember when scepticism, like an overflowing stream, rushed through our land. It penetrated alike into the cabinet, the office, the shop, the employments of agriculture; the circulation of the Bible was stopped; the bench, the bar, the schools of medicine and of merchandise, the mechanic and the farmer, were infected with the mania. Our boys must set up for free-thinking before they were capable of thinking at all. To laugh at the Scriptures was quite as necessary for a fine gentleman as to defraud his humble creditors by petty acts of dishonesty. A scrap of Paine's stolen ribaldry was a sufficient answer to the Christian bigot. In short, a vast multitude of people in these United States agreed in crying down the Bible, and crying up the philosopher of infidelity.

The transition was too violent. The shock to national habit and the national conscience altogether insupportable. People, awakened from their dream, discovered that when they threw away the Bible they were "without God," and that without God they were "without hope in the world."

A revulsion, forcible in proportion to the extreme into which they had been driven, was the natural result; and the tide of opinion set in strongly in a contrary, *i. e.* in a Christian direction— a direction in which it continues to run at this day, and so may it continue to run till that day when our Lord Jesus Christ "shall take to him his great power and reign."

To the current of public opinion, returning into its wonted channels there was another cause, which powerfully co-operated in aiding the same general effect.

In some parts of the country infidelity was found to be intimately associated with odious politics, and straightway those very men who, if left to themselves, had been thorough infidels, became vigorous Christians, that they might be removed as far as possible from every point of communion with "Jacobins;" insomuch that in a great town, among the descendants of the pilgrims, whose public worship had fallen into disrepute, and was much neglected among the higher orders, it became a fashion to go to "church," which fashion has continued: though whether the ministrations which they support have anything in common with the faith of their fathers or with the Word of God, or can in any manner assist a sinner who desires to know what he shall do to be saved, is a question on which none but the most melancholy negatives can be given. Besides, in many sections of the land, there have been manifest effusions of the Holy Spirit of God. He has been as the rain, and he has been as the dew—sometimes more powerfully and sometimes more gently influencing the hearts of men. Many, we have reason to hope, were brought safely under the bond of God's covenant; and many, we have reason to fear, have turned like the "dog to his vomit, and like the sow that was washed to her wallowing in the mire."

These things concurred in giving to the public feeling an irresistible impulse. With all the secret enmity which prevails against true religion, as implacable and bitter as ever, there is great external respect shown to the forms and professions of Christianity. "Infidel" is now a term of reproach. Such being the state of society, can we imagine that all who name the name of Christ do it in simplicity and truth? from the constraining power of his love? Among the ten thousand hail masters which fill our ears are there no Iscariot voices? No lips which convert the token of tender affection into the medium of treason? No hearts which are apparently with the disciples and in reality with the adversary? No hand which meets the hand of Jesus in the dish, and is prepared to make merchandise of his blood? Should a "mighty wind" from heaven "shake our fig-tree," would not the ground be strewed "with her untimely figs?"

To speak plainly, are there not multitudes among professed Christians, whose sole or chief motive is the reputation which they enjoy? Who are held to their allegiance purely by the tie of popularity? There is some credit attached to the Christian name; and while that credit lasts, none are more strenuous Christians. But should the times change—should God in his providence permit the enemy again to come in like a flood—should Christianity be accounted infamous, or be subjected to heavy worldly sacrifices or personal perils—alas! alas! for the visible church! How would her ranks be thinned by desertion! and the Captain of salvation be left with those few followers to whom he has "given the white stone and the new name!" (Those synagogues, indeed, nicknamed rational churches, would lose nothing. Times of apostasy are always propitious to the recruiting service of Satan, and apostates the first to grasp at his bounty-money, and to cry, "Who is like unto the beast?"—"Who is able to make war with him?" But) How many of whom we had reason to "hope for things that accompany salvation would draw back unto perdition?" Examine quickly, while the hour of forbearance is not yet exhausted ye who are allured by the respectability of religion into a profession of the faith. You who are at best receiving honour one of another, and your name at present must be erased from the *album*, the list of those who believe on the Son of God.

In the next place, our Lord Jesus Christ, when he "ascended up on high, received gifts for men," which he distributes in his sovereignty as it hath pleased him. Among these corruption finds much fuel for unhallowed profession. To particularize:

1. The ministry of the Word.

By the very nature of the case, as well as by the institution of the Redeemer, this office exercises a powerful influence upon the Church and on society, and has a proportional degree of honour connected with it. True, where it is stripped of the support of a civil establishment, it can seldom boast any *golden* charms. A man may often shave more gold out of a block of timber than he can from his services in the ministry; but there are men not a few, whose ambition lies in another direction, and who regard as dross all money beyond the supply of their immediate necessities. Now, to such men of a literary turn and of decent moral habits, the pulpit presents what would be called a fair object of secular ambition. To appear once or twice a week in a marked distinction—to enjoy prerogatives which custom at least has rendered inviolable (the effectual and only safeguard of many a preacher)—to exhibit the resources of intellect with the attractions of taste and the coruscations of genius—to enforce valuable moral truth by eloquence, which shall be followed in the public assembly by silent admiration, and out of it by applause and celebrity—and a respect and influence unattainable in ordinary stations—what carnal heart is proof against these temptations? It is woeful to consider that the devil has, through these means, succeeded in planting his servants down in stations which were intended for Zion's watchmen. Love to the souls of men and to the Saviour of their souls—a sense of their dire responsibility for the blood of men, and an honest desire to be faithful, never entered the minds of some who have yet rushed fearlessly into the ministry. The calling is reputable; they wish to sustain its repute in the eyes of the world; they receive honour from men; it is the aliment of their hope, and the object of their anxiety. Faith in our Lord Jesus Christ they have none. Not a thievish publican nor a strolling harlot who are not nearer the kingdom of God than they, and their ultimate reckoning will be dreadful beyond description.

Besides the pulpit, there are other talents of which our Lord shall exact an account. It is distressing to think that for the most part he will exact it of those who never fairly brought them into exercise; and on the other hand, that many whom he never employed have industriously run into forbidden paths. I know not a more unchristian doctrine, nor one more pregnant with practical mischief, than the doctrine which takes the part of the *gifted brethren*. These brethren, if they invade not your pulpits, which, thanks to the good order established in some churches, they cannot do, nevertheless lay hold of the public praying societies. On all occasions they are ready—on all occasions foremost. They are compared with the ministry, and sometimes not to the advantage of the latter. In process of time they begin to try their hand at exhortation—next at preaching—and where, do they say, is the mighty difference? And thus with self-complacency do they edge onwards, until the ministry is surprised by the intrusion and pollution of those to whom God never gave talent nor man cultivation. Mistake me not. I am no enemy to prayer nor to praying societies. But I am an enemy to that withdrawing of men out of their proper place. I am an enemy to whatever would fill them with an improper conceit of themselves. I am an enemy to this giving undue honour to those to whom it is not due, and to converting the worship of God into a vehicle for the vanity of man, and of the smallest of men. There is much ground to fear that many a man's condemnation will be found on his distinction at a praying society. He wished to be noticed—he *was* noticed. To be talked of—he *was* talked of. To be praised—he *was* praised. He sought honour of men—he got it, and it is all he is likely to get. He "sought not the honour that cometh from God only," and will be found at last to have not been even a believer in Jesus Christ.

I have not time to trace the different forms in which, under religious pretences, "men receive honour one of another," to the detriment of all sound principle and the destruction of their own souls. It remains to show,

II. Why the prevalence of such a temper is inconsistent with the faith of our Lord Jesus Christ.

1. It involves a principle essentially sinful.

God alone is the universal monarch, the single fountain of true honour, throughout the universe. When we seek our honour in any other quarter, to the neglect of that which cometh from him alone, we enter into a conspiracy against his throne. We exalt into his place, and give the glory due to his name, to creatures, to men, and often to bad men. We love, we pursue, we worship a phantom. We set up the stumbling-block of our iniquity in our hearts—commit that high rebellion which he has visited from age to age, and now visits, and will continue to visit till the consummation of all things, with his sharpest rebukes, his heaviest curses. To "receive honour from one another, while we seek not the honour that cometh from God only," is to cherish in our hearts the very core of corruption, to identify ourselves in our characters and interests with the fallen spirits, and to expose ourselves infallibly to their fate. What can be conceived more horrible, more utterly at variance with the faith of our Lord Jesus Christ, more deserving of eternal damnation, than to declare practically that we have found a more bountiful benefactor—a nobler object of our praise—a more sufficient portion for our hearts—a richer source of good, than the living God. And what do they do less, who seek their " honour one of another," in preference to that " which cometh from God only?"

2. Receiving honour from men necessarily implies criminal conformity to the world of sinners.

That which we most respect, admire, and love, we are prone to imitate. It is a law of our being, and has its place, and exerts its force, in the formation of spiritual as well as other character. If you receive honour from the world, as contradistinguished from the honour which cometh from God only, you must of necessity be like the world—*i. e.*, be most unlike God, who calls " his people into the fellowship of his son Jesus Christ." The world also exercises a stern, despotic power over its votaries. You must obey its maxims; you must adopt its modes; you must speak its language; you must cultivate its temper; you must be the friend of its friends, and the enemy of its enemies; or its honour will be denied to you, and you will be excommunicated from within its pale. The world will not throw away its honours upon those who undervalue them: and why should it? I do not mean that you must abjure a religious profession: profess what you please, but go no farther, or not so far as to war with its doctrines, and renounce its practices. You may have as much of a religious air, and be as devout in your religious observances as you think proper, and lose none of your honour from men. The world knows that you may have all these—often more of their appearances than many whom it cannot endure—and be sound in its interests all the while. Keep it company, and wear its image, and it will never quarrel with you for walking in the *broad way* with a Christian mark. But the moment you open your heart to one particle of the love of God, or faith in our Lord Jesus Christ, you are ruined, you are hated, despised, proscribed. Now, how can this friendly correspondence with the world, without which it is vain to look for its honours, consist with the condition and character of a true believer? How can it admit that gracious singularity which is mocked on earth, but displays unutterable glories before the angels of God? How does it accord with being "pilgrims and strangers, who seek a better country, that is, an heavenly?" How with that state of separation which their God hath commanded: "Come ye out from among them, and be ye separate, and touch not the unclean thing, and I will receive you, and be a father unto you, and ye shall be my sons and my daughters, saith the Lord Almighty?" Brethren, the thing is impossible. And so it is decided, "if any man love the world, the love of the Father is not in him." As receiving "honour one from another" is, by the terms of the text, in opposition to "seeking that honour that cometh from God only," and as it implies a participation of all those tempers and feelings which are exactly the reverse of all the teachings and influence of the Spirit of God, it follows that, so long as a man continues thus to receive honour, so long as he lays such a stress upon human approbation, it is simply and forever impossible that he should be a believer in Jesus Christ, or have the smallest share in his salvation, or one single hope towards God, which will not perish as infallibly as the leaf fades and falls in autumn.

This receiving honour one of another deceives men by its specious form

The love of honour is a principle of our nature, as it came from the hands of its Divine Maker. He framed us for glory, honour, and immortality. But its beauties are all laid waste, and its direction wholly perverted, by that universal destroyer, Sin. Yet the principle, though depraved, remains, is found to operate most strongly in the most ingenuous spirits, and has actually gone so far as avowedly to dispute the empire with the law of God. We hear it confidently stated, as if it were a moral axiom, that there are two laws for society—religion, and the law of honour; and that when a man disregards the sanctions of one, he is amenable to the other. A notable expedient for a sinful worm, to improve the moral government of God his Maker! Besides, we are bound, even by the law of God, to render "honour where honour is due." Great private worth and public services command, and should command, our most respectful homage. But the misery is, that this homage and this love of honour twine round about the soul, and terminate without looking farther. It makes the man forget his immortal destiny—forget the crown of righteousness—forget the righteous Judge, and cleave to earth, and the voice of earthly praise, as to the perfection of his bliss. This principle is most observable in political and military men. I shudder when I think the applauses of our country are avowedly the motives and the reward of our most distinguished men; and when I see the public press commending the greatness and magnanimity of the sentiment and diffusing the moral pestilence through a thousand streams into the very heart of the community—and that, too, in many instances, under the control of men called Christians, but who seem to forget, on these occasions, that God, or his glory, has any any claim on their presses. O happy for them, if God too were to forget all the indignities which they have put upon his name. I have assigned a reason which makes it very hard for Christianity to thrive in a camp or in a cabinet: and it is quite a rarity, an eighth wonder of the world, to find a godly soldier or statesman. How melancholy the reflection, that from the field of honour, in the very centre of their glories, our bravest men are often summoned in an instant to their eternal reckoning, without having, perhaps, had in their lives one serious thought of the God with whom they have to do! Alas! what will the honour derived from men avail them at his bar? My heart sickens at the thought, and finds no relief but from the assurance that they are in the hands of one who will do them no injustice.

4. Finally, the sin of which I speak—making the honour that cometh from men to compensate and supersede that which cometh from God only—cannot be excused as a sin of infirmity. The strength of physical passions, the suddenness and violence of temptation, have here no place. It is a sin of *calculation*. The whole soul enters into it; habits are formed by it; and habits do not spring up like mushrooms—they grow by slow degrees. The last, though at all times a feeble apology for crime—surprises, the being taken unawares—is swept away. It is a deliberate, systematic rebellion against God. It is the indulgence of wilful transgression, which is utterly inconsistent with every gracious principle, and, where it reigns, marks without a peradventure, an unbeliever in the Lord Jesus Christ.

And now, my friends, if these things are true, and that they are is just as certain as that God hath spoken to us, how wide a scope and how terrible a necessity do they create for the examination of our own hearts! Who does not, in some shape or other, fall under the accusation of the text? Be persuaded to make diligent search; for while it stands against a single individual, it infallibly shuts him out of the kingdom of God. Should an angel be commissioned by revelation to go among the hearers of the gospel—the professors of the religion of Jesus Christ—and put his mark upon the foreheads of all who are under the ban of the text, whose forehead would be without a stigma? Would it be thine? Why, then, does thy bosom heave and thy heart palpitate? Why wilt thou not learn betimes to seek the honour that cometh from God only? How long shall the opinion of men usurp its place? How long will ye seek in political or fashionable life that applause which the Lord abhors, and may, and without his great prevention will, draw after it your eternal destruction? Where is the man who has made even honourable politics his pursuit, whose religious sensibilities were not blunted, and his conscience of rectitude warped? Who has carried into the vortex of the political whirlpool a mind uncontaminated with the corruption that is in the world, and brought it out again equally pure?

Among all the votaries of fashion in whom the religious sense is not wholly obliterated, who has attempted to conciliate the service of God with the honour that cometh one from another and succeeded? Whose garments have not smelt, whose visages have not been blackened, by the infernal fire which they have been compelled to approach? Who has not learned some maxims, or indulged some practice, which has put a wider separation between God and them, and prepared them for a deeper plunge into transgression when the next opportunity should offer? Shall I propose the question? Are there any whose lips have received the hallowed symbols of the body and blood of Jesus the Saviour, and whose feet, ere the taste of that holy pledge had died away, have gone greedily into the same excess of riot with those who walk in the vanity of their minds? In a word, are there none whose consciences whisper to them that the inspiring motive to all their religious appearance and profession has been the applauses of their fellow-men? What shall I say to them all? Awake! arise! flee! flee for your lives from this treacherous ground that stretches over the edge of the bottomless pit! Soon may the voice of that thunder be heard which shall shake it into fragments beneath your feet, and you are irrevocably ingulfed. Even now the cry of despair from some who were gay and careless as any of you can be, rings in my ear. They were taken unprepared, and hurried away with all their reasonings, their decencies, their mistaken religion, and have found their error when the hope of redemption was past! See that this be not your case. See to it soon; see to it immediately. To-day is the accepted time; to-day is the day of salvation. Be not deceived. Yet a little while, and "the Lord Jesus shall be revealed from heaven in flaming fire, taking vengeance of those who know not God and obey not the gospel." The Lord grant that you may be able to stand before him in that final and fiery visitation.

SERMON XVIII.

APOSTOLIC COMMISSION.

LUKE xxiv. 47.

"And that repentance and remission of sins should be preached in his name among all nations, beginning at Jerusalem."

The work which the Father had given the Lord Jesus to do was now finished. He had gone through the several stages of his humiliation, and had ceased to be the "man of sorrows and acquainted with grief." He had magnified the law and made it honourable, and brought in everlasting righteousness, even the righteousness of God, for the justification of men. He had put away sin by the sacrifice of himself, pouring out the blood of his cross as a ransom for their souls. He had passed through the gates of death; had remained in his territories long enough to prove the fact of his having died, and to work the overthrow of his kingdom; had risen in his majesty, and repassed as a conqueror those barriers through which he was led as a prisoner; had frustrated, defeated, and made an open show of the hosts of hell, and was just about ascending in the glory of the Captain of salvation up to his native heavens, there to appear in the presence of God for us! How awful the pause; how tender yet terrifying the crisis! Methinks the cry is heard to the farthest verge of Creation, "Now is come salvation, and strength, and the kingdom of our God, and the power of his Christ." The partition-wall is tottering to its base, and presently will be heard the crash of its fall. The gates of heavenly light are to be unbarred to the world, and floods of living water from the rock of Zion, are to cool and refresh and invigorate the nations. The tabernacle of God is to dwell with men; they are to become his people; he is to be their God; he is to dwell among them, to walk in the midst of them, to cast out the prince of this world, and to bring back the days of primeval glory and blessedness. What! is all this to be effected in our world? Yes! in our world! Why, it is full of crimes and curses; it is overrun with the enemies of God. Devils and devilish men have the rule here. The soil is yet reeking with the blood of the Prince of life. Not a bosom heaves nor a tear starts under the guilt of this "deep damnation." How then shall this marvellous revolution be accomplished? Gather together the wise men, the philosophers; ask them whether the scheme is practicable, whether these fairy visions can be realised. The wise men! the philosophers. They are deep in the great apostasy; they are themselves ringleaders in treason, leaders of the bands of rebels: they are as ignorant as they are criminal. Away with their fooleries! Let me hear the Son of God breathe this portentous silence, "Not by might, nor by power, but by my Spirit, saith the Lord." He who controls the spirits of all flesh issues forth the command in its simple majesty, that repentance and remission of sins should be preached in his name among all nations, beginning at Jerusalem. Observe, my Christian friends, the grandeur of this commission. The Lord Jesus speaks like one who had the "spirits of all flesh" under his control. The magnitude of the object, the difficulty of the enterprise, the feebleness of the means, are not so much as mentioned. "Let there be light," was not uttered with more decision at the first creation, than is this charge to his apostles at the second. The speaker and the energy were the same. It was all worthy of God manifest in the flesh, and so surely as his lips have pronounced the words the effect must follow. The disciples felt their power. Eleven men, without arms or armies, influence, connections, wealth, or literature, are sent to subdue the nations. Not a remonstrance, a scruple or a doubt, is heard from their lips. "I am with you always, I will give you a mouth and wisdom which all your adversaries shall not be able to gainsay or resist," hushed every fear, resolved every difficulty, filled them with courage, crowned them with success.

The text embraces three topics of most interesting inquiry; the extent of the apostolic commission, the substance of their message, and a singular circumstance connected with the commencement of their labours. They were charged with an embassy to "all nations."

They were to "preach repentance and remission of sins in the name of Jesus," and they were to "begin at Jerusalem."*

I. The substance of their commission: "To preach repentance and remission of sins in the name of Jesus."

"Repentance" is a term of great latitude. It primarily signifies, "a change of mind:" and this general idea adheres to every form of its application. When the Jew was commanded to "repent," his whole notions concerning the person and salvation of the Messiah were to undergo a revolution. "Repent ye, for the kingdom of Heaven is at hand." All his preconceived opinions of the Christ as a temporal deliverer, a magnificent conqueror, by whom his nation was to be rescued from the domination of the Romans, and placed at the head of the whole earth, were to be abandoned.

When the Gentile was commanded to repent, all his ideas concerning the religion of his country, of his ancestors, were to be inverted: "Surely our fathers have inherited lies, vanities, and things wherein there is no profit." Both Jew and Gentile were enjoined to alter entirely the nature of their conceptions of truth and happiness.

What sort of an enterprise was this? Judge ye who know how difficult it is to root out an ancient prejudice from the mind of man. Who can estimate the sacrifice which it costs his "vanity?" how little, how feeble, how paltry the success of similar attempts, upon "any thing" consecrated by established modes of thinking and feeling. Particularly, how hopeless must the experiment be, when it is directed against men's ideas of national superiority. Their climate and their country the finest in the world! their persons the handsomest, the bravest, the most skilful! their religion the best, the most divine! all their institutions of the highest order! For example: we are accustomed to applaud ourselves as "the most enlightened people in the universe;" and our institutions, both civil and political, as excelling all others; as perfect, although we are every now and then in the habit of mending, or trying to mend them. Should any one now attempt to reason us out of our prepossessions, to persuade us that the objects of our admiration are in reality detestable, and that we never shall know what decency, and dignity, and pre-eminence mean, until we throw them all away,

* The third topic was reserved for a second sermon, which was never written.

trample them under foot, and open our ears to a new set of instructions, and our hearts to a new set of perceptions altogether. What reception, suppose ye, would this apostle of revolution meet? How many would he persuade? What other effect could he hope to produce, than to arm the community against him, as an insane man?

Now, then, judge from your own sensations what the ambassador of the cross had to hope, when, attacking opinions and prejudices infinitely stronger than those of civil policy or political predilections, he preached to men the necessity of changing, radically, their whole convictions of truth and happiness!

Nor is the necessity of such a change less at this moment, nor will it be less while the world endures, than it was at the first promulgation of the gospel. Be not startled at this assertion! Say not, "The Jews had misunderstood and perverted the Scriptures of their own prophets; they were dreaming about a Messiah, such as their vain imaginations had formed him; and to reap any benefit from him, they must be recalled to a sound mind." The Gentiles, again, had lost altogether the knowledge of the true God. They had run into all excess of riot in their madness upon their idols, and must be reclaimed from these vanities to the living and true God. To both Jew and Gentile, therefore, the doctrine and the duty of repentance was strictly applicable; and so it is to these unhappy men who, in the darkness of paganism, are without God. But to us—to Christians, who have imbibed from our infancy those important truths which were new both to Jews and Gentiles, the doctrine of this *repentance* is superfluous. Stay a little and consider. The effect of Jewish carnality and pagan idolatry was to separate between them and their God; to make them forget the end of their being; to drench them in sense; to chain them to this world; and, finally, to "drown them in destruction and perdition." Are we, with all our superior light, with all our commiseration for Jewish blindness and heathen degradation, in no danger of the same sin, and of the same ruin? Are none of our affections estranged from God, the sovereign good, and set on lying vanities which cannot profit? Are not the minds of many called Christians as far from just ideas concerning the spiritual character and work of our Lord Jesus Christ, as the grossest and most obstinate Jews? and their hearts as full of "abominable idolatries," as the most debased and polluted Pagan? Deceive not your ownselves. The Most High regards not the form, where he sees the substance of idolatry. You may look with contempt and abhorrence upon a wooden or golden god in the shape of a man, or a "four-footed beast, or a creeping thing." Is it any thing better, suppose ye, when it has the devotion of all your faculties, the ardour of your whole hearts, your undivided love and worship, in the shape of a dollar, or a guinea, or a bank note? When the all-seeing glance of God, your Maker, strikes through the bosoms of this assembly, does he perceive there no perverted principles, no unhallowed emotion, no lust of the flesh, nor lust of the eye, nor pride of life? Cannot he single out any who place their happiness in these things as if they were the chief good? Stand forth, ye idolaters, ye evangelized, and therefore most criminal idolaters, and hear his voice, fresh from the heavens, to you, "Repent," or perish. Change all your principles and judgments, or not a man of you shall see the kingdom of God. You may stand high in the respect of the world, but know ye not that the friendship of this world is enmity with God. If any man, therefore, will be the friend of the world, he must be the enemy of God. And what will ye do, when he shall meet you as a bear robbed of her whelps?

But the repentance which my text enjoins, and the apostles preach, is not merely such an alteration in men's views as amounts to a rational and speculative conviction of truth, of duty, and of happiness. Without this they shall in vain hope to enter the kingdom of God. But this alone will not insure their admittance. You may be, in these matters, as orthodox as the devil, and as far from heaven.

The repentance which is expected from us goes much deeper, and makes more thorough work. It teaches us to view our errors, not merely as mistakes, but as sin; as having led us just as far towards ruin as we wandered from God. It sinks into the heart, turns it inside out, shows the evils which lurk there, reaches the very source of all our iniquities, the corruption of our nature; makes us sensible that we are unlike the holy God, unmeet for his fellowship, at enmity with him, exposed to the perdition of his frown. If left to its own operation it would be the sorrow of the world, which works melancholy, despair, death. But it is directed by a kindlier and holier influence. It creates,

Y

1. Godly sorrow for sin: as against all that is good, and pure, and kind, in the Infinite One; against all his authority, all his patience, all his grace. That our hearts should be a fountain, and our lives a channel, of such floods of ingratitude, filth, rebellion, fill us with dismay, and the most unfeigned compunction.

2. It fills with hatred of our sins. Hatred, as those things which have dishonoured the majesty in the heavens, and have rendered us accomplices in treason, with the spirits of the pit—hatred as at those things which have abused the divine mercies, despised the divine judgments, caused our Lord Jesus Christ to shed his most precious blood—hatred, as being emphatically the destroyers of soul, of body, of hope: which made the devil, which kindled hell, and will consign to its untold wo all over whom they reign.

3. This repentance leads to a confession of sin; deep, humble, unaffected. No apologies, no extenuations. "Behold, I am vile; what shall I answer thee; if thou Lord should mark iniquities, O Lord, who shall stand—God be merciful to me a sinner," is the language of a broken, a contrite, a repenting heart.

4. This repentance involves a forsaking of sin and return to God. It is he who forsakes, not who conceals his sin, that shall find mercy. The true penitent forsakes his sin wholly and universally. He makes no reserve for a favourite lust. Compromise is out of the question. Is it not a little one? will never be heard from his lips. Whatever he discovers to be provoking to the eyes of the Lord's glory will be renounced. If it be a right arm, a right eye, dear as one's own soul, it must be cast away; it must be nailed to the cross, and there left to die as our Lord died, a lingering, painful, shameful, accursed death.

Finally. It is a divorce, not a temporary separation, that he seeks. Whatever constituted sin's claim to dwell with him, or rule over him, that must be extinguished. Never more shall his former lusts in his ignorance find a welcome in his bosom. It is henceforth consecrated as a temple of God, and contains no room, no not so much as a corner, for allowed retreat to his enemy. The expelled devil returns not to his house with seven spirits more wicked than himself. The voice of the Son of God, "I charge thee come out of the man and enter no more into him," is peremptory, and Satan must obey.

What a marvellous revolution is here! The man's views, principles, habits, changed! Views, principles, habits, which had grown with his growth and strengthened with his strength!—to which he was strongly attached as his nature would permit! in accordance with which he not long ago sought his happiness! which he judged to be as firm as truth itself! All changed! Radically changed! Changed so as to hate what he loved and to love what he hated! By what process of reason was it effected? What motives enforced, what efficiency ensured it?

Marvel not, my brethren! The secret is very simple, but its energy is all divine. The text contains it. The apostles succeeded; the gospel now so succeeds, by coupling with the doctrine of repentance that of the "remission of sin."

That men are sinners conscience dictates, but her dictates are dark, ill-boding, full of fears and undefined terrors. Hence all her suggestions are melancholy, sour, sullen, very apt to breed superstition, but of cheerful religion absolutely barren. Of forgiveness she knows nothing. This is the blessed discovery of the gospel; and plain as it appears to us, because the gospel hath put it in meridian light and glory, it would have confounded the angels of heaven to all eternity had they been asked whether there is forgiveness with God. It is one of his deep things which he hath revealed unto us by his Spirit. All ye know or can know of it is from this revelation. Let us then inquire at the mouth of the Lord himself what is that forgiveness which he bestows and which he commanded his apostles to preach.

1. It is forgiveness or remission of sin, in which term we comprehend every offence of which God is the object. Now of this he alone is the proper judge. Its thanklessness, its malignity, the height, and length, and breadth, and depth of its evil, the Infinite Mind only can measure. A creature can see and feel it chiefly in the penalty which God has annexed to it; and therefore a part only, and but a small part, can come at once under his observation. To the Eternal Mind, its hideousness and its horrors, from its first introduction through everlasting ages, are all minutely and exactly present. Now that he should be the only being in his own universe who should have thoughts of pardon! How good, how kind, how gracious! What an emphasis does it impart to his name! "The Lord, the Lord God, merciful and gracious, long-suffering, slow to

anger, forgiving iniquity and transgression and sin." Verily, it sprang up in the bosom of his own love. Heaven would not have had the compassion, nor hell the impudence, to sue for our pardon. God alone shall be exalted in this matter; God alone is the forgiver. Let his great name have all the glory!

2. That remission of sin which the gospel proclaims is most free; it is forgiveness according to the riches of his grace. There is indeed something gratuitous in the very idea of forgiveness. It supposes in the forgiver the right of exacting his due, and of his waiving that right with respect to the person of the offender. Of course he must receive it as a free, unconditional gift. How could it come to us in any other way? Who among the sons of men, that rightly considers the case, can have the hardihood to talk or think of compounding with his God? Whose mind is so profane as to insult him with the offer of his best deeds as a price for his favour? You might as well imagine that the gift of God can be purchased with money. Your good deeds, your virtues, your penitence! How much will they cover of the ground of your transgressions? Large and respectable as they may appear in your partial eye, what figure shall they make before him "whose eyes are as a flame of fire?" What but extort from your astonished lips that exceeding great and bitter cry, "We are all as an unclean thing, and our very righteousness are as filthy rags." Yet here is the main difficulty with an awakened conscience; first, to persuade of the fact that there is forgiveness with God; next, to persuade it, his forgiveness is absolutely free. No point do the Scriptures labour more—none do they set in a greater variety of lights—none exhibit in more various attitudes. They display—O let me speak of it with all reverence, for I have no other word!—they display the anxiety of the Holy One for what? Why, that sinful man may believe that he is merciful, and that his mercy is infinitely free! "Turn ye, turn ye, why will ye die, O house of Israel?" "Turn, and I will not cause mine anger to fall upon you, for I am gracious!" "Ho! every one that thirsteth, come to the waters!" Come poor, come wretched; come with nothing to recommend, with everything to disqualify you; only come, and take the water of life freely.

3. The remission of sin is *full*. The covering is sufficient to wrap yourselves in, the bed is long enough for you to repose your-

selves upon. He takes praise to himself that when he forgives, it is of *all trespasses*, and your gladdened hearts should re-echo the praise, "Bless the Lord, O my soul! and all that is within me bless his holy name;" who forgiveth all thine iniquities! God is as really God in his forgiveness as in his vengeance. He will no more be compared with the children of men, with the sons of the mighty, in his grace, than in his severity. So indeed it must be if ever you enjoy the comfort of pardoned sin; for if the divine forgiveness do not completely cover the whole ground of our transgressions—if it leave but one sin, original or actual, out of its provision—we have that one sin to answer for, and so no flesh should be saved. This one sin would be our unsheltered, our vulnerable point, in which guilt would thrust in his mortal dart. Oh! it is our strong consolation, that when God forgives he forgives like God. "When he pardons he will abundantly pardon." Go with your half-forgiveness, limited, conditional pardons, with reserves and limitations, unto the souls of men. It may be, it may become them—it is like themselves. That of God is absolute and perfect, before which our sins are as a cloud before the east wind and the rising sun. Hence he is said to do this work with his whole heart and his whole soul—$\chi\alpha\rho\iota\zeta\epsilon\sigma\theta\alpha\iota$, freely, bountifully, largely, to indulge and forgive unto us our sins, and to cast them into the bottom of the sea (Mic. vii. 19), into the bottomless ocean, an emblem of infinite mercy. Remember this, poor souls, when you are to deal with God in this matter.*

4. The forgiveness of sins is final. In the justification of a sinner, God, the gracious one, pardons once for all—pardons for ever! Pardon would be of no use to us, were it not irreversible: it would no sooner be gained, than lost. The Lord doth not so deal with his pardoned ones; give them just to taste the sweetness of his mercy, that their own sinfulness may the next moment fill their mouths with the bitterness, and their hearts with the horrors of the curse. His bounty is of another order altogether. His gifts and his calling are without repentance, *i. e.* unchangeable. His love is everlasting, and so is the life which he bestows upon them. They are united with his dear Son; their lives entwine with his

---

* Owen's 130th Psalm, p. 240, oct. Glasgow.

life. Whatever reaches them to destroy them, must first kill their Redeemer. "Because I live," is his gracious promise, "ye shall live also." They are kept by the power of God, through faith unto salvation; therefore they shall never perish. There is, there can be, no condemnation for them—they shall have everlasting life.

SERMON XIX.

NON-CONFORMITY TO THE WORLD.

ROMANS xii. 2.

" Be not conformed to this world; but be ye transformed by the renewing of your mind, that ye may prove what is that good, and acceptable, and perfect will of God."

Many of my hearers will take instant alarm from the uncourtly and unfashionable language of the text. They will assume, as granted, that they are to be lectured away from society, shut out from all the innocent and joyous freedoms of life, and persuaded to spend their days in the recesses of a nunnery, or the cells of a cloister. But, softly, there are no nunneries nor cloisters in the Bible; there are scarcely any in our country, and if there were ever so many, it would be rather hopeless to try the experiment of making converts of either sex from among this audience. Take heed, however, that your prejudices do not assail the word of your God; that you stop not your ears, and steel not your hearts against his counsels. You are here in his presence, and it may cost you your souls if you turn away from his admonition. It cannot indeed be denied, that his commandment and the principles of his children are infinitely at variance with a multitude of things which the world calls harmless; nor that it may appear to be your duty, your bounden, your imperative duty, to make a secession even from the innocences of the world, to take a firm stand, and to make a full stop, in a career plausible, popular, reputable, for which many ingenious things may be pleaded, but which are not fit for a Christian who is not of the world, but whom Christ hath "called out of the world;" let it be sulky, or cold, or abusive, as it pleases, and that without infringing at all upon your active duties, or upon your allowed, which are your greatest social comforts. Your souls are too precious to compliment away to your giddy neighbours, and eternal life too infinitely valuable to be put in jeopardy by your desire to please them. Then let us see what the apostle means by being " not conformed to this world,"—what is that " transformation by the renewing of our mind," so zealously pressed upon us: and what is the connection under which he has placed it—" that ye may know what is that good, and acceptable, and perfect will of God."

I. Let us look at the nature of that " non-conformity to this world," which the text enjoins.

This world emits a bad savour in the records of God. Wherein, in trespasses and sins, says the apostle, " ye walked according to the course of this world, according to the prince of the power of the air, the spirit that now worketh in the children of disobedience." The course of this world, then, is directed by the prince of darkness; and in directing it, he employs all the faculties of their souls, and all the members of their bodies, " as instruments of unrighteousness unto sin." The world is at this moment full of demoniacs, the evil one takes as complete possession of their persons, and abuses them to as ignoble purposes, as ever he did their bodies in the days of our Lord's humiliation. Oh that men who are estranged from God would *believe* the terrifying truth! Yes, in that fair, and gentle, and courteous, and polished form, dwells the spirit that organizes all the rebellion against God, all the misery of man; all that he fears and has reason to fear; and causes that lake of *fire and brimstone*, into which his intention is to plunge his votaries. Do you wonder, then, that the Scripture has said, " whoever will be the friend of the world is the enemy of God." Under his evil control the world, like a rebellious province, has set up for itself; and acts as if it were perfectly independent of the divine government. It has its own institutions, statutes, and customs— its own pursuits—its own ethics—its own penal code, and its own recompenses. It covers the very same ground which is covered by the law of God; but is, of course, perfectly hostile and contradictory both to the law and the Lawgiver. Here, then, is the cause and origin of all those injunctions of the Scriptures, concerning our non-conformity to the world. It is in necessary and perpetual collision with the authority of our rightful Sovereign. Obedience to the one infallibly excludes obedience to the other. And it is most idle and ridiculous to attempt their conciliation; the very attempt proves its author to be an enemy to God, and a slave to the usurper.

The case, my friends, admits of but one alternative: you must either take your part with the world, and share in its guilt and condemnation, or you must " come out from the world, and be separate," *i. e.* you must be Christians wholly or not at all. No middle character can be allowed. If you are not for the Saviour, you must be against him. If you do not "gather with him" you must be numbered among those who "scatter abroad." Neither the kingdom of heaven nor the kingdom of hell tolerates a neutral character. "If Jehovah be God, follow him; and if Baal be God, follow him." But to halt between two opinions marks the feebleness of present indecision, and will only conduct to future ruin.

Yet it is not from all intercourse with the world that lieth in wickedness that the authority of Jesus Christ prohibits you. For then, as saith the apostle, "ye must needs go out of the world." But in your separation from it you must show a character which the world never forms, and cannot understand; must show that while you are in it you are not of it—that you do not love it—that your commerce with it is of pure necessity, and that you are going rapidly as time can carry you to that glorious home, where it shall never more show its face. You must be separated from and have no communion with those things which distinguish the world from the redeemed of the Lord, and which qualify you for the career of that graceless society whose "steps take hold on hell, leading down to the chambers of death."

1. There must be a renunciation of the maxims of the world.

These maxims, without exception, centre in the creature, and are bounded by time. There is not one of them which regards an immortal destiny. "Let us eat and drink, for to-morrow we die," is the sum of its philosophy. And were it true—did the spirit of man, like that of a beast, go downward—there is nothing to arraign its wisdom nor to demonstrate the prudence of a very different course. But if, on the contrary, we are immortal beings, than which nothing can be more certain, then to have all our principles of action shaped only to the requisitions of a mortal life, is the extreme of folly and madness; and the farther we can be from so great a delusion, the better for us. Now for example:

It is one of the maxims of the world, that if we are virtuous, *i. e.* if we render to every man his due, cultivate the mild and beneficent affections, do good actions, and are free from gross iniquities, it is enough. No more will be required of us by God himself, and we may sit down at our ease in the calm and undisturbed hope of unquestioned bliss.

Brethren, let me deal very plainly with you on this point, for it is in reality the rock on which a great portion of men make shipwreck of their souls; and I would observe that it confines all your accountability to the second table of the law, leaving the first, all your duties and your relations to God, unprovided for. Who knows not that amiable and beneficent tempers are an essential part of the religion of our Lord Jesus Christ? But who knows not that, separated from the connection under which his word has placed them, torn asunder from supreme love to God from which he has made them to spring, they are at best but a milder form of rebellion against him? How often must you be reminded that mutual acts of kindness, the various good offices of life, are simply necessary to the existence of society among rebels, and that the man who may be most distinguished for them may himself be the most obnoxious rebel among the whole, and may be condemned for abetting and encouraging others in their rebellion? Was such a plea ever of any value before the tribunals of men? Has it not appeared that the most humane, beneficent, and even righteous among a band of transgressors, was himself a principal culprit? And did the abuse of these good qualities in the service of rebellion for one moment arrest the most condign punishment? And shall we impute to the perfect government of God a blunder which cannot find a place among the imperfect governments of men? Besides, what becomes of the rights of God your Maker? Where is the obedience to the first and greatest commandment: "Thou shalt love the Lord thy God with all thy heart, and with all thy strength, and with all thy mind?" Is this to be trodden under foot with impunity? Are you to go all your lives long forgetful of the infinite good, and when called to account escape under the pretext that you were kind to rebels like yourself? Never to bestow a thought upon the eternal world, and to step as a matter of course into all its blessedness? Never to have any concern about glorifying God here, and to be taken up from the mire of your pollutions unpardoned, unwashed, unsanctified, into the full possession of his glory hereafter? O more than sottish! Who hath bewitched you, children of men? And do I not speak to many, who, with the gospel of salvation freely and fully proclaimed in their hearing, have yet no other hope of divine acceptance than this absurd and stupid lie? Believe not the world. Her theology is not for sinful man. To behave decently on earth is no passport for heaven. It may do well enough among the blind and clumsy judges here, but will infallibly be detected by the keen-eyed righteousness beyond the grave. "That which is born of the flesh is flesh;" but "except a man be born of the Spirit, he cannot enter into the kingdom of God." Hope for no change, for no mitigation. If the Lord Christ speaks true, you shall find, when there is no rectifying mistakes, that every man of you who has all that the world pronounces enough, and has no more, will be forever shut out from the kingdom of God.

2. Where the world cannot succeed in expelling *religious* sensibility altogether, there is another maxim calculated to neutralize its power and render it ineffectual: "You need not be so strict; this great precision only does harm; it makes religion unamiable, and yourselves odious. Why cannot you enjoy in moderation and with dignity the innocent freedoms which form the zest of society, and not put on that sombre air, and keep at so chilling a distance from all the relish of life?"

In this way do men contrive to make void the law of God by their manner of representation. To fear God and do his will, is "strictness" and "hurtful precision." To preserve tenderness of conscience, is to be "unamiable and odious." To follow the multitude, is to "enjoy with moderation and dignity only innocent freedoms;" and to avoid all appearance of evil, is to have "a sombre air and to keep at a chilling distance from the relish of life." So they wrap it up. To make short work of all these fair words and false pretences, do those who use them really love the law of God? and is it only against extravagant and fanatical excesses that they set their faces? Or is their opposition in very deed pointed at all to that "holiness without which no man shall see the Lord?" Is it not precisely the image of God which they cannot endure, and his authority which they would gladly set aside? Would they not rob you of all the comforts of a good conscience? of all the sweets of a peaceful walk with God? and persuade you to exchange them for the giddy whirl, for the idiot laugh, for the midnight debauch, and whatever belongs to that mental and bodily dissipation which "is like the crackling of thorns under a pot," noisy for a moment and gone forever? Among the other things which form the "zest of society," you must pollute your conscience, corrupt your morals, and dishonour "the glorious and fearful name of the Lord your God" by a little "innocent" gambling. You must also participate in that rational and elegant amusement which the abandoned and thieves select for their special entertainment, the play-house—all, lest your religion should appear unamiable. Were the Lord Jesus now on earth, should he not pass with our fashionable judges as morose, petulant, impertinent, a perfect stranger to polished manners, an enemy to all the cheerfulness and the graces of life? His apostle Paul would be derided as a fanatic; and John, the beloved disciple, would be pitied as a well-meaning enthusiast, endurable only because he was weak. In short, my friends, if you mean to be Christians, you "must walk as Christ also walked." Your ears must be deaf alike to the open enmity and the hollow friendship of the world. You must have nothing to do with their plausible maxims—parleying is half a surrender. You must put down your foot decisively in the King's highway, the way of holiness, in which "the elders obtained a good report," and which is your short and only way to the kingdom.

3. When guilt, who pays no regard to etiquette, bursts in upon the conscience, raises his rugged voice, and reads his fearful lectures, the world has another maxim to soothe him down and to keep all quiet within: "God is a merciful God; we injure his name by ascribing harshness and rigour to him. He pities his poor, feeble creatures, compassionates their infirmities, takes delight in forgiving their faults, and will not be extreme to mark what is amiss."

How false and foul a conclusion, coupled with the most blessed truth that can sound in the ears of an awakened sinner! He is merciful. The dimensions of his mercy, its height, and depth, and length, and breadth, it is not for the creature to scan. The gospel alone however has revealed it in all its magnitude and freedom.

But it is not to that mercy as thus revealed that the world appeals. Jesus Christ and his merit and grace find no place among its maxims. The creed of the world and that of the Unitarians are perfectly agreed. Shut out the Saviour; make no use whatever of him as "the way, and the truth, and the life;" know nothing, believe nothing, say nothing, of that "new and living way which he hath consecrated by his blood," and all the rebels together will be loud in their praises of the divine mercy. But all this cry about the mercy of God is to encourage sinners who continue in their sins. It has nothing in common with the salvation of our Lord Jesus Christ, who saves his people *from* their sins. It creates a deceitful hope, a lying persuasion, that a man may live habitually neglectful of God, of his immortal soul, of his eternal interests, and after all have a just confidence in the divine mercy. Believe it not—shut your ears against so popular and fatal a delusion. It is not he who palliates, but he who confesses and forsakes his sins— he who turns from them wholly, impartially, forever, and turns his feet unto God's testimonies—that shall find mercy. Have as much as you please of this divinity of the world. It is reprobate silver; it will never make you rich unto everlasting life, nor buy one shred of clothing to cover your nakedness. The "blood of Jesus must cleanse you from all sin; the righteousness of Jesus must be your spotless robe; the spirit of Jesus must be your sanctifier; or in that great and terrible day of the Lord you have nothing to look for but to "be condemned with the world."

2. To renounce in words the maxims of the world, will be of little avail, if we do not also renounce its practices.

The world has a method of forming a conscience of its own, and a moral law to correspond with it, so that whoever observes this law, however he may disregard and insult the law of God, is to be respected as a correct and honourable man. For example:

You may spend a life in utter forgetfulness of God and his worship—in the most positive unbelief, and the most marked contempt of our Lord Jesus Christ—in habitual and even studious neglect of his great salvation, and every thing referring to its existence, and you never break the chain of your harmony with the world. These things give no uneasiness to a worldly conscience, nor disqualify you in the least for worldly honour and confidence. Nay, more: you may convert the Sabbath-day, the day which the

Lord emphatically calls his own, into a season for secular business, or carnal amusement—you may even profane the name of the Lord your God—you may bestow your highest affections upon as many idols as you can find places for in your heart—it breaks no scores with a worldly conscience, nor depreciates you in the least in the eyes of worldly men. If you live in a commercial country, you may defraud the government of its just dues—may make false entries of your goods. If your country be neutral, may furnish forged papers for your vessel, to suit either belligerent, as circumstances shall require—may crown the whole with some *hard swearing*, which old-fashioned men call *perjury;* you may break, as it is termed, may convey your property fraudulently out of the reach of its true owners; may bring multitudes of the poor, the widowed, and the fatherless, who trusted in your integrity, to the extreme of wretchedness—and when you have secured a human acquittal, by laws perhaps not a whit more righteous than your own principles, may erect your crest, may turn round and look full in the face the very persons you have ruined; may insult them with the ostentatious display of your wealth, and receive not a hat the less. If you have spirit to carry the matter so high, you may disturb domestic peace, and then blow out the brains of the injured, for breathing upon your *honour*. The skirts of the world's conscience are very large, and its bowels of charity very strong, for all who side with it against the puritanical practices of "fearing God and keeping his commandments." But now hear a moment what He who is to be your Judge hath said: "Be not deceived: Neither fornicators, nor idolaters, nor adulterers, nor abusers of themselves with mankind, nor thieves, nor covetous, nor drunkards, nor revilers, nor extortioners, shall inherit the kingdom of God." His law is made, and its penalty enacted, "for the lawless and disobedient, for the ungodly and for sinners, for unholy and profane, for liars, for perjured persons, for murderers, and if there be any other thing that is contrary to sound doctrine." He has said that the wicked, whoever they be, by whatever names they go, and under whatever sanctions they may shield themselves, "shall be turned into hell;" if you mean to take up your bed there and to know, by awful experience, what it is to "dwell with everlasting burnings," why then go, "be conformed to this world," and divide its recompense. But if not, if you are set for another course, and for another issue, if you design to meet the Lord in the air, when all that belongs to the world will be poor and contemptible enough, then see, in the

II. Place, the necessity of the transformation mentioned in the text. "Be ye transformed in the renewing of your mind."

Your speculative opinions, and your practical judgments, on those vital questions which affect your relations to God, and the salvation of your soul, must be exactly the reverse of the maxims and habits of this world. You must change sides: do it effectually, decidedly, visibly. You are to enquire, not what is fashionable, but what is right; not what is reputable or passable among men, but what the Lord God hath spoken; you must, in a particular manner, come out for the name of our Lord Jesus Christ, and for the truth which is according to godliness. Let me address a word to those who are sensible of their duty, and yet shrink from the performance of it. "How long halt ye between two opinions?" If your opinion is fixed on the great matters of your eternal hope, of what are you ashamed or afraid? Smothered regard our Captain disdains. Do not imagine that if you are really his disciples ye can escape detection by the world, or that it will spare you the more, or hate you the less. Wo be unto you if it should! Are you afraid, when you look around you and observe the mighty difference between the character of professing Christians, and the requisitions of your Divine Master, that you too, will one day fall back and bring a blot upon that "worthy name whereby ye are called?" It is a salutary fear; but may be worked up to a grievous temptation. It should inspire caution; not keep among the ranks of unbelievers, and apparently in the interests of enmity against God. To omit the plain duty of leaving the world that lieth in wickedness, is not the way to find freedom or peace. Cast you fears of falling upon him who has said, "my grace is sufficient for thee;" start from your lethargy and "run with patience the race that is set before you, looking unto Jesus, the author and finisher of your faith."

And let these careless professors, whose lives lay a stumbling-block before their more conscientious brethren, suffer the word of reproof and exhortation. You are justly liable to part of that same rebuke which our Lord gave to the Jewish lawyer; not indeed for "taking away the key of knowledge," but to the other and severer part of his charge, "you go not into the kingdom of heaven yourselves, and them that would enter in ye hinder." Is it not enough to dishonour the Saviour under the pretence of being his friends, but must you keep back others from honouring him? Are ye not satisfied with perishing alone—must you strive to make your neighbours bear you company? Is the taste of their blood sweet to you? or will it be pleasant to sink down to death under the weight of their ruin, superadded to your own? rather seek to encourage them; to cheer their drooping hopes; to revive their fainting spirits; to "strengthen the hands that hang down, and confirm the feeble knees; and make straight paths for your feet—lest that which is lame be turned out of the way, but let it rather be healed." O how delightful to enter the palaces above, with a friend on either side! To hear a saved one, whom perhaps you never knew, acknowledge, if it had not been for this man's firmness—for that woman's tenderness—for yonder person's fidelity, I had perhaps missed my road, been led astray in the paths of the seducer, and had never been here? Think you that such things will not add to the lustre of your crown, to the intensity of your bliss, to the beauty of your heaven? As you value all the three, be persuaded by a close imitation of Jesus Christ, to help and not to hinder others in the prosecution of their high calling.

This transformation must be by the "renewing of your mind." Outward things alone will not do. "Bodily exercise profiteth little." The resolution must be radical, and within the soul. That Holy Spirit, who is the vicegerent of Jesus Christ, must apply his power to create men anew; or after all their reformation, their hearts will be still hankering after "the lust of the flesh, the lust of the eye, and the pride of life." Trifle not with eternal things. Never imagine that what man can see and understand is enough. Though, if you have not what he can see and understand, there is a fatal deficiency. "Your light must so shine before men, that others, seeing your good works, may glorify your Father which is in heaven." But in order to effect so divine a result, marvel not if we perpetually ring in your ears that proclamation of the Master, "Ye must be born again!" Your faculties must be turned away from the objects of sinful pursuit, to the will and the work of your reconciled God and heavenly Father. Like the great High Priest of your profession, you must "delight to do the will of God."

Your affections too must be changed, and must change their objects. "If ye, then, be risen with Christ," to a new and holy life, "seek those things which are above, where he himself sitteth at the right hand of God. Set your affections on things above, not on things on the earth. For ye are dead, and your life is hid with Christ in God." In fine, this "renewing of your mind" will make you "spiritually minded, which is life and peace."

III. The connection under which this non-conformity to the world is placed in the text demands your serious attention: "That ye may prove what is that good and acceptable and perfect will of God."

So long as men live conformably "to the course of this world," they labour under an incapacity, criminal indeed, but still an incapacity, of clearly perceiving what the will of God is, and especially that it is good and acceptable and perfect. The motives which govern them, the influences which act upon them, the objects of their preference, all conspire to draw a thick film over their moral vision. So that the most conclusive scriptural demonstrations do not operate with their proper force, nor can the strongest scriptural light make their way plain before their face. They still grope in the dark, and though "the light shineth in darkness, the darkness comprehendeth it not." They still profess their honesty, avow themselves sincere inquirers after truth, and wonder that they come no nearer to a satisfying conclusion; or perhaps they do come to a conclusion, and equally wonder to find all the plain simple-hearted Christians in the world are against them. I have only to say, that one beam of the glory of God in Christ Jesus darting into their minds, will instantly put to flight this boasted honesty, this pretence of sincere inquiry, and make them see and own the inconceivable deceitfulness of their own hearts. Under the power of his renewing grace their vision is purified. The images which it forms are in their proper place and position. Obscurities are enlightened, entanglements are unravelled, doubts resolved, and the wonder now is at the former blindness. The words of God have an evidence and an efficacy altogether surprising. The will of God there is no difficulty, generally speaking, of determining with the greatest precision; particularly all that revealed will which affects the substance of our faith, our duty,

z

and our hope. They who believe his testimony the most firmly, receiving it upon his own authority as undisputed and indisputable truth, make the most rapid and eminent progress. They ask no questions but "what said my Lord unto his servant?" and they are enabled to perceive both what he does say and that it is all good, and of such a sort as must be acceptable when it takes place in them, and precisely that which suits their circumstances and promotes the end for which it was intended, being therefore every way perfect. It is just what they themselves would wish it. They have nothing to diminish, to add, nor to alter. They complain, indeed they have reason to complain, often and bitterly, of "sin that dwelleth in them—of the lusting of the flesh against the spirit—of the law in their members warring against the law of their mind, and bringing them into captivity to the law of sin and death." But of the law, of the will of God, not a whisper of complaint—no lamentation about its breadth or strictness—none about its spirituality, "searching even to the dividing asunder of the soul and spirit." They know nothing of what some men call a milder form of grace. They ask for no dispensations, no relaxation. Their unanimous verdict is, that God's "commandments are not grievous; that the law is holy, and the commandment holy, and just, and good." With these views of the divine will, "they go from strength to strength, their path being that of the just, which shineth more and more unto the perfect day."

Such, my brethren, is the non-conformity to this world enforced by the text, and such its fruits. Say, then, if there is not a most lamentable and ruinous difference between what we are and what we should be. Who is there that, like Enoch, "walks with God?" Who makes it his main study to be "conformed to the image of the first-born?" and inquires, conscientiously, into the state and progress of his conformity? Who "crucifies the old man with his deeds, the flesh with the affections and lusts?" If we were to judge from the appearance, and of professing Christians, we should certainly conclude that it is a part of their duty to be as unlike God and as like the world as possible. Look at their spirit; is it not the spirit of the world?—at their affections; are they not the affections of the world?—at their pursuit; are they not the pursuits of the world?—at their law of morals; is it not the world's law? Have they any better or higher motive or standard of conduct than the prevailing fashion? Away with evasion! Come to the matter of fact. How do you stand with respect to the law of God?—to the active faith of our Lord Jesus Christ? that faith which purifies the heart, and which works by love? Why do you turn pale at the thoughts of death? Why shiver with terror in the prospect of the judgment-seat and the judicial process? To a Christian actively engaged in his vocation, the "appearing of the Great God our Saviour" ought to be and is a "blessed hope." Why does the very idea of it fill you with trepidation? Ah! my dear friends, be assured all is not right. There is something rotten and ruinous in your condition, and must be rectified if you would have a hope that shall not put you to shame. Rouse up, all ye who have any regard for your heavenly Master! Rouse up in his strength! shake off your indolence and the entanglements which enwrap you! Many of you are convinced, that to your own peace and to your Redeemer's glory it is necessary that the distance between you and the mere people of the world be greatly widened. Stifle not convictions while you repress the urgencies of duty. Do what the heathen sage advised a young man to do, dare—dare to snap your trammels—dare to be singular—dare to "obey God rather than man." You will lose nothing either of comfort or of dignity. "The peace of God which passeth all understanding will keep your hearts and minds in Christ Jesus." The ministering spirits will descend from on high to help and honour those who honour God. He will himself cast his compassionate and complacent regards upon you, and will abundantly sweeten all the mortifications which may be poured into your cup. Jesus hath said, "Where I am, there shall my servant be also." The full grace of which promise you shall enjoy in the ecstasy of your hearts when he shall take you to himself to be with him in safety; and you shall see the world with its gods, its glories, and its worshippers, consuming together in the last fire!

SERMON XX.

THE FOUNTAIN OF LIFE.

JOHN vii. 37.

"In the last day, that great day of the feast, Jesus stood and cried, saying, If any man thirst, let him come unto me and drink."

The blessed Jesus was ever employed in doing good. To save the souls of men was the benevolent purpose for which he came into our world, and which he continually prosecuted during the whole of his ministry. Love to our ruined race prompted him to leave the bosom of his Father, to empty himself of his glory, to become a man of sorrows and acquainted with grief. With all the tenderness of faultless humanity, he sympathized with even the bodily distresses of those whom he came to redeem, and lent a willing hand to their relief. But on their spiritual miseries his thoughts were principally set. Of these he saw perfectly the deadly nature and the alarming extent. To these he called perpetually the attention of men; for these he proclaimed himself a sovereign Physician, and offered freely his almighty aid. In this labour of love his life was spent. He omitted no opportunity of exercising it, and the same principle which animated all his kind and gracious actions, now leads him to Jerusalem at the feast of tabernacles.

This feast, which God ordained to commemorate the travels of his people in the wilderness, where they dwelt in tents or tabernacles, was one of the three solemn occasions on which all the males of Israel were obliged to appear before God at Jerusalem. Accordingly, vast multitudes resorted thither from every part of the land. The city, and especially the temple, was thronged. On the eighth, which was the last and greatest day of the feast "it was customary for the priests to surround the altar with their palm-branches, and to pour out water in the temple, as an expression of the general desire of the Messiah's appearance, and the pouring forth of the Spirit by him." The Redeemer seized this occasion of claiming publicly the honours of his character, and inviting the Jews to faith in his name. He ascends a small eminence from which he might command a view of the people, and be himself both seen and heard. How august the scene! Was there ever such an assembly and such a minister? The incarnate God preaches to the tribes of Israel! How awful and venerable his aspect! What majesty and love beam from his countenance! What grace flows from his lips! Be still every tumult! be hushed every unhallowed passion! be collected all wandering thoughts, while the Saviour speaks! "Look," says he, "from ordinances to the God of ordinances—from the symbol to the thing signified. Behold in me the accomplishment of the prophetic promise, 'The Lord whom ye seek, shall come into his temple suddenly, even the Angel of the covenant whom ye delight in.' Are you longing for the Messiah promised to the fathers? I that speak unto you am he. Do your thirsty souls need to be refreshed by the waters of the sanctuary? I am the Fountain of life. 'If any man thirst let him come unto me and drink.'" Happy nation! had they known their privileges when the Lord of the temple was present in the temple and explained his own institutions!

But we must not confine to the Jews the Saviour's grace. To all who enjoy the gospel he offers the same invitation. To us he cries, and we are warned not to turn away from him that speaketh from heaven; to every one of us he cries, "If any man thirst, let him come unto me and drink!"

How rich, how free, how adorable his grace is, will appear from considering the persons invited, and the invitation itself.

I. Let us attend to the persons invited. They are the thirsty.

No man can be so senseless as to imagine that the Redeemer speaks of a bodily thirst. He is addressing sinners on the things which belong to their eternal peace, and as that great Prophet whom the Lord God had promised to raise up in the midst of Israel. The meaning of his language must, therefore, correspond with the importance of his object, and the dignity of his character. His words undoubtedly relate to the state of men's souls, and suppose that there is in the minds of those with whom he is dealing, an uneasiness and anxiety analogous to that painful sensation which arises from extreme thirst. The strong terms in which this state of mind is characterized, have induced the current opinion, an opinion adopted indeed, though very negligently, by even great and good men, that the Lord Jesus here invites none but such as are thirsting after an interest in his everlasting righteousness. How many of those who, driven from every other hope, were endeavouring to fix their trembling eye upon the Redeemer's atonement, have heard as a sentence denounced in thunder against them, this interpretation of the text! "Alas! I fear that I have not the spiritual thirst which is here required, and am therefore excluded from the gracious warrant," has often been the language of exercised people. These are certainly included, but they may not monopolize the warrant: and in truth they are frequently the first to decline it, as not belonging to them. If the words imply anything, they imply that those who have never yet drunk of the water of life, which is in Christ as in a fountain, may come and drink. But surely, they who have learned the vanity of every portion but a reconciled God—who have learned that it is Christ Jesus alone by whom the reconciliation is effected—who have learned to renounce every refuge of lies, and count all things but loss and dung that they may win Christ, and be found in him, not having their own righteousness, are already quickened by the Spirit of grace and truth; have already been refreshed from the fountain of living waters. While, therefore, the text encourages such to apply continually to the fulness of the Redeemer, let us not restrict its freedom by appropriating it to them alone. Christ does not say, " If any man thirst for righteousness—for deliverance from the guilt and power of sin—for communion and fellowship with God, let him come unto me or else let him stay back;" but simply, and in the most unqualified manner, " If any man thirst, let him come unto me and drink." Is it necessary to prove, that there is in mankind, universally, a principle which brings them all within the compass of the gracious offer? The fact is as clear as noonday. They all thirst, and insatiably too, they thirst for happiness. This, indeed, is a propensity congenial to the soul, and coeval with its existence. It was implanted in man when God "breathed into his nostrils the breath of life." It was intended to answer the most exalted end, by leading him perpetually to God, the uncreated source of bliss. When he fell, the propensity remained, but the direction was lost. The moment man left the way of God and duty, he left the way of peace and joy. His understanding is so blinded that he knows not how to find it again. His strength is so enfeebled that he is unable to remeasure his steps, to remount the heights of glory from which he fell—and his will and affections are so depraved, that he is not more unable than unwilling to return. From this sad condition of doubt, disquietude, helplessness, and misery, his thirst for happiness impels him to flee. He gropes, he struggles: but he gropes at midnight. He struggles with obstacles which he can neither remove nor surmount. Bewildered in the dreary mazes of an inextricable labyrinth, without light to cheer, without a clue to guide him, he wanders from creature to creature; and after all his labour and all his toil, finds himself as far as ever from the object of his wishes. Deplorable situation! He can do nothing but tread the same insipid, lifeless, hopeless track. Fainting with thirst, he can find nothing to revive his drooping spirit, nothing to cool the fever of his tongue. Utterly ignorant of God and his consolations, he knows not where or how to obtain that grace which alone can relieve him from his trouble. But his necessities are not silent. Ten thousand wants lift up their voices, and send their cry to the very heavens. Pitiable, my brethren, is the note of wo: and so importunate was the entreaty of human wretchedness, that the Son of God, out of pure compassion, left the throne of his glory, and clothed himself with mortality, that he might apply a remedy to our otherwise incurable evils, and deliver us from becoming the victims of eternal death. In consequence of what he has done and suffered, he has opened a fountain of living waters, and invites all poor sinners, who are perishing with thirst, whether they believe it or not, to come and drink. That you may be more firmly convinced of this delightful truth, turn to the beginning of the fifty-fifth chapter of Isaiah's prophecy, and there you will see that a similar invitation is extended to every one who hears the gospel, even though he totally disregards the great salvation which it reveals. "Ho, every one that thirsteth, come ye to the waters, and he that hath no money; come ye, buy, and eat; yea, come, buy wine and milk," the choicest blessings, "without money and without price," without merit or recommendation. Mark what follows. "Wherefore do ye spend money for that which is not bread? and your labour for that which satisfieth not?" Do they, who are seeking Christ Jesus, spend their time, and their talents, and their labour, in pursuing vanity? Assuredly not! There cannot be a more exact description of those who seek everything else but Christ; and, therefore, he adds, with infinite tenderness, "Hearken diligently unto me, and eat ye that which is good, and let your soul delight itself in fatness." And in the same unlimited manner he speaks in the text, "If any man thirst, let him come unto me and drink."

Having seen who are the persons invited, let us now attend,

II. To the invitation itself.

Since human misery was designated by the metaphorical term, thirst, the remedy to that misery is very properly exhibited under the idea of drinking. The command of Christ is, therefore, nothing else than a command to receive from him all the happiness our souls can wish. As if he had said, "Miserable men, who are searching for happiness, but have missed the way, expect not from the creature that solid and permanent enjoyment which is to be found in the Creator alone; quit the broken cisterns which can hold no water; come to me; I only am the portion of the immortal soul; my fulness is abundantly adequate to gratify your largest wishes; come, take, taste, drink, and live for ever. "He that believeth on me," as the Scripture hath said, "out of his belly shall flow rivers of living water."

Without insisting on a number of remarks which naturally occur on this copious and interesting subject, let us direct our attention to the following important truths, that are plainly inculcated in the text. That Christ Jesus requires perishing men to place their confidence in him only. That his salvation is exactly fitted to their necessities—and that it is freely offered.

1. Christ Jesus requires perishing men to place their confidence in him alone.

It is a principle uniformly taught in the Scriptures—a principle which cannot dwell too frequently upon our recollections, nor too powerfully affect our hearts—that the great Redeemer is the only hope of sinners, and therefore in this, as well as in every other invitation of the gospel, he keeps out of sight every thing but his glorious self. The new covenant is so constituted, that let men view it in any direction they think proper, the first object which meets their eyes is the divine Head of the covenant; and of all the blessings with which this covenant abounds, though immense in their magnitude, infinite in their number, inestimable in their value, the soul can neither enjoy nor see any, till faith not only look but enter through Christ the door. Accordingly, the chief and favourite theme of the gospel is the Lord Jesus. Mark his own invitation in the passage before us. What instructions does he give to poor sinners who are dying with thirst? Does he bid them first to drink as much as they can from the polluted waters they may have in themselves, and if they be not then satisfied, to come to him and supply the deficiency? Or, to strip the text of metaphor, does he bid them do what they can to obey the divine law, and when they find their righteousness inadequate to answer its high demand, to come to him and receive from his righteousness so much as will make up the defect of their own, and render the compound an oblation worthy of God's acceptance? No such thing! Christ declares to men their misery; he declares himself their Saviour, and not a syllable do we hear of their own righteousness. This indeed is a doctrine very unpalatable to the unrenewed nature, and rouses into opposition all the enmity of the carnal heart. But it is among the first lessons in the divine life, and if we do not effectually learn it, all our other learning is of trifling moment. Little do sinners know the indignity they offer to the Son of God, and the injury they do to their own souls by endeavouring to associate themselves with him in the work of their redemption. Brethren, deceive not yourselves. Christ will not give his glory to another. He will not share with you the honour of your salvation. He must have all the praise, or he will have none. You must depend entirely on him or entirely on yourselves. Christ is the way, and the only way to the Father and to everlasting life. You must be either wholly in this way or wholly out of it. There is no medium. You cannot combine the old and new covenants, and climb to heaven partly by one and partly by the other. If you please yourselves with such an idea, shame and destruction will be the end of your hope. Foolish men! Abandon the vain attempt!

You must tear Jehovah from his throne before you succeed. And what do you intend by this mad behaviour? Is not the righteousness of Christ sufficient? Is it not perfect? Is it not spotless? Do you think that this glorious robe cannot beautify, nor cover, nor secure you, unless it be patched with the filthy rags of your own righteousness? If the Lord Jesus will adorn you with his righteousness, you may well part with your own, and you will be infinite gainers by the exchange; for,

2. His salvation is exactly fitted to your necessities.

In forming an estimate of these necessities, we may not credit the report of our own hearts, for they are "deceitful above all things, and desperately wicked." We must appeal from their partial sentence to the judgment of "the law and the testimony." Now what account does the divine Word give of men in a natural state? It represents them as spiritually dead—as covered with defilement and loathsomeness—as far from God and hope—as unfruitful in righteousness, and, in consequence of these things, like briars and thorns, whose end is to be burned. What eye that looks back upon the original beauty, and dignity, and bliss of man, and surveys the dread havoc that sin has made, can refuse a tear over the ruins of our pristine glory? What eye that looks around, and sees no arm to deliver from these depths of disgrace and woe, will refuse a flood of tears at the gloomy prospect? But let the sigh of anguish be turned into the shout of joy, for Jesus the deliverer comes, and salvation, complete, everlasting salvation, is in his hand.

He saves from spiritual death. "And you hath he quickened," says the apostle, "who were dead in trespasses and sins." "The hour is coming," said he to the Jews, "and now is, when the dead shall hear the voice of the Son of God, and they that hear shall live." He sends forth his Holy Spirit and breathes upon the dry bones, and flesh and sinews come upon them, and life enters into them, and they stand up upon their feet. He gives them to drink of the river of the water of life, not merely a temporary draught, which may relieve them for a moment and fail them hereafter, but imparts it in such abundance that they never again thirst. He bestows upon them that precious faith which unites them inseparably to himself, and forms a channel through which streams from his fulness flow perpetually into them, and flow so copiously as to send forth from themselves rivers of living water.

Farther, Christ Jesus not only quickens but sanctifies. Sanctification is indispensably necessary to fit us for seeing the Lord, for relishing the employments of heaven. But ah! how polluted is the unrenewed soul! Hear how Jehovah himself describes it:— " As for thy nativity, in the day thou wast born thy navel was not cut, neither wast thou washed in water to supple thee; neither wast thou salted at all, nor swaddled at all—but thou wast cast out in the open field to the loathing of thy person." (Ezek. xvi. 4, 5.) And there mightest thou have lain and perished for ever, had not the Redeemer had compassion on thee. Yet even from this pollution mayest thou be washed in the fountain opened for sin and uncleanness. The Lord God has promised to all who credit his testimony respecting his Son, " I will sprinkle clean water upon you, and you shall be clean from all your filthiness, and from all your idols will I cleanse you." But this purifying water can be obtained only in Christ Jesus. All who are now in glory, without a single exception, " washed their robes and made them white in the blood of the Lamb." Here too must you be washed or you must die. 'Tis the unchangeable decree of an unchanging God. And be not discouraged. The diseases of the soul, though terrible beyond conception, are not so noisome and inveterate as to baffle the healing energy of this sacred fountain. The blood of Jesus cleanses from all sin, and it can cleanse from yours, though it equalled the united pollutions of all the redeemed who ever lived or shall live hereafter.

By performing in our favour such miracles of mercy, our Almighty Friend restores us to the divine image and approbation—brings us near to God, and inspires us with the sweet hope of everlasting life. Holiness is the divine image, and God must love what is like himself. True, our highest earthly attainments are stained with many a blot, and cannot abide the severe scrutiny of Him who chargeth his very angels with folly. But personal holiness, though it forms the lineaments of the divine image on the soul, and is our qualification for heaven, is not our title to it. This is the imputed righteousness of our Redeemer. We have nothing to do with God but in Jesus Christ, neither has God as a God of mercy any thing to do with us but in Jesus Christ, and we are complete in him. In his righteousness, and therefore in his people's righteousness, not even Jehovah's eye can discern a blemish.

Thus, in receiving him by faith, we who once were afar off are brought nigh by the blood of his cross—nigh in the acceptance of our persons with God—nigh to him as a reconciled Father—nigh in fellowship and communion with him. We have boldness and confidence in approaching his throne of grace, for every step in our way to the mercy-seat is sprinkled with the blood of our great Paschal Lamb; and shielded by the faithfulness of him who cannot lie, we are perfectly safe from the blow of the destroying angel. Tell me, ye who are strangers to the Saviour, how do you expect to obtain access to the living God? Lay the word of truth before you—lay your hands upon your hearts—listen to the monitor within, and say, is not the plan which brings you near by Christ Jesus, a glorious plan? Children of deception, who look for this privilege from any other quarter, be assured that if God is true, your "hope shall be as the spider's web," and your "confidence shall lead you to the king of terrors."

But to those who trust in his merit and grace, the kindness of our great High Priest goes still farther. He does not only quicken and sanctify their souls and bring them near to God, he also frees them from the reproach of unfruitfulness.

The human heart is naturally a dry, a barren, a rocky soil—not one heavenly temper, not one good disposition, can flourish there. All the graces of the divine life are plants of foreign growth. They are rooted in the soul *by* none but Jehovah the Spirit, and *in* none but those whom he savingly unites to the Lord Jesus. Here again we see see the fitness of Christ's salvation to our wants. Is there present, a sinner whose heart is so hard and barren that not one holy thought can spring from it? Thus runs the rich promise, "I will pour water upon him that is thirsty, and floods upon the dry ground. I will pour my spirit upon thy seed, and my blessing upon thine offspring; and they shall spring up as among the grass, and as willows by the water-courses." (Is. xliv. 3, 4.) Let the heart be hard, let it be stubborn and impenetrable as the flint, the streams which issue from the fountain opened for the house of David pierce and soften and fructify the most unyielding and barren soil. Then faith and all the kindred graces strike deep their roots, spread wide their branches, unfold their blossoms, diffuse their fragrance, and bear much fruit to the glory of God. Nor is this an honour and a happiness of short duration. The righteous do not resemble those plants of rapid growth, which start almost immediately from the seed into maturity, and as quickly fade and die. They are like the palm-tree, stately, majestic, permanent—like trees planted by the rivers of water, which bring forth their fruit in their season, and whose leaf doth not wither. Thus they continue, ripening by grace for glory, till Christ transplant them into the paradise of God. Here, therefore, let me introduce the last remark on the fitness of his salvation.

It was observed, that in consequence of their guilt, their pollution, their distance from God, and their unfruitfulness, sinners are like briers and thorns whose end is to be burned. Dreadful idea! "Who can dwell with devouring flames? Who can dwell with everlasting burnings?" This is all we can expect on our own account, yet from this tremendous fate the salvation of Christ, and that alone, can deliver us. The moment we draw the breath of life, the curse of a violated law seizes and binds us with chains too strong for the might of all the angels in heaven, and reserves us as criminals for the day of slaughter. But our great Redeemer bursts these chains, looses this iron grasp, sets the captives at liberty, and puts into their mouths a song of triumph. Faith in his precious atonement is not only connected with the important blessings that have been mentioned, but secures to their happy possessors an unfailing title to eternal joy. For by this faith we have " our fruit unto holiness, and the end everlasting life." Christ cannot disappoint the hope of them who trust in him, and he hath said, " Whosoever believeth on me hath everlasting life, and I will raise him up at the last day. Who, then, shall lay anything to the charge of God's elect? Shall God that justifieth? Who is he that condemneth? Is it Christ that died? Yea rather that is risen again, who also sitteth at the right hand of God." Reprobate the suspicion, and be persuaded that " neither death, nor life, nor angels, nor principalities, nor powers, nor height, nor depth, nor any other creature, shall be able to separate believers from the love of God which is in Christ Jesus our Lord."

Adorable salvation! Who would not wish to partake of it? Who would not exult in the faintest dawn of hope that they *may* partake of it? "But what shall we give, what shall we do, to purchase an interest in it?" Give! Do! Misguided men! Nothing. It is not only treasured up in Christ Jesus—it is not only adapted in the most glorious fitness to all your wants, but, in the 3d. Place, It is *free*, absolutely free. And bless God that it is so. Did it require anything to be merited on our part, we might bid an eternal adieu to heaven and happiness. The salvation of Christ cannot be deserved. Infinitely precious, its value surpasses all desert. Every thing about it is infinite. It saves from infinite guilt, infinite pollution, infinite wrath, and infinite wretchedness. It confers on all who enjoy it, infinite dignity and infinite bliss. All the works of all sinful men, from the beginning to the end of time, could not merit the smallest portion of it. The best services of the unregenerate are iniquity, and deserve to be "punished with everlasting destruction from the presence of the Lord, and from the glory of his power." If you are resolved to merit at the hand of God, you shall get, indeed, what you merit; but it will be in hell. The new covenant has no conditions to be performed by us. These were fulfilled by Christ the Mediator. It is, therefore, to us a covenant of grace. But if you think that you must merit something to put you in possession of its blessings, you change its very nature—you transform it immediately into a covenant of works, and then, as the apostle says, "grace is no more grace."—"But must we not repent before we may come to Christ?" No! you can never repent as you ought, till you be interested in his love, and influenced by his Spirit. The tears of true repentance flow from the eye of faith. "They shall look on me whom they have pierced, and shall mourn."

"Are we, then, to be furnished with no qualifications that may fit us for receiving the gospel salvation?" None but the utter want of every good quality. Christ Jesus "came not to call the righteous;" he did not expect to find men so; he expected to find them "altogether filthy," and therefore he came to call "sinners to repentance." Tell me, ye who strive to wed the covenant of works with the grace of the gospel, if a man were lying, panting, fainting, dying with thirst, so feeble that he could not move a limb to help himself, and if some kind friend were to carry him to a pure and wholesome stream, and to put the water to his lips, would he merit anything by drinking it? 'Tis just so, brethren, with the salvation of Christ. Unconnected with him you must perish! And you are so far from being able to do anything to merit an interest in the blessings of his purchase, that you cannot perform a single action which will be honoured with the approbation of God, till you drink of the water of life, and your souls be invigorated by its quickening efficacy.

These, my friends, are important truths; and in bringing them by a close application home to your own consciences, the first question that occurs is, Have you drunk of these living waters which are in Christ Jesus? Too many of you, I fear, if they will act honestly, must reply, that till this hour they have never tasted them. With such of you, my brethren, I have some weighty business. God sent you into this world to glorify him: and as you are sinners, he requires you to glorify him by believing the record he has given of his Son, and securing your happiness by thus obeying his will. Has this been your employment? Far, very far from it. You must have been seeking happiness, indeed, with the most unwearied perseverance. But have you found it? Your conduct declares that you have not. Why else, ye young, ye giddy and ye gay, why this perpetual round of amusement and vanity? Why do ye run from one enjoyment to another, and studiously avoid conversing with yourselves? Why labour to outstrip, in a race of folly, the close pursuit of a vexing conscience? Why endeavour to banish from your minds every settled thought about an eternal world? Is it not because that world wears a gloomy appearance, because all beyond the grave is dreary and cheerless? Ye young, ye giddy, and ye gay, be faithful to yourselves. Lay your hands upon your hearts, and own the truth. Have you not sometimes felt in your own souls, a vacuum which all your amusements could not fill? Has it not sometimes happened, even in your most heedless moments, that reflection—an unbidden and unwelcome guest—has stolen into your bosoms, and whispered the alarming suggestion, that all is not right? Is it not this which makes the idea of God, eternity, heaven, and hell, to trouble you? Is it not this which sheds a freezing terror through your souls? Or are you so benumbed as never to be conscious of such emotions? God grant that you may awaken from this deadly sleep before you open your eyes in that place of torment where the Lord hath forgotten to be gracious, and where his tender mercies are shut up in his wrath.

And you, who, more advanced in years, are sick of the frolic of youth, and plunge with ardour into the busy scenes of active life, has happiness taken up her abode in your breasts? If strangers to the Redeemer, you cannot say so. Why else strive to join house to house, and field to field? Why form plan after plan, and scheme after scheme, to augment your wealth, and honours, and grandeur, in the hope of more complete and contented enjoyment? why be so dejected at the failure of your projects or at the other ills of life, and seek in the gratification of sense relief from the gnawings of an anxious mind? Your acknowledgment may not correspond with the language of the fact, but the fact speaks truly, and declares plainly that the acquisitions of manhood are as unable to satisfy the soul as the trifles of early days. Do not pretend that you labour only for future days, nor flatter yourselves with the expectation of spending quietly, and peaceably, and happily, the evening of your age. To old age be our appeal. Say, hoary sinner, who hast passed through youth and riper years, and approached the confines of eternity, where is thy happiness? The turbulence of passion may have subsided—the vexations of active business may be over—and in these respects you may possess a tranquillity. But if the turbulence of passion has subsided, if the vexations of active business are over, the capacity of enjoyment is also gone. State, then, fairly, both sides of the question, and you will find that you have nothing left. What now strengthens the feeble knees and lifts up the hands that hang down! When the grasshopper is become a burden—when the shadows of the night grow large and long—when the sprightliness of youth has vanished and the vigour of manhood failed—when the king of terrors lifts his unerring arm and threatens to strike the blow which will shatter to atoms thy clay tabernacle, and hurry its lingering inhabitant to the tribunal of God—what revives the fainting spirit? The streams of earthly consolation are already dried up, and wilt thou yet hug to thy bosom, with unavailing fondness, the wretched remnants of its fleeting joy? "O more than sottish!" Be persuaded, all of you who are unacquainted with the gospel, to abandon the hope of finding happiness in created comforts. You are perpetually disappointed, and yet continue to deceive yourselves by imagining that if you miss your object here, you will meet it yonder. But when you arrive at the longed-for spot, the airy phantom eludes your embrace and mocks your hope. But do not blame the creature nor think I mean to blame it. The creature is your friend. The creature bears a testimony for God. Eternal truth has told you, that nothing below can be a suitable portion for the immortal soul; and that when you betake yourselves to the creature in this view, you flee to "a refuge of lies." All the creatures re-echo the important monition, and loudly cry, "It is not in us!" Quit then, quit immediately these "broken cisterns, which can hold no water." Haste with the speed of men who know that eternal glory is the depending stake—haste to Jesus, "the Fountain of living waters." Here "taste and see that the Lord is good."

Ye young, ye giddy, and ye gay, listen to the voice of the great Redeemer, who tenderly invites you to the heavenly draught. The water which *He* gives will effectually quench that fearful thirst which must afflict you whilst you are unacquainted with his grace. It will abundantly repay every sacrfice he requires you to make; for it will be in you "a well of water springing up to everlasting life," and he requires you to renounce nothing but what is really your misery and will prove your ruin. Not only the Word of God asserts, the experience of ages also demonstrates, that "Wisdom's ways are ways of pleasantness, and all her paths peace." Ask the Christian and he will inform you, that, let the devil, and the world, and the corrupt heart say what they will, there is, beyond all controversy, "peace and joy in believing."

Let those who are in middle age reflect seriously on the indispensable necessity and inestimable value of this water of life. My friends, you must drink or you must perish, and the salvation of Christ Jesus will not only secure your own souls, but will extend its divine influence to every circumstance and every relation. Are you blest with comforts? This is the embalmer of joy. Are you harassed with anxious solicitude? This is the sweetener of care. Are you visited with trials? This is the cordial of affliction. Is the favour of God the truest dignity and only bliss of man? This will wash you from all your pollution, and render you fair in his sight. O shut not your eyes upon your own mercies! "Now is the accepted time, now is the day of salvation."—"To-day if ye will hear his voice harden not your hearts."

Are there here any old persons who have never embraced the glorious Saviour? My brethren, your guilt is great, and as your glass is almost run, your day of grace cannot be long. Yet even you, who are at the eleventh hour, are entreated to come and drink of the water of life. You have much reason to be terribly alarmed, but none to despair. The rich warrant proclaims, "whosoever will, let him come." Start from your stupid lethargy and flee at this critical moment to the Saviour of souls. He can save even you, for his grace is sovereign, and it is almighty. If you cast yourselves upon it, all shall yet be well. You are come near to that dread valley, where burning sands swallow up the shallow rivulets of earthly comfort. But the streams that flow from our Rock, Christ, will follow you through these sands—will accompany you into the dark and dreary vale of the shadow of death—will support, and strengthen, and cheer your spirits, till you arrive in safety and triumph at the celestial Canaan.

Is any one saying, in the bitterness of his soul, "Oh that I could obtain a draught of this divine, this living water! I see, I feel, that all the creatures, though well suited to answer the end for which they were given, are too gross in their nature, too limited in their extent, and too short in their duration, to satisfy my vast desires. I see that sin has ruined me, that I cannot help myself, and that without Christ I am lost forever. O that he would visit me with his mercy!" Are these your views, your fears, your wishes? Then to you, in a peculiar manner, is the word of this salvation sent. If Christ has made you sick of sin, it is the most pleasing symptom that he has begun to draw you to himself; and you may soon find, to your unspeakable joy, that he has drawn you much farther than you can now believe. It is the sweet pledge that he will send his word and heal you, that he will set you in a large place, and enable you to shout the praises of your redeeming God. Be not discouraged by your weakness, for a "bruised reed he will not break, and smoking flax he will not quench, till he send forth judgment unto victory." Let not your guilt terrify you, for "though your sins be as scarlet, they shall be white as snow; though they be red like crimson, they shall be as wool." Think not the stain of your filthiness too deep to be washed out, for "the blood of Jesus cleanseth from all sin."—"Fear not, only believe." Throw yourself upon his sovereignty, lay hold upon his promise, "Him that cometh to me, I will in no wise cast out." Say not, "I would, but cannot, hold fast of the promise." Your own ability is out of the question. You are not to consider what *you* can do, but what *Christ* can do. None embrace the gospel offer but they whom he enables to do it; and whenever a poor sinner stretches out his frail trembling hand towards the free promise, Christ incloses it in his own hand, and clasps it round the promise in so firm a grasp, that neither earth, nor death, nor hell can ever loose it. "Trust," then, "in the Lord forever, for in this Lord Jehovah there is everlasting strength; and they who believe on him shall never be confounded."

Finally. Let all the disciples of Jesus, who have been drinking at the fountain of living waters, be careful not to undervalue their privilege, nor to throw contempt upon its adorable Author. Christians, have you, as the children of God, free access to the pure streams of uncreated bliss; and will you so injure your own souls, and dishonour your Redeemer, as to grovel in the polluted and poisonous waters of sinful pleasure? Shrink with horror from the idea! Have you, as the children of God, free access to all the fulness which is treasured up in Christ Jesus, and will you ever be at a loss where to apply for the relief of your wants? Let it be your study to improve this unspeakable gift of God. His nature, his attributes, his names, his covenant, his promises, his ordinances, are to his people so many "wells of salvation," and their faith is never rightly employed, but in drawing water from them. The graces of the divine Spirit cannot divinely grow unless they be divinely cherished. The new creature is of heavenly birth, and must be nourished with heavenly food. As well might you expect that an infant should advance to youth, to manhood, to age, without continual supplies of provision, as that you should grow from babes, to men and fathers in Christ, without the perpetual aids of his Spirit and grace. Why do Christians become languid and faint? Why do they yield to temptation? Why are they vanquished by indwelling sin? It is because they so unfrequently visit the fountain of living waters. Let us learn, my brethren, to live not so much upon what we have received, as upon what Christ has to give. "Be strong," says the apostle, not in the grace which is in yourselves, but "in the grace which is in Christ Jesus." Relying upon his all-sufficiency, we shall find that "they who wait on the Lord," and they only, "shall renew their strength; they shall mount up with wings as eagles; they shall run, and not be weary; they shall walk and not faint."

SERMON XXI.

THE GOSPEL OFFER.

JOHN vi. 37.

" Him that cometh to me, I will in no wise cast out."

These words are part of a most interesting discourse which our Lord addressed to a number of his hearers, whom, shortly before, he had miraculously fed. Highly delighted with such an abundant, cheap, and seasonable supply, when they were worn out with fatigue, and fainting through hunger, and hoping, it seems, to be again feasted, by the repetition of the miracle, they soon renewed their visit to the Saviour. The Lord Jesus immediately saw, (for how could Omniscience not see?) the baseness of the principle by which they were actuated. "Ye seek me," said he, "not because ye saw the miracles, but because ye did eat of the loaves and were filled." Not because your souls were lost in astonishment at the power, and your hearts melted with the love, of God, displayed in my ministration, but because your animal senses were gratified. My brethren, would to God there were not ground to fear that many who now profess the name of Christ, are governed by no better motives.

The Redeemer, however, who lost no opportunity of doing good, did not neglect to improve the present occasion. After discovering to these people his profound knowledge of their hearts, he leads their views from temporal to eternal things—from anxiety about their bodies, to concern for their souls. Under the metaphor of bread, he opens up his mediatorial character and office, illustrates the spiritual nature of his salvation, and strongly inculcates their absolute need of it. The farther he advances in his important instructions, the closer he brings his doctrine to their consciences. Having pointedly charged them with unbelief, that he might at once alarm their fears, and humble their pride, he solemnly tells them, "All that the Father giveth me shall come to me;" and to encourage their hopes, he adds, "Him that cometh to me, I will in no wise cast out." Can tongue express, can heart conceive, the glory, the riches, of this precious promise? On this promise, many who are now singing the song of Moses and the Lamb, once hung their fainting spirits, and it carried them safely through guilt, through temptation, through death. Is its freedom restrained? or its grace diminished? or the power of the Promiser abridged? No. It is made by the same Saviour, to the same kind of sinners, and conveys the same invaluable blessings. It holds up to the most daring offender, who will avail himself of the offer, a free, a full, an irrevocable pardon. It infolds in its spacious bosom all the benefits of the everlasting covenant—all that man can receive, or God bestow. Can any human heart remain insensible to such wondrous condescension? Can you hear with indifference, that Jesus, the Prince of life, the Lord of glory, stoops so low as to present such sweet invitations to the chief of sinners? O that "He who has the key of David, who openeth and no man shutteth, and shutteth and no man openeth," would send forth his light upon those truths which will demand your attention, while we inquire what is meant by coming to Christ, and endeavour to unfold the annexed promise.

I. We are to inquire what is meant by coming to Christ.

To come to Christ is, in general, to believe in him; and to believe in him is to "receive and rest upon him alone for salvation as he is offered in the gospel."

This coming to Christ supposes several things.

1. That we are by nature strangers from God, and feel the misery of our destiny. While our first parents continued in their integrity, they were honoured with free access to their Creator; but the breach of their fidelity ruined this divine privilege, and produced in their minds an alienation from their God. His righteous judgment made their choice their punishment, prohibiting them from that intercourse with himself which they laboured to

shun; and the flaming sword of the cherubim, and what is more terrible, "the decree of justice," barred up forever all approach to Jehovah by the old covenant. That this is our forlorn condition, and that there is no possibility of approach to God acceptably but by the new and living way which the Redeemer has opened, the very nature of his mission and his earnest invitation declare. Approaching to God by Jesus Christ supposes that we feel our distance from him, and farther, that we feel the misery of our estrangement. I need not tell you that when Adam fell he lost not only his dignity but his happiness. His mind, which was filled with light, serenity, innocence, bliss, and joy, became the abode of darkness, inquietude, guilt, wretchedness, and sorrow. He has transmitted to us the doleful inheritance. Offenders in our offending parent, "we are by nature children of wrath." By losing the favour of God we lost our all; we were degraded from his children and friends into the children and drudges of the devil. The temple of the Lord of hosts is converted into a den of thieves. A crowd of fiends, attended by every vile and hateful affection, has entered the soul of man. Enmity against God headed the gang, and the standard of rebellion is erected in that very spot which was once the palace of the King of kings. Can such a state be happy? Can it possibly not be miserable? God is the pure and only source of blessedness, and woe and death are as invariably the effects of distance from him, as darkness and cold, of distance from the sun. But a considerable part of man's misery is, that his apostacy has blinded his eyes and deadened his sensibility. He sees not that sin has robbed him of his beauty in defacing the image of his God. He sees not that sin has obliterated his fair title to eternal life. He feels not that sin, like a venomous reptile, is gnawing his vitals and infusing a mortal poison. These things, however, he must know, or he will not, he cannot, come to Jesus Christ. It is his office to save sinners, and to save *from* sin. But surely they who discern neither danger in the state nor deformity in the character of a sinner, and who roll sin itself "as a sweet morsel under their tongues," will not, while under the influence of such views, think the gospel salvation any favour. Nobody, who is not conscious of a disease, will thank you for a remedy. It is, therefore, the first work of the Holy Spirit to convince of sin. In this work he rouses the conscience from its torpitude—he quickens the soul into life—he opens the eyes that were shut in spiritual death—he unmasks the sinner to himself—but ah! how great the alteration! Like a palsied limb, which, on the recovery of health, feels the acutest pangs shoot through every nerve, the sinner now finds himself inconceivably wretched. He finds himself under the curse of a broken covenant, and therefore exposed to the vengeance of an angry God, exposed to the horrors of everlasting ruin. As the human mind is engaged in a perpetual search after happiness, the first question on such a discovery will be, how shall I escape the destruction which threatens me? It is more than probable that, unacquainted as yet with the wiles of Satan and the deceitfulness of his own heart, a person in this condition will betake himself to the law, which in its original form said, " Do and live," and try to help himself by his " good works." He will form resolutions of amendment, and fondly hope to atone for the folly and guilt of his past, by the wisdom and sanctity of his future conduct. But if the Lord intend to be gracious to him, he will not be allowed to trust in that "refuge of lies." The Holy Spirit will show him that if he stop there, he is undone forever; and therefore coming to Jesus Christ supposes,

2. A sense of our utter inability to assist ourselves.

Under the divine instruction men learn wonderful lessons. The sinner had been convinced that he was guilty, he is now carried a step farther, and sees that he is filthy. His eyes are turned inwards upon his heart, and he is made acquainted with facts of which he had not the least suspicion, when he was told by the divine word, he would not believe what is proved to be too true, "that he is all as an unclean thing"—that his "very righteousness," as he had simply imagined them, "are as filthy rags"—that his heart is a nest of abominations, "a cage of unclean and hateful birds." His loathsomeness in his own sight and in the sight of a holy God, who is "of purer eyes than to behold iniquity," added to his danger, renders him doubly miserable. He gets a glimpse of the infinite evil of sin. He is sensible that nothing short of a spotless obedience to the divine law will be accepted by the Lawgiver. He is sensible, too, that a satisfaction must be made for the innumerable instances in which he has violated its precepts. What can he do? Were he to obey perfectly hereafter, all his obedience is a *debt*. There is no surplus to satisfy for past offences.

But instead of giving perfect obedience, he is incapable of performing *one* acceptable action. Sin is so mingled with all he does, that his best deeds, the incense of his purest offerings, are "a smoke in Jehovah's nostrils." And to put the finishing stroke to his self-confidence, he is obliged to subscribe the humiliating doctrine which tells him, that the broken law spreads its broad curse over his very righteousness. In the anguish which these views must excite, no wonder that he despairs of helping himself—no wonder that he is troubled and terrified with the apprehension of a God absolute and unreconciled. He can enter into the spirit of that passionate exclamation, "What shall I do to be saved?" The business, however, is not finished. The Lord is tearing him from the old root, but has not yet ingrafted him into Christ the living Vine. He has hitherto looked only at the high demands of God's law, and his own unworthiness, weakness, and vileness; but he has not looked at the blessed Mediator. Coming to Jesus Christ supposes then,

3. A view of him as that very Saviour whom we need. When the soul is sinking under the weight of guilt, and every moment fears that the black cloud of divine wrath will burst over his devoted head, how reviving, how transporting the thought, that the "blood of Jesus Christ cleanseth from all sin!" This precious truth, my brethren, is the only thing which can revive the dying hope of a convinced sinner. A Saviour! Delightful sound! A Saviour who has made an atonement for sinners! May I depend upon this heavenly information? Yes, for "his blood cleanseth from all sin." What! from *all* sin? Will it cleanse from *my* sin? It will. In the mingled emotions of wonder and joy, a sinner cannot but long to be better acquainted with this celestial Friend. He opens the volume of inspiration, and there he obtains all the intelligence he can wish. He is told that in the glorious Redeemer there is a fulness to relieve every want. Does he find himself debarred by the flaming sword of justice from approaching to God by the old covenant? He is told that Jesus Christ is the new and living Way to the Father. Does he need a justifying righteousness? He is told that Jesus Christ has "brought in an everlasting righteousness." Nay, that he is himself "the Lord our righteousness." Does he need strength? He is told that Jesus Christ is the Lord our Strength also. Does he need to be purified from his pollution?

He is told that by pleading the merits of Jesus Christ he may expect the accomplishment of that gracious promise, "I will sprinkle clean water upon you, and you shall be clean; from all your filthiness and from all your idols will I cleanse you." Oh! my brethren, how does a sight of glorious Christ tarnish all other glory! It sickens a man to the covenant of works—it makes him say of the covenant of grace, of which Jesus Christ is the Surety and the Head, "It is well-ordered in all things and sure; it is all my salvation and all my desire." But as a bare sense of the suitableness of the Mediator is different from surrendering ourselves up to him, coming to Jesus Christ is,

In the last place, the rolling of our guilty souls, with all their vileness and all their unworthiness, upon his rich sovereign grace.

When a man, into whose mind God hath shined so as to give him an insight into the great things of which we have been discoursing, looks at himself and sees nothing but death there—when he looks at the law and sees nothing but death there—when he looks at the creature, and sees nothing but emptiness and barrenness and death there—when he looks at Jesus Christ and sees in him light, and life, and grace, and all the fulness of Deity, he cannot but say, in the prospect of going away from Christ, "Lord, to whom shall I go? thou hast the words of eternal life." He reasons as the lepers of old, "If I sit here, I die; if I go back, I shall die; if I push forward and make an experiment of his grace, I can but die." These exercises are the suggestions of the blessed Spirit. They terminate upon a *whole* Christ, upon Christ in all his offices. With these exercises, and with "the everlasting arms underneath him," the sinner casts himself down at the feet of Jesus. Happy, thrice happy they, whose souls are exalted into such humility—who willingly lay their honours in the dust, and set the crown upon the Redeemer's head. Nor is this the characteristic of a few; it is the common temper of all God's children—a temper which you must have, if you ever see his face in peace.

To prevent poor sinners from thus coming to the Saviour, Satan leaves nothing unattempted. When he cannot lull them any longer in a state of security, he commonly endeavours to persuade them that they have sinned away their day of grace, and that Christ will not receive them. But "he was a liar from the beginning." Fear not, trembling soul; impudent as he is, you may stop his mouth. He cannot, blessed be God, he cannot erase from your Bibles the gracious declaration of the text, "Him that cometh to me I will in no wise cast out." The unfolding of this promise is the

II. Topic to which your attention was invited.

"Him that cometh to me I will in no wise cast out," *i. e.* I will undoubtedly receive him. I will not cast him from me *now*. Whatever has been his past character—whatever the aggravations of his guilt—whatever are his present fears—whatever the temptations of Satan, I invite him to the arms of my love; I promise him a welcome reception.

This however is not all. Jesus will not only admit you into his favour *now*, but he will not cast you out of it *hereafter*. Those whom "he once loves he loves to the end." He gives to all his people "eternal life, and they shall never perish—no future backslidings, no provocations, will induce him to forsake them utterly. If they "break his statutes, and keep not his commandments, then will he indeed visit their transgressions with the rod and their iniquity with stripes." If, like refractory children, they attempt to run from home, he will scourge them back to their Father's house; but he administers his corrections with a parent's hand; he intends to teach them how bitter sin is—to make them live more by faith, and nearer himself. His chastisements are no proof that they have lost the privilege of their adoption, for "nevertheless," says he, "my loving kindness will I not utterly take from him, nor suffer my faithfulness to fail." And why not? Because of their good behaviour? That would be a dreary doctrine. Far otherwise. "My covenant," he adds, "will I not break, nor alter the thing that is gone out of my lips." (Ps. lxxxix. 31, 34.) And a clause of this covenant is, "I will put my fear in their hearts, that they shall not depart from me." (Jer. xxxii. 40.) "Therefore there is no condemnation to them who are in Christ Jesus." As a consequence, it follows that those who come to Christ he will not cast out of his kingdom of glory. The connection between faith in the Lord Jesus and eternal life is as infallible as God can make it; we can no more disjoin them than we can separate truth from the divine nature. And this is a principle so clearly revealed in your Bibles, that it would be needless to attempt its proof.

Pause then a moment, and ask yourselves what an immortal

being can wish that the Redeemer does not promise in the text? Say, is it not your wisdom, is it not your honour, is it not your happiness, to surrender your hearts and devote your lives to this heavenly Suitor? What greater wisdom than to secure that good part which shall not be taken from you? So that, happen what will, all shall be well with you. What honour should be so ardently courted as that of becoming the sons of God?—of shining in the robes of imputed righteousness?—of wearing through eternity a crown of glory? What happiness like that which lies in Jehovah's favour? for it is life, and his loving kindness is better than life.

"Precious blessings! but we dare not contemplate them only at a distance. We have so often turned our backs upon them and their adorable Author, that we fear there is no hope for us," may perhaps be the language of some present. Why, my friends, why indulge such a fear? You have all the encouragement imaginable to believe that he will freely pardon even *your* transgressions, and adopt you into his family.

For, in the first place: The salvation of sinners is the object and the business of his mediation. "The Son of man is come to seek and save that which was lost." For this very purpose he was set up from everlasting, and commissioned into our world: nay, it is so peculiarly his office that he received his name from it. "Thou shalt call his name Jesus, because he shall save his people from their sins." Who are his people? Certainly they to whom "he gives power to become the sons of God." And who are these? "As many as believe on his name." Stretch forth, then, the withered arm; endeavour to lay hold on his covenant; let your hope lift up her languishing head; for the Redeemer is never employed in work more suitable to his character than when he confers on such as *you* the blessings of his grace. You have, therefore, nothing less to animate your souls than the express design of the scheme of salvation, and all the perfections of God, which are pledged for the security of those who embrace it.

2. As it is the business, so it is the delight of the Lord Christ, to save even the *chief* of sinners. It was in the prospect of this blessed work, that when the council of peace was held in eternity, "he rejoiced in the habitable parts of the earth, and his delights were with the sons of men." The conversion of a sinner produces great joy in heaven, and the first smile brightens on the countenance

of the Son of God. This heavenly personage, this incarnate God, is never so much grieved, nor considers himself treated with so much dignity, as when sinners refuse the offers of his love. If they will not listen to his expostulations, he leaves them with regret. "How shall I give thee up, Ephraim?"—"How shall I deliver thee, Israel?"—"How shall I make thee as Admah?"—"How shall I set thee as Zeboim?"—"Mine heart is turned within me; my repentings are kindled together." (Hos. xi. 8.)

The Lord Jesus is well pleased to be employed by sinners in transacting their eternal interests. Be persuaded to put your souls, and all their concerns into his hand. You cannot commit them to a better, nor a more faithful agent. You cannot find a more powerful friend, nor a more effectual pleader. He is minister plenipotentiary in the court of heaven; and they whose cause he undertakes, shall undoubtedly succeed. Rob not the Saviour of his glory, but let your redemption add a new trophy to the triumphs of his grace.

3. He has actually saved sinners as unlikely as yourselves to obtain his favour. The Scriptures tell us of a Manasseh, whose murders made the streets of Jerusalem run down with innocent blood, and who, nevertheless, became a wondrous monument of redeeming grace. They tell us of a Mary Magdalen, in whom dwelt seven devils, and yet they could not prevent a gracious visit from Christ. They tell us of a Paul, who was a persecutor, blasphemous, and injurious, "but he obtained mercy." They tell us of those who were guilty of crucifying the Lord of glory, and yet this blackest of guilt was washed away in the blood of sprinkling. Were you to enumerate the vile abominations which have disgraced and rendered miserable our nature, and to present the list to the redeemed in heaven, how many would say, "And such were *we!*" Oh, sinner! the path you wish to tread, has been trodden by millions before you, and like you. You injure the freeness and fulness of the Redeemer's grace, by hesitating a moment about his willingness to save you.

4. Christ has told you—in the text he tells you, that he is as willing, as he is able, to save to the uttermost, all that come to God by him. And where has he contradicted himself? "Him that cometh to me," is the unlimited proclamation, "I will in no wise cast out." Nay, he has gone farther; he has not only said, he has

sworn, and sworn by himself (the most solemn oath that God can take,) that he will not reject you. But by your questioning his willingness you give him the lie; you believe the devil and your own deceitful hearts, and believe them at the expense of Jehovah's truth. Away with this false humility. It dishonours God, and is fraught with poison to your own souls. It is the most inveterate enemy the Redeemer has—seize this traitor and nail him to his cross. The great Mediator has promised to receive you. That is enough—take him at his word. He has put no qualification in his warrant—see that you put none there. Fix your eye upon his atonement—bring his promise to his throne, plead it there, "Lord, do as thou hast said." Such a cry has never been, shall never be unanswered; it pierces the third heavens, and brings Jesus to the relief of the soul. And in all your supplications, remember that the salvation of Christ is absolutely free; a quality which it could not have if it excluded any who are willing to submit to it There is not one way to life for little, and another for great, sinners. Are your iniquities heinously aggravated? Then you have more need of the Saviour! Then the honours of his love will be more magnified in your salvation! Then you will be more deeply indebted to his grace! The redeemed will all shout, but you will shout upon a higher note, "to him that loved us, and washed us from our sins in his own blood—be glory and dominion forever and ever." (Rev. i. 5, 6.)

As the whole of this discourse has been practical, the improvement shall consist in a very few obvious reflections.

1. If coming to Jesus implies the several things which have been mentioned, it highly concerns all who have hitherto lived contented with a mere profession, to realize their misery and their danger. My brethren, you seem to forget that a "form of godliness" will not save your souls. All who have any respect for the system of divine truth, profess to believe, though the conduct of too many belies their creed, that there is no salvation detached from faith in the Lord Jesus Christ. Now what will it profit you, that this precious principle is inscribed in every page of your Bible, and has a place in your understandings and memories, if it do not, by the blessing of God, deeply affect, and thoroughly renew your hearts? Let me ask you, and let conscience, as in the presence of Jehovah, put home the question, Have you felt your-

selves wretched, aliens from God, children of wrath, under the curse, and obnoxious to the vengeance of his holy law? Have you found yourselves polluted, your power to do good entirely lost, and inherent depravity contaminating and poisoning, like the pestilence, what you once imagined your best works? Have you utterly despaired of doing any thing to relieve yourselves from your woful condition? Have your minds been illuminated to see the glory of the Redeemer's person, the suitableness and the necessity of his offices, the freedom and the fulness of his grace? Are you pleased with the plan of salvation; that wondrous plan which puts the crown upon the Mediator's head, and lays your honours and your importance prostrate in the dust? Have you surrendered your hearts, and consecrated your lives, to this almighty Saviour? If you are his people indeed, if your are the just expectants of a happy immortality, you certainly know something of these things. If you do not, it is to be hoped you will not dare, in virtue of a mere profession, to seat yourselves, to-morrow, at the table of the Lord. Allow me, my friends, to deal plainly with you; and do you deal plainly and honestly with yourselves. The table shall be spread, but only for the children of the kingdom—the Master comes, but he calls not for you—you have not the wedding garment; you have no invitation from Zion's King to this feast of love; and at your peril be it, if you go uninvited. Nay, if you know nothing of those exercises of the soul on which our reflections have dwelt this evening, you are not only unbidden to our gospel repast, but the whole of your religion is a dead form, an empty shell, a religion for this world, and it will attend you no further than this world. It will leave you at death, when you will most sadly need comfort and support. "Be not deceived: God is not mocked. If any man be in Christ, he is a new creature."—"You must be born again"—you must have a justifying righteousness, and sanctifying grace; without this " no man shall see the Lord." Without this, no splendid profession, no extensive knowledge, no exalted privileges, will benefit you in the most trying hour. All these you may have, and yet go down to the grave with a "lie in your right hand." O that you were wise to know, "in this your day, the things that belong to your peace."

2. Will Jesus Christ reject none who come to him? then all

who perish, perish by their own fault. Christ and all the benefits of the everlasting covenant are now offered to the chief of sinners. To every one in this assembly, whatever his character, whatever his crimes, the free promise of eternal life is presented. Nay, wherever the joyful sound is heard, the gracious proclamation announces peace and pardon through the blood of Jesus. By this blood a fountain is opened for the house of David, and for the inhabitants of Jerusalem. "Ho! every one that thirsteth, come ye to the waters!"—" Whosoever will, let him come and take the waters of life freely!" Whatever, therefore, you may pretend; however plausible the excuses by which you satisfy your consciences while you despise the blessed Saviour; the truth is, (for He who cannot lie hath said so,) "You will not come to him that you may have life." You are, then, your own destroyers; and at the awful appearance of your Judge, guilt will stop your mouths; or should you attempt to speak, your mouths will condemn you. The Lord now waits to be gracious; but remember, that if you persist and die in your unbelief, "there remaineth no more sacrifice for sin, but a certain fearful looking-for of judgment and fiery indignation which shall devour the adversaries."

3. Since Jesus Christ will cast out none who come to him, let it be your care, Christians, to live by faith upon him. May the most inveterate rebel against God look for forgiveness and acceptance through the Mediator's atonement? and shall not his children, who are already justified by that atonement, have boldness and confidence in their approaches to his throne? You have many corruptions to subdue—many trials to sustain—many foes to resist—and therefore, if you expect to succeed, you must have many errands to the throne of grace. And be not now strangers at that throne—spread before it all your weaknesses and all your wants. Pour out, into the bosom of your Father, all your anxieties and all your griefs. Do you feel your lusts strong, and your graces weak? Do not spend your time in lamenting your feebleness, but betake yourselves to him who is not only the Lord your righteousness, but the Lord your *strength*. Does your great adversary seem to be let loose upon you? Does he, as a ravenous lion, terrify you by his roarings? Does he, as a skilful and malicious enemy, discharge into your souls his fiery darts? Run instantly to the Captain of your salvation—he has an arm that is full of power.

In our text he has pledged himself to secure you; and as he cannot deny himself, his faithfulnes will be your shield and your buckler.

Have you acted treacherously towards your Lord? Have you grieved him by backsliding from him? And has he, in righteous indignation, withdrawn from you the light of his countenance? Humble yourselves under his mighty hand, but do not mistake the meaning of his providence. He chastens, because he loves you. He says with inexpressible tenderness, "Return, ye backsliding children, and I will heal your backslidings." Answer his call, "Behold! we come unto thee, for thou art the Lord our God." (Jer. iii. 22.) Whilst the tear of ingenuous shame starts in your eye, fix it on his everlasting righteousness—let your trembling hand again lay hold of his covenant—bow at his footstool—plead his promise—you shall not be disappointed, for it is a truth more stable than the heavens, that "them who come to him he will in no wise cast out."

SERMON XXII.

THE GOSPEL NO CAUSE OF SHAME.

ROMANS i. 16.

"I am not ashamed of the gospel of Christ, for it is the power of God unto salvation to every one that believeth."

ZEAL for the glory of his Divine Master was the most prominent feature in the character of the apostle Paul. Hurried away by the blind impulses of ignorant superstition and inveterate malice, he had formerly persecuted with unrelenting fury all who named the name of Jesus. The account which he gives of himself exhibits the most hideous picture of frantic impiety. " I verily thought with myself that I ought to do many things contrary to the name of Jesus of Nazareth. Which thing I also did in Jerusalem; and many of the saints did I shut up in prison, having received authority from the chief priests; and when they were put to death I gave my voice against them. And I punished them oft in every synagogue, and compelled them to blaspheme; and being exceedingly mad against them, I persecuted them even unto strange cities." (Acts xxvi. 9-11.)

Under these circumstances, who would have thought, according to human judgment, that the conversion of Paul was a probable, not to say a possible, event? Assuredly, had he been governed by worldly motives, we never should have heard of him as a Christian, far less would his name have shown with such splendour on the list of apostles. But what obstacles can arrest the power of Christ, or prevent him from bringing to himself in the moment of love the " chosen vessels" of mercy. No sooner does divine grace take possession of the soul than the heart of stone melts—the fury of persecution subsides—the murdering sword is cast away—the first breath of penitence cries, " Lord, what wilt thou have me to do?"—Saul the persecutor becomes Paul the apostle. With an ardour proportioned to his former enmity, " he now preaches the faith which once he destroyed"—he plants the standard of the Messiah in that very city which witnessed his rebellion, and was the scene of his cruelty—he glories in the cross of Christ—he sees clearly all the dangers which attend such a profession, and all the calumny and odium which are heaped upon those who make it. But unappalled by danger, unmoved by calumny, he throws to his adversaries the gauntlet of defiance. " Why," says he, " should I blush for my Redeemer? Let them blush who never saw his glory nor felt his love. But I, who know both, " am not ashamed of the gospel of Christ;" and I have the best reason not to be ashamed of it, for, let men reproach it as they please, " it is the power of God unto salvation to every one that believeth."

In this noble testimony which Paul gives to the gospel, he speaks with the warmth and eagerness of a man who felt its importance and certainty. Enlarged views of the gracious scheme it unfolds impressed him with the deep conviction that it alone can bear the weight of an immortal soul. Enraptured with the heavenly prospects it opens, not only in this world but beyond the grave, his heart glowed with fervent gratitude to their adorable Author; and unable to repress his devout affection, he cries out, " I am not ashamed of the gospel of Christ." This was not more the heroism of an inspired apostle than it is the temper of all believers. They have in their own bosoms the same divine principle which animated the faith and hope and magnanimity of Paul. 'Tis true, in them it may not be equally active, nor its operations of equal extent; but the principle they have and must have. Born of the same Father—united to the same Redeemer—guided by the same Spirit, they must have the same disposition. However weak their faith, however faint their hope, however dead their frame, it is their " unaltered wish" to glorify their Saviour. And could you see their inmost souls, you might read there, in very legible characters, " I am not ashamed of the gospel of Christ." Too often, indeed, their actions are wholly inconsistent with their character and sentiments. They shrink from the frown or sneer of "a world that lieth in wickedness." But of this timidity they ought to be ashamed. It is the fruit of their unbelief—the badge of their folly—the chastisement of their sin.

That they may not be left to act so unworthy and ungrateful a part should be the constant study and prayer of Christians; and they will find the subject of our present attention fraught with sweet and powerful motives to "hold fast," not merely their faith, but "the profession of their faith, without wavering;" for it naturally leads us to take a view of the gospel of Christ—to notice some of the reasons for which carnal men are ashamed of it—to display the Christian temper by showing what is comprehended in *not* being ashamed of it—and to illustrate the argument by which the bold profession of it is defended.

In prosecuting the plan which has now been proposed, and depending upon that gracious aid, without which we can do nothing, let us,

In the first place, take a brief view of the gospel of Christ.

Gospel, as is commonly remarked, signifies glad tidings; and the term is appropriated, with peculiar propriety, to the revelation of divine mercy as it is manifested in Christ Jesus.

The gospel well deserves to be termed glad tidings in a variety of respects, as it answers to complete satisfaction the most important questions that man can ask. It resolves our doubts about the nature and character of God—about the dispensations of his providence, about a future state, about the misery of our present condition, and about the method of our recovery.

1. The gospel of Christ informs us about the nature and character of God.

That man, who was created in the divine image, and honoured with the divine favour and communication, should so fatally degenerate as to forget the first lesson which was taught to his species, a knowledge of the God who made him, is not a more melancholy proof of his depravity than it is a part of his misery. Credulity itself could scarcely have believed that human reason, which originally was pure and clear, should be so debased and blinded as to mistake entirely the nature and plainest attributes of God, and to ascribe any of them to the creatures of his hand. But the fact is unquestionable. The dreadful apostacy of our race plunged us into such woful ignorance, that we groped in darkness, even at noon-day. I should abuse your understandings should I attempt to prove that the heathen world was overspread with the grossest superstition and idolatry. I should waste your time in recapitulating the opposite opinions which were entertained of God, not only by the multitude, but also by the greatest philosophers. Whether there is one great and glorious being, who centres in himself all the perfections of Deity, or whether these are distributed amongst more than one, is a question about which the philosophers hesitated, and which the vulgar decided in favour of Polytheism. Such a decision must necessarily draw after it a train of fatal errors respecting every part of the divine character, and every relation it bears to us. Its practical effects are briefly, but elegantly and strikingly, summed up by our apostle, when he tells us, in the close of this first chapter of the epistle to the Romans, that men " changed the glory of the incorruptible God into an image made like to corruptible man, and to birds, and four-footed beasts, and creeping things, and worshipped and served the creature more than the Creator, who is blessed for ever." Even they, who, a little more enlightened, condemned idolatry, and were inclined to favour the doctrine of the unity of God, were much at a loss concerning other matters of the highest moment. Is God a Spirit? Is he the author of evil? If not, is he so necessarily holy that he must punish sin? Is there any possible way of escaping his righteous indignation? Will he certainly bring us into judgment for all our actions, or only for some? Does he take notice of our thoughts? How is he to be worshipped? Ought we to worship him at the hazard of mistaking the acceptable mode, and thus bring upon ourselves new and accumulated guilt; or ought we to omit it altogether? On these and other important questions the wisest of the heathens said the least; and they who were most positive most frequently erred. So truly does the apostle say, that " professing themselves to be wise they became fools," and that " the world by wisdom knew not God." From this frightful state of doubt, suspense, and perplexity, the gospel of Christ delivered the world. It chased away the clouds which wrapped in darkness the human mind, and poured upon the gloom of midnight a flood of day. This gospel declares that God is One. " Hear, O Israel! the Lord our God is ONE JEHOVAH. It also declares how he is one, in revealing to us the mystery of the adorable Trinity—the wonderful mystery of three equal divine persons subsisting in one undivided essence; a mystery of dread importance, of which the knowledge is absolutely necessary to our eternal happiness, but which mere reason never could have conjectured, far less discovered. The gospel declares that " God is a Spirit, infinite, eternal, unchangeable, in his being, wisdom, power, holiness, justice, goodness, and truth." In his *being*, and therefore as he could have no beginning, so he can have no alteration nor end, but must continue the same, in all the glory of his nature, to-day, yesterday, and forever. In his *wisdom*, and therefore all things, even the most secret thoughts, are open to his sight, and shall all be conducted to the best and noblest end. In his *power*, and therefore the determinations of his wisdom can never be frustrated, but shall certainly be carried into complete execution. In his *holiness*, and therefore he cannot be the author of evil; he must hate sin with a perfect hatred; he cannot allow it to pass with impunity, but must punish it as infallibly as he is God. In his *justice*, and therefore while he supports the dignity of his laws and the rights of his government, and vindicates the honours of his character, his decisions must be according to truth, and so perfectly equitable as to shut the mouth of every offender. In his *goodness*, and therefore we may be assured that "he does not afflict willingly, nor grieve the children of men;" that the innocent cannot suffer; that they who do suffer must be sinners, and the authors of their own misery; and that there is here laid a foundation on which even the guilty may hope to be delivered from the condemnation to which their consciences tell them they are liable, provided the deliverance can be effected in a consistency with all the divine attributes. And in his *truth*, so that neither his promises nor his threatenings can possibly fail.

Farther, the gospel of Christ declares that God is to be worshipped—that he is to be worshipped in spirit and in truth; secretly and openly; that to neglect this duty is death; and that it cannot be acceptably performed, but in the mode prescribed in the revelation of the covenant of grace.

As the account which divine revelation gives of the nature and character of God far exceeds, both in value and extent, all the accounts to which uninspired philosophy can pretend; so the marks of decided superiority are stamped with equal clearness upon the account which it gives of the government of God. I therefore observe,

2. That the gospel of Christ affords us true and interesting views of Divine Providence.

How great was the confusion and perplexity of the acutest observers of the moral world, when, unaided by revelation, they attempted to develop the mysteries of Providence; and how vain were all their efforts to extricate themselves from their difficulties, can be a secret to none who are acquainted with the state of mankind before the promulgation of the gospel. That God, the Creator of the universe, governs it with unerring wisdom, almighty power, and unceasing care, is a proposition so plain to those who know their Bibles, and with which conscience so immediately closes, that we are apt to imagine no man can refuse, for a moment, his cordial and unhesitating assent. Yet even this proposition, all clear and commanding as it is, was much controverted by pagans of old, and as if God meant to stain the pride of human reason, it is controverted at this hour by many who reject the scriptures of truth. Amongst the heathen, Divine Providence was a subject which seldom occupied the thoughts of the vulgar, and about which the wise were perpetually quarrelling. Some denied, in the gross, God's creating power and goodness. Some, though they ascribed to him the power of creating, were for excluding him entirely from governing, the world; fondly and impiously dreaming that all things are driven at random by blind fatality, or blinder chance, and that God concerns himself neither in human affairs, nor in anything else. Others, measuring Infinite Wisdom and power by their own ignorance and feebleness, and unable to comprehend how a single mind can attend to the varied, and multiplied, and intricate affairs of a universe, wished to rid the Deity of fatigue, and contrived to parcel out the world amongst a number of divinities, to each of whom they assigned a peculiar province. And the few who, more sound in their judgments, and more sober in their inquiries, admitted God's superintendence over the works of his hands, and laboured to shun the dangers of a contrary opinion, were yet puzzled and confounded by the occurrences of every day. When they adverted to the different classes and characters of men, they felt that to reconcile their situations, in the common course of events, with a good, a wise, an equitable providence, was a task too hard for their deepest thought and most diligent research. If anything is to be gathered from a general notion of God's character, and the first dictates of reason and conscience, it is this general maxim, that evil ought to be punished, and good rewarded. But when men, guided by the mere light of nature, turned their attention to the actual administration of Providence, how awful and disheartening was it to find that this leading character of an upright governor was apparently contradicted by almost every act of his government. When they saw iniquity at ease, and prosperity taking up her abode in the dwellings of the wicked—when they saw plenty open her treasures, and pour upon their heads her choice, her balmy blessings—and honour crowning their lives with her most flattering distinctions: especially when they saw, on the other hand, that men, to their discernment unblemished in their characters, and venerable for their virtues, were frequently reduced to struggle with the complicated ills of life—to languish under disease, or pine in poverty—to become the victims of oppression and falsehood, or to sink beneath a load of injuries; when they observed these things what could they say? Renounce the doctrine of a providence they could not without renouncing their reason; and they could hardly retain it without renouncing their senses. Who will help them in this sad dilemma? Who will answer a question like the following: "Do not such dispensations look like a bounty on crimes and a penalty on innocence?" The difficulty is great and serious: it is so great that reflection upon it staggered the faith, and almost overturned the steadfastness of one who was favoured with divine revelation. "Verily," said Asaph, in the agony of his soul, "Verily, I have cleansed my heart in vain, and washed my hands in innocency." (Ps. lxxiii. 13.) Nor were his doubts removed, nor the rebellion of his heart subdued, "till he went into the sanctuary of God." As for those who had not revelation, the only thing which could in the least alleviate their painful anxiety is the idea of future retribution. But this idea, as we shall hereafter see, was at most the trembling conjecture of a probable fact, and by no means the firm and solid conviction of an undoubted reality. But had the conviction been ever so firm, difficulties which we cannot now mention, still remained. If philosophy was required to solve them, she shrunk from the unequal attempt; or if she undertook it, it was only to betray her feebleness, and to mock the expectation of her followers.

But here, when every human resource failed, the gospel of Christ stepped in, and with all the dignity and ease of heavenly truth, untied those gordian knots which bade defiance to the ingenuity of man. I do not mean to say that the gospel disclosed all the secrets of the divine government. There are many things which we may not, should not know. Things of which the knowledge is graciously concealed from us, as it could serve no purpose but to render us miserable. There are many things which we could not know. Things so deep and mysterious as to be far beyond the reach of any created intellect. And therefore, intruding curiosity may start a thousand difficulties which no mortal can remove. But this is no prejudice to the gospel. Its discoveries are adapted, with infinite wisdom, to our circumstances. It unfolds so much of the plan of Divine Providence as is necessary and useful—so much as may justify, even to our frail understandings, "the ways of God to men"—as may teach the wicked the most alarming lessons—as may strengthen and animate the faith, and hope, and peace of the believer.

The gospel informs us, that as God "created all things for himself," so he "upholds them by the word of his power," and rules them by the counsel of his will. It informs us that he framed, in eternity, the plan of all his operations; and that *Providence* is nothing but the gradual development of this plan, at such seasons, and in such degrees, as to his wisdom appears fit—that the plan is unalterable in itself: "I am Jehovah, I change not; my counsel shall stand," says he, "and I will do all my pleasure,"—that it is so infallible in its execution, as not to be hindered for a moment by any impediment whatsover; for "he doth according to his will in the armies of heaven, and among the inhabitants of the earth; and none can stay his hand, or say unto him, what dost thou?"—that it is so boundless in its extent as to comprehend all things, even objects the most minute, and incidents apparently the most trifling. "The hairs of your head," they are the words of our Redeemer, "the very hairs of your head are all numbered;" and "a sparrow shall not fall to the ground without your Father." That nothing can happen but in a subserviency to the end which God has in view—that all second causes, though operating in different ways, and even though hostile in themselves to this end, are combined effectually to promote it. "Surely the wrath of man shall praise thee, and the remainder of wrath thou wilt restrain." The gospel bids us not to wonder if we cannot account for many proceedings of the Governor of the universe, since his "way is in the sea, and his path in the great waters, and his footsteps are not known." It bids us not to be stumbled if we see the "wicked spreading like a green bay tree," high in power, and wantoning in plenty; because this is not the way in which God expresses his approbation and favour, as his word declares, and innumerable facts prove: for nothing is more certain than that inward happiness is far from being a necessary attendant upon outward prosperity, and because wise and valuable purposes are accomplished by this dispensation. Were God to cut off immediately the notoriously wicked, he could not bring all his sons to glory, many of whom are to spring from them, and are to receive, and love, and honour that Redeemer whom their fathers rejected, and hated, and vilified. In the mean time he makes them, though they know it not, the instruments of building up his church, and by loading them with benefits, he renders their impiety the more inexcusable, their guilt the more flagrant, and his justice in punishing them the more conspicuous. If, in righteous indignation, he sometimes scatter their wealth, and stain their honours, and blast their prospects, and bring upon them the swift and fearful recompense of their crimes, he teaches men that "verily there is a God who judgeth rightly." Thus, both his long-suffering and his vengeance throw a lustre on his wisdom. Were all punished, men would forget an hereafter. Did all escape, they would think that God had forsaken the earth, and whatever they did, the Lord regarded not.

On the other hand, as the gospel tells us that external felicity is not always a mark of the divine favour, so it bids us not be surprised if we see good men labouring under the pressure of calamity. It silences the voice of murmuring, by giving us to understand, that considering the infinite evil of sin, however God may frown upon even the righteous, he treats them far more gently and tenderly than they deserve. "Wherefore doth a living man complain, a man for the punishment of his sins?" (Lam. iii. 39.) As if the prophet had said, "What! out of hell, and yet complain? Blush, O man, for thy ingratitude! Tremble for thy presumption!" But the gospel farther informs us, that we greatly mistake in concluding a man miserable because he is poor, or despised, or oppressed—

that the peace and pleasure of a Christian are a peace and pleasure, which, as the world cannot give, so it cannot take away—that even in calamity the "consolations of God" impart more gladness and better enjoyment than can be felt or known by the wicked "when their corn and their wine abound." It informs us that all things, even the most unpromising, "shall work together for the good of them who love God, and are called according to his purpose," that afflictions are the discipline of their Father's house, and that the exercise of this discipline towards them is at once a proof and a privilege of their adoption, for "whom the Lord loveth he chasteneth, and scourgeth every son whom he receiveth,"—that he makes affliction an instrument by which he "purges away the dross, takes away the tin, and purifies the gold of his people,"—by which he mortifies their corruptions and quickens their graces—by which he weans them from a criminal attachment to this world, and teaches them that as they profess to be citizens of heaven, they should justify their title to the exalted character by "setting their affections on things above,"—and finally, the gospel informs us, that their sufferings shall not only be blessed to them here, but shall be abundantly repaid hereafter, when Jehovah shall finish the present dispensation of things by giving to the wicked the exact and impartial due of their iniquities, and bringing the righteous to "Zion with songs," when "everlasting joy shall be upon their heads," when "sorrow and sighing shall flee away," and God himself shall wipe away all tears from their eyes. I therefore remark,

3. That the gospel of Christ affords us the truest information about a future state.

The gospel informs us that we shall live hereafter—that as soon as the soul is separated from the body by death, it repairs to the tribunal of God, where it receives a sentence which fixes its eternal destiny—that this sentence, however, is but the first part of the divine proceeding—that God has appointed a day in which he will openly judge the world by Jesus Christ—that at this awfully interesting period the trump of God shall burst the caverns of the dead, and startle into life the slumbering dust—that the bodies of men thus raised shall be reunited to their souls—that after this new union they shall be summoned, amidst the dread solemnities of a descending God and the convulsions of a dissolving universe, before the judgment seat of Christ—that there they "must give an account of all the deeds done in the body, whether they be good or whether they be evil"—that infinite equity will pass upon every individual an irreversible decision—that then the scene will be forever closed, when the "wicked shall go away into everlasting punishment, but the righteous into life eternal."

When men consider themselves immortal beings, and believe that their present state has a most serious influence upon the happiness or misery of an eternal existence, it becomes a subject of important investigation to know what their state is, and how they may be sure of future bliss.

To obtain true satisfaction, let them not run to philosophic schools—let them not trudge through the pathless desert of wild conjecture—let them not be duped by the high pretensions of learned ignorance. Miserable comforters are they all! The Bible alone can help them in their straits; and, therefore, we may observe,

4. That the gospel of Christ opens to our view the nature of our present condition.

Vain was every exertion to account for the introduction and prevalence of sin, and to discover the extent of its direful consequences. The gospel reveals to us the dreadful secret. It informs us that man was at first created pure, spotless, and transcendently happy—perfectly innocent—shining in the rays of his Creator's glory—surrounded with delights, and dignified with the homage of an obedient world, there was nothing which could give him one painful emotion. All within was serene and joyous—all without secure and peaceful. That in this situation his God entered into a covenant with him by giving him, as the test of his gratitude and his duty, a law which was admirably fitted to promote his happiness. That the condition of this covenant was perfect obedience to the divine law. That eternal life and glory were promised as the high reward of fidelity; and death, in the largest meaning of the word, death temporal, spiritual, and eternal, was threatened as the tremendous penalty in case of unfaithfulness. That this covenant was made with our first parents, not as individuals, but as a nature, as the public representatives of their future family, who should therefore stand or fall with them, live in their life, and die in their death. That God marked, as the pledge of their obedience, a certain tree, from which he commanded them to abstain. That, regardless of his command, abusing the liberty with which he had endued them, and yielding to the suggestions of Satan, an apostate spirit, they plucked the forbidden fruit—they transgressed the covenant of their God—they fell from their integrity. That at the instant of their fall the broken law arrested them, and they became exposed to all the horrors which its curse contains. That by their disobedience they broke down the sacred hedge which divine faithfulness had placed around them. That sin, with all her hellish train, rushed through the breach into our world, and from that fatal moment to this has spread desolation and woe amongst men. But this is not all. The gospel informs us, that we are, every one of us, " by nature children of wrath," deriving from our first parents both guilt and depravity; and that this is the corrupted source from which all actual transgressions proceed. That, in consequence of our guilt and pollution, we are odious and loathsome in the sight of a holy God, and have in our hearts a principle of enmity against him. That "dead in trespasses and sins," we can do nothing to help ourselves, as we can do nothing but sin. That no created power can help us, or loose us in the least from our connection with the violated covenant. That while this connection subsists we can expect nothing but what the covenant has to give, and that this is nothing but " the fiery indignation which shall devour the adversaries."

This information, if viewed in itself, is dreadful—enough to strike the chill of death into every heart—and were the message of God to stop here, instead of bringing glad tidings, it would convert our world into a very hell. But it is one of the benevolent characteristics of the religion of Jesus, that it smites only to heal; it lays open the disease, that it may apply the remedy. And hence we remark,

Lastly, That the gospel of Christ reveals a method of recovery from our ruined condition.

Had Gabriel, who stands in the presence of God, been asked, "Can sinful men be saved, and the honour of his Creator be preserved?" his silence would have proclaimed his inability to answer. It is one of the first dictates of reason, that a criminal ought to atone for his crime. But what atonement, what satisfaction, can a sinner make? His offence is infinite—all that he has, all that he can do, is a debt. Will repentance help him? Alas! the law knows not of repentance. It fixes the penalty with the transgressor; and if God be faithful to himself, the penalty must be executed. And now, when all prospect of escape is cut off, who shall screen the offender from wrath? Shall not despair blacken his countenance, and harrow up his soul? Oh no! at this season of need, the gospel of Christ leaps down from heaven, and brings speedy and effectual relief. It is the sum of her reviving message, "Deliver him from going down to the pit; I have found a ransom." In the explication of this transporting news, the gospel informs us that God, out of mere mercy, resolved to save a number of sinful men, and to save them in a way which should bring all the glory to his sovereign grace; that as he could not dispense with the sanction of his law, and as man was utterly unable to give the satisfaction which the law required, the Second Person of the glorious Trinity voluntarily offered to assume our nature, to become the substitute of all whom the Father should give him, and who should believe upon his name, and in that character to obey perfectly the divine law, and endure the whole of the terrible punishment which their sins deserved; and thus pave the way for restoring them to divine favour and making them certain heirs of eternal life. That in the fulness of time, fixed by infinite wisdom, the Lord Jesus actually came into our world—that being born in an extraordinary manner, he was not one of Adam's represented children—was neither guilty, nor pollutted—was not exposed to the curse, nor bound by the obligations of the law, and that he consented to be made under it as the representative of his people, both in its obligations and in its curse. That having graciously submitted to be made thus under the law, he did perfectly obey it, through a life of labour, temptation, and suffering. That at his death he did make himself an offering. That stretched upon the accursed tree, and deprived of the light of his Father's countenance, he drank the dregs of his Father's wrath; received into his soul the bitter anguish which would have been our portion through eternity; and struggled, at the same time, with all the malice and all the madness of hell. But being Jehovah in our nature, his sufferings, though short, were of infinite value, and completed the purchase of our redemption. His own arm defeated the hosts of darkness—his expiring breath proclaimed his victory—and the cross of Calvary stood the bloody trophy of his conquest.

The gospel informs us that, though our Redeemer died, he rose again, and ascended up, visibly, into the highest heaven—that he appears there at this moment, as the intercessor of his people, presenting in their room his everlasting merits—that there he manages all their concerns—that thence he sends down his Spirit to work effectually in their hearts, and to prepare them for being with him in glory.

The gospel further informs us, that the salvation which Jesus Christ has procured is freely offered to the chief of sinners; that whosoever will, may come and receive it, and be forever happy; and that if any to whom it is preached, shall perish at last, they will have nothing to blame but their own wilful, obstinate unbelief.

[*The application is wanting.*]

SERMON XXIII.

ON STEADFASTNESS IN RELIGIOUS SENTIMENT.

EPHESIANS iv. 14.

"That we henceforth be no more children, tossed to and fro, and carried about with every wind of doctrine, by the sleight of men, and cunning craftiness, whereby they lie in wait to deceive."

The unity of Christians in the faith, the growth and strength of their character, have much importance attached to them by the Lord Jesus, and appear, if we may use the expression, to lie very near his heart. After his ascension to the throne of his glory, one of the first acts of his intercession, and of the power of his exalted state, was to make provision for the continuance and increase of these graces. "When he ascended up on high, he led captivity captive, and gave gifts unto men: and he gave some, apostles; and some, prophets; and some, evangelists; and some, pastors and teachers; for the perfecting of the saints, for the work of the ministry; for the edifying of the body of Christ, till we all come in the unity of the faith, and of the knowledge of the Son of God, unto a perfect man; unto the measure of the stature of the fulness of Christ." What the particular connection is between his people's advancement in knowledge and spiritual attainments, and the degree of happiness in their unseen witnesses, or what especial influence it may exert upon the general economy of his kingdom, in the invisible world, we do not know, nor is it useful if it were proper to inquire. But we do know, from the passage just read, that whatever is great or magnificent in the office of an apostle, or prophet, or evangelist; whatever is useful or honourable in a pastor or teacher, it was and is conferred upon them, not for their own sakes, but for the sake of "his body, the church." We are furnished with ordinances, and means in every variety, that there may be no hindrance to our profitting in the school of Jesus Christ—that we may habitually enlarge our knowledge of those things "which the angels desire to look into;" and as fellow-students with them of "the mystery of God," may grow in the intelligence which they value and in fitness for their fellowship, when, after a few days spent here, in "absence from the Lord," we shall join their society in his presence and service.

Surely, if such is our destination—if these the prospects which cheer us in this vale of tears—if our hearts are set upon their invigorating refreshment and peerless dignity—nothing can worse become us than indifference about our progress in the Christian lesson; nothing should fill us with deeper shame than the poor account which most of us have to give of the pains wasted upon our spiritual education, and of our slowness of heart to understand our Lord's instructions. On nothing should our eagerness be prompted, our ambition fired, and our efforts expended, more than on this, "that we henceforth be no more children, tossed to and fro, and carried about with every wind of doctrine by the sleight of men and cunning craftiness, whereby they lie in wait to deceive."

It may be of advantage to us to consider, somewhat more minutely, this description of religious children—the contrast which ought to mark our characters—and the means and motives to our solid improvement.

I. Our notice is drawn to the characters of these religious children. The apostle states it to consist principally in two things: *fickleness* in matters of faith, and *facility* of deception by designing men.

1. *Fickleness* in matters of faith—being "tossed to and fro, and carried about with every wind of doctrine."

There always has been and always will be a desperate and deadly conflict between truth and error, nor can there can be any compromise between them. The bastard charity of the day is very clamorous to make us give up all that we account most precious, or at least to compound with and not to molest their contraries.

But the demand is absurd and the concession impossible. It is the nature of truth to be the most intolerant thing conceivable. That truth is and can be but one. And the Liar plays off his most ancient, most extensive, and most successful game, when he can sow in the church the seeds of all sorts of discordant principles touching the faith and hope of sinful men. In this, it is true, God does as he does in other cases, bring good out of evil. "There must be heresies among you," *i. e.* divisions on account of the truth, "that they which are approved may be made manifest among you." Thus it fared with the churches in the days and under the eyes of the apostles themselves. The apostle Paul was constantly in armour combating for the faith that had been delivered once for all to the saints. Every gross corruption of the gospel, every foolish and fantastic whim invented and broached by men of reprobate minds, or of distorted imagination, infested the churches in as great a variety as at any later period. Perhaps modern times cannot reckon a single deviation from the gospel, which in form or in substance was not a curse of the apostolic age. No sooner were the pestiferous notions started, than crowds started and ran after them. If any thing, in the mean while, struck the fancy of one who was or who wished to be a leader, a part of the crowd would turn aside after him. Some of them, after fatiguing themselves in the pursuit of every vanity, would perchance return to a sober mind, and re-adhere to the cause which they had deserted. Others again, though cured of one extravagance, were just as ready to fall into another as the occasion recurred; and many, proceeding from one step to another in their evil course, at last made shipwreck of the faith altogether, and became downright apostates; abandoning the grounds of their confidence before God and the communion of his people, and "perishing at last in their own corruption."—"These were they who separated themselves; sensual, not having the spirit."—" They went out from us," says John, " but they were not of us; for if they had been of us they would have continued with us; but they went out that they might be made manifest that they were not all of us."

It is no otherwise yet. Old errors of every sort, which have been exploded long ago, revive, are new-dressed, and recommended to the acceptance of the religious world. I say "old errors," for the devil's wit is not inexhaustible; and therefore his delusions, plausible though they be, are only stale artifices newly tricked up to catch the ignorant and the conceited. All that the "rational Christianity" of the day glories in as its own discoveries, has many centuries ago been cast out of the Christian Church as "heresies of perdition." But come when they will, and how they will, they are sure of a ready reception, and many abettors among those who are "tossed to and fro, and are carried about with every wind of doctrine." They, indeed, call themselves "philosophers," and "liberal inquirers;" but the apostle calls them by their true name, "babies," and will allow them no place among inquirers but the place of those "who are ever learning and never coming to the knowledge of the truth." Learn what they will, the truth is what they do not learn and never can perceive. They have no fixed first principles; nothing to keep them firm and steady in the hour of temptation, or to prevent them being led away by the error of the wicked. In the calm sunshine, while there is no disturbance of the church's tranquillity, they mingle with the multitude and pass for Christians. But when the storm gathers, the waters swell, the winds blow, they are shaken from their own stedfastness. They never were secured to the rock of safety, but lay loose and idle upon the surface. Now the trial hath reached them, and without strong moorings, without grapplings, without anchors, without any fastenings, they are swept out of the Christian roads, and are the sport of the waves and the winds on the trackless ocean. Soon are they scattered away from the rock; and while they run, swift as the evil blast can drive them, towards certain destruction, they are elated, ignorant as they are, with the rapidity of their course, until they are suddenly dashed among the breakers, or engulfed in the billows, or absorbed in the quicksands. Thus terminates their adventurous speculation, and the last news of the poor souls is, "they perished!"

I have been referring to those errors, in the success of which the Destroyer goes directly to his proper work, the irretrievable ruin of men. But a capital error seldom comes alone; so there are many smaller deviations from the soundness of the faith which attend the steps and prepare the way for that which strikes at the foundation of entire Christianity. It is melancholy and almost incredible to see what a mere puff of wind is sufficient to drive many a gallant looking vessel out of her course; and the odds are infinitely against her, but before she recovers it, she falls among enemies who decoy her to her ruin. Without figure, you often find those who, upon the whole, are friendly to the truth; yet, by the merest trifle in the world—something which appears to them ingenious when it is only absurd—something which is recommended by a respectable name—something of which the whole attraction is its supposed novelty—turns them aside from "the old paths where is the good way."

The swarms of little sects which spring up and die almost as soon as they are known, yet for the time being vex the friends and furnish matter of exultation to the foes of evangelical doctrine, owe their origin for the most part to a paltry individual vanity. The peace of the church is broken; her strength is divided; the vigour of her sons is impaired by foolish contentions. The wily adversary does not let the occasion slip. Many who set out with an apparent trifle, do not end till they have made inroads upon the substantial truth; and Christians are called to struggle with an enemy who has already penetrated their camp. On such fickle beings you never can count; they want that sobriety of mind, that Christian common sense, which is proof against such small attacks, and is infinitely better for preserving the order and the truth of God pure and entire, than the finest genius and the profoundest learning can be without it.

2. Liableness to imposition by the arts of the insidious is another character of these religious children.

Error, when seen in its true colours, is rather apt to deter than to allure. Nor is there, perhaps, a single one which, if exhibited without disguise, would ever succeed in making proselytes. Even children would be too sagacious for such dupery. Accordingly, its approaches are conducted with caution and address. It is very careful not to alarm suspicion or excite prejudice. Concealment is its very life. Its abettors will pretend that your faith and theirs, however they may differ upon speculative points, come nearer to each other on all questions of practice than you are ready to admit. They will enumerate a number of things which no man in his senses ever thinks of disputing; and when there is no gainsaying them in these matters they will leave you, if they are master-workmen, to draw the inference that, after all, they cannot be so far wrong as some would persuade you; well knowing that the great obstacle to your conversion is surmounted when you are brought, by this piece of craft, to form a favourable opinion of their tenets. But you have already entered into temptation; you have already set your foot in the path which goes down to death, and if God in his great mercy do not enable you to make a speedy retreat, your ruin is inevitable. Take it then at the very beginning, as a simple rule, and of easy and sure application. The man who equivocates in religious matters, who declines giving you a prompt explanation of his views, and rather evades your inquiries than meets them, that man is a deceiver and an Antichrist. Truth was not intended to be smuggled. A city set on a hill cannot be hid, nor is a lighted candle to be put under a bushel. "Preach the word," is the commandment of our Lord Jesus Christ; and the teacher who does not do it frankly, so that men may not only understand his meaning, but cannot possibly misunderstand it, when treating of our eternal peace, is an enemy to our happiness and to our Lord. Avoid him as you would a pestilence. My contempt and horror embrace all those, who, after years of public ministrations, leave their people in doubt what their sentiments are. Truth is not with them the infinitely important interest. Their prospect is that of a fearful reckoning with that Saviour, "who came into the world that he might bear witness to the truth;" and even here it is the duty of his church to spew them out of her mouth.

3. Another artifice of those who lie in wait to deceive, is the wrapping up of their deceptions in scriptural phrases, and even in the language which is consecrated by the usage of the Christian church. Every thing sounds fair and looks well; has a pious air, and apparently a sound sense; and they may notwithstanding be inculcating the most damnable errors, and converting the very Word of God into a vehicle for the poison. Undoubtedly the inspired word expresses revealed truth in the most precise and proper manner. And the objection to these men is, not that they quote the scriptures, but that they quote them fraudulently. The cheat lies here—the passages quoted have, from time immemorial, borne in the Church of God a definite sense. You of course understand them in that received sense. But you are not aware that these apostles of error take them in quite a different sense, they and you use the same terms, but you do not intend the same thing; and when they think you are not drilled quite enough, they will never have the

candour to undeceive you. They will let out in other places and at other times, as far as they judge it prudent, what their meaning is; and in the meanwhile you are become so accustomed to hear this perversion of Holy Writ, that your minds are debauched from the simplicity of Christ, and you imperceptibly slide into the pit they have digged for you. Sometimes, indeed, this trick overshoots the mark. It is related of John Taylor, the famous Arian of Norwich, that he gave mortal offence to an Arian congregation in London by the use of Scripture language. His hearers, like people of that class everywhere, were not much acquainted with their bibles, and mistook him for an old-fashioned puritan! Thus the common sense of mankind, even of Arians themselves, when they are not put on their guard, decided that whatever the Bible teaches, it does not teach Arianism.

4. A fourth stratagem of deceivers is an affectation of unbounded liberality and charity.

Nothing is so odious in their eyes as bigotry. Why must you claim the exclusive privilege of being in the right? Why is not another man's opinion as good as your own? Why not allow your neighbours the privilege of which you are so tenacious, the privilege of thinking for themselves? Why must your charity be confined to sects or principles? Cannot a man be distinguished for Christian virtues, and exemplary in the discharge of his Christian duties, a sincere lover of the truth, and ardent in the pursuit of it, unless all his ideas of propriety be squared by your own rule? How terrible that the religion of peace should set friends quarrelling? How unworthy of the good will which the gospel was intended to cherish, and of the generous philanthropy of its Divine Author! All this is very fine, no doubt, for plausible talk; but in the mouths of the crafty nothing but talk; yet its effect is to overthrow the faith of some, who from want of discrimination, from a softness of mind, from not suspecting any mischief with so benevolent a face, from not having nerves to withstand a little raillery, from the joint power of ridicule and flattery, run headlong into the arms of a fiend, and from a dread of bigotry adopt ruinous heresy. On all which I crave leave to submit a remark or two.

(1.) They who are so very anxious about the liberty of thinking for themselves, mean in reality the liberty of thinking *for* you and thinking *through* you. Who hinders them from thinking and speaking too? Who meddles with their thoughts or their speech until they invade the sanctuary of our own faith? Then if they be resisted—if everything is not yielded to them as a matter of course —if we exercise the right of thinking and speaking—they are vastly indignant. Then come forth the lamentations about the lack of charity, and all the whinings about "bigotry" and "persecution," of which the true grievance is that they cannot provoke something which might appear worthy of the name. But do you shut your mouths and allow them to have all the representation in their own way—let them without contradiction or opposition spread their doctrines and instil their poison throughout the community—and you will doubtless be lauded for your liberality and charity.

(2.) My second remark is, that, after all, the truths of the gospel are not matters of human opinion, nor have you any right to treat them so. They are facts about which our appeal must lie to the veracity of God speaking in his word. He has committed them to us as a sacred deposit, which we are ordered to keep pure and entire, contending earnestly for them, and are not at liberty to make a compromise of them with any opinions whatsoever.

(3.) Once more. This profession about "liberality" and "charity," is a mere artifice of imposture. No men have less of it than they whose boast of it is the loudest. How do they exult and triumph in the misconduct of any who hold sounder principles than themselves? Now, if the apostle understood the nature of charity when he said that she rejoiceth not in iniquity, they who do so rejoice proclaim that they are utterly destitute of its influence.

You shall find these advocates for charity, when they are in mixed companies, all gentleness, all forbearance, with nothing but the milk of human kindness; but when they are by themselves, to use the expression of one who had been once of their party, "bitter enough." In short, of all the sects which are abroad in the world, not excepting even the followers of the Man of Sin, there are none which occasionally evince more virulence and violence of feeling, nor a more persecuting temper, than these same smooth-tongued praisers of charity. Of all the bigots on this earth, let me be farthest from the bigot to modern liberality.

Let us now turn our eyes for a moment,

II. To the contrast which we ought to exhibit to these religious children. "That ye be no more children." We should then display,

1. *Intelligence.* I know not how it has come to pass, but such is the fact, that hearers of the gospel are prone to take their profession upon trust. They think, or act as if they thought, that any particular acquaintance with its principles and proofs, belongs exclusively to the ministry. They commit the interests of their property to the lawyer; of their bodies to the physician; and as for their immortal souls, the clergyman may look after them, if he pleases. In this spirit of listlessness do they hear the gospel, and forget it almost as soon as heard. But for diligent inquiry—for ascertaining with their own eyes and understandings what are revealed truths, on points too of infinite moment—for searching the scriptures daily, whether these things which they are taught from the pulpit are really so, why its what no *genteel* professor ever thinks about. The consequence is, and must be, that they are mere children in the most important of all knowledge—even men of high respectability for talents and research in other things, betray the most surprising ignorance of the Bible. No wonder that they are carried about by every wind of doctrine, and fall helpless victims into the snares of those who lie in wait to deceive. At the same time, if they happen to get any crude and undigested notions of Christian truth, they are as obstinate and positive in maintaining their own hasty views, as if they had studied the scriptures all their lives long. My friends, this will not do. Have you not immortal souls? Do you know when they will be required of you? Are you fully aware of their natural condition; and what is requisite to their eternal happiness? On all these questions the Bible treats plainly and decisively. It fairly warns you that a mistake is very possible, very common, and infinitely dangerous. Is it a waste of time, think you, to know what it really does determine? Is the message of the great and terrible God, to men, to *you*, to you *personally*, to be thrown aside with less ceremony than a daily newspaper, and without an effort so much as to understand what he says? And all your awful concern in it to be tossed away with a carelessness which makes the angels tremble? Do you consider, while you indulge this supineness, while you neglect to become proficients in the knowledge of that wisdom which cometh from above, you are habitual breakers of God's commandments, in as high and in a higher degree, than if you were common drunkards, thieves, adulterers, and prostitutes? Rouse from your

slumbers, or you may see stranger things than publicans and harlots going into the kingdom of God before your faces, and leaving you, with all your decencies, your morals, your accomplishments, your respectability, to beg for admission and be refused. Strive to enter in at the straight gate. Aim at being not only Christians, but intelligent Christians. Study that great charter of your salvation, the Bible, until, by God's rich blessing, you shall "always be ready to give a reason of the hope that is within you," and no longer be ranked as children, nor be considered as an easy prey to them who lie in wait to deceive.

2. The second attribute of Christian character as opposed to the infirmities of children, is *firmness*.

In religious, as in other life, the plausible are the least solid and the least to be trusted. They who have arrived at what the scriptures call *perfection*, who have grown up into Christian manhood, are not to be moved away from the hope of the gospel by smooth stories and bland professions; nor to be cajoled out of their faith concerning our Lord Jesus Christ, by pretenders to new illumination, or more expansive charity. "Beloved," says John, "believe not every spirit, but try the spirits whether they be of God; because many false prophets are gone out into the world." And they are to try them by their doctrines, especially, adds the apostle, try their doctrines concerning the person of our Lord Jesus Christ. "Every spirit that confesseth that Jesus Christ is come in the flesh, is of God; and every spirit that confesseth not that Jesus Christ is come in the flesh, is not of God." Do you think the insipid, the frigid notion, that Jesus Christ was born like any other man, gives you the meaning, or touches the emphasis, of his "coming in the flesh?" A Christian, that is, a settled, established Christian, is not thus to be fooled and wheedled out of the true doctrine of his Redeemer, and of eternal life along with it. Ten sheep-skins, ever so artfully put on, cannot conceal the insidious wolf. His voice betrays him, and the real sheep flee from him. It is no new thing for Satan to be transformed into an angel of light; nor his ministers as ministers of righteousness. A well-trained Christian will use the freedom to look under this angel mask—to inquire how far the resemblance to ministers of righteousness goes—and by faithfully and fearlessly applying the apostle's rule, will speedily detect both the devil and his ministers.

He has told us how these gentry, the ministers of Satan, must be treated. "If there come any unto you," viz. with the pretensions of a teacher, and "bring not this doctrine," the doctrine of Christ as come in the flesh, "receive him not into your house, neither bid him God speed, for he that biddeth him God speed, is partaker of his evil deeds." He carries his master's mark in his forehead. Christians, who are enlisted under the Captain of salvation, are to allow no place to such an Antichrist—far less do anything to encourage him. There must be no half measures—no parleying—no pausing. Shut your doors upon him, saith the inspired direction, and let him go where the devil and his doctrines are in better repute. If not, if you are frightened by the terror of an ill name, if you are unable to stand the small shot of Antichrist, and begin to tremble and tamper when the breath of the evil one approaches you—look well to yourself; you are in a fair way of changing your professed service, of being disowned by Jesus Christ, and linking yourself forever with the devil and his angels. Let it be known, Christians, openly known, so that there can be no mistake, that you have neither hearts, nor hands, nor ears, for any, who, upon whatever pretext, would unsettle your faith on the Son of God. So that men may save you the pain, and themselves the judgment, of trying to break up your trust for eternity, and of persuading you to lay another foundation "than that is laid, which is Jesus Christ."

III. The means of our preservation and solid improvement are very obvious and simple.

1. Be students of the Holy Scriptures; search them; dig in them as for hidden treasures, and you shall find that which will make you wise to salvation, while the scorner seeketh wisdom and findeth it not. But remember that he who gave them for a light to your feet and a lamp to your paths, must open your eyes before you shall see wonderful things in his law. Sweet, and blessed, and freely given are his gracious teachings. "Did not our hearts burn within us," said one disciple to the other, "while he talked with us by the way, and while he opened to us the scriptures."

2. Repress vain curiosity. Inquire not into the reason of those things which are to be received on the credit of the divine testimony. Be satisfied that the Lord hath said it, and ask no farther.

They, "who boldly intrude into those things which they have no seen," may pretend what they please; but you have the highest authority in earth or heaven for being assured that "they are only vainly puffed up by their fleshly mind," and with all their knowledge or speculations, can do you nothing but harm.

3. Open not your ears to the suggestion of new light and new discoveries in religion. "The true Christ is no new Christ." He is the same yesterday, and to-day, and forever. There is no room for discoveries in God's revelation for the salvation of men. The revelation is itself the discovery. You are not to look for a new way to heaven. Jesus Christ is the way, and the truth, and the life; no man cometh to the Father but by him. This has been the divine method from the very beginning. That which a thousand years ago brought his sons and daughters to glory, viz. the making the Captain of their salvation perfect through sufferings, must bring you thither, or your arrival there is hopeless. And as to the new light, which is the boast of those who turn aside from the holy commandment delivered unto them, rely upon it, it is nothing but a new edition of old darkness, only resembling more than it did the dunnest smoke of hell.

4. Keep especially clear of uncommon pretenders to charity. Satan will mask his designs so long as he can, and so will all his ministers. Believe that God is love, that he is the great and essential Charity. Be satisfied then with as much charity as he has shown, and do not think of improving upon your Maker, by entertaining and expressing a more charitable opinion of sinners than himself. He hath said, and will make it good, and see that your charity do not trench upon his truth, he hath said, gainsay it who will, "He that believeth not shall be damned."

IV. Lastly, we have abundant motives for our Christian cultivation.

The angels are our fellow-students, and in some particulars of their education Christians have the preference. Their first knowledge of God's gracious design of forming Jews and Gentiles into one family with themselves, under Christ the head, they got from the church, and probably from the revelations made to Paul. "To the intent," says that great proficient in sacred things, "that now unto the principalities and powers in heavenly places might be made known *by the church* the manifold wisdom of God." If the thought of being scholars in the same school, and learners of the same things, with those blessed beings, does not raise in your minds the glory of your studies, and cause you to strain every nerve in patient and persevering application, that you may be fit to hold converse with them when you shall throw off this body, it is not for the speech of earth to tell the baseness of your spirits; eternity must find the proper expressions.

Moreover, every advance in true scriptural knowledge advances you at the same time in righteousness and true holiness, deepens and brightens the features of the divine image, and is a step in your heavenly promotion; for "they that be wise shall shine as the sun" in the kingdom of their Father.

Farther, every victory over error renders every succeeding one more easy. "Resist the devil and he will flee from you." And when the chief has taken himself to flight, his subalterns will not be long in quitting the field. It is the *first* attack in which they are most furious, and lay the basis of their future success. Foiled here, they become less troublesome. Satan and his servants have something else to do with their time and talents than to waste them upon fruitless attempts.

Once more. Not only will your duty become easier in proportion as you faithfully perform it, but every advantage gained over the foe, draws you into closer communion with our Lord Jesus Christ. It is in his strength that you withstand and conquer. His glory gains by every achievement performed in his name. You press hard upon his steps as a victorious Saviour, and are safe, as you are near him. He notes and he rewards your efforts. "To him that overcometh," is his magnificent promise, "will I grant to sit down with me on my throne, even as I also overcame and am set down with my Father on his throne."

Wherefore, my beloved brethren, be stedfast, immovable, always abounding in the work of the Lord, forasmuch as ye know that your labour is not in vain in the Lord. Amen!

FUNERAL ORATION

ON THE

DEATH OF GENERAL WASHINGTON.*

FELLOW-CITIZENS,—The offices of this day belong less to eloquence than to grief. We celebrate one of those great events, which, by uniting public calamity with private affliction, create in every bosom a response to the throes of an empire. God, who doeth wonders, whose ways must be adored but not questioned, in severing from the embraces of America her first-beloved patriot, has imposed on her the duty of blending impassioned feeling with profound and unmurmuring submission. An assembled nation, lamenting a father in their departed chief; absorbing every inferior consideration in the sentiments of their common loss; mingling their recollections and their anticipations; their wishes, their regrets, their sympathies, and their tears; is a spectacle not more tender than awful, and excites emotions too mighty for utterance. I should have no right to complain, Americans, if, instead of indulging me with your attentions, you should command me to retire, and leave you to weep in the silence of woe. I should deserve the reprimand were I to appear before you with the pretensions of eulogy. No! Eulogy has mistaken her province and her powers when she assumes for

---

* Delivered in the Brick Presbyterian Church, in the City of New York, 22d February, 1800.

her theme the glory of Washington. His deeds and his virtues are his high eulogium. His deeds most familiar to your memories—his virtues most dear to your affections. To me, therefore, nothing is permitted, but to borrow from yourselves. And though a pencil more daring than mine would languish in attempting to retrace the living lines which the finger of Truth has drawn upon your hearts, you will bear with me, while, on a subject which dignifies everything related to it, "I tell you that which you yourselves do know."

The name of Washington, connected with all that is most brilliant in the history of our country and in human character, awakens sensations which agitate the fervours of youth, and warm the chill bosom of age. Transported to the times when America rose to repel her wrongs and to claim her destinies, a scene of boundless grandeur bursts upon our view. Long had her filial duty expostulated with parental injustice. Long did she deprecate the rupture of those ties which she had been proud of preserving and displaying. But her humble intreaty spurned, aggression followed by the rod, and the rod by scorpions, having changed remonstrance into murmur, and murmur into resistance, she transfers her grievances from the throne of earth to the throne of heaven, and precedes by an appeal to the God of battles her appeal to the sword of war. At issue now with the mistress of the seas—unfurnished with equal means of defence—the convulsive shock approaching—and every evil omen passing before her—one step of rashness or of folly may seal her doom. In this accumulation of trouble, who shall command her confidence, and face her dangers, and conduct her cause? God, whose kingdom ruleth over all, prepares from afar the instruments best adapted to his purpose. By an influence which it would be as irrational to dispute as it is vain to scrutinize, he stirs up the spirit of the statesman and the soldier. Minds, on which he has bestowed the elements of greatness, are brought by his providence into contact with exigencies which rouse them into action. It is in the season of effort and of peril that impotence disappears and energy arises. The whirlwind which sweeps away the glowworm, uncovers the fire of genius, and kindles it into a blaze that irradiates at once both the zenith and the poles. But among the heroes who sprung from obscurity when the college, the counting-house, and the plough, teemed with "thunderbolts of war," none could, in all respects, meet the wants and the wishes of America. She required, in her leader, a man reared under her own eye; who combined with distinguished talent a character above suspicion; who had added to his physical and moral qualities the experience of difficult service; a man who should concentrate in himself the public affections and confidences: who should know how to multiply the energies of every other man under his direction, and to make disaster itself the means of success—his arm a fortress and his name a host. Such a man it were almost presumption to expect; but such a man all-ruling Heaven had provided, and that man was Washington.

Pre-eminent already in worth, he is summoned by his country to the pre-eminence of toil and of danger. Unallured by the charms of opulence—unappalled by the hazard of a dubious warfare—unmoved by the prospect of being, in the event of failure, the first and most conspicuous victim, he obeys her mandate because he loves his duty. The resolve is firm, for the probation is terrible. His theatre is a world; his charge, a family of nations; the interest staked in his hands, the prosperity of millions unborn in ages to come. His means, under aid from on high, the resources of his own breast, with the raw recruits and irregular supplies of distracted colonies. O crisis worthy of such a hero! Followed by her little bands, her prayers and her tears, Washington espouses the quarrel of his country. As he moves on to the conflict, every heart palpitates, and every knee trembles. The foe, alike valiant and veteran, presents no easy conquest nor aught inviting but to those who had consecrated their blood to the public weal. The Omnipotent, who allots great enjoyment as the meed of great exertion, had ordained that America should be free, but that she should learn to value the blessing by the price of its acquisition. She shall go to a "wealthy place," but her way is "through fire and through water." Many a generous chief must bleed, and many a gallant youth sink at his side, into the surprised grave; the field must be heaped with slain, the purple torrent must roll, ere the angel of peace descend with his olive. It is, here, amid devastation, and horror, and death, that Washington must reap his laurels, and engrave his trophies on the shields of immortality. Shall Delaware and Princeton? Shall Monmouth and York? But I may not particularize; far less repeat the tale which babes recite, which poets sing, and Fame has published to a listening world. Every scene of his action was a scene of his triumph. Now he saved the republic by more than Fabian caution; now he avenged her by more than Carthaginian fierceness; while at every stroke her forests and her hills re-echoed to her shout, "The sword of the Lord and of Washington!" Nor was this the vain applause of partiality and enthusiasm. The blasted schemes of Britain, her broken and her captive hosts, proclaimed the terror of his arms. Skilled were her chiefs, and brave her legions; but bravery and skill rendered them a conquest more worthy of Washington. True, he suffered in his turn repulse, and even defeat. It was both natural and needful. Unchequered with reverse, his story would have resembled rather the fictions of romance than the truth of narrative: and had he been neither defeated nor repulsed, we had never seen all the grandeur of his soul. He arrayed himself in fresh honours by that which ruins even the great—vicissitude. He could not only subdue an enemy, but, what is infinitely more, he could subdue misfortune. With an equanimity which gave temperance to victory, and cheerfulness to disaster, he balanced the fortunes of the state. In the face of hostile prowess; in the midst of mutiny and treason; surrounded with astonishment, irresolution, and despondence; Washington remained erect, unmoved, invincible. Whatever ills America might endure in maintaining her rights, she exulted that she had nothing to fear from her commander-in-chief. The event justified her most sanguine presages. That invisible hand which girded him at first, continued to guard and to guide him through the successive stages of the revolution. Nor did he account it a weakness to bend the knee in homage to its supremacy, and prayer for its direction. This was the armour of Washington; this the salvation of his country.

The hope of her reduction at length abandoned; her war of liberty brought, in the establishment of independence, to that honourable conclusion for which it had been undertaken; the hour arrived when he was to resign the trust which he had accepted with diffidence. To a mind less pure and elevated, the situation of America would have furnished the pretext as well as the means of military usurpation. Talents equal to daring enterprise; the derangement of public affairs: unbounded popularity; and the devotion of a suffering army, would have been to every other a strong, and to almost any other an irresistible temptation. In Washington they did not produce even the pain of self-denial. They added the last proof of his disinterestedness, and imposed on his country the last obligation to gratitude. Impenetrable by corrupting influence; deaf to honest but erring solicitation; irreconcilable with every disloyal sentiment; he urged the necessity, and set the example, of laying down in peace arms assumed for the common defence. But to separate from the companions of his danger and his glory was, even for Washington, a difficult task. About to leave them forever, a thousand sensations rushed upon his heart, and all the soldier melted in the man. He who has no tenderness, has no magnanimity Washington could vanquish, and Washington could weep. Never was affection more cordially reciprocated. The grasped hand; the silent anguish; the spontaneous tear trickling down the scarred cheek; the wistful look, as he passed, after the warrior who should never again point their way to victory —form a scene for Nature's painter and for Nature's bard.

But we must not lose, in our sensibility, the remembrance of his penetration, his prudence, his regard of public honour and of public faith. Abhorring outrage; jealous for the reputation; and dreading the excesses, of even a gallant army, flushed with conquest, prompted by incendiaries, and sheltered by a semblance of right, his last act of authority is to dismiss them to their homes without entering the capital. Accompanied with a handful of troops, he repairs to the council of the States, and through them surrenders to his country the sword which he had drawn in her defence. Singular phenomenon! Washington becomes a private citizen. He exchanges supreme command for the tranquillity of domestic life. Go, incomparable man! to adorn no less the civic virtues than the splendid achievements of the field. Go, rich in the consciousness of thy high deserts! Go, with the admiration of the world, with the plaudit of millions, and the orisons of millions more for thy temporal and thine eternal bliss!

The glory of Washington seemed now complete. While the universal voice proclaimed that he might decline with honour every future burden, it was a wish and an opinion, almost as universal, that he would not jeopard the fame which he had so nobly won. Had personal considerations swayed his mind, this would have been his own decision. But, untutored in the philosophism of the age, he had not learned to separate the maxims of wisdom from the injunctions of duty. His soul was not debased by that moral cowardice which fears to risk popularity for the general good. Having assisted in the formation of an efficient government which he had refused to dictate or enforce at the mouth of his cannon, he was ready to contribute the weight of his character to insure its effect; and his country rejoiced in an opportunity of testifying that, much as she loved and trusted others, she still loved and trusted him most. Hailed by her unanimous suffrage the pilot of the state, he approaches the awful helm, and grasping it with equal firmness and ease, demonstrates that forms of power cause no embarrassment to him.

In so novel an experiment as a nation framing a government for herself under no impulse but that of reason, adopting it through no force but the force of conviction, and putting it into operation without bloodshed or violence, it was all important that her first magistrate should possess her unbounded good will. Those elements of discord which lurked in the diversity of local interest; in the collision of political theories; in the irritations of party; in the disappointed or gratified ambition of individuals; and which, notwithstanding her graceful transition, threatened the harmony of America, it was for Washington alone to control and repress. His tried integrity, his ardent patriotism, were instead of a volume of arguments for the excellence of that system which he approved and supported. Among the simple and honest whom no artifice was omitted to ensnare, there were thousands who knew little of the philosophy of government, and less of the nice machinery of the constitution; but they knew that Washington was wise and good; they knew it was impossible that he should betray them; and by this they were rescued from the fangs of faction. Ages will not furnish so instructive a comment on that cardinal virtue of republicans, confidence in the men of their choice; nor a more salutary antidote against the pestilential principle, that the soul of a republic is jealousy. At the commencement of her federal government, mistrust would have ruined America; in confidence she found her safety.

The re-appearance of Washington as a statesman excited the conjecture of the old world, and the anxiety of the new. His martial fame had fixed a criterion, however inaccurate, of his civil administration. Military genius does neither confer nor imply political ability. Whatever merit may be attached to the faculty of arranging the principles, and prosecuting the details, of an army, it must be conceded that vaster comprehensions belong to the statesman. Ignorance, vanity, the love of parodox, and the love of mischief, affecting to sneer at the "mystery of government," have indeed taught that common sense and common honesty are his only requisites. The nature of things and the experience of every people, in every age, teach a different doctrine. America had multitudes who possessed both those qualities, but she had only one Washington. To adjust, in the best compromise, a thousand interfering views, so as to affect the greatest good of the whole with the least inconvenience to the parts; to curb the dragon of faction by means which insure the safety of public liberty; to marshal opinion and prejudice among the auxiliaries of the law; in fine, to touch the mainspring of national agency, so as to preserve the equipoise of its powers, and to make the feeblest movement of the extremities accord with the impulse at the centre, is only for genius of the highest order. To excel equally in military and political science has been the praise of a few chosen spirits, among whom, with a proud preference, we enrol the Father of our country.

It was the fortune of Washington to direct transactions of which the repetition is hardly within the limits of human possibilities. When he entered on his first presidency, all the interests of the continent were vibrating through the arch of political uncertainty. The departments of the new government were to be marked out and filled up; foreign relations to be regulated; the physical and moral strength of the nation to be organized; and that at a time when scepticism in politics, no less than in religion and morals, was preparing throughout Europe to spring the mine of revolution and ruin. In discharging his first duties, that same intelligent, cautious, resolute procedure, which had rendered him the bulwark of war, now exhibited him as the guardian of peace. Appropriation of talent to employment, is one of the deep results of political sagacity. And in his selection of men for office, Washington displayed a knowledge of character and business, a contempt of favouritism, and a devotion to the public welfare, which permitted the General to be rivaled only by the President.

Under such auspices, the fruit and the pledge of divine blessing, America rears her head and recovers her vigours. Agriculture laughs on the land: Commerce ploughs the wave: Peace rejoices at her home; and she grows into respect abroad. Ah! too happy to progress without interruption. The explosions of Europe bring new vexations to her, and new trials and new glories to her Washington. Vigilant and faithful, he hears the tempest roar from afar, warns her of its approach, and prepares for averting its dangers. Black are the heavens and angry the billows, and narrow and perilous the passage. But his composure, dignity, and firmness, are equal to the peril. Unseduced by fraud; unterrified by threat; unawed by clamour; he holds on his steady way, and again he saves his country. With less decision on the part of Washington, a generous but mistaken ardour would have plunged her into the whirlpool, and left her till this hour the sport of the contending elements. Americans! bow to that magnanimous policy which protected your dearest interests at the hazard of incurring your displeasure. It was thus that Washington proved himself, not in the cant of the day, but in the procurement of substantial good, in stepping between them and perdition, the servant of the people. The historian of this period will have to record a revolt raised by infatuation against the law of the land. He will have to record the necessity which compelled even Washington to suppress it by the sword. But he will have to record also his gentleness and his lenity. Deeds of severity were his sad tribute to justice; deeds of humanity the native suggestions of his heart.

Eight years of glorious administration created a claim on the indulgence of his country, which none could think of disputing, but which all lamented should be urged. The ends which rendered his services indispensable being mostly attained, he demands his restoration to private life. Resigning to an able successor the reins which he had guided with characteristic felicity, he once more bids adieu to public honours. Let not his motives be mistaken or forgotten. It was for him to set as great examples in the relinquishment, as in the acceptance of power. No mortified ambition; no haughty disgusts; no expectation of higher office, prompted his retreat. He knew that foreign nations considered his life as the bond, and his influence as the vital spirit of our Union. He knew that his own lustre threw a shade over others, not more injurious to them than to his country. He wished to dispel the enchantment of his own name. He wished to relieve the apprehensions of America, by making her sensible of her riches in other patriots; to be a spectator of her prosperity under their management; and to convince herself, and to convince the world, that she depended less on him than either her enemies or her friends believed; and therefore he withdrew.

Having lavished all her honours, his country had nothing more to bestow upon him except her blessing. But he had more to bestow upon his country. His views and his advice, the condensed wisdom of all his reflection, observation, and experience, he delivers to his compatriots in a manual worthy of them to study and of him to compose. And now, when they could hope to enjoy only the satisfaction of still possessing him, the pleasure of recounting his acts, and the benefit of practising his lessons, they accompany his retirement with their aspirations that his evening may be as serene as his morning had been fair, and his noon resplendent.

That he should ever again endure the solicitudes of office was rather to be deprecated than desired; because it must be a crisis singularly portentous which could justify another invasion of his repose. From such a necessity we fondly promised ourselves exemption. Flattering, fallacious security! The sudden whirlwind springs out of a calm. The revolutions of a day proclaim that an empire was. However remote the position of America; however peaceful her character; however cautious and equitable her policy; she was not to go unmolested by the gigantic fiend of Gallic domination. That she was free and happy, was crime and provocation enough. He fastened on her his murderous eye; he was preparing for her that deadly embrace in which nations supine and credulous had already perished. Reduced to the alternative of swelling the catalogue of his victims, or arguing her cause with the bayonet and the ball, she burst the ill-fated bonds which had linked her to his destinies, and assumes the tone and attitude of defiance. The gauntlet is cast. To press on is perilous; to retreat destruction. She looks wistfully round, and calls for Washington. The well-known voice, that voice which he had ever accounted a law, pierces the retreats of Vernon, and thrills his bosom. Domestic enjoyments lose their charm; repose becomes to him inglorious;

every sacrifice is cheap, and every exertion easy, when his beloved country requires his aid. With all the alacrity of youth he flies to her succour. The helmet of war presses his silver locks. His sword, which dishonour had never tarnished nor corruption poisoned, he once more unsheathes, and prepares to receive on its point the insolence of that foe whose intrigue he had foiled by his wisdom.

It must ever be difficult to compare the merits of Washington's characters, because he always appeared greatest in that which he last sustained. Yet if there is a preference, it must be assigned to the Lieutenant-General of the armies of America. Not because the duties of that station were more arduous than those which he had often performed, but because it more fully displayed his magnanimity. While others become great by elevation, Washington becomes greater by condescension. Matchless patriot! to stoop, on public motives, to an inferior appointment, after possessing and dignifying the highest offices! Thrice favoured country, which boasts of such a citizen! We gaze with astonishment; we exult that we are Americans. We augur every thing great, and good, and happy. But whence this sudden horror? What means that cry of agony? Oh! 'tis the shriek of America! The fairy vision is fled: Washington is—no more!

"How are the mighty fallen, and the weapons of war perished!"

Daughters of America, who erst prepared the festal bower and the laurel wreath, plant now the cypress grove, and water it with tears.

"How are the mighty fallen, and the weapons of war perished!"

The death of Washington, Americans, has revealed the extent of our loss. It has given us the final proof that we never mistook him. Take his affecting testament, and read the secrets of his soul. Read all the power of domestic virtue. Read his strong love of letters and of liberty. Read his fidelity to republican principle, and his jealousy of national character. Read his devotedness to you in his military bequests to near relations. "These swords," they are the words of Washington, "these swords are accompanied with an injunction not to unsheath them for the purpose of shedding blood, except it be for self-defence, or in defence of their country and its rights; and in the latter case to keep them unsheathed, and prefer falling with them in their hands, to the relinquishment thereof."

In his acts, Americans, you have seen the man. In the complicated excellence of character he stands alone. Let no future

Plutarch attempt the iniquity of parallel. Let no soldier of fortune; let no usurping conqueror; let not Alexander or Cæsar; let not Cromwell or Bonaparte; let none among the dead or the living; appear in the same picture with Washington; or let them appear as the shade to his light.

On this subject, my countrymen, it is for others to speculate, but it is for us to feel. Yet in proportion to the severity of the stroke, ought to be our thankfulness that it was not inflicted sooner. Through a long series of years, has God preserved our Washington a public blessing; and now that he has removed him forever, shall we presume to say, "What doest thou?" Never did the tomb preach more powerfully the dependence of all things on the will of the Most High. The greatest of mortals crumble into dust the moment he commands, "Return, ye children of men." Washington was but the instrument of a benignant God. He sickens, he dies, that we may learn not to "trust in men," nor to "make flesh our arm." But though Washington is dead, Jehovah lives. God of our fathers! be our God, and the God of our children! Thou art our refuge and our hope; the pillar of our strength; the wall of our defence, and our unfading glory.

Americans! This God, who raised up Washington and gave you liberty, exacts from you the duty of cherishing it with a zeal according to knowledge. Never sully by apathy or by outrage, your fair inheritance. Risk not, for one moment, on visionary theories, the solid blessings of your lot. To you, particularly, O youth of America! applies the solemn charge. In all the perils of your country remember Washington. The freedom of reason and of right has been handed down to you on the point of the hero's sword. Guard with veneration the sacred deposit. The curse of ages will rest upon you, O youth of America, if ever you surrender to foreign ambition or domestic lawlessness, the precious liberties for which Washington fought, and your fathers bled!

I cannot part with you, fellow-citizens, without urging the long remembrance of our present assembly. This day we wipe away the reproach of republics, that they know not how to be grateful. In your treatment of living patriots, recall your love and your regret of Washington. Let not future inconsistency charge this day with hypocrisy. Happy America, if she gives an instance of universal principle in her sorrows for the man, "first in war, first in peace, and first in the affections of his country!"

AN ORATION,

COMMEMORATIVE OF THE LATE

MAJ.-GEN. ALEXANDER HAMILTON.[*]

SAD, my fellow-citizens, are the recollections and forebodings which the present solemnities force upon the mind. Five years have not elapsed since your tears flowed for the Father of your country, and you are again assembled to shed them over her eldest son. No! it is not an illusion—would to God it were: your eyes behold it,—the urn which bore the ashes of Washington is followed by the urn which bears the ashes of Hamilton. Cruel privation!—but I forbear. God's "way is in the sea, and his path in the great waters, and his footsteps are not known." It is not for mortals to repine,—much less to arraign. Our Hamilton is removed; and we have nothing left but to recall his image; to gather up his maxims, and to profit by our affliction. Accompany me, therefore, to a short retrospect. I feel that I shall not justify an appointment too imposing to be declined. Your own hearts must supply my deficiency. I aspire to nothing more than a faint outline of the man whom you loved.

Presages of his future eminence were evolved by the first buddings of intellect in Alexander Hamilton. The course of the boy,

---

[*] Pronounced before the New York State Society of the Cincinnati, on Tuesday, the 31st July, 1804.

like that of the man, was ardent, rapid, and beyond the reach of his contemporaries. History will hereafter relate that he was numbered among statesmen at an age when in others the rudiments of character are scarcely visible. In the contest with Great Britain, which called forth every talent and every passion, his juvenile pen asserted the claims of the colonies against writers from whom it would derogate to say that they were merely respectable. An unknown antagonist, whose thrust was neither to be repelled nor parried, excited inquiry; and when he began to be discovered, the effect was apparently so disproportioned to the cause, that his papers were ascribed to a statesman who then held a happy sway in the councils of his country, who has since rendered her the most essential services; and who still lives to adorn her name.* But the truth could not long be concealed. The powers of Hamilton created their own evidence; and America saw with astonishment a lad of seventeen in the rank of her advocates, at a time when her advocates were patriots and sages. A distinction thus nobly acquired, and ably maintained, was a pledge to the commonwealth, which he lost no time in redeeming. His first step from the college was into a military post; his second into the family and confidence of Washington. Here he had opportunities of studying a man, from whom no other man was too great to learn; of analyzing those rare qualities which met in his character; and of nourishing his own magnanimity by free communication with the magnanimity of his chief. His sound understanding, his comprehensive views, his promptitude, application, and patience would have endeared him to a man less discriminating than Washington; but to him they were inestimable, and they speedily sunk the patron in the friend. The pair became inseparable. While others were indulging in wonted gaiety, they were closeted on matters of state; and the pensive brow of the youth was often the first intimation of serious design in the veteran.

It was impossible for such a pupil, in such a school, not to be conspicuous. The materials furnished by Washington's experience, by his consummate prudence, by the disclosure of his plans, and of the springs of national operations, fostered the genius of

* John Jay, Esq.

Hamilton, and fitted him for command. His agency in the correspondence of the commander-in-chief, and in directing the movements of the army, is for the research of his biographer. I pass over his personal valour, not only because it never was disputed, but because the possession of it, as being one of the most common of military attributes, is not so much the praise of a soldier, as the want of it is his infamy. But be it remembered with pride, that he was as humane as he was brave. He knew how to storm an enemy's entrenchments, but not how to sacrifice a suppliant. His gentleness assuaged martial rigour; nor was his sword polluted by a drop of blood wantonly or carelessly shed.

The capture of Lord Cornwallis having secured our independence, there was nothing to protract the war, but a few measures proper to save appearances, and to prepare for acceding, with decorum, to preliminaries of peace. It became, of course, a subject of solicitude to reflecting young men, who had no profession but that of arms, how they should procure an honourable subsistence, and be useful to the community, when that profession should be superseded. Among these was Hamilton. Encumbered with a family, destitute of funds, and having no inducement to continue in the army, he sheathed his sword, and at the age of twenty-five applied to the study of the law.

To most men, sudden alterations of habit are seldom advantageous, often ruinous. To Hamilton they did but introduce an acquaintance with his own inexhaustible mind. Hardly had he exchanged the camp for the bar, when he burst forth in the lustre of a civilian; and gave a promise, which he more than fulfilled, of excelling in jurisprudence, as he had excelled in war.

But it was not for Hamilton to detach his private pursuits from the public welfare. Scenes were about to open in which it would need his resource and his energy. The war of independence had terminated gloriously; the states had risen to their natural position; their career of prosperity had commenced, but their struggles were not over. Resentments, jealousies, and the farce of an advising government, kept them in jeopardy. That foresight, moderation, and firmness; that comprehension of the public interest, and of the means of promoting it; that zeal, and vigilance, and integrity, which were indispensable to our safety, the inspiration of God had assembled in the soul of Hamilton. To many who now hear me it is familiar, that after the conclusion of peace, some of our citizens, impelled by their temper, their cupidity, or both, were meditating violence against the property and persons of all who had remained in this city during the war. The generous Hamilton revolted. No consideration of private friendship or hazard could prevail with him to connive at faithlessness and revenge. He remonstrated against a scheme of which the policy was as false as the spirit was malignant. His voice was authority, for it was honour and truth. The public listened, and the infatuation was at an end.*

To these agitations succeeded a more perplexing difficulty. The confederation, framed under the pressure of common danger, proved unequal to its object whenever that pressure was removed. Thirteen republics, with an internal organization which commanded their whole moral and physical force; connected by a fictitious tie under a head without a single effective power, afforded a spectacle of which it is hard to say, whether it was more ludicrous or melancholy. Such a condition of things could not last. The very first occurrence which should put the will of congress at issue with the will of one of the larger states, would have dissolved the phantom, and shown America to be, what the discerning at home and abroad already perceived her to be in theory, a nation; in fact, a number of rival and hostile sovereignties. The evils to be apprehended from such a conflict were alarming; and they were approaching with no less certainty, than it is certain that the principles of human action are not to be altered, nor suspended by compact. The failure of a request from Congress for permission to levy a small duty upon imports, was hastening a crisis which the mighty mind of Hamilton proposed to avert. With the express intention of making an effort to retrieve our affairs by establishing an efficient general government, did he consent to be nominated as a candidate for the legislature of this state. The design was magnanimous. It embraced the only expedient to prevent our ruin; but it was confided to a few chosen friends. For such was the national inexperience and the popular jealousy, that the least suspicion of his purpose would have blasted

---

* On this subject it would be less a compliment to mention, than an injury to omit, the name of his excellency George Clinton, Esq., then governor of the state; whose honourable, independent, and successful exertions to restrain our citizens, cannot be remembered but with respect and veneration.

his reputation as an enemy to freedom. Oh, Hamilton! equally pure and disinterested were all thy plans, though often misunderstood and calumniated! And now, when there is no more room for suspicion, let his country, in judging of them, not forget that the very measure which, at first she would bitterly have execrated, has been her salvation. Yes, it is indubitable, that the original germ out of which has grown up her unexampled prosperity, was in the bosom of Hamilton. From the abortive attempt of Congress already mentioned, proceeded a commercial convention; and to the report of that body, which, as he foresaw, was unable to extricate the nation, do we owe the federal convention. Here, Americans, was the constellation of your heroes and your statesmen. Here your Washington presided, and your Hamilton shone. What weight the first of these names added to every thing which received its sanction, and what a conciliating charm it diffused through the States, you need not to be informed. But you ought not to be ignorant, that the benefit arising from the signature of Washington substantiates a claim on your gratitude to Hamilton; as it was the advice of the latter, previously consulted, which persuaded the former to accept a seat in the convention. A prudent secrecy covers the transactions of that august assembly. But could the veil be drawn aside, you would hear the youth of thirty fascinating with his eloquence the collective wisdom of the States, and instructing the hoary patriot in the recondite science of government. You would observe all the emotions of his manly heart occupying, in turn, his expressive features; and see, through the window in his breast, every anxiety, every impulse, every thought directed to your happiness. The result is in your hands; it is in your national existence. Not such, indeed, as Hamilton wished, but such as he could obtain, and as the States would ratify, is the federal constitution. His ideas of a government which should elevate the character, preserve the unity, and perpetuate the liberties of America, went beyond the provisions of that instrument. Accustomed to view men as they are; and to judge of what they will be, from what they ever have been, he distrusted any political order which admits the baneful charity of supposing them to be what they ought to be. He knew how averse they are from even wholesome restraint; how obsequious to flattery; how easily deceived by misrepresentation; how partial, how vehement, how capricious. He knew that vanity, the love of distinction, is inseparable from man; that if it be not turned into a channel useful to the government, it will force a channel for itself; and if cut off from other egress, will issue in the most corrupt of all aristocracies —the aristocracy of money. He knew that an extensive territory, a progressive population, an expanding commerce, diversified climate, and soil, and manners, and interest, must generate faction; must interfere with foreign views, and present emergencies requiring, in the general organization, much tone and promptitude. A strong government, therefore,—that is, a government stable and vigorous, adequate to all the forms of national exigency, and furnished with the principles of self-preservation, was undoubtedly his preference; and he preferred it because he conscientiously believed it to be necessary. A system which he would have entirely approved, would probably keep in their places those little men who aspire to be great; would withdraw much fuel from the passions of the multitude; would diminish the materials which the worthless employ for their own aggrandizement; would crown peace at home with respectability abroad; but would never infringe the liberty of an honest man. From his profound acquaintance with mankind, and his devotion to all that good society holds dear, sprang his apprehensions for the existing constitution. Convinced that the natural tendency of things is to an encroachment by the States on the Union; that their encroachments will be formidable as they augment their wealth and population; and, consequently, that the vigour of the general government will be impaired in a very near proportion with the increase of its difficulties; he anticipated the day when it should perish in the conflict of local interest and of local pride. The Divine mercy grant that his prediction may not be verified!

But whatever fears he entertained for the ultimate safety of the federal constitution, it is, in every respect, so preferable to the old confederation, and its rejection would have been so extremely hazardous, that he exerted all his talents and influence in its support. In the papers signed Publius, which compress the experience of ages, and pour original light on the science of government, his genius has left a manual for the future statesman. And they will be read with deeper interest when it is considered that, eloquent and powerful as they are, they were written under the pressure of business, amidst the conversation of friends, and the interrogatories of clients. Alas! the spirit which dictated them is fled; the hand which penned them moulders in death!

His voice co-operated with his pen. In the convention of this state, which met to deliberate on the federal constitution, he was always heard with awe, perhaps with conviction, though not always with success. But when the crisis arrived—when a vote was to determine whether New York should retain or relinquish her place in the Union; and preceding occurrences made it probable that she would choose the worst part of the alternative, Hamilton arose in redoubled strength. He argued, he remonstrated, he entreated, he warned, he painted, till apathy itself was moved, and the most relentless of human things, a preconcerted majority, was staggered and broken. Truth was again victorious, and New York enrolled herself under the federal standard.

The government happily erected, was now to be organized. Every eye fixed upon Washington for the first magistrate. He knew it, and hesitated. The competition between his love of retirement, his former resolutions, and the new state of affairs, held him in painful suspense. But the judgment of Hamilton preponderated, and he yielded to the public wish.

That faithful adviser, whom he had consulted upon every question of moment, and who never gave him an unsound advice, could not be omitted in the original administration. The department best suited to him, because the most arduous, was the treasury. He had already passed from the warrior into the jurist, and he was now to appear in the new and very different character of a financier. A losing commerce, a famished agriculture, an empty purse, and prostrate credit, would have overwhelmed the ordinary man; but they only brought into action the resources of Hamilton. His plans for redeeming the reputation of the country, by satisfying her creditors; and for combining with the government such a monied interest as might facilitate its operations, were strenuously opposed. But as it is easier to cavil than to refute, to complain than to amend, the opposition failed. The effect was electrical. Commerce revived; the ploughshare glittered; property recovered its value; credit was established; revenue created; the treasury filled.

This great fiscal revolution enriched numbers who held a large amount of the public paper, purchased at a season when the unpromising state of the public faith had set it afloat in the market at a most ignoble price. None could have fairer opportunities of acquiring a princely fortune than the financier himself. So inviting was the occasion, and the disposition to profit by it so little at variance with the common estimate of honourable gain, that few supposed it possible to resist the temptation. The fact being presumed, every petty politician erected himself into a critic; while the gazettes, the streets, the polls of election, resounded with the millions amassed by the secretary. It is natural that the idolators of gold should treat the contempt of it as a chimera; but gold was not the idol of Hamilton. He had formerly relinquished his own claims to compensation for military services, that obloquy might not breathe an impeachment of his motives in espousing the claims of his brother officers.* And from this proud eminence which he then ascended, he was not now to be seduced by the attractions of lucre. Exquisitely delicate toward official character, he touched none of the advantages which he put within the reach of others; he vested not a dollar in the public funds.

Although his particular province was the treasury, his genius pervaded the whole administration; and in those critical events which crowded each other, had a peculiar influence upon its measures. The French Revolution, which our fondness mistook for the birth of virtuous freedom, stood before him, from the beginning, in that hideous form which it has since unmasked. Not to be duped by hollow pretences, he was active in arresting the course of an insolent minister; and not to be biased by popular frenzy, he secured that dignified ground to which the United States were led by the proclamation of neutrality. Without his

---

* Being a member of congress, while the question of the commutation of the half-pay of the army for a sum in gross was in debate, delicacy, and a desire to be useful to the army, by removing the idea of his having an interest in the question, induced him to write to the secretary of war, and relinquish his claim to half-pay; which, or the equivalent, he accordingly never received. Neither did he ever apply for the lands allowed by the United States to officers of his rank. It is true, that having served through the latter periods of the war on the general staff of the United States, and not in the line of this state, he could not claim the allowance as a matter of course. But having before the war resided in this state, and having entered the military career at the head of a company of artillery raised for the particular defence of this state, he had better pretensions to the allowance than others to whom it was actually made. Yet has it not been extended to him.

aid, great Washington himself might have been borne down by the torrent, and the nation implicated in war, to gratify the resentment and ambition of France.

Internal embarrassment soon added fresh honours to Hamilton as a statesman. The western insurrection, which had rejected the condescending proposals of government, was to be quelled by force. A more serious question had not occupied the cabinet, as nothing had hitherto occurred to try the strength of the national arm. It was now to be ascertained how far the turbulent might trifle with the law, and what reliance they might place upon armed opposition. Incalculable consequences hung upon the precedent. Feeble measures would have surrendered the peace, perhaps the life, of the Union; but feeble measures were contemplated. That timidity which shrinks from decision; that economy which accounts every thing less precious than money; and that covered treason which favoured the rebellion, would have ordered out a detachment that might have been met and defeated.

The penetration of Hamilton was not to be eluded, nor his firmness to be shaken, by any argument in support of so dangerous an experiment. "If you wish," said he, "to maintain the authority of the laws; to prevent the repetition of similar outrages; to spare your treasure and your blood; let the insurgents, let the continent see, that it is never to admit of a doubt whether the national shall be obeyed or not. Teach them this lesson by employing a force that shall put resistance out of the question." This sage and humane policy was adopted by Washington; and the rebellion disappeared without effusion of blood.

After the restoration of order, Mr Hamilton remained but a short time in office. His numerous services gave him, perhaps, a right to retire when the state might be safely intrusted to other hands. But one reason of his retreat deserves particular notice, because it involves a mischievous and disreputable principle. A general error in popular systems, is a frugality which computes nothing but pence. The affairs of a nation, however, cannot be ably conducted without able and independent men. But such men, in a country where the demand for active talent is greater than the supply, will always hold their fortunes in their own hand: nor are we to expect that they will submit to the toils and responsibility of public office, with a support utterly disproportioned both to their station and their means of providing for themselves. No people is in jeopardy from the liberality of their civil list; but when this is niggardly, able men withdraw in succession, and the state falls at length into the hands of the weak or the wicked, whose want of capacity or of integrity squanders on one occasion the public revenue, and on another overloads it with the expenses of war. The last of these consequences God forbid we should experience; the first was exemplified in the history of Hamilton. He entered into public service with property of his own, the well-earned reward of professional talent; he continued in it till his little funds were dissipated; and left it to get bread for a suffering family. It was surely enough that he had impoverished himself while he was enriching the commonwealth; but it was beyond measure insulting to charge him, under such circumstances, with invading the public purse. Nobody believed the charge; and least of all, the slanderers who brought it. But Washington was vilified, and how should Hamilton escape! The virtuous saw with regret that he stooped to repel it, and with anguish that, in regard to a private aberration, his defence contained a disclosure of which they admired the ingenuousness, but deplored the occasion, while they wept over a spot in a blaze of excellence.

Large and lucrative practice at the bar promised to replace his pecuniary sacrifices in official life. But a new distress of his country drew him again from his professional engagements. Our remonstrances against the injuries committed by France had proved unavailing; and her rude and humiliating requisitions had fired the national spirit. Little was to be expected from the generosity, and less from the rectitude, of a government framed upon the maxims of the new philosophy. Tribute or the sword was the only choice of the States, and it would have been a libel on the war of independence to have hesitated a moment. A provisional army, with Washington at their head, was summoned into the field; but the condition on which he suspended the acceptance of his own commission was, that Hamilton should be his associate. The end of this stipulation could not be misunderstood. He not only designed to have his age relieved from some heavy cares by his younger friend, but, in the event of his own decease, to leave the sword of America in the hands of a man whom nothing could overreach, nothing intimidate, nothing corrupt.

Subsequent adjustment of our dispute with the French Republic, was accompanied with the discharge of the provisional army, and with Hamilton's second return to his profession. Here, unwearied in diligence, and unrivalled in fame, he filled up the residue (ah, too transient!) of his invaluable days. But, as you have truly been told, though he had withdrawn from public life, he was not an hour absent from the public service. It did not belong to a man absorbed in his country's welfare, to look with indifference on the course of her affairs. Office he wanted none. None in the gift of the nation would have moved him from his purpose. He reserved himself for crises which he feared are approaching; such crises, especially, as may affect the integrity of the Union. How he was alarmed by every thing which pointed at its dissolution; how indignant were his feelings and language on that ungracious topic; how stern and steady his hostility to every influence which only leaned toward the project, they will attest with whom he was in habits of communication. In every shape it encountered his reprobation as unworthy of a statesman, as fatal to America, and desirable to the desperate alone. One of his primary objects was to consolidate the efforts of good men in retarding a calamity which, after all, they may be unable to avert; but which no partial nor temporary policy should induce them to accelerate. To these sentiments must be traced his hatred to continental factions; his anxiety for the federal constitution, although, in his judgment, too slight for the pressure which it has to sustain; his horror of every attempt to sap its foundation, or loosen its fabric; his zeal to consecrate it in the affections of his fellow-citizens, that, if it fall at last, they may be pure from the guilt of its overthrow—an overthrow which may be accomplished in an hour, but of which the woes may be entailed upon ages to come.

With such dignified policy he joined the most intense application to his professional duties. But the description of these is not my province. How he resolved the most intricate cases; how he pursued general principles through their various modifications; how he opened the fountains of justice; how he revered the rights of property; how he signalized himself in protecting the defenceless; how judges, and jurors, and counsel, and audience, hung on his accents, let them declare who have entrusted their fortunes to his hand; let them declare who have wondered that any man should be thought great while Hamilton appeared at the American bar.

But enumerations were endless. He was born to be great. Whoever was second, Hamilton must be first. To his stupendous and versatile mind no investigation was difficult—no subject presented which he did not illuminate. Superiority in some particular belongs to thousands. Pre-eminence, in whatever he chose to undertake, was the prerogative of Hamilton. No fixed criterion could be applied to his talents. Often has their display been supposed to have reached the limit of human effort; and the judgment stood firm till set aside by himself. When a cause of new magnitude required new exertion, he rose, he towered, he soared,—surpassing himself as he surpassed others. Then was nature tributary to his eloquence! Then was felt his despotism over the heart! Touching, at his pleasure, every string of pity or terror, of indignation or grief; he melted, he soothed, he roused, he agitated; alternately gentle as the dews, and awful as the thunder. Yet, great as he was in the eyes of the world, he was greater in the eyes of those with whom he was most conversant. The greatness of most men, like objects seen through a mist, diminishes with the distance; but Hamilton, like a tower seen afar off under a clear sky, rose in grandeur and sublimity with every step of approach. Familiarity with him was the parent of veneration. Over these matchless talents, probity threw her brightest lustre. Frankness, suavity, tenderness, benevolence, breathed through their exercise. And to his family!—but he is gone: that noble heart beats no more; that eye of fire is dimmed; and sealed are those oracular lips. Americans! the serenest beam of your glory is extinguished in the tomb.

Fathers, friends, countrymen! the death of Hamilton is no common affliction. The loss of distinguished men is at all times a calamity; but the loss of such a man, at such a time, and in the very meridian of his usefulness, is singularly portentous. When Washington was taken, Hamilton was left; but Hamilton i taken, and we have no Washington. We have not such another man to die. Washington and Hamilton in five years! Perceav-d America! Thou art languishing beneath the divine displeasure. Let this truth awfully impress my hearers, that when the Almighty God is about to " shake terribly the earth ;" when he ha bidden scourge to follow scourge, and vengeance to press on vengeance, one of his means is to deprive a nation of their ablest men. Thus bereft of counsel, their affairs run into confusion, and bring forth misery. I invent nothing; I only repeat the admonition of Holy Writ: "For behold, the Lord, the Lord of hosts, doth take away the mighty man, and the man of war, the judge, and the prophet, and the prudent, and the ancient, the captain of fifty and the honourable man, and the counsellor and the cunning artificer, and the eloquent orator." The disastrous consequences are impotent governors and ruthless anarchy. For the prophet continues: "I will give children to be their princes, and babes shall rule over them. And the people shall be oppressed, every one by another, and every one by his neighbour; the child shall behave himself proudly against the ancient, and the base against the honourable."

Fathers, friends, countrymen! the grave of Hamilton speaks. It charges me to remind you that he fell a victim not to disease or accident,—not to the fortune of glorious warfare; but how shall I utter it? To a custom which has no origin but superstition, no aliment but depravity, no reason but in madness. Alas! that he should thus expose his precious life. This was his error. A thousand bursting hearts reiterate—This *was* his error. Shall I apologize? I am forbidden by his living protestations, by his dying regrets, by his wasted blood. Shall a solitary act into which he was betrayed and dragged, have the authority of a precedent? The plea is precluded by the long decisions of his understanding, by the principles of his conscience, and by the reluctance of his heart. Ah! when will our morals be purified, and an imaginary honour cease to cover the most pestilent of human passions? My appeal is to military men. Your honour is sacred. Listen. Is it honourable to enjoy the esteem of the wise and good? The wise and good turn with disgust from the man who lawlessly aims at his neighbour's life. Is it honourable to serve your country? That man cruelly injures her, who, from private pique, calls his fellow-citizen into the dubious field. Is fidelity honourable? That man forswears his faith who turns against the bowels of his countrymen weapons put into his hand for their defence. Are generosity, humanity, sympathy, honourable? That man is superlatively base, who mingles the tears of the widow and orphan, with the blood of a husband and father. Do refinement, and courtesy, and benignity, entwine with the laurels of the brave? The blot is yet to be wiped from the soldier's name, that he cannot treat his brother with the decorum of a gentleman, unless the pistol or the dagger be every moment at his heart. Let the votaries of honour now look at their deeds. Let them compare their doctrine with this horrible comment. Ah! what avails it to a distracted nation that Hamilton was murdered for a punctilio of honour! My flesh shivers! Is this indeed our state of society? Are transcendent worth and talent to be a capital indictment before the tribunal of ambition? Is the angel of death to record, for sanguinary retribution, every word which the collision of political opinion may extort from a political man? Are integrity and candour to be at the mercy of the assassin? And systematic crime to trample under foot, or smite into the grave, all that is yet venerable in our humbled land? My countrymen, the land is defiled with blood unrighteously shed. Its cry, disregarded on earth, has gone up to the throne of God; and this day does our punishment reveal our sin. It is time for us to awake. The voice of moral virtue, the voice of domestic alarm, the voice of the fatherless and the widow, the voice of a nation's wrong, the voice of Hamilton's blood, the voice of impending judgment, calls for a remedy. At this hour, Heaven's high reproof is sounding from Maine to Georgia, and from the shores of the Atlantic to the banks of the Mississippi. If we refuse obedience, every drop of blood spilled in single combat will lie at our door, and will be recompensed when our cup is full. We have then our choice, either to coerce iniquity, or prepare for desolation; and in the mean time to make our nation, though infant in years, yet mature in vice, the scorn and the abhorrence of civilized man?

Fathers, friends, countrymen! the dying breath of Hamilton recommended to you the Christian's hope. His single testimony outweighs all the cavils of the sciolist, and all the jeers of the profane. Who will venture to pronounce a fable, that doctrine of "life and immortality," which his profound and irradiating mind embraced as the truth of God? When you are to die, you will find no source of peace but in the faith of Jesus. Cultivate for your present repose and your future consolation, what our departed friend declared to be the support of his expiring moments: " A tender reliance on the mercies of the Almighty, through the merits of the Lord Jesus Christ."

Hamilton! we will cherish thy memory, we will embalm thy fame! Fare thee well, thou unparalleled man, farewell — for ever!

Edinburgh: Printed by A. & W. R. Wilson, 135 High Street.

BOOKS PUBLISHED BY OGLE & MURRAY.

THE LETTERS AND JOURNALS OF ROBERT BAILLIE, Principal of the University of Glasgow, 1637-62. A new Edition, with an Account of the Author's Life and Writings. By DAVID LAING, Esq. Three vols., royal 8vo, cloth. Published at £2, 8s., reduced to £1, 10s.

THE PRESBYTERIAN'S ARMOURY. Containing the WORKS OF GEORGE GILLESPIE, RUTHERFORD'S LEX REX, BROWN'S APOLOGETICAL RELATION, and CALDERWOOD'S PASTOR and PRELATE. Three vols, royal 8vo, cloth. Published at £2, 4s, reduced to £1, 11s. 6d.

THE WHOLE WORKS OF GEORGE GILLESPIE. With Memoir by Rev. Dr HETHERINGTON. Two vols, royal 8vo, cloth. Published at £1, 9s., reduced to £1, 1s.

RUTHERFORD'S LEX REX, BROWN'S APOLOGETICAL RELATION, CALDERWOOD'S PASTOR AND PRELATE. One vol., royal 8vo, cloth. Published at 14s., reduced to 10s.

THE ASSEMBLY'S SHORTER CATECHISM, Catechetically Illustrated and Practically Applied. Adapted for Public and Private Instruction. By an Elder of the Free Church. *Second Edition*. 12mo, cloth. Price 2s. 6d.

"To parents and teachers this book will be a precious help, and Gospel ministers we are sure will earnestly recommend it. It is so well fitted to be useful to families, that we hope soon to see on the title-page, the TENTH THOUSAND."—*Scottish Guardian.*

AN EXPOSITION UPON THE PROPHET JONAH, in several Lectures preached at Oxford by GEORGE ABBOT, D.D., Archbishop of Canterbury, 1611. A new Edition, with Memoir. Two vols. in one, post 8vo. cloth, lettered. Price 6s.

"It is with much pleasure that we behold a reprint of this valuable work. In genuine worth it is to many works of a like kind as the solid weight to the 'small dust of the balance.'"—*Eclectic Review.*

AN EXPOSITION OF THE EPISTLE TO THE HEBREWS. By the Rev. ROBERT DUNCAN, Minister at Tillicoultry, 1728. A new Edition, revised, post 8vo, cloth. Price 4s.

"At once learned and luminous, and well calculated to assist the Student and Divine."—*Ulster Banner.*

DE FOE'S MEMOIRS OF THE CHURCH OF SCOTLAND. With Preface by DAVID LAING, Esq. Royal 8vo. Price 1s.

SUPPLEMENTARY VOLUMES TO EDWARD'S WORKS. Two vols, royal 8vo. Published at 28s., reduced to 15s.

Containing NOTES ON THE BIBLE, MISCELLANEOUS OBSERVATIONS, TYPES OF THE MESSIAH, and SEVENTEEN OCCASIONAL SERMONS.

Gentlemen who may have the eight volume edition of Edward's Works, or the one printed at New York in four volumes, are respectfully informed that the above matter is wanting in these editions; and those intending to complete their Sets are respectfully requested to do so without delay, as the impression was originally limited, and a considerable portion is already disposed of.

THE PHILOSOPHY OF THE PLAN OF SALVATION. A Book for the Times. By an AMERICAN CITIZEN. 12mo, bds., 1s., cloth, 1s. 6d.

"The book before us is one of singular merit. As a piece of clear, vigorous, consecutive thinking, we scarcely know its superior."—*Free Church Magazine.*

"This is really an original book. Every sentence is pregnant with thought, and every idea conduces to the main demonstration."—*United Presbyterian Magazine.*

THE DEATH OF DEATH IN THE DEATH OF CHRIST. A new Edition, revised. To which is annexed a Vindication from the Objections of Richard Baxter. By Dr JOHN OWEN, 12mo, cloth. Price 3s. 6d.

THE WARRANT, NATURE, AND DUTIES OF THE RULING ELDER IN THE PRESBYTERIAN CHURCH. By the Rev. SAMUEL MILLAR, D.D. 12mo, cloth. 2s. 6d.

THE WORKS OF THE REV. JAMES FRASER, of BRAE. Containing the DOCTRINE OF SANCTIFCATION, and SERMONS ON SACRAMENTAL OCCASIONS. 12mo, cloth. 6s.

FISHER'S MARROW OF MODERN DIVINITY. With Notes by BOSTON. 12mo, cloth. 3s. 6d.

Now Ready, in Two thick vols., 8vo., cloth, lettered, Price £1, 1s.,

LECTURES
ON THE
GOSPEL ACCORDING TO LUKE,
BY THE
REV. JAMES FOOTE, D.D.,
LATE MINISTER OF THE FREE EAST CHURCH, ABERDEEN.

Third Edition, Revised.

THESE Lectures, CXXXVII. in number, will be found very useful and suggestive to Clergymen who may be engaged in a Course of Lectures on Luke's Gospel. They are the production of one who possessed a discriminating understanding, a mature judgment, and earnest piety; and are the result of extensive reading, careful examination, and diligent research.

The following are extracts from a few of the criticisms on the former editions:—

"They are admirable specimens of the good old Scottish style of lecturing, whereby the people of the North were wont to be so thoroughly indoctrinated in Scriptural knowledge. . . . Ministers, students, and teachers will especially find here plentiful materials to aid them in their study or exposition of Gospel truth or duty."—*English Presbyterian Messenger.*

"Mr Foote's style is clear, his manner earnest, his exegesis generally satisfactory. His doctrine is that large Biblical Calvinism which finds room for and appropriates the elements of truth that are in the Arminian scheme."—*Christian Treasury.*

"These Lectures may be regarded as a standard work in Theology and Biblical interpretation. It would be difficult, in our language, to point to a work on the Gospel of Luke so ample in its details and illustrations, and, at the same time, so thoroughly to be relied on for its sound and orthodox views of Christian Truth."—*Evangelical Magazine.*

"These Lectures consist of a history, the most important to be found in the Testament—the history of Divinity on earth,—a history in which there lives not a human being who is not virtually interested. But then we have a continuous history, not, as usual, a lecture on this or the other passage, but a consecutive description of the life, works, and death of our blessed Redeemer. In this respect, so far as we know, it stands alone; and we are almost inclined to assert that no mere worldly man could begin this fascinating history, illustrated in the very interesting style of the author, without a desire to conclude it,—how much more must it be acceptable to the genuine Christian."—*Glasgow Examiner.*

EDINBURGH: OGLE & MURRAY AND OLIVER & BOYD.
LONDON: HAMILTON, ADAMS, AND CO.
AND ALL BOOKSELLERS.

www.ingramcontent.com/pod-product-compliance
Lightning Source LLC
Chambersburg PA
CBHW051850300426
44117CB00006B/335